T0136673

EMPIRICAL
STUDIES
OF
PROGRAMMERS

HUMAN/COMPUTER INTERACTION

A Series of Monographs, Edited Volumes, and Texts

SERIES EDITOR

BEN SHNEIDERMAN

Directions in Human/Computer Interaction
Edited by Albert Badre and Ben Shneiderman

Online Communities:
A Case Study of the Office of the Future
Starr Roxanne Hiltz

Human Factors In Computer Systems
Edited by John Thomas and Michael Schneider

Human Factors and Interactive Computer Systems
Edited by Yannis Vassiliou

Empirical Studies of Programmers
Edited by Elliot Soloway and Sitharama Iyengar

Human–Computer Interface Design Guidelines
C. Marlin Brown

EMPIRICAL STUDIES
OF
PROGRAMMERS

Papers presented at the
First Workshop on Empirical Studies of Programmers
June 5–6, 1986, Washington, DC

edited by
ELLIOT SOLOWAY
Yale University

SITHARAMA IYENGAR
Louisiana State University

ABLEX PUBLISHING CORPORATION
NORWOOD, NEW JERSEY

Library of Congress Cataloging in Publication Data

Workshop on Empirical Studies of Programmers
  (1st: 1986: Washington, D.C.)
  Empirical studies of programmers.

  (Human/computer interaction)
  Bibliography: p.
  1. Electronic digital computers—Programming—Congresses.
2. Computer programmers—Congresses. I. Soloway, Elliot.
II. Iyengar, Sitharama. III. Title. IV. Series: Human computer
interaction (Norwood, N.J.)
QA76.6.W688   1986   005'.092'2   86-3526
ISBN 0-89391-388-X

Ablex Publishing Corporation
355 Chestnut Street
Norwood, New Jersey 07648

Contents

v

Preface

While considerable effort has already been expended on studying "programs," comparatively little has been expended in studying the "programmer." (We use the terms "program" and "programmer" here as generic entities; they stand for specifications, documentation, etc., and designer, maintainer, etc., respectively.) In studying either entity, the hope is that insights can be gained that would facilitate improved productivity and improved quality of software. Broadly speaking, the basic assumption of researchers who study programmers is this: By understanding how and why programmers do a task, we will be in a better position to make prescriptions that can aid programmers in their task. For example, if we can understand how a maintainer, say, goes about comprehending a program, we should be in a good position to recommend changes in documentation standards that would enable the maintainer to more effectively glean from the documentation the necessary information. Similarly, recommendations for software tools and education should also follow.

It's one thing to say that studies of programmers are needed, but quite another to actually carry out such studies! By its very nature, this type of research requires a complex mix of skills and talents: The researcher needs to be well versed in the technical issues of computing, as well as the technical issues of carrying out empirical research. For example, *what* questions are worth pursuing? One needs a healthy degree of sophistication in both programming and psychology in order to recognize and appreciate what are the important research issues. Moreover, one needs a solid grounding in computing in order to develop the all-important "stimulus materials" for the study. Finally, one needs to be sensitive to the human element; how can we design an experimental setting that will elicit the behaviors we want to observe? Thus, actually carrying out productive research in this multi-disciplinary field is no mean feat! And, it is important: With computers—and software—controlling all sorts of life-critical systems (e.g., nuclear power plants, defense systems), we desperately need ways to insure the development of the highest quality software possible. Thus, there is a heady sense of excitement in going out to conquer this important, and relatively unexplored, territory: There is precious little known about programmers—the field is wide open.

This workshop developed out of discussions, started in 1984, between Ben Shneiderman, Elliot Soloway, and Ram Iyengar. We felt that there was a definite need to "bring the people together"—to facilitate a meeting of the minds, where *face to face* sharing of ideas could take place. With some trepidation, born of recognizing the difficulties in actually bringing such a meeting to fruition, we put out feelers for sponsors, papers, and attendees. The response we received was, quite frankly, exhilarating! Three universities (Yale University, University of Maryland, Louisiana State University) quickly stepped forward as sponsors, as did the Software Psychology Society. The call for papers drew in more than 50 papers. And, demand for a "ticket" to the workshop has been extremely intense. This volume, then, represents the hardcopy output of the First Workshop on Empirical Studies of Programmers, held in Washington, DC, on June 5–6, 1986. While the Software Psychology Society of Washington, DC, has been a pillar of support for this sort of research for some 10 years, and while research on this topic has appeared in various journals (e.g., *International Journal of Man-Machine Studies, Communications of the ACM*) and conferences (e.g., the SIGCHI Conferences on Computer-Human Interaction), this is the first workshop to focus solely on the topic of empirical studies of programmers. Moreover, given the strong, genuine interest in this first workshop, we foresee a successful Second Workshop!

The papers included in this volume cover a wide range of topics and employ a wide range of methodologies: from studies about student programmers to studies about professional programmers; from carefully controlled studies that examine a specific topic to analyses of verbal protocols that range over a variety of topics. Besides the refereed papers, of which there are 15, there is an invited paper by keynote presenter Ben Shneiderman that attempts to both look at where the research on programmers has come from and where it is going. There are also invited position papers, by Victor Basili, Elliot Soloway, and Bill Curtis, for a panel session entitled "Future Directions of Empirical Studies of Programmers."

By and large, the research reported here can be viewed as examining "programming in the small." While million-line programs are commonly found in industry, software of such magnitude has not as yet received significant attention by researchers in this field. However, it is reasonable that this comparatively young field should first attempt to get its "sea legs" by focusing on relatively more constrained problems. Moreover, prescriptions for improving the software process can be drawn from (and are often explicitly stated in) the papers in this volume. Thus, we are pleased and excited by the research reported here. We have no illusions about this research: It is clearly only a first step. However, we sense a momentum building: Studying the programmer is not only a legitimate endeavor, but it is an important one—while others may be satisfied with simply making prescriptions about what programmers should and should not do, researchers of the sort represented in this volume are bent on making prescriptions based squarely on empirically tested theories.

And last, but definitely not least, it is with great pleasure that we recognize and thank those that helped bring about this workshop. We would like to thank the institutions who lent their names and resources to our workshop: Yale University, University of Maryland, Louisiana State University, and the Software Psychology Society of Washington, DC. And, we would like to thank the people who worked, cajoled, and laughed—all necessary ingredients in making this enterprise work: Ben Shneiderman, Sylvia Sheppard, Mark Weiser, Stuart Zweben, and Bill Curtis, and the other members of the program committee: John Anderson, Victor Basili, Ruven Brooks, H.E. Dunsmore, Marc Eisenstadt, Thomas Green, Richard Mayer, Roy

Pea, S. Kundu, Emmanuel Girad, and Dominique Potier, for all their assistance. We would like to thank Stan Rikfin for the super job he did as local arrangements chair. Craig Van Dyck, Barbara Bernstein, and Walter Johnson from Ablex Publishing Corp. provided invaluable support in actually bringing this volume to fruition. And, finally, we would like to thank all those who submitted papers, those who attended the workshop, and those who wanted to attend but were not able: It makes it all worthwhile to know that there are lots of people who share our curiousity about how programmers really do do it!—*E.S. and S.I.*

KEYNOTE ADDRESS

CHAPTER 1

Empirical Studies of Programmers:
The Territory, Paths, and Destinations

Ben Shneiderman
Department of Computer Science
University of Maryland
College Park, MD 20742

ABSTRACT

This paper attempts to describe the varied intellectual territory that programmers work in. It offers several paths for researchers who wish to explore this territory: controlled experiments, observational or field studies, surveys, and cognitive theories. Finally, this paper suggests several important destinations for researchers: refining the use of current languages, improving present and future languages, developing special purpose languages, and improving tools and methods.

1. INTRODUCTION

Computer programming is a challenging and exciting adventure for many people. It offers the joyous experience of creation and the sweet taste of success as a reward for correct performance. Satisfaction is especially strong if the effort has been long and tiring due to errors. The strong reinforcement of programming is enhanced by the sense of power in controlling the computer and the mastery of a small, personally-defined world.

Programming, like music, blends esthetics and technology. The high-level plan, the middle-level concepts, and the low-level details must be correct and in harmony with each other. Discordant data structures or missed notations are jarring.

Success in programming has been traditionally measured in terms of efficient use of storage and machine resources, accuracy of the numeric results, adherence to specifications, adaptability to change, and portability. These are vital criteria, but questions about the human dimension have become equally important: Is the program readable by other programmers who must test, debug, or maintain it? Is the programming language learnable, convenient for expressing certain algorithms, or comprehensible to novice users? Are design methods, flowcharts, documentation aids, or browsers helpful?

Measures of human performance in programming have become valued not only for the guidance they provide for professional or novice programmers, but also for the evidence they provide about complex human cognitive processing. Empirical studies of programmers are a golden opportunity for psychologists to study human problem-solving and contribute to the refinement of programming languages, training, tools, and design methods.

This paper offers a personal view of the territory covered by empirical studies of programmers, describes possible research paths for exploring this territory, and suggests some appealing destinations.

2. THE TERRITORY

Like the surface of the earth, there is great diversity in programming. Researchers must recognize the differing needs of the warm beaches of student programming, the dense forests of real-time control software, and the jagged mountains of expert systems programming. The following sections categorize the terrain, offering researchers a decomposition of concerns. No research project can cover all the territory. Progress will be made incrementally by ideas that protect student programmers while they acquire skills, support testing for real-time systems, or help professionals maintain complex knowledge bases.

2.1 Programming Phases

Programming begins with the formulation of a problem to be solved. The early stages might be called requirements analysis or preliminary design. This is followed by specification of what the program should do, but not how it should be done. Then the detailed design sets the stage for coding statements in a programming language. After personal or peer review, the program can be tested to see if it adheres to the specifications. If not, debugging is performed to isolate and repair bugs. Most programs must be revised or extended as part of a maintenance process.

This neatly described process is violated more often than not. Some programs may go through six identifiable stages, while others go through eight or ten. Sometimes coding of known components begins before full specification is done. Sometimes testing of prototypes is necessary to formulate the requirements. In short, programming has many variant forms and multiple stages (Curtis et al., 1986; Weiser & Shneiderman, 1986; Shneiderman, 1980).

Language design issues are related to programming phases. Some languages may ease readability, thus supporting maintenance, but they are tedious and lengthy to compose. Some languages offer great flexibility in data or control, thus simplifying design, but making debugging very difficult. If we understand these differences, we can redesign languages and support tools to maximize performance. For example, abbreviations or template selection can speed program creation, but to support readability the editor produces a complete display of keywords and automatic indentation.

2.2 Programming Situations

A program might be created by one person who uses it only once, for example, for an amateur astronomer to compute the sighting angle for Halley's comet. In another situation, three or four people might construct software for a small business to do weekly inventory. At another extreme is the thousand programmers who build the air traffic control system that is used daily for life-critical decision-making tasks. Personal use software that is run only once does not require documentation, may not need to be modular, can be easily tested, and does not cause loss of life if an error is made. Working in large groups on complex software requires a different attitude towards the choice of variable names, documentation strategies, management structure to permit changes, modular decomposition, and testing. Researchers must take into account the different programming situations.

2.3 Program Size and Complexity

Some programs have only ten lines, while others, such as the space shuttle software, have 10 million lines. Some programs use one array, while others have databases supported by data dictionaries listing 10 thousand variable names. Some programs use only input and print statements, while others have rich patterns of control flow, elegant coroutines, and multiple real-time interrupts.

Some programs take only an hour to compose, others take many years of effort by large teams of programmers. Complexity may range over six orders of magnitude.

Clearly, the programming process must be vastly different across these terrain. BASIC may be acceptable for short programs with 10 variable names, but when long programs are written more meaningful variable names, better modular decomposition, and richer control and data structures are necessary. Can one programming language be flexible enough to meet the needs of these differing conditions? Are there dangers in scaling up from a small prototype to a large system?

2.4 Skill Levels

Graduates of six-week courses may call themselves programmers, but their skills are vastly different from the thoughtful professional with ten years of experience. Some languages may be suitable for novices, but unacceptable for professionals because of limitations in features. Languages with many features may overwhelm novices, but be attractive to experts. Can one language have enough flexibility to be suitable for beginners and experts?

Expertise has many dimensions. Programmers may be expert in the syntax of a specific programming language, in certain algorithms (e.g. string manipulation, graphic data structures), or in an application area (e.g. payroll, banking, or chemistry). Some programmers are exceptional at design, while others excel at debugging (Weinberg, 1971).

There are underlying cognitive style, learning style, or personality differences that contribute to skill and influence effectiveness. Increased attention is being paid to individual differences among programmers and to complementary personalities in forming teams (Buie, 1985). Can personality tests be used to form teams or predict success in programming?

Unfortunately, we still have only poor methods for evaluating programmer skill, as demonstrated by performance differences of 20 to 1 and more for professionals in the same organization and job title (Curtis, 1981; DiPersio, Isbister & Shneiderman, 1980). Is there hope for developing a reliable ability test? How can peer ratings or supervisor evaluations be made more accurate? Can we measure quality and productivity for programmers?

2.5 Programming Languages

The number of widely used and documented computer programming languages is approximately 200, yet the variety is impressive (Sammet, 1978). They range from languages with 30-40 keywords to languages with more than a thousand variant commands. There are languages for special purposes such as steel structure analysis or music composition, and languages for general use such as PASCAL, FORTRAN, or C. There are interpreted and compiled languages, textual and visual languages, procedural and non-procedural languages, fixed and extensible languages, and interactive and batch languages. Researchers must recognize the style of programming promoted by each language and consider design suggestions within that context. Indentation rules may be helpful in PASCAL but confusing in APL. Rules for modular design or parameter passing in COBOL may be unsuitable for LISP or PROLOG.

Experimental results have influenced Ada and other recent languages, but designers still work largely from intuition. A major research project to investigate the impact of programming language design on productivity and error rates and to develop an understanding of the cognitive processes in programming could have a dramatic influence on future programming languages.

2.6 Programming Tools and Methods

Programming is greatly influenced by the available tools. The advent of interactive usage changed the preferences in programming languages, design and debugging methods, and teaching strategies. The emergence of syntax-directed editors, browsers, interactive design aids, dynamic debuggers, etc. changed the nature of programming. The highly argumentative discussions about the design of these tools could be made more productive and scientific by the inclusion of empirical data about usage. When does rapid response time aid programming? How might large screens be a hindrance? Do graphical or visual displays of data structures or program execution really help?

There are also a diverse set of programming methods, such as the ones proposed by Jackson, Warnier-Orr, Mills, or Parnas. These methods are often vaguely defined and require interpretation when they are applied. A better understanding of when each method is most effective would be a major contribution.

3. THE PATHS

Explorations of the territory are increasingly well-planned, guided by practical considerations, and directed by a theoretical framework.

3.1 Controlled Experiments

There are many ways to do research on programmers, but the discipline of controlled psychologically-oriented experiments produces reliable and authoritative results. No single experiment can conclusively answer all our questions, but a series of well-designed and narrowly focussed studies will clarify an area of concern. Each experiment is a small tile in the emerging mosaic of human performance in programming (Shneiderman, 1980; Platt, 1964).

Effective and influential studies are built on a solid theoretical foundation and a knowledge of realistic concerns in practical programming situations. These dual bases lead to a lucid and testable hypothesis followed by the identification of a small number of independent variables to alter and a small number of dependent variables to measure. The outcome should suggest refinements to the theoretical foundation and guidance to the professional practitioner.

Successful experiments require great care in the selection of subjects, assignment to groups, choice of tasks, design of materials and instructions, diligence in administration, wisdom in applying statistical techniques, and skill in writing up the results (Brooks, 1980, Moher & Schneider, 1981).

At least one pilot test of the materials and procedures is necessary for refinement, but successful studies often develop only after a series of preliminary experiments. The high variability in human performance with complex cognitive tasks such as programming often obscures the modest differences from the independent variable treatments. Refinement of the dependent measures can help and within-subjects designs are also effective.

Controlled experiments can be so rigid and artificial that the laboratory-like conditions do not reflect or apply to the reality of programming. Each step in improving controls and eliminating biases may also be a step that removes the results from validity and applicability. The knowledgeable experimenter will also blend the discipline of controlled experimentation with a sensitivity for individual performance, a curiosity about extreme scores, and an awareness of anecdotal results that may lead to novel hypotheses.

3.2 Thinking Aloud and Observational Studies

The precision and rigidity of controlled experimentation may be inappropriate when a researcher is exploring new domains in which the independent and dependent variables are unclear. Thinking aloud or observational studies are applicable when the tasks are so complex and varied that setting precise goals for subjects would invalidate the experiment (Lewis, 1982). Typical situations are early stages of program design or exploratory debugging.

The subjects can be videotaped, audiotaped, or simply observed for critical incidents or frequency of reference to specific terms or processes (Littman et al., 1986; Brooks, 1977). Observational studies in realistic setting can lead to discovery of work styles that can be helpful to others or suggest novel software support tools (Adelson & Soloway, 1985; Grantham & Shneiderman, 1984).

The danger of observational studies is that they take a large amount of experimenter time and that resulting conjectures may not be widely applicable. Furthermore, cause and effect relationships cannot be easily demonstrated. Still they are a valuable tool that should be considered.

3.3 Field Studies, Surveys, and Data Capture

Other less formal approaches can contribute valuable insights to the programming process. Field studies to capture performance during professional or student programming are helpful in identifying baselines of normal behavior (Saal & Weiss, 1977; Knuth, 1972). Surveys can elicit useful opinions of what programming methods, tools, languages, etc. are beneficial. Machine logging of response times, frequency of use of programming language features, frequency of use of programming tools such as dynamic debuggers, etc. can also help to clarify actual programmer activity.

There is a great opportunity to conduct grand national "clinical trials" of programming languages, tools, or methods. Similar to clinical medical trials, data would be conducted on a large number of programmers in a large number of programming situations. This enormous database would be available for many researchers to explore hypotheses, probe for unexpected correlations, and compare performance over time as changes are made. A realistic clinical trial might take five years and cost $10-20 million dollars, but the benefits are potentially much greater.

3.4 Theories

No area is more important to the health and growth of empirical studies of programmers than the development of cognitive theories of programming. No one theory will encompass all of programming. Many smaller theories are necessary. Some theories may address only the use of conditionals by novice child programmers. Other theories may suggest effective maintenance procedures for professionals working on parallel processing algorithms. Some theories are broadly conceived and explanatory (a framework for describing or teaching programming), while more narrowly focussed theories can be predictive (a mathematical model for predicting the time to locate a bug as a function of program complexity).

The syntactic/semantic model of long-term memory is an explanatory model, but as it is refined it has the potential to become more predictive (Shneiderman & Mayer, 1979; Shneiderman, 1986) (Figure 1). In this model, syntactic knowledge is the language-dependent details for carrying out actions or defining objects. This knowledge is arbitrary and acquired by rote memorization; therefore it is difficult to retain in long-term memory. For example, the choice of the exponential operator (single asterisk in APL, double asterisk in FORTRAN, up-arrow in BASIC, or a function in LISP or PASCAL), iteration keyword (DO, FOR, LOOP, or REPEAT), or use of semi-colons (to terminate or separate statements) is language-dependent and arbitrary. This knowledge must be frequently rehearsed to preserve retention.

By contrast, semantic knowledge is meaningfully acquired by reference to previous knowledge, by example, or by analogy. There is a logical structure to semantic knowledge that is independent of the specific syntax used to record it. Semantic knowledge is further decomposed into computer and task-related domains. Computer knowledge has to do with the actions and objects in the computer domain. The low-level actions might be assignment, iteration, conditional execution, input, output, synchronization, etc. Higher level actions are algorithms for sweeping through an array, for sorting items, or for recursive binary tree search. Computer objects include the low-level data types such as booleans, integers, strings, real numbers, etc. Higher level objects include arrays, records, stacks, or threaded trees.

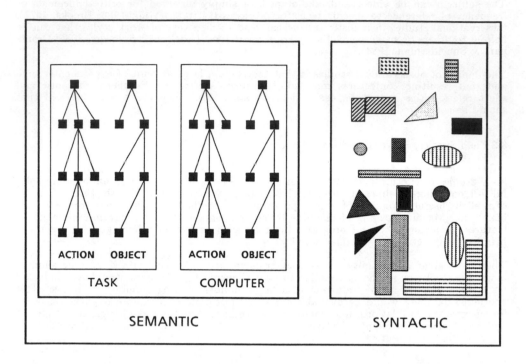

Figure 1: The long-term knowledge necessary for programming as portrayed in the syntactic/semantic model. Syntactic knowledge is arbitrary, poorly structured, learned by rote memorization, and must be rehearsed to ensure retention. Semantic knowledge, which is subdivided into computer and task domains, is organized into objects and actions, meaningfully acquired, stable in memory, and language independent.

The semantics of the task domain can also be decomposed into objects and actions. If the task domain is stock market portfolio management then the actions might include opening or closing a portfolio, buying or selling stocks, and tabulating or displaying performance over a three-month period. The objects might include portfolios, customers, stocks, buy or sell orders, transaction dates, and prices.

Successful programmers must master the syntax of a specific programming language, the semantics of computer programming, and the semantics of the task domain. Novice programmers may be familiar with a task domain (for example, inventory control or satellite orbit determination), but must acquire the semantics of computer programming and the syntax of one or more programming languages. Professional programmers must become proficient in the task domain before they can begin design. It's hard to say which challenge is greater.

Any model is an abstraction of reality. The syntactic/semantic model is not a perfect representation of a programmer's knowledge or cognitive process, but it has been helpful in sorting out the differences between novice and expert programmers, teaching programming, writing textbooks, understanding bugs, and preparing documentation. Still it is a rough model that needs refinement and verification (Barfield, 1986; Wiedenbeck, 1986; Adelson, 1981; McKeithen et al., 1981; Shneiderman, 1977). A variant model based on plans and goals has been formulated by Soloway and his colleagues (Soloway et al., 1983; Soloway & Ehrlich, 1984; Rist, 1986).

4. THE DESTINATIONS

Some explorations are justifiable just for the joy of discovery. Understanding human performance in computer programming is a satisfying process and it has important benefits for improving the practice of programming and for sharpening our model of human cognition. As a computer scientist, my primary goal is the former, but my secondary goal is the latter. I am proud to consider myself as twenty percent experimental psychologist, but my approach has been to apply empirical techniques to the benefit of computer programming practices, languages, tools, and management practices.

Contemporary programming languages are a remarkable achievement. They provide a notation for precise expression of complex and useful processes. This notation is parsable by a computer and yet more or less readable by people. This balance generates remarkable power to accomplish intellectual, commercial, educational, and entertainment tasks. These successes might be attributed to clever choice of a small number of control and data structures, the provision of facilities for modular decomposition of large problems, and the capacity for extensibility by function and data type definition.

These successes are tempered by many weaknesses, or shall I say, opportunities for improvement. Contemporary programming languages often take long to learn, are error-prone, and can be tedious to compose with. There seem to be insufficient mechanisms for level structuring, weak facilities for checking correctness, and poor tools for maintenance. In short, there are many destinations available for the energetic researcher.

4.1 Refining the Use of Current Languages

The most direct means for improving programmer productivity and program quality is by making incremental improvements in the use of current languages. The following brief list offers some ideas about where research efforts might lead to rapid and substantial improvement:

- better use of mnemonic variable names: more meaningful and distinctive mnemonic variable names can be helpful in comprehending programs. This effect becomes noticeable when the number of variable names grows beyond 10-15 and when the programmers are unfamiliar with the task domain. There is a danger about excessively long variable names as they can interfere with comprehension. A range of variable name lengths in a program may support recognition. An in-depth study of naming policies, hierarchical naming strategies, and name documentation methods would be useful. What makes a name memorable? Is it distinctiveness in a name set or familiarity to the user or close linkage to meaning?

- program formatting: Indentation has often been cited as an aid to comprehension, but it can have negative effects in breaking up the semantic units of a program in favor of syntactic units. A modest level of indentation (2-4 spaces) has been shown to be beneficial (Miara et al., 1983). The use of blank lines to show modular organization is also helpful. The use of multiple fonts and characters sizes is being explored as an aid to program comprehension (Baecker & Marcus, 1986). How should programs be shown on screens vs. paper? Would color coding be helpful?

- comments, documentation, flowcharts, and diagrams: embedded comments, external writeups of program structure, pseudocode design documents, control flow oriented flowcharts, structure charts, and data structure diagrams are promoted as aids to program composition or comprehension. For the knowledgeable programmer, these aids are helpful when they reveal information that is difficult to extract from the program text; for example when one sheet of paper shows the relationship among thirty program modules (Shneiderman, 1982). Merely reiterating the program in a detailed visual form may produce a lengthy distracting document. What aids, for which people, for which tasks are most effective (Sheppard, Kruesi & Curtis, 1981)?

7

- modular design by data and procedural abstraction: program organization plays a key role in comprehensibility and modifiability. The top-down design, information hiding, data abstraction, procedure abstraction, and reusable component approaches to modular design offer promising possibilities that have not yet been fully exploited. Little attention has been paid to the motivation for these approaches as a function of human cognitive skills. How might modularity for novice programmers differ from modularity for experts? When is a linearly organized program more comprehensible than a modular program? When does a program reach the point of excess modularity? How should variables be shared among modules?

- group processes and team organizations: although it is difficult to perform carefully controlled experiments on group processes and team organizations the evidence is strong that one of the most effective means for rapid improvement in productivity and quality is by structured walkthroughs or design inspections (Freedman & Weinberg, 1982; Basili & Reiter, 1979; Fagan; 1976). Group processes provide an opportunity to communicate program designs, educate junior team members, increase motivation, and facilitate cooperation. Still, these methods are under utilized and poorly understood. Social and industrial psychologists might be helpful in developing and studying these techniques.

4.2 Improving Present and Future Languages

Researchers are often more attracted to the creation of a new language rather than the refinement of current languages. Commercial programmers and managers are more interested in improving specific features and enhancing current languages. There is plenty of opportunity for both.

- control structures: the contemporary IF-THEN-ELSE and DO-WHILE patterns are effective in many cases but they become clumsy when nesting is deep and complexity is great (Sykes, Tillman & Shneiderman, 1983; Sime, Green & Guest, 1977). More powerful CASE, SELECT, or SEARCH commands might accomplish the work of several lower level control structures. Backtracking, recursion, co-routining, concurrent and parallel control, object-oriented, interrupt handling, and error handling control structures have yet to be adequately explored.

- data declarations: composite data types, such as a record or a stack of arrays, are a major contribution, but more elaborate data typing facilities will be helpful in the next generation of languages. Level structuring and modular design of data types, as is done in database systems, may become available in standard programming languages. How can the semantics and syntax be made comprehensible? Empirical studies can shed light about what makes one data structure more or less cognitively complex (Iyengar, Bastani & Fuller, 1985).

- direct manipulation programming: the text-oriented style of contemporary programming languages will be complemented by more visually-oriented styles of programming (Shneiderman, 1983). Programmers would see representations of objects and actions in the task domain. By pointing, dragging, and drawing the programmer would create programs for later execution. Such programs may be easy to understand, simple to debug, and rapid to revise. Direct manipulation depends on an analogically appealing, task domain-related, visual representation of the objects and actions of interest. Definition of actions is by pointing, dragging, or drawing, instead of typing command strings. Execution of actions is rapid, incremental, and reversible.

The Xerox Star and Apple Macintosh offer many of the aspects of direct manipulation for carrying out tasks, but are weak in supporting programming. The Wang Decision Processing and Spinnaker's Delta Drawing packages provide some of these features. There are currently many efforts to develop visual or direct manipulation programming environments (Iseki & Shneiderman, 1986; Glinert & Tanimoto, 1984; Halbert, 1984).

- spreadsheets: these powerful tools enable users to do much of the work that formerly required programming in a procedural language. Spreadsheet programs offer direct manipulation of an accountant's model of reality and provide a variety of powerful operations in a relatively simple manner. But spreadsheets are to the 1980's what COBOL was to the 1960's. The computer science community has largely ignored this fundamental and important innovation (Shneiderman, 1985). It seems there is a great opportunity to learn from the VisiCalc, LOTUS 1-2-3, Multiplan, etc. designs and to contribute to their evolution. This visual representation of the world of action may be useful model for designing rule-based systems, array computations, or data structures.

4.3 Developing Special Purpose Languages

General purpose programming languages are often deficient in handling some novel set of features. This leads designers to propose special purpose languages. Sometimes these languages survive to serve a small community, but often the ideas eventually influence extensions to general purpose languages. Important destinations for researchers include contributions to the development of these special purpose languages:

- rule-based and logic programming: a currently hot topic in computer science is the design of rule-based and logic programming languages. Unfortunately, the designers of these systems have not absorbed the lessons of structured programming, modular design, or human factors. The resulting systems are often difficult to program in, error prone, and hard to comprehend. Substantial improvements are possible by modular organization of facts and rules, use of visual presentations, and improved notations.

- dialog management systems: traditional procedural programming languages do not provide adequate facilities for creating complex interactions. Dialog management systems, also called user interface management systems, separate the design of the user interface from the underlying programming tools. The interaction style can be changed be merely altering a few lines of the specifications. The design of dialog management systems will be one of the most important topics for the next decade. Creating a user interface for dialog management systems is a further challenge.

- sound, voice, graphics, videodisk, and animation: traditional programming languages also fail to provide adequate facilities for novel interaction techniques using sound, voice, graphics, videodisk, and animation. New programming languages or extensions will be needed to accommodate these features.

- robot and physical device control: when three-dimensional reality and timing constraints are part of the task-domain new languages will be necessary to support convenient programming. Programs may become cartoons or be created by physically moving a robot arm through a specific motion to paint a car door or place an integrated chip on a circuit board. Modular design and editing of these programs is a provocative challenge.

4.4 Improving Tools

Effective tools amplify the user's power to do work. A pressing goal is to provide programmers with more powerful tools to cope with the increased complexity of modern systems and the higher quality and reliability that customers demand.

- syntax-directed editors: editors can be designed to reflect the objects in programs (procedures, variable names, or keywords), instead of merely dealing with strings of characters. During program composition, a syntax-directed editor can guide the programmer to create syntactically correct programs by offering a choice of permissible structures or templates. Benefits arise through reduced keystrokes, fewer typographic errors, and hopefully fewer slips in converting a design into a program. Disadvantages include greater demands on the hardware, some distraction for the expert user, and some clumsiness in current interfaces.

- semantics-directed editors/browsers: modern programming development tools enable users to conveniently edit or display programs. A hierarchical browser shows a table of contents of the modules in a program and the user can see the code in the module by just pointing and clicking on the module name (Shafer et al., 1986). Similarly, placing the cursor on a variable name and pressing a single key can result in a display of the data declaration for the variable. Changes to a variable name in a declaration can result in changes to the variable name everywhere it is used in the program. Finally, maintenance tools can aid in the automatic rewriting of programs. For example, elimination of all code related to a specified output variable would help in trimming a program while conversion of a scalar variable to an array would help in expanding a program.

9

- testing and debugging tools: the highly personal styles of testing and debugging are giving way to disciplined approaches supported by useful and convenient tools. The design of such tools would benefit from human factors studies of how people do testing and debugging, as well as from studies of user interface design for exploratory tasks (Weiser & Lyle, 1986; Spohrer & Soloway, 1986).

- resuable libraries of code: the opportunity to reuse program or design components is attractive to managers who wish to speed development, reduce costs, and ensure reliability. The benefits are potentially great, but most observers feel that the reality is far short of the potential. Software tools to support reuse are beginning to be developed, but the social structure of programming has to be considered as well. First, there must be benefits to the person whose code is reused and to the person who reuses code. Second the atmosphere of trust needs to be enhanced by information about who developed the code, who maintains it, who else has already successfully reused it, and thorough documentation of the inputs and outputs.

5. CONCLUSION

The term programming covers a fascinating and broad territory that invites exploration by courageous and bold research pioneers. The paths are still rough, but the increasing traffic smooths out the bumps and leaves clearer signposts for future travelers. The destinations are attractive: the chance to improve programming practice and to comprehend complex human problem-solving.

Acknowledgements: I greatly appreciate this opportunity, offered by Elliot Soloway and Sitharama Iyengar, to scan the horizon and report to my colleagues. It gave me the chance to reflect on 15 years of papers by fellow researchers and students. I felt warmed and encouraged while reviewing the work of hundreds of bold researchers who have ventured from narrow professional domains to blend psychology and computer science. But this is just the beginning. The greatest opportunities are still ahead. I appreciated the helpful comments from Richard Furuta, William Gasarch, Jim Hendler, Susan Humphrey, Sitharama Iyengar, and Elliot Soloway.

REFERENCES

Adelson, Beth (1981). Problem solving and the development of abstract categories in programming languages, *Memory and Cognition 9*, 422.

Adelson, Beth and Soloway, Elliot (1985). The role of domain experience in software design, *IEEE Transactions on Software Engineering SE-11*, November 1985.

Baecker, Ron and Marcus, Aaron (1986). Design principles for the enhanced presentation of computer program source text, *Proceedings of the ACM SIGCHI '86: Human Factors in Computer Systems*, Available from ACM, New York, NY.

Barfield, Woodrow (1986). Expert-novice differences for software: implications for problem-solving and knowledge acquisition, *Behavior and Information Technology*, to appear.

Basili, V. R. and Reiter, R. W. (1979). An investigation of human factors in software development, *IEEE Computer 12*, 12, December 1979, 21-38.

Brooks, Ruven (1980). Studying programmer behavior experimentally: The problems of proper methodology, *Communications of the ACM 23*, 4, April 1980, 207-213.

Brooks, Ruven, Towards a theory of the cognitive processes in computer programming, *International Journal of Man-Machine Studies 9*, (1977), 737-751.

Buie, Elizabeth (1985). Jungian psychological type and programmer team building, *Proceeding of IEEE COMPSAC '85*.

Curtis, Bill (1981). Substantiating programmer variability, *Proceedings of the IEEE 69*, July 1981, 533.

Curtis, Bill, Brooks, Ruven, Soloway, Elliot, Black, John, Ehrlich, Kate, and Ramsey, H. Rudy (1986). Software psychology: The need for an interdisciplinary program, *Proceedings of the IEEE*, to appear.

DiPersio, Tom, Isbister, Dan, and Shneiderman, Ben (1980). An experiment using memorization/reconstruction as a measure of programmer ability, *International Journal of Man-Machine Studies 13*, 339-354..

Fagan, Michael E., Design and code inspection to reduce errors in program development, *IBM Systems Journal 15*, 3, (1976).

Freedman, Daniel P. and Weinberg, Gerald M. (1982). *Handbook of Walkthroughs, Inspections, and Technical Reviews*, Third Edition, Little, Brown and Co., Boston, MA.

Glinert, Ephraim and Tanimoto, Steven L. (1984). Pict: An interactive graphical programming environment, *IEEE Computer 17*, November, 1984, 7-25.

Grantham, Charles and Shneiderman, Ben (1984). Programmer behavior and cognitive activity: An observational study, *Proceedings ACM Washington, DC Chapter Annual Technical Symposium*.

Halbert, Daniel (1984). Programming by Example, Ph. D. dissertation, Department of Electrical Engineering and Computer Sciences, University of California, Berkeley, CA. Available as Xerox Report OSD-T8402, Palo Alto, CA.

Iseki, Osamu and Shneiderman, Ben (1986). Applying direct manipulation concepts: Direct Manipulation Disk Operating System (DMDOS), University of Maryland Department of Computer Science Technical Report.

Iyengar, S. S., Bastani, F. B., and Fuller, J. W. (1985). An experimental study of the complexity of data structures, In Agrawal, J. C., and Zunde, P. (Editors), *Empirical Foundations of Information and Software Science*, Plenum Press, New York, NY, 225-239.

Knuth, Donald (1972). An empirical study of FORTRAN programs, *Software: Practice and Experience 1*, 105-133.

Lewis, Clayton (1982). Using the "Thinking-aloud" method in cognitive interface design, RC9265, IBM Yorktown Heights, NY, (February 1982).

Littman, David C., Pinto, Jeannine, Letovsky, Stan, and Soloway, Elliot (1986). Mental models and software maintenance, In Soloway, Elliot and Iyengar, Sitharama (Editors), *Empirical Studies of Programmers*, Ablex Publishers, Norwood, NJ.

McKeithen, K. B., Reitman, J. S., and Hirtle, S. C. (1981). Knowledge organization and skill differences in computer programmers, *Cognitive Psychology 13*, 307.

Miara, Richard J., Musselman, Joyce A., Navarro, Juan A., and Shneiderman, Ben (1983). Program indentation and comprehensibility, *Communications of the ACM 26*, 11, November 1983, 861-867.

Moher, Tom and Schneider, G. Michael, Methods for improving controlled experimentation in software engineering, *Proceedings of the Fifth International Conference on Software Engineering*, Available from IEEE, (1981), 224-233.

Platt, John (1964). Strong inference, *Science 146*, Number 3642, October 16, 1964, 347-353.

Rist, Robert S. (1986). Plans in programming: Definition, demonstration and development. In Soloway, Elliot and Iyengar, Sitharama (Editors), *Empirical Studies of Programmers*, Ablex Publishers, Norwood, NJ.

Saal, H. J. and Weiss, Z. (1977). An empirical study of APL programs, *Computer Languages 2*, 3, 47-60.

Sammet, Jean E. (1978). Roster of programming languages 1976-77, *ACM SIGPLAN Notices 13*, 11, November 1978, 56-85.

Shafer, Phil, Simon, Roland, Weldon, Linda, and Shneiderman, Ben (1986). Display strategies for program browsing: Concepts and an experiment, *IEEE Software*, to appear.

Sheppard, S. B., Kruesi, E., and Curtis, B. (1981). The effects of symbology and spatial arrangement on the comprehension of software specifications, *Proceedings of the Fifth International Conference on Software Engineering*, 207-214. Available from IEEE, Piscataway, NJ.

Shneiderman, Ben (1986). *Designing the User Interface: Strategies for Effective Human-Computer Interaction*, Addison-Wesley Publishers, Reading, MA, to appear.

Shneiderman, Ben (1982). Control flow and data structure documentation: Two experiments, *Communications of the ACM 25*, 1, January 1982, 55-63.

Shneiderman, Ben (1980). *Software Psychology: Human Factors in Computer and Information Systems*, Little, Brown and Co., Boston, MA.

Shneiderman, Ben (1977). Measuring computer program quality and comprehension, *International Journal of Man-Machine Studies 9*, 465-478.

Shneiderman, Ben and Mayer, Richard (1979). Syntactic/semantic interactions in programmer behavior: A model and experimental results, *International Journal of Computer and Information Sciences 7*, June 1979, 219-239. Reprinted in Curtis, Bill (Editor), *Human Factors in Software Development*, IEEE EHO 185-9, (1981).

Sime, M. E., Green, T. R. G. and Guest, D. J. (1977), Scope marking in computer conditionals - a psychological evaluation, *International Journal of Man-Machine Studies 9*, 107-118.

Soloway, E. and Ehrlich, K. (1984). Empirical studies of programming knowledge, *IEEE Transactions on Software Engineering SE-10*, 5, 595-609.

Soloway, E., Ehrlich, K., Bonar, J., Greenspan, J. (1983). In Badre, A. and Shneiderman, B. (Editors), *Directions in Human-Computer Interaction*, Ablex Publishers, Norwood, NJ, 27-54.

Spohrer, James C. and Soloway, Elliot (1986). Analyzing the high frequency bugs in novice programs. In Soloway, Elliot and Iyengar, Sitharama (Editors), *Empirical Studies of Programmers*, Ablex Publishers, Norwood, NJ.

Sykes, F., Tillman, R., and Shneiderman, B. (1983). The effect of scope delimiters on program comprehension, *Software: Practice and Experience 13*, 817-824.

Weinberg, Gerald M. (1971). *The Psychology of Computer Programming*, Van Nostrand Reinhold, New York, NY.

Weiser, Mark and Lyle, Jim (1986). Experiments on slicing-based debugging aids, In Soloway, Elliot and Iyengar, Sitharama (Editors), *Empirical Studies of Programmers*, Ablex Publishers, Norwood, NJ.

Weiser, Mark and Shneiderman, Ben (1986). Human factors of computer programming, In Salvendy, G. (Editor), *Handbook of Human Factors/Ergonomics*, John Wiley & Sons, Inc., New York, NY to appear.

Wiedenbeck, Susan (1986). Processes in computer program comprehension, In Soloway, Elliot and Iyengar, Sitharama (Editors), *Empirical Studies of Programmers*, Ablex Publishers, Norwood, NJ.

TECHNICAL SESSION PAPERS

CHAPTER 2

Comprehension Differences in
Debugging by Skilled and Novice Programmers

Leo Gugerty
Gary M. Olson
University of Michigan
Ann Arbor, MI 48109

ABSTRACT

Two experiments investigated expert-novice differences in debugging computer programs. Subjects used a microcomputer to debug programs provided to them. The programs were in LOGO in Experiment 1 and Pascal in Experiment 2. We found that experts debugged more quickly and successfully than novices, largely because they generated high quality hypotheses on the basis of less study of the code. Further, novices frequently added bugs to the program while trying to find the original one. We also described some of the debugging strategies the subjects used. At least in these simple programs, experts' superior debugging performance seemed to be due primarily to their superior ability to comprehend the program.

INTRODUCTION

Debugging is a central part of computer programming. Programs seldom work when first coded. Many superficial syntactic errors are easy to find, especially with the aid of a compiler or interpreter. But a substantial number of bugs require concentrated problem solving. Though various debugging strategies and tricks are often taught in programming classes, much of the skill of debugging is learned through the experience of writing programs and getting them to run.

We report two studies of expert and novice programmers working at debugging a program written by someone else. While programmers often work at debugging a program they have written themselves, frequently individuals who are part of programming teams must work on the code generated by others.

What kinds of strategies and skills are required to debug a program written by someone else? Obviously, one main component is knowledge of programming

Funding for part of this research was provided by the Reading and Learning Skills Center, University of Michigan. The first author was also supported by an NIMH Training Grant to the University of Michigan Experimental Psychology Department. We would like to thank the following people who assisted in this research: David Sodergren, Elisabeth Feldman, Rebecca Goodman, Karen Goldschmidt, Arnold Chiu, and Bridget Barrer.

constructs. One strategy a programmer can use is to comprehend what the program actually does and what it is supposed to do. Places where the actual program does not match the programmer's best model of how the program should work are potential bugs. Johnson and Soloway's PROUST model uses this strategy to successfully debug novice programs in limited domains (1).

Rasmussen (2) has identified two other major troubleshooting strategies, called topographic and symptomatic search, which may also be used in debugging. In topographic search, a programmer uses clues in the output or tests of internal program states to narrow the possible location of a bug to a small part of the program. In symptomatic search, the programmer uses prior debugging knowledge and recalls a bug that has previously caused symptoms like the current ones.

The comprehension, topographic, or symptomatic strategies, or some combination of them, can be used to generate hypotheses as to what the bug is. These can be checked by editing the code, running the program, and studying the consequences, or by engaging the desk checking.

How might experts and novices differ in their debugging of someone else's program? It is possible that experts could outperform novices at each of the three main debugging strategies. With respect to comprehension, experts greater knowledge of programming concepts, such as **program plans** and **rules of programming discourse** (3) will likely lead them to understand what the program does much more readily than a novice. In addition, experts may know more particular strategies for focusing in on the bug via topographic search; or they may use the ones they know more effectively. Finally, if experts are debugging in a familiar domain, they would be expected to have a larger mental "library" of symptom-bug associations and thus do better at symptomatic search.

Jeffries (4, 5) reported findings from an informal study of debugging behavior that supports the existence of comprehension differences between experts and novices. She compared six experts and four novices on the debugging of short Pascal programs. Her experts were graduate students in computer science, while the novices had just finished their first programming course. Each subject debugged two short Pascal programs, each of which contained a number of bugs. Subjects worked with a print-out of the program and a print-out of output from test runs -- they did not use a computer. Experts found more of the bugs and found them faster. Experts spent a large proportion of their time on comprehension of the program, and constructed a much more complete representation of the program. They also remembered details of the program better than novices did. Novices and experts seemed to use similar strategies while debugging, but the experts had much superior comprehension skills. Because of the small number of subjects she tested, no statistical evaluation of her findings was reported.

In our experiments we also focused on the contrast between expert and novice programmers. We defined expertise the same way Jeffries did. In the first experiment, we taught subjects the LOGO graphics language and had them debug several simple LOGO programs. We used LOGO because we felt its modular, graphical nature would make it easy to follow the debugging behavior of subjects. In the second study, expert and novice Pascal programmers debugged a Pascal program. We switched languages to evaluate the generality of the findings from Experiment 1.

EXPERIMENT 1

Method. The subjects in this experiment were 18 novices and six experts. The novices were just finishing their first or second course in Pascal, while the experts were advanced graduate students in computer science.

None of the subjects knew LOGO prior to the experiment. Thus, the first phase of the study consisted of teaching each subject the LOGO programming language and the LOGO graphics programming environment on an Apple II computer. Subjects were taught individually or in small groups in a session that lasted approximately two hours. Subjects were taught the basic commands of the LOGO language, the basics of the programming environment, and then were asked to write and debug a short LOGO program. The subset of LOGO used in this experiment was very similar to Pascal, which all the subjects knew. Therefore, the main things that subjects learned in the training were the LOGO graphics commands and programming environment.

Following training, each subject debugged three programs. The subject's task was to correct the program so it produced the correct graphical output. All debugging was done on-line. Each defective program was read in from a floppy disk, and the subject was given a print-out of the defective program to look at. Further, the subject was given a drawing of what the program was supposed to draw. A 30-minute time limit was imposed for the debugging of each program. Subjects were not told how many bugs the program contained. Subjects were asked to think-out-loud while engaged in debugging. The session was also videotaped, primarily to record the information that appeared on the computer screen.

There were three different programs, ranging in length from 16 lines to 49 lines. Each program was supposed to draw a simple figure or design on the screen. One bug was put into each program. Three different types of bugs were used: incorrect graphics-procedure parameter, missing graphics interface statement, and global-local variable error. Each of the bug types was combined with each of the programs to produce nine different buggy programs. Figures 1 through 4 show the three programs, the three bugs, and the correct output for each program. All of the buggy programs were syntactically correct and produced graphical output when run. An individual subject saw each program and each bug type once, and across subjects all combinations of program and bug type were used equally often. Order of presentation was also counterbalanced.

This first experiment was a preliminary study, and the experts and novices were run at different times. One of the three programs was slightly modified for the experts, and some small procedural changes were made. However, these slight differences do not account for the contrast in behavior between experts and novices in this study.

Results. Since the programs were fairly simple, most subjects were able to find the bugs most of the time. Experts found the bug 89% of the time, while novices found it 72% (t (22) = 1.62, .05 $< p <$ .10). However, experts found the bugs much faster than novices. The mean time to find the bug was 7.0 minutes for experts and 18.2 for novices (t (22) = 3.27, $p <$ .01).

All subjects began each debugging session by studying the program. This included studying the printed copy we gave them or a listing of the program on the screen, studying the intended drawing, and -- often but not always -- running the program to see what the flawed output looked like. At some point a subject got an idea as to what the bug might be, and tested this idea by editing the program and running it. We used this set of acts -- editing and running -- to operationalize hypothesis testing.[1] Overall, novices tested 4.5 hypotheses per program, while experts tested an average of 1.9 (t(22) = 2.58, $p <$.05). Looking only at those subjects who were successful, novices went through an average of 3.8 hypotheses, while experts went through 1.5 (t (22) = 2.19, $p <$ .05). Experts had fewer hypotheses because they often tested the correct hypothesis on their first try. 56% of the experts' attempts to debug a program were solved with their first hypothesis, whereas novices found the correct hypothesis first only 21% of the time (t (22) = 2.54, $p <$ .02). Thus, one reason the novices took longer to debug these programs was that their initial hypotheses were often not correct. This led to more hypotheses and longer debugging sessions.

Running the program is an important debugging behavior, since it can provide several different kinds of diagnostic information: it can aid in comprehension, it can allow for reasoning backwards from symptoms in the output to potential problems in

---

[1] Editing the program to put in test writes or LOGO PAUSE statements did not count as a hypothesis test.

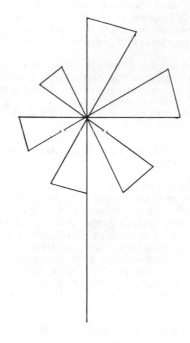

```
TO TRI  :SIDE
FD  :SIDE
RT  105
FD  (:SIDE * .52)
RT  105
FD  :SIDE
RT  150
END

TO PETALS :SIDE
REPEAT 6 [TRI :SIDE RT 60 MAKE "SIDE (:SIDE * .9)]
END

TO PINWHEEL
MAKE "SIZE 50
CS PU FD 40 PD
PETALS :SIZE
BK  (2 * :SIZE)
END
```

*The underlined variable should read :SIDE

FIGURE 1

EXPERIMENT 1 : PINWHEEL Program with VARIABLE Bug* and Correct Output

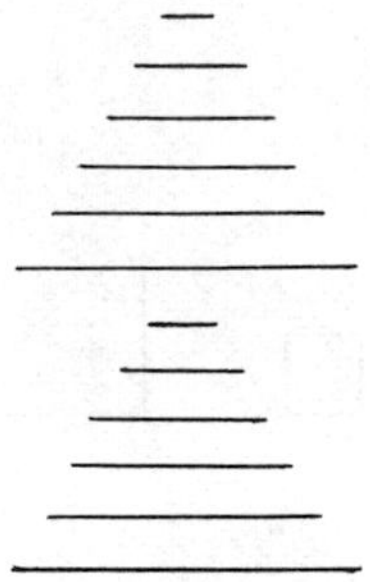

```
TO LINE : SIDE
FD :SIDE  BK :SIDE
END

TO TRILINES :SIDE
IF (:SIDE < 2) [STOP]
LINE :SIDE
PU
RT 60 FD 5
PD
TRILINES (:SIDE - 5)
END

TO DOUBLE
MAKE "SIZE 30
CS LT 90
REPEAT 2 [BK (:SIZE / 2) TRILINES :SIZE]
END
```

*The underlined statement should be followed by LT 60

FIGURE 2

EXPERIMENT 1 : DOUBLE Program with INTERFACE Bug* and Correct Output

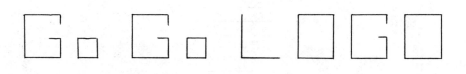

FIGURE 3

EXPERIMENT 1 : Correct Output for MESSAGE Program

```
TO O :SIDE
REPEAT 2 [FD :SIDE RT 90 FD (:SIDE * .85) RT 90]
RT 90 FD (:SIDE * .85) LT 90
END

TO SPACE :N
PU
RT 90
FD (:N * 1.2 * :SIZE)
LT 90
PD
END

TO G :SIDE
FD :SIDE
RT 90
FD (:SIDE * .85)
RT 90
FD (:SIDE * .25)
PU FD (:SIDE * .25) PD
RT 90
FD (:SIDE * .25) BK (:SIDE * .25)
LT 90
FD (:SIDE * .5)
RT 90
FD (:SIDE * .85)
BK (:SIDE * .85)
RT 90
END

TO MESSAGE
MAKE "SIZE 20
CS PU LT 90 FD 100 RT 90 PD
G :SIZE
SPACE 1
O (:SIZE * .5)
SPACE 2
G :SIZE
SPACE 1
O (:SIZE * .5)
SPACE 2
FD :SIZE BK :SIZE
RT 90
FD (:SIZE * .85)
LT 90
SPACE 1
O :SIZE
SPACE 1
G :SIZE
SPACE 1
O :SIZE
END
```

*The underlined parameter should be 0.4

FIGURE 4

EXPERIMENT 1 : MESSAGE Program with PARAMETER Bug*

the program, and it can allow one to test hypotheses about what the bug might be. Overall, experts ran the program more often that novices: an average of once every 1.9 minutes during their session compared to the novices' once every 2.9 minutes ($t(22) = 2.15$, $p < .05^2$). Prior to their first hypothesis test, experts ran the program an average of 3.3 ($+3.5$) times, and novices 2.8($+2.5$) times.[3] Given the variability of these data, the number of runs prior to the first hypothesis appears to be related much more to individual differences among the subjects than to their level of expertise. Thus, prior to testing a hypothesis, novices ran the program roughly as many times as experts did. However, since experts tested hypotheses earlier than novices, they actually ran the program more often in real time.

So far we have described experts' and novices' debugging in terms of behaviors such as testing hypotheses and running the program. Now we will describe some of the strategies our subjects used to guide their debugging behavior. These strategies were identified through inspection of the protocols. We have not yet completed the process of counting how often these strategies were used by experts and novices[4], but we will briefly describe what seem to us to be the most important types of strategies subjects used.

Subject often simulated the execution of parts of the program. They would draw or act out with their hands the results of the graphics routines, or make notes about the value of variables at various stages of the programs. Sometimes the simulations seemed to be purely mental, in that subjects would mention that they were doing a simulation but carry out no overt acts.

Another important strategy was working backwards from symptoms. Subjects would first run the program, and after comparing the actual and desired results, identify one or more problems. Then, based on their previous study of the program, they would look at the part of the program which they thought produced the incorrect output. Working backwards is one kind of topographic strategy for guiding the initial search for the bug.

Another strategy which provides overall guidance is elimination. Here the subject examines one or more of the procedures in a program by simulation, or as is possible in LOGO, by running the procedure separately. Procedures which seem correct are eliminated from consideration.

After using a strategy such as working backwards or elimination to focus on a particular part of the program, subjects would sometimes do a detailed simulation and compare the simulated and desired outputs in order to find the bug.

Another way of obtaining detailed information about a program is adding test writes -- statements which print out the value of certain variables at a particular location in the program.[5] We have tabulated the data for this strategy, and novices used it at least as much as experts. Novices used test writes on 45% of the programs, and experts 33% ($X^2 = 0.8$, n.s.).

Another strategy subjects used during the later stages of debugging, after the bug had been localized to a particular statement of the program, was to try changing parts of the statement without a clear idea of the result. For example, subjects might try a new value for a LOGO graphics statement. Then they would adjust the value depending on whether or not it made the output closer to the desired figure. Subjects would sometimes make three or four adjustments before finding the correct parameter. This strategy is best called an empirical approach.

Once a hypothesis about the bug had been tested and found to be correct, the

[2]The t-test was performed on the reciprocals of the times in order to normalize the distributions.
[3]The figures in parentheses are 95% confidence intervals.
[4]This involves detailed analysis of more than 60 videotaped sessions.
[5]In LOGO, this can be done using the PAUSE statement.

subject was done. However, suppose the subject made an editing change, ran the program, and the output was still defective. The subject would need to decide whether this particular change contributed to a partial solution of the original defects in the output. If the subject were unsure, or if the subject were convinced this was **not** the bug, the prudent thing to do would be to change the program back to what it had been originally. This would prevent additional bugs from being added to the program.

Novices often added their own bugs. We defined adding bugs as testing an incorrect hypothesis which changed the program's output and not undoing this change before testing the next hypothesis. We were conservative in counting new bugs. Changes due to incorrect hypotheses which had no effect on the program's output were not counted. For novices, adding a bug was correlated with being unsuccessful at debugging. When novices failed to get the program to work in the allotted time, 92% of the time they had added at least one bug of their own. When they **did** get the program to work, they had added a new bug only 23% of the time (t (17) = 5.46, $p <$ .01[6]). In contrast to this novice behavior, only once did an expert ever add a new bug to the program (and interestingly enough, did not debug the program within the time limit).

To summarize Experiment 1, the first hypothesis that a subject tested after a period of studying the program was consistently better for the experts than for the novices. This suggests that in part the superior debugging performance of experts was due to their better ability to comprehend a program. Our evidence is less clear about strategy differences. Novices used test writes as often as experts did, and ran the program as often as experts did prior to testing a hypothesis, an important component of the working backwards and elimination strategies. Novices often generated further trouble by failing to undo incorrect hypotheses.

In Experiment 2, we looked to see whether a similar pattern of results emerged when experts and novices debugged a program written in Pascal, a language subjects already knew when they came to the laboratory.

EXPERIMENT 2

Method. The subjects were 10 novice programmers who had just finished their first or second course in Pascal and 10 expert programmers who were advanced graduate students in computer science.

All subjects in this experiment knew Pascal. The study was conducted on an IBM PC using the Turbo Pascal programming environment. Since this specific environment was unfamiliar to the subjects, a 25-minute training session was used to familiarize them with the environment and allow them to use its various editing, debugging, and file manipulation tools.

Prior to training on the programming environment, each subject read a Pascal program for comprehension. Their understanding of this program was measured by having them (a) answer short questions about the program and (b) label the functions of various sections of the program. There were two different programs for this phase, with half of each group of subjects given each. This phase of the experiment was part of a transfer design that will not be further described here (since there was no evidence

---

[6]These data were analyzed by calculating a single score for each subject that represented these tendencies. Since each subject debugged three programs, a score of + 1 was assigned to those cases where they (a) failed to find our bug and added a new bug or (b) found our bug but did not add any new bugs. -1 was assigned to the other two combinations. Thus, to the extent that the scores of individual subjects were significantly greater than 0, the hypothesis that finding our bug and adding new bugs were independent could be rejected. The t-test is a test of just this: the extent to which the mean score for 18 novices exceeded 0.

of transfer).

The program to be debugged was a 46-line Pascal program that read in data from a file, manipulated the data, and printed out results. There was a single bug in the program that produced an incorrect value for a counter variable. The program, with the bug, is shown in Figure 5. Subjects were given a listing of the program and a printed copy of the data file, both of which were also available to them in on-line files. They were also given a printed description of the purpose of the program, a copy of the correct output, a calculator, and a note pad. They were allowed 40 minutes to try to get the program to run correctly. Subjects were not told how many bugs there were. Unlike Experiment 1, they were not asked to think out loud. Experts and novices were treated identically in this experiment.

During the debugging session, an observer monitored where the subjects were looking, recording the activity times on a second microcomputer located across the room from the subject. The observer recorded on the keyboard where the subject was looking, using the following categories: screen, keyboard, statement of purpose, program listing, data-file listing, correct answers, calculator, note pad, reference materials, and other. All of the materials were fixed in standard locations in the subject's workspace to simplify the monitoring process. The observer's keystrokes were time stamped, providing a record of how long a subject looked at each location. For one pilot subject, two observers logged the subject's looking. The two observers agreed on 95.6% of the keystrokes, and all of the disagreements were minor.

Results. Experts were better at the preliminary comprehension task than novices. The two preliminary programs used were not equally easy to understand ($F(1.16) = 10.5$, $p < .01$). However, there was no interaction between program and expertise. Overall, experts answered 11.3 of the 13 comprehension questions correctly, while novices were correct on 8.5 ($F(1.16) = 7.56$, $p < .02$).

In the debugging task, nine of 10 experts found the bug in the allotted time, while only five of 10 novices did ($X^2 = 3.81$, $.05 < p < .10$). When the bug **was** successfully found, experts were much faster than novices. The mean time to solution was 14.2 minutes for the experts and 33.1 minutes for the novices ($t(12) = 5.18$, $p < .01$).

Experts and novices differed in their testing of hypotheses, where a hypothesis test was defined as making an explicit editing change in the program and then running it. As in the first experiment, experts' hypotheses were of better quality than novices; and this enabled the experts to test fewer hypotheses than novices before finding the bug. Overall, novices tested an average of 2.2 hypotheses per program and experts tested 1.1 ($t(18) = 2.11$, $p < .05$). Of the subjects who successfully debugged the program, novices went through 1.8 hypotheses, while experts went through 1.2 ($t(12) = 1.78$, $.05 < p < .10$). Looking at the quality of the hypotheses, the initial hypothesis tested was correct for seven of the experts and only two of the novices ($X^2 = 5.1$, $p < .025$). Furthermore, experts were much quicker at testing hypotheses. They made their first test an average of 12.9 minutes into the session, while novices made theirs only after 24.3 minutes ($t(16) = 3.46$, $p < .01$)[7].

What were experts and novices doing prior to testing their first hypothesis? For each subject we had a complete record of what they were paying attention to. Two of these categories were (a) studying the program (either on the screen or on the printed sheet) and (b) studying the description of the purpose of the program. Experts and novices devoted the same proportion of their time to these activities prior to testing their first hypothesis. Experts spent 58% of their time studying the program and 14% studying the statement of purpose, while novices spent 63% of their time studying the program and 9% studying the statement of purpose. The other categories of behavior were all very low in frequency (see Table 1)[8]. Thus, experts and novices did not

[7]One expert and one novice failed to test a single hypothesis (by our definition) during the 40-minute period.
[8]Novices also spent 9% of their time, on average, making notes and looking at the notepad. However, this was mostly due to two subjects who spent more than 23% of their time in this activity.

```
Program debug (datafile, input, output);
const
    ncollege = 5;
    maxncategory = 12;
type
    dim2 = array[1..maxncategory, 1..ncollege] of integer;
    dim1 = array[1..maxncategory] of integer;
var
    datafile : text;
    rating : dim2;
    rank : dim1;
    sum, category, ncategory, college : integer;
    finalrate : real;
procedure readdata (var rating :dim2; var rank :dim1; var ncategory :integer);
    var category, college : integer;
        begin
            assign (datafile, 'college.dat'); reset (datafile);
            category : = 1;
            while ( (not eof(datafile)) and (category < = maxncategory) ) do
                begin
                    read (datafile, rank[category]);
                    for college : = 1 to ncollege do
                        read (datafile, rating[category, college]);
                    readln (datafile);
                    category : = category + 1;
                    if (category > maxncategory) then
                        begin
                            writeln ('Data file too long for arrays rating & rank');
                            halt    {the program}
                        end
                end;
            ncategory : = category
        end
begin
    readdata (rating, rank, ncategory);
    writeln ('college number   overall rating');
    for college : = 1 to ncollege do
        begin
            sum : = 0;
            for category : = 1 to ncategory do
                sum : = sum + (rank[category] * rating [category, college]);
            finalrate : = sum / ncategory;
            writeln (college:8, finalrate:17:1)
        end
end.
```

*The variable NCATEGORY is 1 too large when it is passed out of the READDATA procedure. This can be fixed in a number of ways.

FIGURE 5

EXPERIMENT 2: The Buggy DEBUG Program*

TABLE 1

Allocation of Subjects' Attention Prior to First Hypothesis Test

(expressed as the percentage of time prior to the first hypothesis test)

	Novices*	Experts*
Program (hardcopy or on screen)	63.3	58.2
Statement of purpose	9.2	14.0
Notepad	9.3	2.3
Program output (on screen)	1.9	4.0
Correct answers	1.0	2.2
Data file (hardcopy or on screen)	0.4	0.6
Calculator	3.9	2.9
Keyboard	3.3	6.1
Operating system messages	2.2	3.4
Error messages	0.0	0.1
Reference materials	0.8	0.3
Other	0.3	0.8

*For the 9 novices and 9 experts who tested at least one hypothesis

24

distribute their activities differently during the time prior to testing their first hypothesis. However, novices took nearly twice as long to get to the point of being ready to test a hypothesis, during which they studied the program and the statement of purpose almost twice as long as the experts (17.3 minutes for novices, 9.3 minutes for experts, $t(16) = 3.28$, $p < .01$).

Experts ran the program an average of once every 4.0 minutes, while novices ran it once every 5.8 minutes ($t = 1.47$, n.s.). This difference was in the same direction as in Experiment 1, but was not significant here. Prior to testing their first hypothesis, experts ran the program an average of 2.4 ($\pm$ 1.0) times, and novices 2.2 ($\pm$ 1.0) times. As in Experiment 1, there were no significant expert-novice differences in the number of runs prior to the first hypothesis test.

Although verbal protocols were not collected in this experiment, the data provided some information about our subjects' debugging strategies. Novices used test writes in three of 10 programs, while experts used them in five of 10 (n.s.). Thus, as in Experiment 1, both groups appeared to use this strategy equally often.

Novices did not always undo incorrect hypotheses. Novices in Experiment 2 tested 15 incorrect hypotheses. Eight times such an incorrect hypothesis was undone, while seven times it was left in the program. Of these seven, three had no adverse effect on the program and four created new bugs.[9] Experts only tested two incorrect hypotheses; and both of these were undone.

As in the first experiment, novices who did not get the program to work in the allotted time had often added their own bugs. Three of the five novices who did not debug the program also added their own bugs, whereas none of the five novices who successfully debugged added their own bug. No expert ever added a new bug to the program.

GENERAL DISCUSSION

Three of our findings were quite surprising to us. First was the fact that prior to generating and testing an initial hypothesis, experts and novices distribute their activities in the same way. We had expected that novices might quickly plunge into experimenting with the program, perhaps pursuing long, blind alleys as they edited the program before really understanding it. Instead, novices studied the program intensively before making any changes. They did not do qualitatively different things than the experts. Rather, they just took longer. Second was the finding that despite studying the program much longer, the novices' initial hypotheses were substantially inferior to those of the experts. These were not long or difficult programs, yet despite this novices seldom found our bug on their first attempt at making a substantive change in the program. Third, we had not at all expected to find that novices make matters even harder for themselves by adding additional bugs in the course of looking for ours. Experts almost never added new bugs to the program.

Why were expert subjects faster and more successful at finding the bug in these simple programs? The overall **pattern** of behavior of the two groups of subjects was not strikingly different. In experiment 2, both experts and novices waited a long time to test their initial bug hypothesis, usually until more than 70% of their total debugging time was up. And both groups spent most of this time studying the program

The evidence from these two studies suggests that a primary reason for the experts' superiority was the ease with which they understood what the program does and is supposed to do. This in turn allowed them to isolate the bug more quickly, as indicated by the frequency with which they found the bug on their first attempt. Novices, on the other hand, while spending nearly twice the time in preliminary study of the program

---

[9]In addition, one subject added a bug inadvertently, through a typing error.

and the statement of purpose, did not have sufficient programming knowledge to focus in on good hypotheses. Moreover, they frequently made the situation worse by introducing new bugs as they edited the program and tested hypotheses. These added bugs were a major predictor of whether or not the program was ever debugged within the given time limit.

These findings are reminiscent of the research of Chase and Simon (6) with expert and novice chess players. In both their work and in ours, the most striking difference between experts and novices is in the domain knowledge they possess. Experts' superior performance is based more on their ability to quickly and effectively encode the stimulus situation than on their reasoning strategies. McKeithen, Reitman, Rueter and Hirtle (7) replicated Chase and Simon's findings with expert and novice programmers. In both realms successfully encoding (comprehending) the problem leads to dramatic differences in problem-solving performance. This is much the same conclusion that Jeffries (4, 5) came to in her preliminary studies of debugging.

In conclusion, these experiments suggest that expert-novice performance differences in debugging are due, at least in part, to the different program-comprehension abilities of these two groups. In the introduction, we also suggested that experts and novices may differ in the use of remembered symptom-bug associations (symptomatic search) and of strategies such as backtracking (topographic search). At least in the LOGO experiment, the expert-novice differences were probably not due to experts' better recall of prior bugs, since both the experts and the novices were unfamiliar with the LOGO graphics domain. However, some of the expert-novice differences in these experiments could be due to experts using topographic search strategies more effectively. This possibility deserves further investigation.

In planning further research in this area, it should be noted that this study shares an important characteristic with most expert-novice studies of problem-solving -- in order to give experts and novices the same stimuli, rather simple materials are used. As a result, the full range of the experts' skills are probably not revealed. These studies revealed differences between experts and novices in the comprehension phase of debugging. But because experts often got the correct hypothesis on their first attempt, the differences in problem-solving behavior following the point at which an initial hypothesis was tested were difficult to study. Many of the problems the novices had after their initial hypothesis test seem mainly due to faulty comprehension or retention of the program, as indicated by the extent to which they inadvertently added new bugs. Testing whether experts and novices display differences in other debugging strategies probably will require using more difficult programs with the experts.

REFERENCES

1. Johnson, W.L. & Soloway, E. (1983). PROUST: Knowledge-based program understanding. New Haven, CT: Yale University, Computer Science Department, Technical Report # 395.

2. Rasmussen, J. (1981). Models of mental strategies in process plant diagnosis. In J. Rasmussen & W. Rouse (eds.) *Human Detection and Diagnosis of System Failures*. New York: Plenum Press.

3. Soloway, E. & Ehrlich, K. (1984). Empirical studies of programming knowledge. *IEEE Transactions on Software Engineering, SE-10*, 595-609.

4. Jeffries, R. (1981). Computer program debugging by experts. Paper presented at the 1981 meetings of the Psychonomic Society.

5. Jeffries, R. (1982). A comparison of the debugging behavior of expert and novice programmers. Paper presented at the 1982 meetings of the American Educational Research Association.

6. Chase, W.A. & Simon, H.A. (1973). Perception in chess. *Cognitive Psychology, 4*, 55-81.

7. McKeithen, K.B., Reitman, J.S., Rueter, H.H. & Hirtle, S.C. (1981). Knowledge organization and skill differences in computer programmers. *Cognitive Psychology, 13*, 307-325.

CHAPTER 3

Plans in Programming:
Definition, Demonstration, and Development

Robert S. Rist

Cognitive Science Program
Department of Psychology
Yale University
New Haven, CT 06520

ABSTRACT

Support for the use of plans in cognitive models of programs was provided by evidence from both novice and expert programmers. For novice programmers, an initial plan-based description of code segments was replaced by syntactic and control based groups as the programs became more complex. An increase in plan use with expertise was also evident. Experts used only plan groupings in their efforts to understand a program.

Cluster analysis of these code groupings showed the precise definition and order of appearance of the program plans, providing an experimental basis for identifying cognitive plans. Three main sources of plan emergence were identified in the novice data: goal based, object based and basic plans. Goal based plans allow the focal segment for a goal or program to be easily identified. The link between the program goal and the code that implements this goal provides the basic plan structure of the program. The rest of the program code supports this basic operation. The conceptual model of the program for experts is centered on this focal segment. This directs attention in the understanding and construction of programs. It gives a human solution to the problems of goal search and selection.

INTRODUCTION

A program is a tool designed for a purpose. As a machine, it has rules of operation that are governed by the syntax and the control structures of the language used. As a goal-directed artifact, it is constructed by the selection of plans that satisfy its purpose. These plans organise the code into well-defined fragments that achieve a goal, cutting across syntactic and control flow boundaries.

A mental model of the program as a machine has been the dominant influence in most recent research. The construction of program algebras and correctness proofs [5, 7] relies solely on issues of control and data flow, deriving correctness from the formal structure of the program. Rich [12] and Waters [21, 22] applied these formal models to discrete program segments by constructing and merging plan fragments in the Programmer's Apprentice Project. The plans realised program goals, but their formal correctness and expression in the program was the focus of attention.

The concept of basic programming plans developed by Soloway and his associates [15, 16, 17] moved further towards a goal description of a program. Such plans are small program fragments that achieve a single, well-defined goal, such as to count or sum a series of numbers. These plans are thought to underlie the development of programming expertise by transforming knowledge about mechanism into correct plans. The basic plans by themselves, however, cannot describe a program; they must be supplemented by a plan and goal description at higher levels of analysis.

A program may be considered as a plan tree that relates program plans to dominant goals. Top-down program design would view a program as growing from the top description node in the tree down to the individual leaves. In such a tree, the program goal represents the highest node. Below this are the standard global plans, such as input, process and output. At each level, goals are split into plans and the process continues until the plans at the lowest level can be translated into code. These basic level plans would be like those discussed by Soloway. The names or descriptions of the modules appear before any specific code. Program descriptions of this kind have been used to provide a detailed analysis of bugs in student programs [18]. The basis for creating such a tree is not clear, since it attempts to capture both plan and mechanism oriented groupings. Analysis by top-down design uses such modules, but does not give a principled definition for their creation.

Development of a program by goal chaining defines these modules as goals that create the program structure, defining instead of simply describing their bounds. The name of the module is created by its specific focal code. In a program that calculates the average, for example, the goal chain begins with the output goal, which creates the calculation goal. This in turn creates the count and sum plans, defined by their focal segments. These central lines of code are defined by goal back-chaining before the abstract and control structure of the program is known. They define the plan structure of the program before details appear. This chain is known and retrieved by experts in top-down design, but the knowledge that created these modules is goal based, not an unspecified decrease in abstraction.

A further advantage of this approach is its ability to deal with plan interactions. In top-down design, an increase in implementation creates a new tree rather than one with more leaves. Plan interactions often require sections of code (other plans) to be moved so that a new plan can be integrated [13, 19, 20]. A detailed plan approach captures the plan dependencies that require the movement, giving a vocabulary to describe these changes.

This experiment investigates the plan structure of programs by both novices and experts. The experts organised code in programs into plan-based groups that supported Soloway's plans and demonstrated the plan and goal tree suggested by a goal analysis. The novices described simple programs in plan terms, but changed to a syntactic or control flow description if the code became difficult to follow. An increase in plan usage was observed over the test period. This replicates the movement found in other expertise studies [4, 9] from surface (syntactic) to deep (plan) structures. A further change was seen in the expert data, where code was grouped by its relation to the focal lines of a code segment, abstracting over the plan roles used by novices. Contiguous sections of basic plans that shared the same role (such as setup or update) relative to the focal code, were defined as a group by the experts.

Three sources of plan development were seen in the novice data. The major source was goal back-chaining, where plans appear as pre-requisite sub-goals, back from previous goals. Definition of a code segment as plan-based was related to the distance between the code and its goal. A second source was down from higher levels of description, where the goal of a section of code may be known, but the intricacies of the algorithm are not well-understood. Small sections of code were labelled as plans before large sections; common plans, such as input and output, appeared early in the development sequence. A third source was the basic level plans, which help to define which plans are known and unknown. As plans are learned, unstructured goal segments are broken down into smaller, plan pieces. Sections of code previously defined by their syntactic relationships come to be defined as implementing a goal.

THE STRUCTURE OF PLANS

Global Plans

Global plan labels are used at the highest levels of program description. The basic structure of a program is to *input* a set of data, *process* the data or calculate a result, and then *output* the result. These descriptions are the first ones learned by students and define simple programs completely, without the need for other plans. As programs grow longer, the simple match is broken but the labels still apply to the larger program. These labels may be termed global plans (gplans), since they describe the program as a whole. They are first learned and provide the beginnings of plan development. As more programs are encountered, the number of these gplans rises slightly to about six, including perhaps validate and update plans.

If we look at detailed plans, the same basic terms are used at all levels of program description, not just the highest. A count must be initialized to zero, then accumulated in a loop (processing) and finally used in some further calculation or output. The global plans consist of plan segments that share the same label, such as all the initializations in a program, created from the plans that stretch through the program. Thus these gplans may also be considered as role definers that provide frames for the creation of new plans.

Basic Plans and Goal Chaining

Goal back-chaining is the solution method in problem-solving that is used when a problem is difficult or novel. Larkin *et al.* [10] examined the solution of physics problems and reported that 'novices solved most of the problems by working backward from the unknown problem solution to the given quantities'. Experts usually worked forward, but for difficult problems the solution method was goal back-chaining.

The first version of a new program, a new problem, is written by a process of goal back-chaining. The program goal creates one or more subgoals which in turn create other and more detailed goals. Once learned, this goal chain can be isolated and retrieved from a plan library for use in writing later versions by top-down design. The initial definition of the plans arise from the goal chaining technique, however. Once the structure of the goals has been identified, these pieces can be used by experts in forward analysis by top-down design. Top-down design arises from the previous analysis, and is only useful when the module definitions are known. The problem of creating the initial modules is not well-addressed by top-down techniques, but depends on abstraction from the pieces defined by a previous goal analysis.

Role	Plans		
	Count	Sum	Average
Init	count := 0	sum := 0	av := 0
Process	count := count + 1	sum := sum + num	if count <> 0 then av := sum / count
Use	calc average	calc average	writeln (av)

Figure 1: Plans: count, sum and average

The interaction of plans with the goal chain may be seen in the *average* plan [15]. This plan makes use of the count and sum plans, shown in Figure 1. Count and sum are basic plans used in a read loop, to count and sum a set of numbers. Their products are use to calculate the average. The process segments of these plans are contained in the read loop (*ibid.*) which is itself a complex plan, involving three components, two reads and an input-controlled loop. The read itself may be a composite plan, consisting of a descriptive prompt and the (focal) read statement.

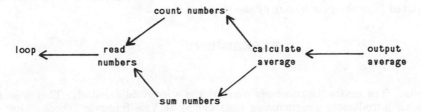

Figure 2: Goal chain for finding the average

These plans describe the plan structure of the *average* program. They may be tied together by constructing a goal chain, to which the plans are attached. The goal chain begins at the task of the program, which is to output the average of a set of numbers (Figure 2). This creates a goal to calculate the average, the focus (process) of the output goal. The calculation goal creates the count and sum goals, which in turn require numbers as input. This creates the need for an input goal and finally a loop to repeat over the numbers. The count and sum plans define the focus for the program; the process section of a plan defines the focus for that individual plan. These chained goals define and structure the plans required for the program by backward goal dependencies. Control flow and (forward) data flow structure their implementation into program code.

Focal Plans and Automation

In more complex programs, the focal segment may be buried at the bottom level of the plan tree, in the most intricate code. In a sort program, for example, the test and order process that compares two elements is focal to the sort. All the other lines of code support this test, nested deep inside the program. The focal line is the driving force of the plan. It may be thought of as the basic difference reducer [11] between the start and the goal states of the problem. The concept of a *kernel idea* in algorithm development [8] is very similar to this focal segment. Focal lines are always beacons [2], but beacons may also be control structures, such as the loop control in a sort.

The focal line usually appears deep inside the program and the plan tree. Top-down design would not encounter it until very late in the design process. Goal back-chaining identifies it quickly and then uses this knowledge to create the modularization used in top-down design. The label of the focal plan is repeated in a chain from the top node to the focal segment, as in the sort program. The overall description of the program is a sort. At the next level it may be modularised into input, sort and output. Within sort it may be divided into loop, calculate index and sort, and so on, each use of the label applying to a smaller section of code until the focal segment is reached.

Knowledge of the focus reflects an increase in expertise. The expert may be characterized by the ability to focus on the most important parts of the program in coding and understanding, exploring the crucial issues before writing any code. Novices are characterized by a forward development of the program with little planning. For them, every line of code is a problem and so they solve these problems (implement the goals) in a simple, sequential manner. Plans are constructed and debugged as required. As expertise develops, some plans are automated (such as input and output) and initially ignored during design, freeing attention for the more difficult segments in validation or processing. Plan schemas are formed that define the information (slots) required and ignore the internal structure of the schema. Plans are selected rather than constructed [1, 2]. Experts can define a particular part of the processing as most important, the focal segment, and accrete a program around this segment. They have both plan templates and sophisticated plan building mechanisms. Finally, plan interactions with other plans and the environment become the focus of attention; plans are compared and evaluated before being used [14].

The goal chain defines the overall structure of the program. Novices focus on construction issues and use this goal information to implement program operators. They work from the code to the goals. As templates form, these goals index code segments and code is retrieved from the plan library by the goal that it realizes.

EXPERIMENT

Design

Subjects. Ten novice programmers were used in a longitudinal study. They were all students in an introductory programming class taught at Yale Summer School. Most of them were seniors in high school. The class was a first introduction to programming using Pascal, for students with no computer experience. The course ran for five weeks and subjects were tested at the end of every week.

The course was based largely on the text *"Introduction to PASCAL"*, by Dale and Orshalik [6] and adopted their top-down approach to program design. Some basic programming plans were taught early in the summer, the count, sum and max plans. The bubble sort program, discussed later, was taught in the third week (see Figure 4).

Seven expert programmers performed the same task. These programmers were all third year computer science graduate students at Yale. Each expert had at least eight years experience in programming. All subjects were paid $5 per hour.

Materials. Twelve programs were used in the study. They ranged in length from 22 to 42 lines of code and over a range of difficulties. All were written in structured, indented Pascal. The simplest calculated the cost of covering a circular area with material, the most difficult performed a two-dimensional bubble sort.

Two sets of programs were isomorphs in the sense that the logical structure of each set was the same, but the variable names and program description had been changed. The first set was the tax-factory isomorph. The tax program calculated the net pay (including overtime) and tax, given the pay rate and the number of hours worked. The rate of pay was changed to the weight of a box and the tax rate calculation to a cartage rate for the isomorph. The factory program calculated basic and overweight cartage rates. The second set of isomorphs was composed of the 'hen' and 'mile' programs, fantasy versions of an averaging program. In the first program, the average number of eggs per henhouse was calculated; in 'mile' it was the average number of miles travelled over a set of trials.

Task. Subjects were given five copies of each program and asked to group the lines of code together that 'did the same things'. The written instructions were

> I am trying to find out how people understand what a program does. Which lines of code did you mentally group together when you were trying to understand what the program did? I want you to write down these lines as a group. I cannot tell you what to use as a basis for this division. Try to think which lines of code *are related* to each other in their action. Then write a short (one to three words) description of why these lines are related.

Each line of code was numbered and subjects created a group by writing these line numbers in a group and then giving the basis or reason for seeing these lines as a group.

This was done for the smallest sized groups first. Then the subject took a new copy of the program and repeated the task, this time using larger sized groups. The size and composition of these larger groups was left unspecified. After sorting the program lines again, the task was repeated until the program was a single group. Thus a hierarchy of clusters was used as the raw data for analysis, not simply the bottom-most level of clustering. Each subject used as many copies of the program as he or she needed; the maximum number of levels used was 6, the minimum 3. The order of grouping was randomized throughout the experiment by asking subjects to alternate the order, from smallest to largest for one program and from largest to smallest for the next. All subjects grouped the first program from the smallest groups up, but were then split into two sets and given a different initial direction for grouping, up or down.

Procedure. The task was explained to the subjects and the materials distributed. The experts were given all the programs and scored them at their own pace. The novices were given a set of programs, usually two, on Thursday or Friday of each week during the course. No time limit was set for the task, which usually lasted from one to two hours.

Difficulty rating. The expert programmers were also asked to rate each program on how difficult it would be for a novice programmer to write. They first sorted the programs, then rated them using a scale of 1 for the simplest and 10 for the most difficult.

Category Definitions

The groups of line numbers were analyzed by sorting them into a set of categories. Short descriptions of each category are shown in this section; a full description may be obtained by writing to the author. Where several sources of information appeared, such as 'an if statement that calculates the average', the most advanced basis (plan here) was used. Where the basis was ambiguous, such as a 'read' description, then the most primitive basis (syntax here) was assumed.

Prologue. The lines preceding the executable code; also the program as a group.

Syntax. The syntactic category of a line of code. These were

- Assignment (may be split by type)
- If
- For
- While
- Repeat
- Read
  - ▸ read, readln, reads (both types)
- Write
  - ▸ write, writeln, writes (both types)
  - ▸ write space, write something

Control. Control groupings are based on the flow of control through the program, realised in Pascal by the looping and selection constructs. A typical example was to place all the if, for, while and repeat lines together as one group, a control group.

Functional. There are only four functional classifications. These apply over all plans in a program. The groupings are

- unnecessary: write space lines plus comments
- assign values: assignments and constants
- give values: assignments, constants and reads
- give values or types: add declarations to the above group

Gplan. Initialize, input, process, calculate and output.

Plan. There are three main types of plans:

- Basic plans are Soloway's plans, at the highest level of detail.
- Goal-based plans derive their structure from the code that supports the focal lines. All the groups labelled as sort, for example, are goal-based groupings. They implement the details required for the matrix sort.
- Objects such as pay and room organise these goal based plans. In a program that calculated the cost and amount of wallpaper needed, for example, input and calculation was needed for three objects (the room, the doors and the

33

windows) before the final area and cost calculations could be done.

Variations. Groups were defined for each program using the rules described above. Since many novice groups did not correspond precisely to these, three variations of plans were allowed:

- merges: a begin or end is merged with the neighbour group
- fragments: the major syntactic part of a plan (such as a while for a read loop) is used as the plan.
- combinations: some common plans are combined, such as input and output.

Coding ambiguous data. The defined groups were matched to the data to provide a count of the number of groups for each basis used by the subjects. Many groups of line numbers could appear as either a syntactic or a plan based group, such as an if/then that calculated the average. These were marked as ambiguous groups and rated by hand. An example of this analysis is shown in Appendix II.

To measure the reliability of the rating technique, two independent raters were used. Both were computer science graduate students at Yale who had not taken part in the study. A set of detailed guidelines on the grouping bases was constructed and given to the two raters. Any difficulties were discussed and the raters then scored the novice 'hen' program groups, sorting the repeated and the not matched groups into the defined categories. Agreement between the raters was 91% for repeated groups and 87% for those not matched. Disagreements were again discussed and the 'mile' program was scored, with agreements of 95% and 91%.

One of these raters and the author then scored all the data, sorting the repeated groups into their categories. For the novices, the total agreement was 94.3%. Agreement for the ambiguous groups was 95.8%, for the groups not matched 92.3%. Agreement for the expert groups was 95.3% overall, agreement for ambiguous groups was 99.3%. The raters thus agreed for almost all the data, demonstrating the definition and precision of the grouping categories. All groups not matched were dropped from further analysis. For the novices, this removed 20.4% of the data; for the experts this was 8.6%.

CATEGORY RESULTS

The overall behavior of the two groups was remarkably similar. The ten novices produced a total of 2087 groups; the seven experts produced 1451 groups. The average number of groups used per program by the novices was 17.4, for the experts 17.3. The average number of levels per program was also similar, 4.28 versus 4.3 for the experts. Novices showed more variability in the number of levels used, with more difficult programs requiring more levels of description ($r = .75$, $p < .001$). There was no similar correlation for the experts.

The categories are shown in Figure 3 with the percentage of matched groups in each category. In describing a program, novices used a mixture of syntactic and plan based groups. Experts used almost solely a plan-based classification. The percent values for each category are shown in Table 1. There was a marked and significant difference in the use of syntax and plan groups by novices and experts.

There were no observable differences for the prologue and functional categories between novices and experts. The control and gplan percentages did show a small, significant difference over expertise. The major differences were the change in plan percentage and the percent of matched groups, both improving with expertise.

Plan use was demonstrated by the high percentage of plan groups and low level of syntax use for the experts. To focus on these effects, a new percentage was calculated for the program groups. Both the prologue and not matched groups were dropped from analysis. In subsequent figures, the five remaining bases sum to 100% of the data used.

34

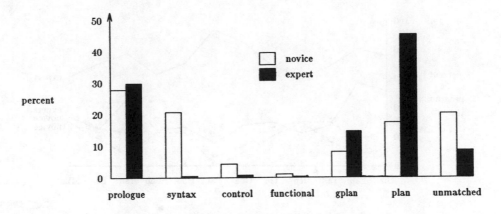

Figure 3: Percent of groups by category

	Novice	Expert	F	Probability
Prologue	27.88	29.84	0.17	
Syntax	20.93	0.55	132.25	*** < .001
Control	4.40	0.75	13.18	** < .01
Functional	1.05	0.13	3.93	
Gplan	8.00	14.74	10.40	** < .01
Plan	17.34	45.34	151.48	*** < .001
Not matched	20.36	8.61	24.16	*** < .001

Table 1: Percent of groups by category

For each program, novices used a mixture of plan and syntactic groupings. Experts used a plan basis for over 97% of the groups. Differences between novice and expert levels were significant beyond .001 (syntax, $F = 204.77$; all plan, $F = 158.24$). The results also showed a strong correlation between plan and syntax levels. As plan levels increased, the level of syntax based groups decreased ($r = -.91$, $p < .0001$).

Plan use may be seen more readily in isolation, as shown in Figure 4. This reveals that the main difference in overall behavior is the amount of plan groupings used, as predicted ($F = 76.47$, $p < .001$). The use of global plans is similar over both novices and experts, increasing slightly with expertise ($F = 5.24$, $p = .05$). The correlation of gplan use between the two groups ($r = .87$, $p < .001$) is more important, and seems more to be tied to the individual programs used than to the level of expertise required.

Correlation with academic performance

The development of plan use seems to underlie expertise. To test this claim more precisely, we may examine whether there was a correlation between plan use and final mark in the course. The overall level of plan use is correlated ($r = .50$, ns; $p (.05) = .549$), but not significantly due to the small sample size. This is not a pure measure of expertise, since it reflects a general (pre-course) preference for plan descriptions.

A more sensitive indicator of plan use is provided by the hen-mile isomorph. We can measure increases in plan use, and thus expertise improvement, by subtracting beginning (hen) plan level values from final (mile) levels. The people who learned plans faster, who had greater plan differences between the isomorphs, did better in the course ($r = .62$, $p < .05$). It is encouraging that such effects appeared, since the sample was small, the time

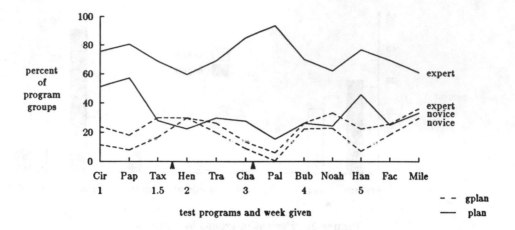

Figure 4: Gplan and plan levels

interval extremely small (five weeks) and the range of final marks restricted to the upper half of the class distribution.

Interaction with difficulty

There was not a consistent upward trend of plan use over time. Initial plan use, for the first two programs, ran at 51% and 57% respectively. Use of gplans added another 10 points to these, meaning that at the start of the course, one week into programming, novices used plan descriptions for about 65% of the program groups. Examining only plan use, this high level fell for the next two programs, from 57% to 28% when the IF statement was introduced and 22% when looping was introduced. The control structure of a program thus had an important effect on a subjects' ability to analyse it in plan terms.

There was a correlation of .61 (p < .02) between the rated difficulty of a program and the use of syntactic groups to describe it; for plan use, this correlation fell to -.43 (ns). The influence of difficulty on understanding is therefore important, but is not simple.

Program differences may be studied in two ways, by using ratings of program difficulty and arguing about their effect, or by ignoring difficulty and using program isomorphs. There were two isomorphs used in the study. The first isomorph, tax-factory, produced no significant results (Table 2). The second isomorph, hen-mile, showed a significant increase in plan use with expertise when difficulty was held constant. A t-test for matched samples was used to measure the difference in mean scores over the test occasions. The hen isomorph showed the predicted behavior. Plan use rose significantly, gplan use did not change and syntax fell in response to increased expertise.

The effect of difficulty may be examined directly by looking at the percent of plan groups in a program similar to, but more difficult than, the averaging program. This is provided by the program 'noah', which included all the code from the hen program and added a check for invalid data and two additional counts. The noah program was presented at the end of week four, one week before the mile program. From Figure 5, it may be seen that the effect of this extra difficulty was to increase the amount of syntactic grouping and so depress plan levels.

The observed level of expertise thus seems to be a function of two, opposing factors. The first is a gradual development of expertise over time, increasing plan use. The second factor is the difficulty of the program, which presents the novice with a new set of plans to

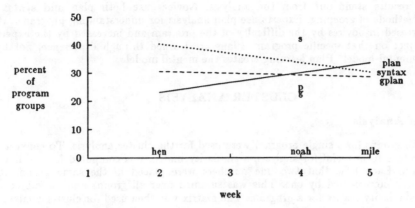

Figure 5: Difference in group levels for the hen isomorph

		First program	Second program	t	Probability
Tax	Syntax	38.41	43.64	0.47	
	Gplan	16.5	18.75	0.47	
	Plan	28.17	25.69	-0.24	
Hen	Syntax	40.14	30.13	-1.42	.1
	Gplan	30.14	33.56	-0.30	
	Plan	22.99	33.56	1.80	* .05

Table 2: Values for program isomorphs

integrate. Initially, these plans are not known and so a syntactic or control grouping is made. Program complexity decreases plan use by forcing a reversion to control based program understanding. An explanation of program behavior needs to be constructed from the code, not interpreted from the recognized plan structure.

The same interaction, with an opposite result, may be seen by looking at another section of the data associated with the bubble sort program. This program was rated as most difficult by the experts, yet showed unexpectedly high levels of novice plan use. The bubble sort algorithm had been taught in class (time is shown in Figure 4) and so expertise on this particular program was high. Contrasts were written to test the effect of difficulty on the three prior test programs and on all four programs. The level of observed expertise was explained for the first three programs by the rated level of difficulty ($p < .001$ for all measures). This relation could not be extended to all four programs. None of the measures proved significantly related to difficulty. The additional factor of expertise on the bubble sort interacted with difficulty to raise the observed level of expertise.

This example shows the specificity of expertise. Although the bubble sort had been taught as an algorithm for one-dimensional arrays, the experience in learning how the program worked contributed to knowledge about program plans and affected the experimental results. Plans appear as a result of experience and learning, not from some gestalt shift. A plan orientation was apparent from the first program, but broke down for more complex programs. Specific plans must be learned by experience with those plans. This gives a possible explanation for the lack of change in the tax isomorph, since the plans involved were specific to that program and not repeated over the study. Reading, looping and counting plans did appear in many of the test programs, and allowed changes in these plans to be observed in changes from the 'hen' to 'mile' isomorphs.

Four results stand out from the analysis. Novices use both plan and syntax as alternate methods of grouping. Experts use plan analysis for understanding programs. Plan use is depressed in novices by the difficulty of the program and increased by the expertise of the subject on that specific program. Plans are learned through experience, not by a change in mental model. Plan learning creates the mental model.

CLUSTER ANALYSIS

Method of Analysis

All the groups for a single program were used for the cluster analysis. To convert the group data to a form useful for analysis, a similarity matrix was computed for the lines in the program. Each time that two line numbers were placed in the same group, their similarity was incremented by one. This was summed over all groups and all subjects to create the similarity matrix for a program. The matrix was then used for cluster analysis.

The cluster trees were labelled by taking the most common descriptions for each group from the data. The groups for each subject were sorted to remove all duplicate groups. These unique groups for each subject were then merged to provide an aggregate description of all the groups and the most common label was used for the tree. Where no group matched, labels are preceded by a '?'.

The shift in conceptualization from syntax to semantics is reflected in the cluster analysis for each of the programs. The cluster trees reveal the shift in much more detail than the aggregate statistics, and may be used to specify the changes noted above. Cluster nodes define the code that implement goals in the expert trees and thus define the plans themselves. Their position and order of emergence give insight into the developmental history of plans.

Goal and Object Groups

The novice and expert clusters for the first and simplest program, 'circle', are shown in Figures 6 and 7. Recall that the percentage of all plan groups in the novice program was 63%; the labels for the cluster tree of Figure 6 reflect this bias and are all plan based.

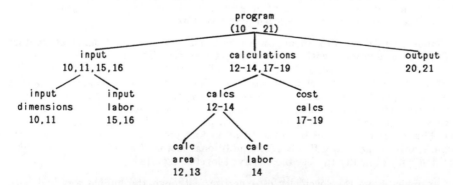

Figure 6: Novice cluster tree for program 'circle'

More specifically, these plans are goal-defined plans. The top level of description consists of the three gplans: input, calculate and output. The details of these share the same description as the gplan and simply implement it in code. The prompt plan is the first basic plan learned; it is used as a chunk here. Note that the goal structures group non-sequential lines together.

The expert clusters shown in Figure 7 are also plan based, but the major structure

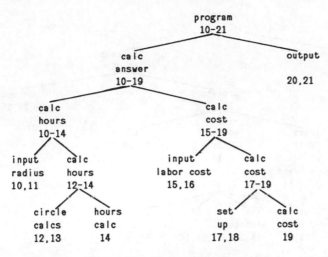

Figure 7:   Expert cluster tree for program 'circle'

comes from the program objects. For each program object, hours and cost, there are input, intermediate and final calculation nodes. These low-level nodes closely resemble those of the novice plan tree, but they have been re-organised into object-based groupings. For experts, objects dominated subordinate gplans.

Plan Development

As programs became more complex, the simple plan definitions are not sufficient for understanding. Other novice cluster trees appear as a mixture of plan and syntactic labels. Gplan descriptions are common, as expected. Plan descriptions tend to be based on a basic plan or a focal node. The order of emergence for plans may be seen by comparing the plan trees for the hen and mile isomorphs in both novice and expert versions. The cluster trees for these programs are shown in Figures 8 to 11. The program code for 'hen' is shown in Appendix 1.

The first cluster tree for program 'hen', Figure 8, shows a mixture of plan and syntactic groups. The plan groups are very localised, however. There are the three gplans: input, process and output, and one group (16,17) based on the count and sum plans. These basic plans do not appear in the data as separate entities and it is only the focal lines that are considered to be plan based. These plan focal lines also make up the focus of the program, since they represent the process segment of the calculate average goal.

Note that the gplan label has been wrongly applied to the prompt plan, lines 12-14. This is incorrect, since it is subordinated to the process node (12-23) and there is more input inside the main loop, at line 20. This second input has been labelled syntactically as a 'read' statement. This could be interpreted as a plan based group, but the label is ambiguous and in the absence of other data, a syntactic basis is assumed. The first read corresponds to the grouping seen in the 'circle' program, where the prompt and read plan appears as a single unit, divided into two parts at a finer level of detail.

The cluster tree for 'mile', Figure 9, alters in both shape and label. The label for the first lines in the program has changed from assign to initialize, showing a shift from syntactic to gplan grouping. The label of the prompt plan has also changed, from the gplan 'input' to the correct plan label, read. These are capitalized in the figure. The WHILE loop (15-21) has developed from an unorganised tree to show an internal, plan-based structure. Three components have been isolated to define the loop: the loop control, the focal updates and the second read. The max calculation has merged with the updates to form a single node. Interestingly, these updates are now labelled as syntactic groups, assign and if, as though the plan based group merge retained these syntactic descriptions as distinctive.

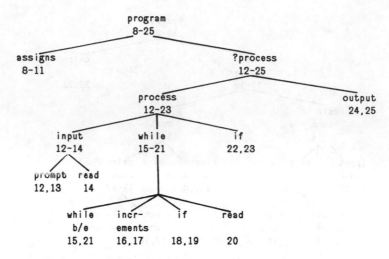

Figure 8: Novice cluster tree for program 'hen'

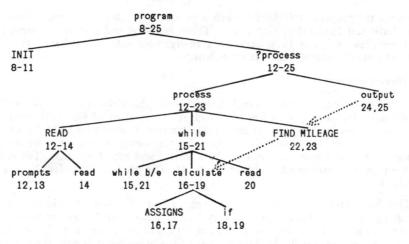

Figure 9: Novice cluster tree for program 'mile'

Most interestingly, the syntactic group (22,23) has changed to a plan label, 'find mileage'. This is the calculation goal for the average plan, to which the updates are subordinate. At this stage in their expertise development, novices show correct gplan and plan use, but in highly restricted locations. The most abstract level of description is labelled by gplans. The first input plan has been identified and labelled as a prompt plan. The goal back-chain has emerged and stretches from the output (24,25) through the average calculation (22,23) to the update calculations (16-19). The plan labels for the program consist only of gplans, the prompt plan, and plans formed by goal back-chaining.

The expert tree for program 'hen', Figure 10, shows the continued development of the novice plans. The program has been split into the output and the processing required for that output. More importantly, the initial read has been subsumed under the update node and merged with the update plan. This reflects a common pattern seen in the shift from novice to expert trees. Novices often place isolated plan initializations far from the focus of the plan they serve. For the *read loop* plan, for example, the first read (outside the loop) was typically grouped with the previous code instead of the loop (Figure 9). The full count, sum and max plans appeared only in the expert groups; novices omitted the initialization.

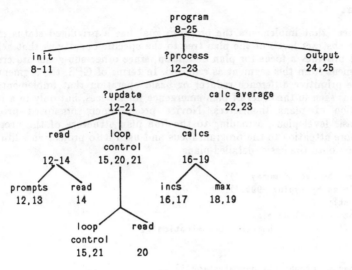

Figure 10: Expert cluster tree for program 'hen'

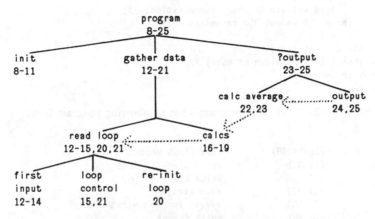

Figure 11: Expert cluster tree for program 'mile'

The last tree, Figure 11, shows the plan tree in a final form. In doing the grouping tasks, the experts changed their responses as a function of familiarity. The task seems to have created a focus on plan groupings that led to learning about the plan structure of the programs. The 'average' focal line has joined its goal, output (24,25). Soloway's read plan has appeared as a separate entity. Loop plans, such as the read loop plan, were identified by every expert, but only appeared for program 'bubble' in the novice data, where there was a sentinel controlled loop.

The code in this plan tree now breaks up into the components suggested by the goal analysis of Figure 2. The backward chain begins with the goal (24, 25) and focal (22,23) lines to output the average. The focal lines of the update plans form the next group, and the read loop completes the processing. All the plans then create the initialization section. The code has been grouped into plans that implement goals specified by goal back-chaining. The same plan knowledge was used by novices, but experts organized these simple plans by specific goal chains and objects. Novices used less fine-grained, global categories that ignored individual plan dependencies, indexing from the gplan to the plan role.

Focus Development

The focal segment that implements the program goal has a priviliged status in the program. It links the abstract levels of the plan tree to the specific operations that achieve the program goal. It provides a focus for plan definition, since other sub-goals are created by program development from this segment as required. In terms of GPS, the segment can be considered as the primitive difference reducer or basic operation that implements the goal. Its influence was seen in the order of plan emergence for novices, but only in a minor way in the definition of plans themselves. Novice programmers organised program understanding by basic level plans, attending to the fine plan structure of the program. Experts payed far more attention to the program focus and used it to project an additional scheme of organization onto the basic, detailed plans.

```
16      write ('Enter the sum of money. ');
17      writeln ('Finish by typing -999.');
18      readln (amount);
19      while (amount <> STOP) do begin
20          writeln ('             Number   Denomination');
21          i := 1;
22          repeat
23              number := amount DIV denomination[i];
24              if number <> 0
25                 then writeln (number, denomination[i]);
26              amount := amount MOD denomination[i];
27              i := i + 1
28          until (amount = 0);
29          writeln('Enter the sum of money');
30          readln (amount)
31          end
```

Figure 12: Section of program 'change' showing program focus

```
                 (16 17 18)          read first amount
                 (19 31)             while there is data
                 (20)                write heading
Basic            (21 27)             scan array
plans            (22 28)             repeat for denominations
                 (23 26)             split amount
                 (24 25)             show denominations used
                 (29 30)             read next input

                 ((21 22 23 24 25 26 27 28) (FIND CHANGE))
                 ((23 26) (*S CALCULATE CHANGE)))
                 ((20 21) (SET UP FOR CHANGE))
                 ((20 25) (*O SHOW CHANGE))
Novice           ((21 27) (*S SCAN ARRAY))
groups           ((21 27) (*S SCAN ARRAY))
                 ((23 24 25) (PROCESS DENOMINATION))
                 ((23 26) (*S CALCULATE CHANGE)))
                 ((26) (UPDATE AMOUNT))
```

Figure 13: Basic and novice plan groupings for 'change' focal segment

A shift in focus may be seen easily in the 'change' program. This program calculated change for an arbitrary amount of money. The focal section is shown in Figure 12. The goal of this program is to output the number of each denomination required. This output goal is realized by lines 24 and 25 in the program. The output is calculated by the focal segment of the program, line 23. An analysis of this section of code by basic plans is revealing. The basic plans involved are the read loop, an index calculation, the repetition over denominations and the output and 'split' plans. The split plan consists of lines 23 and 26; it is a common pattern used in Pascal for splitting a value into single digits. This analysis produces the groups shown in Figure 13. Novices used these basic plans in grouping code; the relevant section of their plan data is shown below the predicted groups.

	(16 17 18)	read first amount
	(19 31)	while there is data
Focal	(20 21)	set up for change
plans	(22 28)	repeat for denominations
	(23 24 25)	check this denomination
	(26 27)	set up for next cycle
	(29 30)	read next input

	((20 21 22 23 24 25 26 27 28) (MAKE CHANGE))
	((20 21) (SET UP FOR CHANGE))
	((20 21 22 28) (SET UP LOOP))
Expert	((21 22 27 28) (*SL SCAN THROUGH DENOMINATIONS))
groups	((22 23 24 25 26 27 28) (FIND CHANGE +F))
	((22 28) (*SL TEST DENOMINATIONS))
	((23 24 25 26 27) (PROCESS DENOMINATION +M))
	((23 24 25 26) (PROCESS DENOMINATION))
	((23 24 25) (PROCESS DENOMINATION))
	((24 25) (*O SHOW CHANGE)))
	((26 27) (PREPARE NEXT DENOMINATION)))
	((26) (UPDATE AMOUNT))
	((27) (UPDATE COUNTER))

Figure 14: Focal and expert plan groupings for 'change' focal segment

Experts did not favor basic plans as the major program groupings. In the relevant section of plan data for the 'change' program, only 5 of the 31 plan groups were basic. The other groups were defined in terms of the focal segment of the program. From this perspective, the program does one primary thing: change a single denomination. The focal group is lines 23-25 as discussed above. The other lines in the code are there only to allow this group to function. The first cycle is prepared by setting up the header and denomination index (20,21), setting up the repeat loop over denominations (22,28), handling a single denomination (23,24,25) and then setting up for the next cycle (26,27). The groups predicted by using this focus are shown in Figure 14, together with the relevant expert plan data. This section has been editted by removing the five basic plan groups from the 31 total plan groups and then deleting any repetitions. The first segment shown and the focal segment were the most common, repeated four times each.

The set of groups shown in Figure 14 shows a well-organized top-down structure. The first group, lines 20 to 28, gives the overall description of the code. Subsequent groups reduce this description by taking out related plans and control structure, focussing the description from eight lines down to, eventually, the goal lines of the program. Knowledge of these plans allows such clean top-down design, a hallmark of expert performance. Novice programmers do not possess this knowledge or focus, and thus need to be treated differently. Top-down design, it seems, is inappropriate for teaching novices programming.

CONCLUSION

The use of plans by both novice and expert programmers has been established in this study. In understanding the code in a program, experts defined code groups on the basis of program plans that the code implemented. Novices used a mixture of syntactic, control and plan based groups, reverting to more syntactic groupings when programs became complex.

Two effects were apparent on the level of observed plan expertise: a trend toward increasing plan use with expertise and decreasing use with difficulty. This plan expertise was not a gestalt shift, but the product of experience with specific plans.

Plan knowledge appeared from three main sources. Gplans were the first plans taught and are used by novices and experts similarly. Focal plan descriptions appeared in both novice and expert trees. Basic plans define the detailed structure of the program. Two more plan bases appeared in the expert data: the program object and program focus as plan organisers. The use of hierarchical data provided a cognitive snapshot of this plan and goal structure.

Four stages in code grouping (mental models) were observed. The first stage used syntactic categories to group data. The second stage based groupings on the control structure of the program. The third stage saw the use of basic plans to organise and describe code. The last stage used the role information of these plans to highlight their relation to the program focus. This last stage resembles top-down design. It was not used by novices and not predicted by Soloway's plan formalism. Top-down design thus seems inappropriate for novice instruction, since the vocabulary to implement it has not yet been developed.

Goal chaining has been advocated as the mechanism for the development of solutions to new problems. In program production, the construction of these chains defines the plan and code required to implement a goal. If the student learns by doing, then goal chaining seems a natural route to the order of plan emergence. Segments of code, defined initially by a mechanistic mental model of the program, are relabelled as achieving a subgoal.

The analysis of gplans and plans revealed an underlying structure. Basic plan roles can be defined in the same terms as the program as a whole. This provides a useful vocabulary for plan description and construction. It also gives a natural definition for the focal segment as the basic process that achieves the program goal.

The definition of focus provides a new perspective on program development and plan learning. It captures the essence of a program or plan long before any details are apparent. The construction of goal chains from this segment create the structure of the program. Program and plan focus reflect the human characteristic of 'knowing what to do next', constraining the number of current goals to a very small set. Goal chaining and plan selection drive both the production and learning of plan segments in programming.

ACKNOWLEDGEMENTS

I wish to express my appreciation to Jim Spohrer for his many ideas and criticisms and assistance in the scoring task; to Dana Kay, for help with the statistics; to David Littman for acting as an independent rater; and to John Black, for his continual support through the experiment. This study was made possible by grant number 66430 from IBM.

REFERENCES

1. Anzai, Y. (1984). Cognitive control of real-time event-driven systems. *Cognitive Science*, **8**, 221-254.

2. Brooks, R. (1983). Towards a theory of the comprehension of computer programs. *Int. Journal of Man-Machine Studies*, **18**, 543-554.

3. Card, S. K., Moran, T. P. & Newell, A. (1980). Computer text-editing: An information-processing analysis of a routine cognitive skill. *Cognitive Psychology*, **12**, 32-74.

4. Chi, M. T. H., Feltovich, P. J. & Glaser, R. (1981). Categorization and representation of physics problems by experts and novices. *Cognitive Science*, **5**, 121-152.

5. Chi, U. H. (1985). Formal specification of user interfaces: A comparison and evaluation

of four axiomatic approaches. *IEEE Transactions on Software Engineering*, Volume **SE-11**, *8*, 671-685.

6. Dale, N. & Orshalik, D. (1983). *Introduction to PASCAL and structured design.* Lexington, MA: D. C. Heath and Company.

7. Hoare, C. A. R. (1969). An axiomatic approach to computer programming. *Communications of the ACM*, **12**, *10*, 576-583.

8. Kant, E. (1985). Understanding and automating algorithm design. *IEEE Transactions on Software Engineering*, Volume **SE-11**, *11*, 1361-1374.

9. Larkin, J. H. (1981). Enriching formal knowledge: A model for learning to solve textbook physics problems. In J. R. Anderson (Ed.), *Cognitive skills and their acquisition.* Hillsdale, New Jersey: Lawrence Erlbaum.

10. Larkin, J, McDermott, J., Simon, D. P. & Simon, H. A. (1980). Expert and novice performance in solving physics problems. *Science*, **208**, *6*, 1335-1342.

11. Newell, A. & Simon, H. A. (1972). *Human problem solving.* Englewood Cliffs, NJ: Prentice-Hall.

12. Rich, C. (June, 1981). *Inspection methods in programming.* MIT AI Technical Report #604. Department of Computer Science, MIT, Boston, MA.

13. Rist, R. & Tien, E. (September, 1985). Program description by levels of abstraction. *Proceedings of the Human Factors Society, 29th Annual Meeting.* Baltimore, MD., 846-850.

14. Rist, R. (1985). Program plans and the development of expertise. *Unpublished pre-dissertation manuscript*, Yale University, New Haven, CT.

15. Soloway, E., Bonar, J. and Ehrlich, K. (1983). Cognitive strategies and looping constructs: An empirical study. *Communications of the ACM*, **26**, *11*, 853-860.

16. Soloway, E. & Ehrlich, K. (1984). Empirical Studies of Programming Knowledge. *IEEE Transactions on Software Engineering*, Volume **SE-10**, *5*, 595-609.

17. Soloway, E., Ehrlich, K., Bonar, J. & Greenspan, J. (1982). What do novices know about programming? In B. Schneiderman & A. Badre (Eds.), *Directions in Human-Computer Interaction.* New York: Ablex Publishing Company.

18. Spohrer, J. C., Pope, E., Lipman, M., Sack, W., Freiman, S., Littman, D., Johnson, L. & Soloway, E. (May, 1985). *Bug Catalogue: II, III, IV.* Research Report #386. Department of Computer Science, Yale University, New Haven, CT.

19. Spohrer, J. C., Soloway, E. & Pope, E. (September, 1985). *A goal/plan analysis of buggy Pascal programs.* Research Report #392. Department of Computer Science, Yale University, New Haven, CT.

20. Sussman, G. J. (1975). *A computer model of skill acquisition.* New York: American Elsevier.

21. Waters, R. C. (1979). A method for analyzing loop programs. *IEEE Transactions on Software Engineering*, Volume **SE-5**, *3*, 237-250.

22. Waters, R. C. (1982). The programmer's apprentice: Knowledge based program editing. *IEEE Transactions on Software Engineering*, Volume **SE-8**, *1*, 1-12.

APPENDICES

Appendix I : Program 'hen'

```
1   program henhouse (input,output);
2   { This program finds the average number of eggs laid by a set of chickens }
3   { in a henhouse. It also finds the best producing henhouse }

4   CONST STOP = -999;
5   VAR    eggs, count, total, max   : integer;
6          average                   : real;

7   begin
8       count := 0;
9       total := 0;
10      max := 0;
11      average := 0.0;
12      write ('Please enter the number of eggs. ');
13      writeln ('Terminate with -999');
14      readln (eggs);
15      while (eggs <> STOP) do begin
16          count := count + 1;
17          total := total + eggs;
18          if eggs > max
19             then max := eggs;
20          read (eggs)
21          end;
22      if count > 0
23         then average := total / count;
24      writeln ('The average is', average:6:2);
25      writeln ('The maximum value is ', max)
26  end.
```

Appendix II : Sample analysis of data

The number of groups in each basis is shown to the right. The basis numbers do not sum to 18, since some groups are repeated in two or more bases. Repeated and unmatched group labels are the subject's, all others are the author's.

```
Subject N3                                        18

Program HEN for PROLOGUE groupings                3
  (((1 2 3 4 5 6 7 26) (NOT PROGRAM))
   ((2 3) (COMMENTS))
   ((4 5 6) (DECLARATIONS)))

Program HEN for SYNTACTIC groupings               4
  (((8 9 10 11) (FIRST ASSIGNMENTS))
   ((18 19) (IF))
   ((19 23) (THEN STATEMENTS))
   ((24 25) (FINAL WRITES)))

Program HEN for CONTROL groupings                 2
  (((16 17) (ASSIGNMENTS INSIDE LOOP))
   ((18 19) (IF INSIDE LOOP)))

Program HEN for FUNCTIONAL groupings              1
  (((12 13) (UNNECESSARY)))
```

```
Program HEN for GPLAN groupings                          4
 (((8 9 10 11) (*N INITIALIZATIONS))
  ((12 13 14 24 25) (*I INPUT OUTPUT +C))
  ((15 16 17 18 19 20 21 22 23) (*PS PROCESS))
  ((24 25) (*O OUTPUT)))

Program HEN for PLAN groupings                           3
 (((12 13) (*P PROMPTS +F))
  ((16 17) (*RC INCREMENTS))
  ((18 19) (*X FIND MAX)))

Repeated matches were found for
 (((12 13) (QUERY))
  ((16 17) (INCREMENT))
  ((18 19) (SUBROUTINE IN SUBROUTINE))
  ((8 9 10 11) (INITIALIZING TO ZERO))
  ((24 25) (OUTPUT)))

All groups not matched are                               6
   (((1 4 5 6 7 26) (BEGINNING END))
    ((1 4 7 21) (BEGIN END))
    ((8 9 10 11 12 13 14 24 25) (MAIN BODY OF PROGRAM))
    ((14 15 16 17 18 19 20) (INPUT))
    ((15 16 17 18) (START OF CONTROL))
    ((15 16 17 20 21 22 23) (SUBROUTINES)))
```

CHAPTER 4

Processes in Computer Program Comprehension

Susan Wiedenbeck

Department of Computer Science
University of Nebraska
Lincoln, NE 68588

ABSTRACT

Beacons are key features in a program which serve as typical indicators of the presence of a particular structure or operation. According to Brooks's top-down theory of program comprehension, programmers do not study a program line-by-line but rather search for beacons to verify their hypotheses about a program's function. This paper reports on an experiment which used a memorization and recall method to study beacons in program comprehension. Novices and experienced programmers memorized and recalled a short Pascal program. The results showed that experienced programmers recalled key lines, or beacons, much better than other parts of the program. However, novices did not recall them better. This supports the idea that certain key parts do exist in programs, and they serve as focal points for comprehension by experienced programmers.

MODELS OF PROGRAM COMPREHENSION

Computer program comprehension is a basic skill which is an important part of other programming activities, including debugging, modification, documentation, and learning. In spite of its central role, the program comprehension process has been little studied empirically, and little is known about it. However, several models of program comprehension do exist, and they can serve as a guide as we begin the empirical study of the comprehension process.

The earliest program comprehension model, proposed by Shneiderman and Mayer (1), was largely bottom-up. According to this model, the programmer studies and interprets small groups of lines and stores the interpretations in his or her memory. As new groups of lines are comprehended, they are assimilated to what the programmer has already understood and stored. Eventually by this incremental process, the whole program, or as much of it as possible, is comprehended. This model and also a similar one proposed by Basili and Mills (2) reject the idea that a program is understood on a line-by-line basis. However, they are basically inductive and driven by the data of the program text.

An alternate theory of program comprehension has been proposed by Brooks (3), and it assigns a much greater role to top-down processes. In this model, comprehension is an iterative process of hypothesis, verification, and modification of hypotheses. The programmer begins by making an overall hypothesis about the program's function from sources such as the program name or a brief description. This general guess about the program's function leads the experienced programmer to expect certain structures and operations to appear in the program, based on his or her knowledge of programming and the problem domain. These expectations form a second, more specific, level of hypotheses about the program.

Once these relatively specific hypotheses about the presence of given structures or operations have been formed, the programmer tries to verify them against the program text. This is done not by studying the program line-by-line but by searching selectively for certain key features which are typical indicators of the presence of the particular structure or operation. Brooks calls these key features "beacons." An example which Brooks proposes is the swapping of values, which he believes is a beacon for a sort. Of course, a swap does not occur in every sort routine, and this illustrates another important point in Brooks's theory. A beacon is associated with a structure or operation with some high probability. If it is found, it tends to strengthen the programmer's current hypothesis about the program's function. If it is not found, the programmer may have to search more carefully, perhaps calling into play knowledge about alternate forms of algorithms and using search techniques such as hand simulation. If this deeper search fails to confirm the presence of the expected structure or operation, the programmer will have to revise, or even reject, the current hypothesis about the program's function.

Beacons are important in Brooks's theory because they form the bridge between the top-down hypotheses of the programmer and the actual program text. This paper reports on an experiment which gathered evidence for the existence of beacons in program comprehension.

PREVIOUS WORK

Jeffries's (4) protocol analysis of novices and experts performing a program debugging task is relevant to the current study because comprehension is a major part of debugging. Expert programmers in Jeffries's study had a common strategy for reading a program. They read it in the order in which it would be executed, main program first, then procedures called by the main program, then procedures called by those procedures, etc. This apparently allowed them to form a top-down representation of the program. At the end of each block of code, some of the experts would stop, review the block, and relate it to the rest of the program. The experts seemed to recognize many frequently-recurring code patterns within the program (e.g., a loop and counter combination) and quickly passed over them. Also, they seemed to use simple but effective heuristics to locate bugs. They skimmed over what they considered to be irrelevant parts and made assumptions about the values of irrelevant variables. They read the code carefully and simulated parts only where they believed a bug to be located. Of course, sometimes these heuristics hurt them, as, for instance, when they skipped over a segment of code where a bug was actually located.

By contrast to the experts, novices read the program from beginning to end like a piece of text. They recognized only the simplest, low-level patterns, such as incrementing a counter, and they had difficulty judging which parts of the program were relevant and which irrelevant to the bug they were searching for. As a result, they spent too much time simulating some parts of the program and not enough time on others.

Although Jeffries's study does not provide direct evidence for the existence of beacons, her finding that experts recognized certain well-known patterns does suggest the idea of beacons. Also, her observation that experts read a program selectively rather than line-by-line is evidence that some kind of conceptually-driven processing does go on in program comprehension.

Psychological research on scripts is also related to the study of program comprehension. A script is a cognitive structure that contains information about stereotyped situations, such as what happens in restaurants and doctors' offices (5). This mental representation of the stereotyped situation affects both thinking and behavior, being useful, for example, in interpreting stories about restaurants and also in acting appropriately when we go to a restaurant. Soloway and researchers in his lab (6,7) have suggested that programmers have script-like knowledge structures, which they call tacit plan knowledge, about stereotyped programming situations. These tacit plans serve to chunk together related information about objects and operations. One example would be a variable plan which includes information about the role of the variable, the manner of its initialization and update, and guards which must be implemented to keep the variable from taking on illegal values.

Finally, some of my own work is related to the study of beacons. A recent experiment (8) tested programmers' ability to recognize and make decisions about short, simple code patterns which occur frequently in programs. Novice and expert programmers were shown an English language description of a program structure or operation (called the prime), followed by a short Fortran code segment. The subject pressed one of two buttons to indicate whether the prime applied to, or was a true description of, the code. Accuracy and reaction time were measured. The primes used were either syntactic (e.g., "DO LOOP") or functional (e.g., "SUM AN ARRAY"). The code segments were very simple and frequently used ones, many of them taken from introductory programming textbooks. As a result of this simplicity and familiarity, one might have predicted that novices and experts would perform about equally well. However, the experts turned out to be somewhat more accurate and very much faster than the novices in all conditions. This difference in performance indicates that experts do seem to learn frequently-recurring patterns extremely well, and this knowledge of frequent patterns is part of what distinguishes them from novices.

METHOD

This experiment investigated the hypothesis that key lines, or beacons, exist as a focus for program understanding. Specifically, a sort program was used; and, following Brooks's suggestion, the lines which swap values were presumed to be the beacon. A memory and recall method was used. It was assumed that, if subjects recalled some part of the program very well after brief study, then that part was a key to understanding.

SUBJECTS

The subjects in this experiment were 12 novice and 12 experienced Pascal programmers, all volunteers. The novices were students in an introductory Pascal class at the University of Nebraska. According to their self-reports, they had taken an average of two programming courses, including the one they were currently enrolled in. Seven students had some additional programming experience, either using Basic on a personal computer or teaching Basic in high school. The experienced group was made up of graduate students in computer science at the University of Nebraska. All were very experienced student programmers and, in addition, 10 had taught programming courses at the university level, and 5 had programmed professionally for periods up to one year.

STIMULI

The stimulus used in this experiment was the Shellsort program which appears in Figure 1. The program is 23 lines long and written in Pascal. It is written in a structured way and indented but does not contain documentation. The swap was presumed to be the beacon (temp := a[j]; a[j] := a[j+incr]; a[j+incr] := temp;).

PROCEDURE

Subjects were run individually or in small groups. The subject was given a hardcopy of the program to study and told to try to understand it and at the same time to memorize it verbatim. The study period lasted 3 minutes. After that, the subject was given 4 minutes to recall the program. Finally, the subject had 3 more minutes to write down what he or she thought the program's function was.

RESULTS

One measure of performance was the number of novice and experienced programmers who correctly identified the program as a sort. To be counted correct the subject had merely to say that the procedure was a sort, not what kind of sort. One hundred percent of the experienced programmers and 67 percent of the novices were correct. A Z-test for the difference between proportions was significant ($Z = 2.36$, d.f. = 22, $p < .05$).

The other measure of performance was the percentage of beacon and non-beacon lines recalled correctly by novice and experienced programmers. A line was judged correct if it was identical to the original except for indentation, spacing, and punctuation. A simple reversal of lines was counted as one wrong. Figure 2 shows the overall results for correctness of recall, and Figure 3 shows the results line-by-line. After determining that the assumptions of the Analysis of Variance had been met, a two-way, repeated-measures ANOVA was run. Level of expertise (novice/expert) and type of line (beacon/non-beacon) were the independent variables, and percentage of lines correct was the dependent variable. There was a main effect of expertise ($F(1,22) = 48.75$, $p < .05$). Type of line was not significant, but there was a significant interaction between level of expertise and type of line ($F(1,22) = 8.38$, $p < .05$). See figure 4 for a graph of the interaction. Newman-Keul's test showed that the pairs of means which differed reliably at the .05 level were: 1) novice-beacon vs. experienced-beacon, and 2) experienced-beacon vs. experienced-non-beacon.

DISCUSSION

All of the experienced programmers and 2/3 of the novices recognized the program as a sort. However, only 2 of the experienced subjects identified it as a Shellsort. In fact, most of the experienced programmers as well as the novice programmers expressed uncertainty about the exact behavior of the complex loops with their many levels of nesting. The fact that subjects comprehended the program in a general, high-level way but apparently did not assimilate all the details seems to point to the idea that they make use of key features in recognition.

Experienced programmers remembered more lines than novices in the recall task. This overall superiority in ability to recall replicates what was found in earlier program memorization studies by Shneiderman (9), Shneiderman and Mayer (1), and McKeithen, Reitman, Rueter, and Hirtle (10). The usual interpretation given to this result is that experienced programmers chunk together several related lines of a well-ordered program and remember them as a unit, rather that treating each line as an independent unit to be remembered separately. Novices lack this chunking ability, treat each line as a separate entity, and thus remember less.

Beacon lines were not recalled significantly better than non-beacon lines if one looks at the novice and experienced groups together. However, dividing them up and looking at the two groups separately, a clear difference emerges. The graph of the interaction between level of expertise and type of line (Figure 4) shows that beacons were recalled very well by experienced programmers but not by novices. This suggests that one element of expertise is the ability to focus on key lines which carry much of the meaning of the program. Notably, the novice and experienced groups differed much less on recall of non-beacons.

The graph also shows that experienced programers recalled beacons better than non-beacons, 77.75 percent recall for beacons and only 47.50 percent for non-beacons. This difference for experienced programmers supports Brooks's theory of the existence of beacons and their focal role in comprehension. In fact, the figures given probably tend to understate the superiority of the beacons. Figure 3 shows the recall percentages line-by-line. Many of the non-beacon lines which were well recalled were syntactic markers, such as "begin" and "end" rather than content lines. Leaving out the syntactic markers, the effect of beacons would be even more pronounced.

One trend in the graph in Figure 4 which needs to be explained is the novices' better recall of non-beacons than of beacons. Originally, the difference between beacons and non-beacons was expected to be relatively small for novices but still in favor of better recall of beacons. This was not the case. The difference was not significant, and in fact novices recalled non-beacons somewhat better than beacons. A close look at the novices' recall percentages shows that novices tended to recall in linear order, remembering best the lines at the beginning of the program and progressively less as they went further into the program. The swap lines were embedded deeply in the program and therefore remembered poorly. The opposite was true for experienced programmers who remembered the swap much better than many lines which preceded it in the program. From this experiment there is no indication that novices use beacons in program comprehension. Yet the fact remains that 2/3 of the novices correctly identified the program as a sort. How they came to this conclusion and the role the beacon may have played for them is still an open question.

CONCLUSION

The results reported above support the idea that there are key features in a program which play a focal role in understanding. Program comprehension is not linear, and each line does not play an equal role. Rather, experienced programmers make use of beacons in recognizing an algorithm. Of course, the fact that programmers use well-known patterns in comprehension does not mean that the rest of the program makes no contribution. On the contrary, it seems that for correct recognition of a program other non-beacon features must be present, even if they are not well understood. The Shellsort is a good example of this. For the swap to be interpreted as part of a sort it probably has to appear embedded inside program loops. However, the loops themselves may not have to be completely understood.

In studying a program, people respond to the task at hand. This is also illustrated by the present experiment. Subjects were given a very short study time during which they had to both memorize and understand the program. The short time forced them to try to recognize the program without fully understanding the complex looping structure. Thus, it seems that using the beacon to recognize the program is something like skimming a text. It gives a general, high-level understanding of the program but is not sufficient for debugging or modification, which require deeper understanding. If the task demands in this experiment had been different, we most likely would have found that subjects could follow through and remember even the complex loops.

This experiment found evidence for the existence of beacons in a sort program. We do not know whether beacons can also be identified in other programs. It seems likely that beacons do exist. However, they may not always be a compact, contiguous group of lines as they were here. Rather, several semi-independent beacons may be spread throughout the program, and all or some combination of them may have to be recognized to understand the program's function. This appears to be a promising area for future study.

ACKNOWLEDGEMENTS

I would like to thank Dr. Nancy J. Evans and Dr. George Nagy for helpful discussions about this research.

REFERENCES

1. Shneiderman, B., and R. Mayer (1979). Snytactic/semantic interactions in programmer behavior: a model and experimental results. International Journal of Computer and Information Sciences, 8, 219-238.

2. Basili, V. R., and H. D. Mills (1982). Understanding and documenting programs. IEEE Transactions on Software Engineering, SE-8, 270-283.

3. Brooks, R. (1983). Towards a theory of the comprehension of computer programs. International Journal of Man-Machine Studies, 18, 543-554.

4. Jeffries, R. A. (1982). Comparison of Debugging Behavior of Novice and Expert Programmers. Pittsburgh, PA: Department of Psychology, Carnegie-Mellon University.

5. Abelson, R. (1981). Psychological status of the script concept. American Psychologist, 9, 715-729.

6. Soloway, E., K. Ehrlich, J. Bonar, and J. Greenspan (1984). What do novices know about programming? In A. Badre and B. Shneiderman (Eds.), Directions in Human/Computer Interaction. Norwood, NJ: Ablex.

7. Ehrlich, K., and E. Soloway (1984). An empirical investigation of tacit plan knowledge in programming. In J. C. Thomas and M. L. Schneider (Eds.), Human Factors in Computer Systems. Norwood, NJ: Ablex.

8. Wiedenbeck, S. (1986). Organization of programming knowledge by novices and experts. Journal of the American Society for Information Science, (To be published).

9. Shneiderman, B. (1976). Exploratory experiments in programmer behavior. International Journal of Computer and Information Sciences, 5, 123-143.

10. McKeithen, K. B., J. S. Reitman, H. H. Rueter, and S. C. Hirtle (1981). Knowledge organization and skill differences in computer programmers. Cognitive Psychology, 13, 307-325.

```
Procedure X (var a: arraytype; n: integer);

var i, j, incr: integer;
    temp: character;

begin
        incr := n div 2;
        while incr > 0 do begin
                i := incr;
                repeat
                        i := i + 1;
                        j := i - incr;
                        while j > 0 do
                                if a[j] > a[j+incr] then begin
                                        temp := a[j];
                                        a[j] := a[j+incr];
                                        a[j+incr] := temp;
                                        j := j - incr
                                end
                                else
                                        j := 0;
                until i = n;
                incr := incr div 2
        end
end;
```

Figure 1: Test Program

	BEACON	NON–BEACON
EXPERIENCED	77.75%	47.50%
NOVICE	13.83%	30.42%

Figure 2: Percentage of Beacons and Non-Beacons Recalled

LINE	NOVICE	EXPERIENCED
Procedure X (var a: arraytype; n: integer);	.25	.25
var i, j incr: integer;	.83	.67
temp: character;	.00	.17
begin	.92	.92
incr := n div 2;	.50	.83
while incr > 0 do begin	.42	.50
i := incr;	.17	.42
repeat	.33	.50
i := i + 1;	.25	.33
j := i - incr;	.25	.33
while j > 0 do	.25	.08
if a[j] > a[j+incr] then begin	.00	.50
temp := a[j];	.25	.83
a[j] := a[j+incr];	.08	.75
a[j+incr] := temp;	.00	.75
j := j - incr	.00	.08
end	.17	.75
else	.42	.75
j := 0;	.35	.67
until i = n;	.08	.33
incr := incr div 2	.00	.25
end	.25	.50
end;	.58	.58

Figure 3: Proportion of Lines Recalled
By Novice and Experienced Programmers

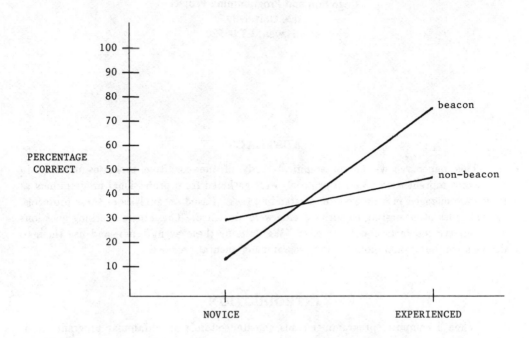

Figure 4:   Interaction of Level of Expertise
and Type of Line

CHAPTER 5

Cognitive Processes in Program Comprehension

Stanley Letovsky
Computer Science Department
Cognition and Programming Project
Yale University
New Haven, CT 06520

ABSTRACT

This paper reports on an empirical study of the cognitive processes involved in program comprehension. Verbal protocols were gathered from professional programmers as they were engaged in a program understanding task. Based on analysis of these protocols, several types of interesting cognitive events were identified. These include asking questions and conjecturing facts about the code. We describe these event types, and use them to derive a computational model of the programmers' mental processes.

INTRODUCTION

When a computer programmer reads and understands an unfamiliar program, he or she is performing a cognitive task of considerable complexity. A thorough understanding of those processes would help clarify the determinants of programmer performance in understanding-intensive tasks such as program maintenance, and provide a principled basis for the design of documentation formats.

In this paper we present a study of the cognitive processes underlying program understanding. Program understanding involves processes at different levels of temporal resolution, stretching from eye fixations and memory accesses at the extreme micro-scale, to decisions about an overall approach to studying the program at the macro-scale. Our earlier work on comprehension processes focussed on the macro-scale description of the subjects' behavior. [9] There we described different strategies that subjects employ to guide their study of the program. Those strategies organize behavior on the scale of minutes and hours. Here we are concerned with events that occur on the order of seconds and minutes, such as identifying the intent behind a line of code, becoming confused about something, or formulating a question. We call these meso-scale events.

Our methodology includes both an empirical component and a theoretical component. In the empirical portion of the study, we gathered "thinking aloud" protocols from programmers as they were solving a program enhancement task. These protocols provide the closest approximation currently available to a trace of the subjects' thought processes. The task required that subjects understand the program that they were enhancing. Some parts of each protocol are concerned with understanding the program, others with planning out the modifications. In this paper our concern is with the understanding portions. We analyzed the understanding parts of the protocols to identify recurring patterns in the subjects' behavior. Here we will focus on two recurring behaviors: asking questions and conjecturing answers. These two behaviors dominate those portions of the protocols devoted to understanding.

In the theoretical portion of the study, we developed a computational model of the subjects' understanding processes, in which questioning and conjecturing behaviors play a functional role. This computational model incorporates processes and representations drawn from research in artificial intelligence. These processes and representations constitute a *cognitive model* of human program comprehension abilities at the meso-scale. The basic structure of the model is a set of knowledge assimilation processes which construct a *mental model* of the target program by combining information gathered though reading the code and documentation with knowledge from a knowledge base of programming expertise. By trying to account for the protocol data within this theoretical framework, we develop a more detailed model of the assimilation processes and representations used in program understanding. Our goal is to develop the model to a level of detail sufficient to specify a computer program which would simulate the subjects' behavior. For the model to be plausible, such a simulation program would have to ask the same sorts of questions and make the same sort of conjectures that human programmers make.

The organization of the paper is as follows: we describe our method of gathering protocol data, then describe our method of protocol analysis, and our empirical results, which consist of several behavior taxonomies. We then present the basic framework of our cognitive model, which we call the *knowledge-based understanding* model. Following this we propose augmentations to this model to account for the protocol data. We end with some concluding remarks.

EXPERIMENTAL METHOD

We video-taped 6 professional programmers as they were engaged in the task of adding a new feature to an existing program. In order to perform this enhancement task, subjects had to develop some understanding of the unmodified program, and they had to plan a modification to that program. The research described here is concerned with the processes by which subjects developed an understanding the original program, and not with how they planned the enhancement.

The subjects consisted of 4 expert level program maintainers and 2 junior level program maintainers; the former had between 3 and 20 years of professional programming experience, while the latter had less than 3 years of professional experience.[1]

---

[1] The subjects included both men and women. To preserve confidentiality, and to simplify the prose, male pronouns are used to refer to subjects throughout the paper. Hence, male pronouns should be understood as gender neutral.

The subjects were instructed to talk freely as they performed the task. In addition, they were asked to tell us whenever they looked at a piece of code or documentation, what they were looking at and why. The interviewer verbally prodded subjects to keep them talking when they fell silent. This technique is called the "thinking aloud protocol". [7] We presented each of the subjects with a Fortran 77 program that managed a small, interactive database of personnel information, henceforth referred to as the PDB program. The program contained 14 routines, for a total of approximately 250 lines of code.

In addition to the code, we provided program documentation consisting of the following components:

- Overview: a brief description of the functionality of the program
- Program Routine Descriptions: each routine was described in terms of its specific function and the roles of its variables
- Hierarchy Chart: the calling structure of the routines was diagrammed
- File Description: the structure of database file was described
- Sample Session: a trace of an interactive session with the PDB was provided

Our intention was to make the documentation of the PDB reflect generic standards for program documentation.

The subjects were asked to make the following enhancement to the code:

The enhancement we are asking you to make would allow the user to restore a deleted record to the data base, during the same session in which it was deleted. The restored record is thus returned to active status and is available for subsequent access.

Three of the 6 subjects completed the task in the allotted 90 minutes.

ANALYSIS OF PROTOCOL DATA

In this section, we describe the approach we used to analyze the protocols. We begin with an informal consideration of a sample vignette from a protocol transcript, to give the reader a sense of the methodological issues involved in analyzing these data. In the following protocol vignette, the subject is beginning to read the code for a subroutine called GETDB. At the start of the vignette he is looking at the first line of declarations in GETDB, which reads:

```
CHARACTER*60 dbase(200,7)
```

This declaration allocates an array of strings, each having maximum length 60 characters. This array is used to hold the database contents during interactive database maintenance sessions. In this transcript, numbered lines correspond to distinct utterances. Lines beginning with "E:" were uttered by the experimenter.

```
[01]  Yes.
[02]  Ok, I'm on page 7 in the code.
[03]  GETDB.
[04]  E: What's going through your mind?
[05]  Ok.  DBASE is a character, star 60.
[06]  Record.
[07]  DBASE is an array: 200,7.
[08]  Why seven?
[09]  Seven fields, I'll bet.
[10]  Right.
[11]  E: Ok. Where are you looking now?
[12]  Ok. I looked back in the documentation.
[13]  E: On page?
[14]  On page 3.
[15]  And DBASE I,J.
[16]  [reads:] Jth field in the Ith record.
[17]  So there's 200 records maximum.
[18]  Explains the 200 records.
[19]  And there are 7 fields.
[20]  So if you want an increase in fields you'd have to increase that declaration
too.
```

How should one analyze this sort of data? There are no hard and fast rules. Our goal
was to extract from these data some clues about the internal cognitive events that we are
unable to observe directly. There are a number of clues in this vignette. For example,
consider lines 5 and 6. The subject notices the datatype of DBASE and then says *record*.
What is he thinking? Does he think that each record is a string sixty characters long?
That would be wrong, but not implausible -- actually it is the fields in the records that are
character*60 strings. How was he led to think about records, so quickly, from the
information in line 5? Or consider lines 7 through 10. He wonders about the 7 rows, then
he correctly guesses the reason. Why does he wonder? How does he guess?

Our approach to analyzing these data grew out of intuitive questions like these. To
make the analysis more systematic, we identified in vignettes like the above fragments with
distinct concerns. For example:

- Line 8 is a question.
- Lines 6 and 9 are conjectured connections between observed details of the code and
  known goals of the program.
- Lines 11 through 16 show the subject actively seeking out specific information.
- Lines 10 and 18 show the subject accepting an explanation for some aspect of the code.

We screened five protocols for vignettes like the one above, in which the subject arrived at
an understanding of something. Whenever possible, we collected vignettes from more than
one subject studying the same part of the program. In this way we assembled a corpus of
16 vignettes, averaging about 29 utterances in length. The vignettes concerned 5 principal
issues in the program, such as the structure of the database, the overall flow of control in
the program, and the record deletion mechanism. We then culled question and conjecture
fragments from these vignettes for closer scrutiny.

Inquiries

Frequently in the protocols we find questions, conjectures and searches and that are
all concerned with the same topic. These can be grouped into a higher order structure
which we will call an *inquiry*. The structure of an idealized inquiry is as follows:

61

1. The subject is reading along, and encounters some fact which prompts him to ask a question.

2. He conjectures answers to his question.

3. He attempts to find an answer, by searching through the code and/or documentation for relevant information, or occasionally, by doing detailed reasoning about the program.

4. At some point he finds something which allows him to draw a conclusion. He then resumes his previous previous activity.

The understanding portions of the protocols consist of inquiries, conversational exchanges with the interviewer, and reading or scanning behavior, where the subject assimilates materials without any apparent difficulties. Conversational exchanges can reveal useful facts about the state of the subject's knowledge, but only rarely do we find evidence of cognitive *events* important to the understanding process occurring during these exchanges. During reading behavior the analysis is confounded by the apparent smoothness of the process; the utterances reveal little more than easy understanding of the intentions behind the code, although interesting conjectures are sometimes made. Inquiries are the richest source of insight into the subject's thought processes, because a rich variety of cognitive events occur, including confusion, questioning, hypothesizing, and concluding.

Below we present three sample inquiries. These have been edited by removing extraneous utterances such as digressions, dialog and some reading aloud, in order to emphasize the inquiry structure. The line numbers reveal where elisions have occured. The first inquiry is extracted from the above vignette, and concerns the explanation of the seven fields in the array DBASE.

```
[1.07] DBASE is an array: 200,7.
[1.08] Why seven?
[1.09] Seven fields, I'll bet.
[1.12] Ok. I looked back in the documentation.
[1.19] And there are 7 fields.
```

The subject reads a line (1.07), formulates a question (1.08), correctly conjectures an answer (1.09), looks in the documentation for confirmation (1.12), and finds it (1.19). In the next example the subject is trying to explain the use of the seventh field, which is a marker field. Initially he is reading this line of code, which sets the marker field:

```
dbase(iptr,7)="deleted"
```

The following inquiry ensues:

```
[2.01] Ok. Field 7 deleted.
[2.03] Ok. I want to find out what field 7 is.
[2.04] I want to go back to the documentation.
[2.05] And see if I can find where it showed me what the fields were.
[2.08] [reads:] Each record consists of 7 fields.
[2.09] Ok, there is a [reads:] status: active or deleted.
[2.13] So delete is no problem at all.
[2.15] Because they have that marker in there to determine if it's
       deleted.
```

The pattern is similar to the first inquiry, but with no explicitly conjectured answers. The final example begins with the subject reviewing his understanding of the program.

```
[3.08] It's a very simple system.
[3.09] It's not complicated.
[3.10] Of course, there's some of these searching mechanisms I haven't
looked at that but...
[3.11] That may be complex, I don't know.
[3.15] Although I probably should look to see...Good thought.
[3.16] Maybe it won't find a record that's deleted.
[3.17] I'll take a look at SEARCH.  Ok.
[3.18] Nothing in there.
[3.19] Look at SEARCH2.
[3.20] SEARCH2. Ah ha.
[3.21] E: What's the "ah ha"?
[3.22] Well  SEARCH2  won't find a record that's been deleted,
        unfortunately.
```

In the course of reviewing his understanding, he formulates a conjecture (3.16), goes to the code for confirmation (3.17-20), and finds it (3.20-22). Here there is no explicit question.

The last two examples show that this notion of an inquiry is an idealization, because frequently one or more of the inquiry components is missing. For example, sometimes the subjects do not always explicitly ask a question. Frequently in these cases we can infer an implicit question which was not uttered, or not uttered as a question. Subjects do not always conjecture answers to their questions; sometimes they have no idea, or perhaps they have but they do not utter it. Sometimes a subject accepts a guess as a conclusion directly, omitting any search or detailed reasoning. There are also aborted inquiries where a question is posed, possibly followed by guesses, but no search is done and no conclusion reached.

Despite these variations, the inquiry idea provides a useful conceptual framework for organizing related questions, conjectures, and searches into a connected, functionally complete whole. In the next sections we will take a closer look at some of the components of inquiries, specifically, questions and conjectures.

Questions

In this section we describe our criteria for identifying questions in the protocols, and then present a taxonomy of question types.

Identifying Questions. The first issue we must address is, what utterances are we calling questions? Some utterances are easily recognizable as questions because the subject employs the English language intonation pattern that marks an utterance as interrogatory, and the transcriber naturally transcribes these utterances with a question mark at the end. For example[2],

```
DBASE is an array: 200,7.
Why seven?
Did they actually delete it though?
```

---

[2]In the presentation of example protocol fragments, we try to include in each fragment just enough of the context surrounding the question to make the fragment comprehensible on its own. Spaces separate distinct fragments.

In other cases, we infer a question when the subject describes an information-gathering goal he is operating from. Here are two different subjects expressing questions which we consider identical to the above pair, only expressed in a non-interrogatory form.

```
So I was going to look over and see if these are from top to
bottom the seven fields.

So I want to find out if the record is still existing there
or gone completely.
```

In the first fragment, the subject is looking at the description of the records in the database to verify his conjecture that the 7 corresponds to the number of record fields. We assume that the conjecture is formulated in response to a question which was not explicitly uttered. In this case the question to which the conjecture "7 is the number of fields" is an answer would be *why seven?*, i.e., the same question asked in the first interrogatory fragment.

Another utterance form which we interpret as a question is the tentative conjecture.

```
Maybe it won't find a record that's deleted.

Since the record to be restored will have been deleted
previously, then it might not be there in the database.
```

We consider these utterances to be equivalent to questions, eg.

```
Will it find a record that's deleted?

Will the record to be restored be present in the database?
```

Question Taxonomy. We analyzed our corpus of vignettes using the above criteria to identify questions. We then developed a rough taxonomy of question types. The categories in this taxonomy are principled in that we can tell which category a question belongs in, but they were not motivated by a pre-existing theory: they were developed in order to provide some structure to the question data. Later we will relate them to a model of the understanding process and try to provide a theoretical basis for these question types. Note that the category names -- what, how, why, etc. -- are chosen because these question words frequently occur in questions of the corresponding category, but *we are not classifying questions simply on the basis of the question word used*. Rather the questions are classified on the basis of what they are asking about. Below we present this taxonomy, together with the defining criterion and examples for each category.

- *Why* Questions: Questions which ask about the purpose of an action or design choice. Eg.,

```
DBASE is an array: 200,7. Why seven?

Why is he putting "deleted" in the DBASE,
  stored in DBASE(ipointer,7)?

It's setting ipointer to zero.
I'd like to know why.
```

- *How* Questions: Questions which ask about the way some goal of the program is accomplished. Eg.,

```
Just trying to figure out how you step down.
If this thing is by number or by last name or how it's basically
  indexed in the array.
They use pointers I suppose.

I'm...what I'm looking at is how they actually get rid  of  the
record in DELETE.
```

```
That means I would have to go back to find out how the Search
routine is implemented.
```

- *What* Questions: Questions which ask what a variable or subroutine is. Eg.,

```
Ok.  I want to find out what field 7 is.
```
```
Then IFINAL points to the last record.
Does it?
```
```
So now I'm going to glance back and see what the heck these
variable names...
```

- *Whether* Questions: Questions which ask whether the code behaves in in a certain way. Eg.,

```
Is this subroutine actually deleting a record or is it just
putting a delete mark there, and the record is still there?
```
```
I need to know whether...
Since the record to be restored will have been deleted
previously,
then it might not be there in the data base.
It's still there in the data base, but it might not be found in
the search process.
```

- Discrepancy Questions: Questions which reflect confusion over a perceived inconsistency. Eg.,

```
So I see six here and I see seven here so I'm not sure what...
```
[I.e., The database description shows 6 fields in a record, while the array which holds the database has 7 fields.]
```
If...I don't understand the difference between the two
different searches.
Why you'd need two.
```

Conjectures

In this section, we look at another inquiry component: the conjectures that subjects formulated about the program. We present samples from our data showing subjects expressing conjectures. Our procedure for analyzing conjectures was similar to that used for questions: we analyzed the vignettes to identify conjectures, and built a rough categorization scheme for the resulting corpus of protocol fragments. For conjectures we developed two orthogonal taxonomies, one based on content and the other on certainty.

Identifying Conjectures. We define a conjecture to be any plausible inference about the program. We will present examples to give a sense of what we mean by *conjecture* at the level of utterances.

In an inquiry, conjectures occur in conjunction with questions; i.e., subjects conjecture answers to their questions. This manifests in the protocol as an utterance expressing a question followed closely by one expressing a conjectured answer, as in the following fragment:

```
DBASE is an array: 200,7.
Why seven?
Seven fields, I'll bet.
```

Since our conjectures and questions as we have defined them are not mutually exclusive, it is also occasionally the case that *same utterance* is classified as both a question and a conjecture, for example,

```
Maybe it won't find a record that's deleted.
```

Thus, a number of the fragments which occur in the conjectures corpus also appear, or overlap with fragments which appear, in the questions corpus.

Not all conjectures appear in obvious inquiries. Sometimes a subject just utters an assertion about the program which we know is a plausible inference because he could not know it for sure based on the materials he has read at that point in time. For example,

[reads:] *If Command equals E* --which is probably the exit command.

```
And this also tells me that records are modified on the basis of
the person's name, which is character length 60.
```

Assertions about the program which we do not classify as conjectures include statements read aloud or paraphrased from the code or documentation, such as

```
It sets it to zero.
```

uttered while reading the code line

```
iptr = 0
```

Conjecture Content Taxonomy.   When we classified the conjectures on the basis of their content, a number of the categories used to classify questions seemed to apply to conjectures as well, specifically, *why, how,* and *what.* The match up between the two taxonomies is not perfect, however. The question categories *whether* and *discrepancy* involve interactions between multiple conjectures, so there is no single corresponding category of conjectures. We also distinguish a subcategory of *what* conjectures called *word* conjectures, which are inferred from meaningful variable names. The categories for the conjecture content taxonomy are presented below.

- *Why* Conjectures: Conjectures about the purpose of an action or design choice. Eg.,

```
Ok.  DBASE is a character, star 60.
Record.

DBASE is an array: 200,7.
Why seven?
Seven fields, I'll bet.

It resets the previous pointer when it comes out to zero.
Just  so  that that record doesn't exist if you access it again
  right away.
```

- *How* Conjectures: Conjectures about the way some goal of the program is accomplished. Eg.,

```
Basically all  it's doing is just putting you down the location
  of the record so I imagine there must be an ID to it let's say.
Just trying to figure out how you step down.
If this thing is by number or by last name or how it's basically
  indexed in the array.
They use pointers I suppose.

And this also tells me that records are modified on the basis of
the person's name, which is character length 60.
```

- *What* Conjectures: Conjectures which ask what a variable is, or what some code does. Eg.,

```
Is this subroutine actually deleting a record or is it just
   putting a delete mark there, and the record is still there?
That I still don't know.
So I want to find out if the record is still existing there or
   is gone completely.
```

```
This almost looks like it's going to be a data entry procedure.
```

- *Word* Conjectures: A subtype of *what* conjectures which are based on meaningful identifiers in the program. These examples show the utterances together with the lines of FORTRAN code that the subject was reading at the time. The relevant identifier is italicized in the code. The utterances reveal that the subject has made inferences about the function of the code. We assume that these inferences are based solely on the meaningful identifiers in the code, since the subjects had not accessed any alternate sources of functional information at the time of these utterances.

```
Then it goes off to get a command.
```
Code Line: CALL *getcmd*(cmd)

```
PUTDB to get rid of the DB and then writes it all out.
```
Code Line: IF (ichnge .GT. 0) CALL *putdb*(dbase, ifinal)

```
Well, I'm going to assume that it gets the file into memory.
I'm assuming that because it gets DB, database.
Just from the name.
```
Code Line: CALL *getdb*(dbase, ifinal, ioerr)

Conjecture Certainty. Not all conjectures are equally certain. Some conjectures one is tempted to call guesses -- a judgement frequently supported or suggested in the subject's language, such as:

```
Seven fields, I'll bet.
```
```
I guess it's a subroutine to read in something.
```
```
Well, I'm going to assume that it gets the file into memory.
```

Other factors which might lead one to call a conjecture a guess are that it is wrong, or that it is correct but the subject couldn't know that for sure based on the information he has seen at that point. Most of what we call conjectures are guesses by these criteria. We were tempted to set up a subcategory of conjecture which is opposed to guesses -- something more certain, called perhaps *answers* or *conclusions*. Presumably this would be something that the subject has seen enough evidence to conclude with full rigor. We have not done this, because the determination turns out to be impossible to make. Even if we know that the subject has looked at the right information, we don't know that he has seen it, or remembered it, or used it in coming up with the conjecture.

Another way of approaching the certainty issue is to define guesses as conjectures which are tentative from the point of view of the subject, and define conclusions as facts which the subject seems to firmly believe. This breakdown is more attractive in that it focusses on the subject's subjective certainty, and is more fruitful in that most conjectures can be unambiguously classified. Here are examples of each type:

- Guesses:

```
DBASE is an array: 200,7.
Why seven?
Seven fields, I'll bet.
```

```
If this thing is by number or by last name or how it's basically
   indexed in the array.
They use pointers I suppose.

In order for somebody to make a modification, you know, it must
   be by name, I would assume.

It would print out the whole record.
I don't know that yet, but that's what I'm assuming it does.
```

● Conclusions:

```
So I assume it's just the name is the key to the...O.K.
Yes, that seems to be reasonable.

So you access records by the name database.

If the pointer is already at that record then it doesn't bother
   to search.
```

OUTLINE OF THE COGNITIVE MODEL

In this section we describe the basic structure of our cognitive model of understanding. The level of description here is intended to be general and noncontroversial. In subsequent sections we will describe augmentations to the model which are needed to account for the inquiry data.

We view programmers as *knowledge based understanders*, a position also taken by several earlier studies. [3, 13] At the coarsest level, a knowledge-based program understander consists of the following three components:

- **a knowledge base**, which encodes the expertise and background knowledge which the programmer brings to the understanding task.
- **a mental model** which encodes the programmer's current understanding of the target program. This model evolves in the course of the understanding process.
- **an assimilation process** which interacts with the stimulus materials (target program code and documentation) and the knowledge base to construct the mental model.

We will briefly consider each component.

The Knowledge Base

The types of knowledge that make up programming expertise have been studied by a number of authors, using both AI [2, 8, 11] and empirical [1, 14] methods. Types of knowledge which have been identified include:

- Programming Language Semantics: the programmer must have understand the language.
- Goals: the understander knows the meaning of a large set of recurring computational goals, such as search, sort, delete from a set, and so on. These goals are described independently of algorithms which compute them.
- Plans: a programmer has a bag of tricks or solutions to problems that he has solved in the past. This includes a small catalog of low level components like running-total-loop or counter which are almost universally known to experienced programmers, to plans that are more domain specific and dependent on the programmer's history, such as converging-iteration loop, heuristic search, and so on. There are plans for actions and for data structures.
- Efficiency Knowledge: programmers have criteria which allow inefficiencies to

be detected (sometimes), as well as techniques for evaluating the resource costs of plans.

- Domain Knowledge: programmers have knowledge of the world, the application domain, and specialized domains such as arithmetic or human-computer interaction.
- Discourse Rules: programmers have knowledge of stylistic conventions in programming, which allow them, for example, to interpret variable and routine names.

We assume that our knowledge base contains all these types of knowledge.

The Mental Model

Next we consider the understander's mental model of the target program. A complete mental model of the program should include the following:

- Specification: an explicit, complete description of the goals of the program
- Implementation: an explicit, complete description of the actions and data structures in the program
- Annotation: an explanation which shows how each goal in the specification is accomplished, and by which parts of the implementation, and what goal(s) in the specification is(/are) subserved by each part of the implementation.

The specification may be thought of as the top layer of a layered network, and the implementation as the bottom layer. We assume that between them are layers of structure which show how the goals are decomposed into subgoals and ordered together. Goals or tasks in adjacent layers are linked by subgoal or *purpose* links. These intermediate layers and purpose links consistute what we are calling the annotation. This kind of network is seen frequently in AI planning models such as [12], and is called a task network or procedural net.

An understander's model would only be complete at the end of the understanding process. During the understanding process the model may, in principle, differ from this final version in a number of ways. It may be incomplete, lacking components or relations between components which are present in the final model. It may contain ambiguities, eg. multiple goals for a piece of code, or multiple implementations for a goal. The ambiguous alternatives may have associated plausibility evaluations. Finally, the intermediate model may also contain vaguely specified components, or even outright errors.

The Assimilation Process

It is the responsibility of the assimilation process to direct the understander to turn pages and aim his eyeballs in certain directions, to take in information from the program and documentation text, and to construct the mental model. If we assume that the complete mental model resembles a procedural net, we immediately have a space of possibilities for how the assimilation process constructs it. It could represent the bottom or implementation layer first and build the annotation from the bottom up by recognizing plans. This is the approach taken in [4] and [13]. Alternatively, the understander could represent the specification first and develop possible implementations top down using a planner or automatic programmer, ultimately matching the possible implementations against the code. This approach is used in [8] and [3]. Our position is that the human understander is best viewed as an opportunistic processor capable of exploiting both bottom up and top down cues as they become available. We will argue that this view is consistent with the inquiry data.

The assimilation process is the most important component of the model for the purposes of this paper, because it is the process most constrained by our data. In the next section of the paper we present a more detailed theory of the assimilation process, which we developed by trying to account for the inquiry data.

EXPLAINING THE DATA

In this section we elaborate the basic knowledge-based understanding model by positing specific processes which can explain the different components of inquiries. By "explain", we mean, provide a computational mechanism which would generate the observed behavior.

Explaining Questions

In this section we present an explanation of the question data within the framework of the knowledge based understanding model. Our explanation relies on three assumptions:

1. The understanding process mixes both bottom-up and top-down elaboration of the mental model.
2. The understander is constantly evaluating the consistency and completeness of the mental model.
3. Questions arise when the model is found wanting with respect to this evaluation.

How and Why Questions. Two types of questions are readily explained within the context of an understander which operates in both bottom up and top down modes: *how* and *why*. Both question types correspond to dangling *purpose* links, that is, parts of the mental model where a complete bridge from specification to implementation has not been built. A goal whose implementation has not been understood, gives rise to a *how* question, eg.,

```
So let's see how it searches the database.
```

A piece of the implementation whose goal is not known gives rise to a *why* questions, eg.,

```
It's setting IPTR to zero.
I'd like to know why.
```

We hypothesize that these questions are generated when the assimilation process evaluates the completeness of the mental model and finds an incomplete portion. *How* questions are generated top down from the program goals, while *why* questions are generated bottom up from the program text.

This picture of dangling purpose links explains how *how* and *why* questions arise, but it does not explain why they are asked when they are. It turns out that the dynamic behavior of these two types of questions is slightly different. Consider some *why* questions:

```
DBASE is an array: 200,7. Why seven?
Why is he putting "deleted" in the DBASE, stored in DBASE ipointer 7?
It's setting ipointer to zero. I'd like to know why.
```

These questions are asked about lines of code or attributes of data structures as they are encountered for the first time. This suggests that subjects are constantly asking themselves *why* about every new implementation detail as they encounter it, and that this constant asking *why* only manifests as an utterance when the subject cannot immediately guess the answer.

How questions, by contrast, tend to be less urgent.

```
So let's see how it searches the database.

I'm...what I'm looking at is how they actually get rid of  the
record in DELETE.

That  means  I would have to go back to find out how the Search
routine is implemented.
```

In the first example, above, the question is asked after the subject has finished understanding a routine which contained a subroutine call to the database search routine. The *how* question was postponed during the analysis of the calling routine. In the second example, the subject has finished reading the record deletion routine and still hasn't seen anything which seemed to accomplish the goal of deleting a record, so he is starting to get worried. His goal of understanding *how* deletion happens has presumably been active for a while. In the third example, the subject had ignored the search routine in his initial reading of the code, but he is led to consider it when planning a modification.

These examples suggest that while *why* questions are asked as soon as an unexplained action or attribute is encountered, program goals with unknown implementations can sit around in the subjects' memories for a while without immediately giving rise to questions. We hypothesize that the urgency of *why* questions is due to a memory effect; i.e., that the subjects are unable to remember an open ended set of unexplained actions. This would be consistent with studies of short term memory, which demonstrate a limit on the number of distinct "chunks" of information which a person can manipulate simultaneously. *How* questions need not be subject to the same limitations, since they can be bound together in a larger conceptual structure, which effectively reduces the number of "chunks". For example, the notion of a database program entails a number of subgoals: the data must be physically represented and stored, there must be a way to find specific records, to add records, modify them, and so on. Since they are all interconnected by the concept *database*, however, they would count as only one chunk. An unexplained action, by contrast, is by definition not connected to the known goals of the program, and would therefore constitute a separate chunk.

What Questions. *What* questions, such as

```
I want to find out what field 7 is.
```

all arise when a reference to an unfamiliar variable, subroutine, or data structure component is encountered for the first time. The answer to a *what* question for a subroutine is the function or goal of the subroutine, i.e., *what does it do?* For a storage location, the answer seems to be the datum that it is this location's job to hold.

The timing of *what* questions is the same as for *why* questions; that is, the question is asked as soon as the unfamiliar implementation object is encountered. This suggests that *what* and *why* questions are associated with the same process, namely, bottom up explanation of the code. The answer to a *what* question is often logically necessary in order to make conjectures about the goal (why) of an action. For example, if we see a subroutine call, before we ask *why* that routine is being called, we want to know *what* is does. If we see an assignment to a variable, we are much more likely to correctly guess the goal of the assignment if we know what the variable's role is. For example, if we see a variable being incremented, and we know that its role is to keep track of the number of records in the database, we might guess that the goal of the increment is to maintain the variable's role in a context in which a new record is being added. *What* and *why* questions are thus not very different: the former are applied to subroutine definitions and variables, while the latter are applied to subroutine calls and design choices such as number of array rows, but in both cases it is the purpose behind an observed code-level entity that is demanded.

Whether Questions. Next we consider *whether* questions. Some examples:

```
Is this subroutine actually deleting a record or is it just
putting a delete mark there, and the record is still there?
```

```
Maybe it [the search routine] won't find a record that's deleted.
```

These examples are both asking for more detail about what a routine does, that is, its purpose. Is the purpose of the DELETE routine to physically delete a record, or to virtually delete it by marking it? Is the purpose of the search to find a record regardless of its status, or to find an active record? We view these as being equivalent to a pair of *what* questions:

```
What does subroutine DELETE do?
```

```
What does subroutine SRCH do?
```

where the subjects conjectured an alternative pair of answers. *Whether* questions, therefore, are an indication that the understanding process sometimes constructs multiple explanations for the same evidence, and that the model evaluation process detects such ambiguous explanation sets and turns them into questions.

Discrepancy Questions. The questions that we have called discrepancy questions do not pertain inherently to any particular content. They arise when the subject has conflicting information about something. For example, in the fragment

```
So I see six here and I see seven here so I'm not sure what...
```

the subject is trying to reconcile two pieces of information. In one part of the documentation he read a description of the array which holds the database, and this array has 7 columns, corresponding to the fields of a record. Elsewhere, he sees a user's view of a record, and he counts six fields. Hence his confusion. The discrepancy is due to an extra field in each record, which the program uses to hold status information about the record. This example shows us that the mental model is evaluated for consistency as well as completeness. Occasional inconsistencies are an inevitable by-product of making plausible conjectures, or jumping to conclusions.

Summary. To summarize, our main hypothesis in this section is that people employ a mixture of top-down and bottom-up understanding. Questions arise when the subject's partial mental model is evaluated with respect to some "well-formedness" criterion and found wanting. Different criteria give rise to different types of questions. *How* and *why* questions arise from incompleteness of goal-plan annotation, *Whether* questions arise from ambiguities; discrepancy questions from contradictions in the mental model. Some questions are more urgent than others; we argue that this arises from a memory requirement that the number of chunks in the mental model be kept small.

Explaining Conjectures

There are two aspects of conjectures which need explaining: where do they come from, and how does a conjecture's status change from *guess* to *conclusion*. We consider each in turn. Conjectures are considerably more complex than questions, however, so the best we can do here is sketch out some of the mechanisms we believe are involved in conjecture generation and illustrate them with examples.

Why & What Conjectures. The next few sections describe several mechanisms that we believe are involved in conjecturing answers to *why* and *what* questions. These mechanisms are not independent, rather, they should be thought of as interacting components which make up the bottom-up explanation process.

Plausible Slot Filling: Consider the following protocol fragment:

```
Ok.  DBASE is a character, star 60.
Record.
```

In this fragment the subject erroneously conjectures that the datatype character*60 implements records. He knows that the database is made up of records, but he knows nothing of how they are implemented at this point, so in his mental model record is an unimplemented goal. He also knows that each record has a few fields: a name, address, phone number, and the like. Our theory of questions tells us that the introduction of the new datatype *character*60* gives rise to a *why* question. In attempting to answer the question, the subject somehow connects the datatype character*60 with the record goal. How does he do this?

Presumably when the subject sees a chunk of storage being allocated, with the name DBASE, and he has in his mental model an expectation that a database is going to be implemented, he will quite easily form the conjecture that that storage is going to hold the database contents. (The mechanism behind that conjecture will be considered later.) When he then tries to assimilate the datatype information, he is dealing with the following facts:

```
DBASE stores database.
DBASE can be decomposed into character*60 elements
The database can be decomposed into records elements.
```

What is needed to form the subject's conjecture is a piece of knowledge which suggests that the elements of the storage and the data correspond. One possibility is the following:

```
Complex Storage Plan:
     slots: S, a complex storage object
            D, a complex data object
            S-elts, a decomposition of S into elements
            D-elts, a decomposition of D into elements
     Goal: store D
     Plan: store D-elts in S-elts
```

This plan is a generalization of many common plans for storing complex data objects. It expresses the notion of element-wise correspondence between complex storage and complex data. We will call very abstract plans like this *generic plans*. There are independent

73

grounds for believing that programmers might have generic plans besides a desire to make this example work: Kant & Newell proposed similar structures called *weak methods* to account for programmers' algorithm design abilities. In this example, we assume that the complex storage plan is active because storage of a complex data object is happening.

The application of this plan to a given situation may be ambiguous, since complex things can have multiple decompositions into elements. For example an array can be taken to be a set of locations, a set of rows, or a set of columns. In this example, the slots `S`, `D` and `D-elts` are bound to `DBASE`, `database`, and `record`, respectively. The subject's "record" conjecture corresponds to binding `character*60` to the `S-elts` slot. We assume that this binding is made because the requirements associated with the unfilled `S-elts` slot of the complex storage plan appear to be compatible with the decomposition of the storage into `character*60` elements. To summarize the explanation, the conjecture arises from a plausible binding of a slot in a generic plan. We call this mechanism *plausible slot filling*.

Plausible slot filling can lead to ambiguity when more than one object can plausibly fill a slot. This is illustrated in these fragments, which are classified as both *whether* questions and *what* conjectures.

```
Is this subroutine actually deleting a record or is it just
putting a delete mark there, and the record is still there?
```
```
Maybe it [the search routine] won't find a record that's deleted.
```

These subjects already already know a good deal about *what* the subroutines they are asking about are, in that they know that they delete and search, respectively. Their uncertainty hinges on a specific point: what set is being searched or deleted from? There are two plausible answers: the set of active records, or the set of all records. This ambiguity gives rise to these *whether* questions.

Abduction: Plausible slot filling presumes the existence of partially instantiated knowledge structures. Where do these come from? In the fragment

```
DBASE is an array: 200,7.
Why seven?
Seven fields, I'll bet.
```

the subject correctly conjectures that the columns in the array correspond to fields in the database records. This conjecture can also be explained as a plausible slot filling. We assume that a plan called `table` is active. `Table` is a specialization of `complex storage` which describes how tabular data can be stored in an array. `Table` has a slot for a decomposition of records into elements, which is plausibly filled by `fields` to produce the conjecture. This leaves us with the problem of explaining how *table* was activated in the first place. Somehow, the information that DBASE is an array enables the conjecture that the *table* plan describes its usage. We assume that the concept *array* is used to index the *table* plan, so the conjecture mechanism involves reasoning from a piece of a plan to the plan itself.

This style of reasoning is known as *abductive inference*, or just *abduction*. Abduction is a plausible inference technique which involves explaining phenomena by using deductive rules backwards to generate possible explanations [10], i.e.,

```
from "Q" and "P implies Q", conclude "maybe P"
```

In program understanding the "rule" is a plan, so the abduction takes the form

```
from "Q" and "the P plan has subgoals Q,R and S",
    conclude "maybe the P plan"
```

In the above example, Q is the array, and P is the table plan, which has array as a subgoal. This kind of abduction, i.e., from subgoals to goals, has been called *motivation analysis* by Charniak [5], who has applied it in the domain of understanding natural language stories.

Symbolic Evaluation: Abduction sometimes depends on other types of reasoning to support it. In the next fragment, the subject has just read this piece of code, which is part of a routine for searching the database for a record with a given name.

```
IF (oldnme .EQ. nome) THEN
    iptr = ioldp
    RETURN
    ELSE
    CALL srch2(dbase, ifinal, iptr, name)
```

The code checks whether name, the name being searched on now, is the same as oldnme, the name most recently searched on. If they are the same, ioldp, the pointer from the last search, is returned as the result of the search. Otherwise, the routine SRCH2 is called. The subject comments:

```
I've noticed now that it keeps track of the previously accessed
 record.
So that if you're already there, it doesn't bother.
It's sort of an efficient way to do things.
Is to keep track of where you are and if they want to go to
 where you are then don't bother searching through the whole
 sequential file again.
Just...you're already there so. Ok.
```

The conjecture here is that the goal motivating this code is efficiency. We consider this to be a recognition of a generic efficiency plan of the following form:

```
IF cheap solution applies
    THEN use cheap solution
    ELSE use expensive solution
```

The recognition of this plan relies on the subject first identifying the branches of the IF as solutions to the same problem, then abductively considering plans which compose alternative solutions using IF. Identifying the first branch as a solution to the search goal requires recognizing that the value of ioldp when name is equal to oldnme is the same as the desired value for iptr. This requires the propagation of assertions about the contents of varables across assignments and case splits, or more generally, simulating the effects of the code to determine *what* it does. This kind of reasoning is called symbolic evaluation.

How Conjectures: The examples considered so far all involve bottom-up *what* and *why* conjectures, and we have found plausible slot filling, abduction and symbolic evaluation playing a major role in generating the conjectures. *How* conjectures are different; they rely on the subject's programming ability. This is not surprising; programming or planning is in effect the inverse of abduction or understanding, just as *how* is the inverse of *why*. Consider the following fragment:

```
Basically  all  it's doing is just putting you down the location
 of the record so I imagine there must be an ID to it let's say.
Just trying to figure out how you step down.
If this thing is by number or by last name or how it's basically
 indexed in the array.
They use pointers I suppose.
```

Here the subject appears to be mentally stepping through various plans in his knowledge base which could implement the goal of indexing records in the database.

Another form of *how* conjecture relies on the conventions of programming called *discourse rules*. In the following fragment,

```
GETNAME types out this and then gets a name.  Alright.
And it apparently searches the database.
So you access records by name in the database.
```

the conjecture in the last utterance is based on just having read a routine which queries the user for an employee name (the database holds personnel records) and then calls a routine called SRCH. The name is one of six parameters passed to SRCH. The subject has not yet read the definition of SRCH. Yet he makes a partially correct conjecture about its function. Presumably the word SRCH gets him to a knowledge structure which defines the goal search. This goal has several conceptual slots or parameters: a set to be searched, a search predicate, and the object which is found. The first two are input slots. In identifying the name as the basis of the search predicate, the subject seems to be relying on a discourse rule which says

```
The parameters to a routine which implement a goal are likely to
play a role in implementing the conceptual slots of the goal.
```

Word Conjectures. Discourse rules play an important role in word conjectures as well. Word conjectures undoubtedly rely on much of the same inferential machinery used to resolve noun phrase reference in natural language understanding, but there are some programming-specific conventions that come into play, and these are captured by discourse rules. The two main rules are:

```
Variables and data structures are named for the data they hold.
```

```
Routines are named for the functions the perform.
```

These rules still leave room for a fair amount of ambiguity in the meaning of names. A name like GETDB, for example, was interpreted by some subjects as meaning "get the database from somewhere", and by others as "get something from the database". These alternatives can be accounted for by an ambiguity about which conceptual slot of get is filled by database. Compound names like GETDB illustrate that the mechanism for mapping words to conceptual structures sometimes has to compose structures, such as get and database in this example. For other words, such as "command", the mapping is simpler: the word "command" is taken to point directly to a slot in a plan for inter-agent communication of programs. Even these words can be ambiguous in that there may be more than one likely referent in the program context. A variable name like "N" suggests the size of a set, but programs often deal with many sets. Heuristics for disambiguating such references may rely on features such as recency of mention in the program text.

Certainty. We turn now to the issue of the certainty of conjectures. Earlier we distinguished two certainty states of conjectures, which we called *guesses* and *conclusions*. The existence of this dictinction tells us that the subject's mental model encodes more that just assertions; it also encodes the belief status of those assertions. These belief states probably take into account the nature of the evidence that led to the assertion; for example a guess about the code which is contradicted by an observation of something in the code must be abandoned, because observations are more compelling evidence than guesses. The idea of *endorsements* [6])seems like a promising vehicle for encoding these sorts of judgements. In an endorsement theory of a domain, a set of rules determines how evidence from different sources is to be combined to yield the belief status of facts in the domain. Sources of evidence in program understanding include documentation, inferences from meaningful names, the code itself, and abduction and planning guesses based on programming knowledge. The mechanism which evaluates the certainty of assertions needs to interact with the mechanism which generates questions in order to tell it when questions have or have not been answered by assertions.

Summary. To summarize, we have identified several processes and knowledge types that are suggested by the conjecture data. These include:

- Plausible Slot Filling to integrate new code objects into prior expectations.
- Abduction to hypothesize plausible explanations for code objects.
- Planning to hypothesize plausible implementations for known goals.
- Symbolic evaluation to determine *what* code does.
- Discourse Rules to draw *what* conjectures from meaningful names, and from the parametrization of routines.
- Generic Plans to encode efficiency knowledge and to support vague initial descriptions of implementation relations.
- Endorsement rules for assigning belief status to assertions.

Explaining Inquiries

The structure of inquiries follows in a fairly straightforward way from the processes we have postulated for questions and conjectures. As facts are added to the mental model, the model is evaluated for consistency and completeness, sometimes resulting in questions. Conjectural processes come into play to suggest answers to the question; sometimes one of these will accumulate sufficient endorsements by virtue of the way it fits with the rest of the mental model to be accepted as a conclusion. Other times, the question leads to behavior intended to yield an answer.

There are several behavioral methods available to answer questions, including reading the code, reading the documentation, or reasoning about the mental model. We surmise that subjects pick a method which is likely to yield an answer with little effort. The effort required to answer a question using a particular method depends on both the question type and the quality of the information source. Reasoning from the mental model requires that the model be well developed in the areas of interest, and that the question be of the *what if* variety. Reading the documentation will be an easy way to find an answer to the extent that the structure of the documentation makes it easy to predict where to look for the answer to a particular question. For example, in the documentation provided to our subjects, *what* questions about variables were always handled by looking at the documentation, because each routine document contained a description of the role of each of the variables used by the routine. Other questions, such as *why* questions about particular lines of code, were not easily answered from the documentation. The difficulty of using the code itself as a source of answers can vary greatly with the textual proximity of the answer to the subject's current focus of attention, as well as the degree to which the subject's mental model allows him to predict where to look for answers, and how to interpret the control flow context in which an answer occurs.

At some point, an accumulation of endorsements from different sources of evidence causes some conjecture to be accepted as a conclusion. This satisfies the model evaluation process which generated the question, and control returns to whatever assimilation strategy was controlling behavior prior to the question.

CONCLUDING REMARKS

We have presented an approach to studying the meso-scale cognitive processes underlying program comprehension. We have shown that data from verbal protocols can be analyzed into fragments which are indicative of cognitively interesting events. We have focussed on two types of events, namely *questions* and *conjectures*, and described how these are organized into a larger event type we call an *inquiry*. We developed taxonomies for questions and conjectures, and then analyzed the various categories to develop crude theories of the mental representations and processes that produced them. We explain the genesis of questions in terms of a process which evaluates the consistency and completeness of the understander's developing mental model. We explain conjectures in terms of abduction and planning processes operating on a variety of types of knowledge. In subsequent research we plan to apply these insights to the development of a computer simulation of human program comprehension.

We envision two potential lines of application of this research, beyond its intrinsic psychological interest. The study of the questions asked by program understanders should be applicable to the design of program documentation standards consonant with understanders' cognitive requirements. Our methodology, or something like it, could be useful for evaluating the effectiveness of proposed documentation standards. A computer-based model of human understanding which exhibited the kind of anticipatory conjectural ability characteristic of our subjects could serve as a prototype of for new, more flexible programming and program specification tools.

ACKNOWLEDGEMENTS

The author thanks Elliot Soloway, David Littman, Jeanine Pinto, James Spohrer, Lewis Johnson, Rob Rist and Robert Farrell for useful comments on earlier drafts of this paper.

REFERENCES

[1] Adelson, B., Littman, D., Ehrlich, K., Black, J., Soloway, E.
Novice-Expert Differences In Software Design.
1984.
First Conference on Human-Computer Interaction, London, England, in press.

[2] Barstow, David.
A Perpective On Automatic Programming.
AI Magazine 1(5):5-27, Spring 1984.

[3] Brooks, R.
Towards a Theory of the Comprehension of Computer Programs.
International Journal of Man-Machine Studies (18):543-554, 1983.

[4] Brotsky, Daniel C.
An Algorithm For Parsing Flow Graphs.
Master's thesis, MIT, March 1984.

[5] Charniak, Eugene.
Motivation Analysis, Abductive Unification and Non-Monotonic Equality .
AI Journal , to appear 1985/6.

[6] Cohen, Paul R., and Grinberg, Milton R.
A Theory of Heuristic Reasoning About Uncertainty.
AI Magazine 2(4):17-24, Summer 1983.

[7] Ericsson, K.A., Simon, H.A.
Protocol Analysis: Verbal Reports As Data.
MIT Press, Cambridge, MA, 1984.

[8] Johnson, W. L., Soloway, E.
PROUST: Knowledge-Based Program Understanding.
In *Proceedings of the 7th International Conference on Software Engineering.* IEEE, Orlando, Florida, 1983.

[9] Littman, D., Pinto,J., Letovsky,S., Soloway, E.
Mental Models and Software Maintenance.
1985.
To appear in: Proceedings of the Conference on Empirical Studies of Programmers.

[10] Pople, Harry E., Jr.
On the Mechanization of Abductive Logic.
In *Proceedings of the Third International Joint Conference on Artificial Intelligence*, pages 147-152. IJCAI, Stanford, CA., August 1973.

[11] Rich, C.
Inspection Methods in Programming.
Technical Report AI-TR-604, MIT AI Lab, 1981.

[12] Sacerdoti, E.D.
A Structure for Plans and Behavior.
Elsevier North-Holland, Inc., 1977.

[13] Shrobe, H.
Dependency Directed Reasoning for Complex Program Understanding.
Technical Report AI-TR-503, MIT AI Lab, 1979.

[14] Soloway, E., Ehrlich, K.
Empirical Studies of Programming Knowledge.
IEEE Transactions on Software Engineering SE-10(5):595-609, 1984.

CHAPTER 6

Mental Models and Software Maintenance

David C. Littman
Jeannine Pinto
Stanley Letovsky
Elliot Soloway

Department of Computer Science
Cognition and Programming Project
Yale University
New Haven, CT 06520

ABSTRACT

Understanding how a program is constructed and how it functions are important parts of the task of maintaining or enhancing a computer program. We have analyzed videotaped protocols of experienced programmers as they enhanced a personnel database program. Our analysis suggests that there are two strategies for program understanding, the *systematic* strategy and the *as-needed* strategy. The programmer using the systematic strategy traces data flow and control flow through the program in order to understand global program behavior. The programmer using the as-needed strategy focuses on local program behavior in order to localize study of the program. Our empirical data show that there is a strong relationship between using a systematic approach to acquire knowledge about the program and modifying the program successfully. Programmers who used the systematic approach to study the program constructed successful modifications; programmers who used the as-needed approach failed to construct successful modifications. Programmers who used the systematic strategy gathered *knowledge about the causal interactions of the program's functional components*. Programmers who used the as-needed strategy did not gather such causal knowledge and therefore failed to detect interactions among components of the program.

1. Introduction

Understanding how a program is constructed and how it functions are important components of the task of maintaining or enhancing a computer program. In an early study of professional, expert maintenance programmers, Fjeldstad & Hamlen [2] discovered that the maintenance programmers they studied spent a major portion of their time "understanding the intent and style of implementation of the original programmer....". Fjeldstad & Hamlen [2] found that, in making an enhancement, maintenance programmers studied the original program

- about three-and-a-half times as long as they studied the documentation of the program and
- *just as long as they spent implementing the enhancement.*

In view of the observation that the professional maintenance programmers spent as much time understanding the program as constructing the enhancement, it is clear that understanding the original program was very important to them.

What it means for an expert maintenance programmer to "understand" a computer program, however, is not clear. Does it mean knowing all the variables used in the program? all the subroutines? all the data structures? how the program behaves when it executes? Equally, it is not clear *how the strategy a programmer uses to study a program affects the knowledge the programmer acquires about the program.* Meyers [3] and Weiser [5], for example, have identified several program understanding strategies, but the relationship between program understanding strategies and the knowledge they lead to is not well understood. In order to investigate the relationship between program understanding strategies and the knowledge programmers acquire when they study programs, we studied professional maintenance programmers implementing an enhancement to an existing program. The results of our program enhancement study lead to three, intimately related, conclusions.

- There are two basic approaches to understanding computer programs.

- The approach a programmer uses to study the program strongly influences the knowledge the programmer acquires about the program.

- The programmer's knowledge about a program directly determines whether the programmer can perform a successful modification of the program.

In this paper we begin to identify the relationship between the manner in which a programmer studies a program, the knowledge the programmer acquires as a result of using a particular program study strategy, and the programmer's performance on a program modification task. We examine two strategies for program understanding, the *systematic* strategy and the *as-needed* strategy. The systematic strategy and the as-needed strategy stem from differences in the extent to which the programmers want to understand the program.

- SYSTEMATIC STRATEGY: The programmer using the systematic strategy wants to understand how the program behaves *before* attempting to modify it. To learn how the program behaves when it executes, this programmer performs extensive symbolic execution of the data flow and control flow paths *between* subroutines. By performing extensive symbolic execution of the data flow and control flow paths between subroutines, the programmer detects *causal interactions among components of the program.* Knowledge of the causal interactions in the program permits the programmer using the systematic strategy to design a modification that takes these interactions into account.

- AS-NEEDED STRATEGY: In contrast to the programmer using the systematic strategy, the programmer using the as-needed strategy attempts to *minimize* studying the program to be modified. This programmer attempts, as soon as possible, to localize *parts of the program to which changes can be made* that will implement the modification. Since the programmer using the as-needed strategy does not approach the modification task with a good understanding of the program when he or she attempts to implement a modification, it becomes necessary to gather additional information while the program modification is performed. The specific questions that arise as a result of attempting to modify the program determine what this programmer learns about the program. Thus, there is no guarantee that he or she will *ever* focus on the data flow and control flow among interacting subroutines. As a result, the programmer using the as-needed strategy is *unlikely to detect interactions in the program that might affect or be affected by the modification.*

Thus, the systematic strategy and the as-needed strategy arise primarily from different goals. The programmer using the systematic strategy traces data flow and control flow through the program in order to understand *global program behavior*; the programmer using the as-needed strategy focuses on local program behavior in order to *localize study of the program.*

Our empirical data show that there is a strong relationship between using a systematic approach to acquire knowledge about the program and modifying the program successfully. We observed that programmers using the systematic strategy and those using the as-needed strategy acquired different knowledge about the program. In particular, programmers who used the systematic strategy gathered *knowledge about the causal interactions of the program's functional components.* Programmers who used the as-needed strategy did not gather such causal knowledge and therefore failed to detect interactions among components of the program. A programmer's success or failure in the enhancement task was directly based on knowledge of the interactions of the program's components: Programmers who used the systematic approach to study the program constructed successful modifications; programmers who used the as-needed approach failed to construct successful modifications.

In the rest of this paper, we explore the implications of using the systematic and as-needed strategies for understanding programs. We show that there is a relationship between the use of a study strategy, the understanding of the program the programmer acquires, and success on an enhancement task. In Section 2, we provide a description of our study and the enhancement task we gave professional programmers. In Section 3, we discuss the knowledge required to construct a successful enhancement. Section 4 introduces the concept of mental models representing the programmers' understanding of the program. In Section 5 we present examples, drawn from our programmers, that illustrate the knowledge acquired through using the systematic and the as-needed strategies. Section 6 reports statistical data supporting the relationship between successful enhancement of the program and the use of the systematic approach to understanding the program. Finally, in Section 7, we discuss some of the conclusions and implications of this study.

2. Methodology

2.1. Subjects
Ten professional programmers from Jet Propulsion Laboratory, California Institute of Technology, participated in this study. Each programmer had at least five years of programming experience. Subjects ranged in professional programming experience from 1 year to 22 years.

2.2. Data Collection
Each subject was interviewed individually. Interviews were recorded on videotape. During each interview, subjects were asked to describe their thoughts as they performed the task. The interviewer prompted the subject and asked questions to ensure that the subject produced a steady report of his or her thoughts.

2.3. The Maintenance Task
We presented subjects with a 250-line, 14-subroutine FORTRAN program that maintains a database of personnel records of the employees of a small company. The personnel database program, **PDB**, permits records to be created, updated, deleted, and displayed. The unmodified **PDB** program does not, however, allow a user to restore a record deleted during a session. The programmer's task, therefore, was to add a subroutine, called **RESTORE**, that permitted the user of the database program to restore records deleted during a session through the use of the **DELETE** subroutine. Subjects attempted to solve the task presented in Figure 2-1.

The Personnel Data Base System provides online personnel information. Today, we ask you to increase the functional capability of the system by making the following enhancement:

Allow the user to restore a record that was deleted during the current session. For example, assume that the user deleted the following record during a session with the Personnel Data Base System:

Soloway,Elliot,M.
177 Howard Ave.
New Haven CT. 06519
203 562-4151
Dunham Labs 322C
436-0606

Deleting a record makes that record unavailable for subsequent access. The enhancement we are asking you to make would allow the user to restore a deleted record to the database during the same session that it was deleted in. For example, a user who had deleted the above record could then restore it during the same session. The record is thus returned to active status and is available for subsequent access.

Figure 2-1: The **RESTORE** Enhancement Task

3. Knowledge Required for Accomplishing the Task

In order to understand a program, a programmer must know about the *objects* the program manipulates and the *actions* the program performs. In addition, the programmer must have knowledge about the *functional components*, comprised of functionally-related actions, which accomplish tasks in the program. Because these aspects of the program do not change as the program runs, but remain static, we call the programmer's knowledge of these objects, actions, and functional components, *static knowledge*. A programmer must also know about causal connections among functional components in the program as the program runs. We call this knowledge about the connections and interactions among functional components *causal knowledge*. In the next section, we outline the specific static and causal knowledge programmers needed to construct correctly a **RESTORE** enhancement.

3.1. Static Knowledge Required

To construct a successful **RESTORE** enhancement, a programmer needs at least four key pieces of static knowledge:

The programmer must know about the objects the program manipulates:

- Each personnel database record contains a *record activity status field* which may be given the value "active" or the value "deleted", depending upon whether the personnel record is active in the database or deleted from it.

The programmer must also know about three primary functional components of the **PDB** program:

- In order to delete a record from the personnel database, the **DELETE** subroutine changes the value in the activity status field in the record from "active" to "deleted".
- Records are never physically deleted from the **PDB** personnel database.

- Since the record search subroutines bypass records marked "deleted", the record search process finds only "active" records.

In short, without knowing that personnel records are deleted by changing the value in the record's activity status field from "active" to "deleted", and that the search subroutines find only "active" records, the programmer cannot construct a successful **RESTORE** enhancement that introduces minimal modifications to the existing **PDB** program.

3.2. Causal Knowledge Required

Causal knowledge about the **PDB** program permits the programmer to reason about how the program's functional components interact during execution. An important aspect of the program's behavior is the way in which data flow and control flow permit structurally separate program components to *interact causally* during execution. In particular, in order to construct a successful **RESTORE** enhancement the programmer must recognize the interaction between **RESTORE**'s need for records marked "deleted" and the sequence in which the record search process and the transaction subroutines, **CREATE, DELETE, SHOW** and **UPDATE**, are called: since the record search process is carried out *before* calling the transaction subroutines, the same record search process must fulfill the precondition of finding the appropriate record for all transactions, *including* **RESTORE**. Unmodified, however, the record search process cannot provide "active" records for **CREATE, DELETE, SHOW** and **UPDATE** and also "deleted" records for **RESTORE**. Therefore, if **RESTORE** uses the same record search process the other transaction subroutines use, then the search process must be modified to fulfill **RESTORE**'s need for a "deleted" record. Unless the programmer knows how the data flow and control flow satisfy preconditions for the transaction subroutines, this interaction between **RESTORE** and the search routines will remain undetected and will hinder the construction of a successful **RESTORE** enhancement.

As programmers studied the **PDB** program, they gathered both static knowledge and causal knowledge about it. We call the programmer's knowledge about the **PDB** program a *mental model* of the program. In Section 4, we introduce the two strategies programmers used to study the program and the mental models they built as a result of each strategy.

3.3. Prototypical Solution for RESTORE task

A prototypical **RESTORE** enhancement to the **PDB** program respects

- the program's modularity and
- the program's calling hierarchy.

Respecting the modularity of the **PDB** program means not adding *new* subroutines to perform the record search process when the user requests the **RESTORE** transaction; respecting the calling hierarchy means calling the record search subroutine at the same point in the program regardless of the record transaction requested by the user of the **PDB** program. To satisfy both constraints, the prototypical **RESTORE** enhancement consists of two modifications to the search subroutine:

- a parameter identifying the requested transaction is passed to the record search subroutines
- the actual search for records in the database are made conditional upon both the record status *and* the requested transaction

Figure 3-1 shows the unmodified code for the primary record search subroutine; Figure 3-2 shows the code for the modified subroutine. Additions to the search subroutine are highlighted in bold: the command *CMD* is passed into the search subroutine and the conditions for successful search are altered. With the modifications shown in Figure 3-2, records are "found" in the database under either of two conditions:

1. the command (*CMD*) is **RESTORE**, a record with the correct search key is found, and the status of the record that is found is "deleted"

2. the command (*CMD*) is *not* **RESTORE**, a record with the correct search key is found, and the status of the record that is found is "active"

While the solutions to the **RESTORE** enhancement task varied somewhat from the prototypical solution illustrated in Figure 3-2, most enhancements were in the same spirit as the solution shown here.[1]

```
SUBROUTINE SEARCH(dbase,iptr,name)

DO 700 I = 1, ifinal
  IF (name(1:ipos-1) .EQ. dbase(i,1)(1:ipos-1)     COMMENT 1
     .AND. dbase(1,7) .EQ. 'active')               COMMENT 2
  THEN iptr = I                                     COMMENT 3
  ...
END
```

COMMENT 1: Compare names
COMMENT 2: Be sure record 'active'
COMMENT 3: Return pointer to record

Figure 3-1: Unmodified Search Subroutine

```
SUBROUTINE SEARCH(dbase,iptr,name, CMD)

DO 700 I = 1, ifinal
  IF (name(1:ipos-1) .EQ. dbase(i,1)(1:ipos-1)             COMMENT 1
  .AND.
       ((CMD .NEQ. 'r' .AND. dbase(1,7) .EQ. 'active')     COMMENT 2
  .OR.
       (CMD .EQ. 'r' .AND. dbase(1,7) .EQ. 'deleted'))     COMMENT 3
  THEN iptr = I                                             COMMENT 4
  ...
END
```

COMMENT 1: Compare names
COMMENT 2: Be sure command *is not* a **RESTORE** and record is 'active'
COMMENT 3: Be sure command *is* a **RESTORE** and record is 'deleted'
COMMENT 4: Return pointer to record

Figure 3-2: Enhanced Search Subroutine

4. Building Mental Models of Programs

We call the knowledge programmers acquire about a program a *mental model* of the program. We define *weak mental models* of a program to be those mental models which contain only static knowledge of the program. We define *strong mental models* of a program to be mental models which contain both static knowledge *and* causal knowledge about it. We observed that strong and weak mental models result from using different strategies for studying the **PDB** program. Programmers using the systematic strategy to study the **PDB** program gathered both static and causal knowledge about it and so built strong mental models of the program. Programmers using the as-needed strategy gathered only static knowledge of the program and therefore built weak mental models.

---

[1]See Soloway, Letovsky, Loerinc, and Zygielbaum [4] for a discussion of the quality of this enhancement.

85

In the next section of this paper, we show that the programmer's use of a strategy to study the program leads directly to the knowledge he or she acquires about the program. In order to illustrate this finding, we present anecdotal excerpts from videotaped interviews with two programmers. The interviews were conducted while the programmers studied the **PDB** program and made their **RESTORE** enhancements. We use the excerpts to illustrate, compare, and contrast the systematic and as-needed strategies and the different knowledge that results from using each strategy. One of the programmers, SYS1, used the SYStematic strategy; the second programmer, A-N1, used the As-Needed strategy. We present a comparison of these two programmers for three reasons:

- SYS1's and A-N1's study strategies are at opposite ends of a continuum: SYS1 studied the **PDB** program very systematically; A-N1 studied the program using an as-needed strategy.

- SYS1's **RESTORE** enhancement was prototypical of successful modifications: by passing a parameter to the record search subroutines indicating whether the user requested the **RESTORE** transaction, SYS1 forced the record search subroutines to return the "deleted" records **RESTORE** required. Nearly every successful **RESTORE** enhancement used this method to provide "deleted" records to **RESTORE**.

- The way in which A-N1's **RESTORE** enhancement failed was prototypical of programmers who used the as-needed strategy: A-N1 did not adjust the record search subroutines to locate "deleted" personnel records when the user requested the **RESTORE** transaction. Therefore, A-N1's record search subroutines could not find the "deleted" personnel records as **RESTORE** requires.

SYS1, the programmer who used a systematic strategy, acquired the static and causal facts about the program, built a strong mental model, and constructed a successful **RESTORE** enhancement. A-N1, who used the as-needed strategy, learned only the static facts, built a weak mental model, and failed to construct a successful **RESTORE** enhancement.

5. The Systematic and As-Needed Strategies Compared

The strategy a programmer uses to understand a program affects both the parts of the program the programmer studies and how the program is studied. Programmers using the as-needed strategy focus on *local facts* about the program. In contrast, programmers using the systematic strategy are concerned with discovering *relationships among parts* of the program in addition to discovering local facts about the program. Below, we examine the following three issues which are central to the two study strategies:

- What are the programmers' goals in studying the program?
- Which functional components does the programmer choose to study?
- Does the programmer study the interactions of the program's components?

The way in which the programmer resolves these three issues determines whether the programmer uses the systematic or the as-needed strategy. In this section, we present examples from interviews with SYS1 and A-N1 that illustrate how programmers using the systematic or the as-needed strategy resolve these three issues, resulting in the acquisition of either static *and* causal information about the program or only static information.

5.1. Programmers' Goals
What are the programmers' goals in studying the program?

Programmers' assessments of their need to understand the **PDB** program differed; some programmers believed that they needed a thorough understanding of the program while others believed that a partial understanding would be sufficient. Programmers chose the systematic strategy if they believed that they would have to understand how the behavior of the enhancement would interact with the behavior of the rest of the **PDB** program. In contrast, programmers who did *not* believe that they had to understand the interactions in the program in order to make their enhancements used the as-needed strategy.

5.1.1. Systematic Strategy: SYS1

Understanding the unmodified **PDB** program was very important to SYS1. Before starting to implement his **RESTORE** enhancement, SYS1 studied the program extensively. The interviewer asked him why he did this; we have paraphrased[2] SYS1's response below:

> SYS1: The easiest way for me to work on a new project is to see how the original programmers were doing it...and carry on with their way, rather than try to work the whole thing my way *because my way may not mesh with their way.* Then we'd have a problem when I put my module or my enhancement in --it might not fit. *If I see how they've done things first, then I can make my enhancement fit.*

This paraphrase of SYS1's remark illustrates his belief that, by understanding how the unmodified program is organized and functions, he would be able to construct a **RESTORE** enhancement whose behavior would "mesh" with the rest of the **PDB** program. SYS1 believed that by understanding how the original program is organized, and how it functions, he could construct an enhancement that would minimize the likelihood of disrupting the functioning of the program.

5.1.2. As-Needed Strategy: A-N1

A-N1 believed that he did not have to understand the whole **PDB** program to construct his **RESTORE** enhancement. A-N1 justified his satisfaction with a partial understanding of the program by observing that the **PDB** program is quite small and therefore unlikely to involve any complex interactions. We have paraphrased his remarks below:

> A-N1: Since this system is small I think I would feel good about modifying the program *without understanding it.* But, if this were a large, really complex system, I really think I would want to understand it better *since there might be some subtle little problem that might exist in the interactions of the subroutines.*

A-N1 realized that in large programs subtle, unanticipated, problems could emerge as a result of modification. The **PDB** program was small enough, and constructed simply enough, that A-N1 did not believe it was necessary to understand it in detail. Though A-N1 recognized that he did not understand the program in detail, he nonetheless believed that his **RESTORE** enhancement would function correctly with the rest of the program:

> A-N1: "...I'm 90% sure the thing [the **RESTORE** enhancement] would work perfectly, *but I wouldn't understand it* [how the enhanced program worked]."

This quotation illustrates A-N1's belief that, since the **PDB** program is small, he could make changes to it without understanding how the program functions as a whole. In contrast, SYS1 wanted to understand the program in order to ensure that his **RESTORE** enhancement would be coordinated, or "mesh", correctly with the original program. In each of the following two sections, **Acquiring Static Knowledge** and **Acquiring Causal Knowledge**, we describe and compare the processes by which the programmers,

---

[2]As a result of stuttering, faltering, and re-organizing thoughts as they speak, our subjects' protocols tend to include spurious expressions, repeated phrases and words, and segments of false-start sentences. These fragmented expressions make reading the protocols difficult. This particular segment of the interview, though very revealing, was long and difficult to read so we have paraphrased it, capturing the intent, omitting only the extra words.

SYS1 and A-N1, attempted to collect static and causal information about the **PDB** program. Following each description of the programmer's information gathering strategy, we provide evidence from verbal protocols that the programmer succeeded or failed to acquire the information necessary to correctly implement the **RESTORE** enhancement, identified in Section **3**.

5.2. Acquiring Static Knowledge
Which functional components does the programmer choose to study?

In this section, we show how SYS1 and A-N1 gathered the static knowledge required for a **RESTORE** enhancement. In Section 5.2.1 we describe the process by which SYS1 gathered static knowledge and the knowledge he acquired. Then, in Section 5.2.2, we show how A-N1 gathered static knowledge essential to performing the **RESTORE** enhancement.

5.2.1. Systematic Strategy: SYS1
Before beginning his **RESTORE** enhancement, SYS1 examined most of the **PDB** program, identifying functional components and their organization. Beginning *at the top of the main routine*, SYS1 read through the code, noting the ordering of the subroutine calls. Initially inferring the function of each subroutine from its name, SYS1 linked these functions together *in the order in which they occur as the program executes*, thus developing an understanding of the global data flow and control flow in the program. After this initial study of the **PDB** main routine, SYS1 returned to each subroutine call, in order, and examined the code associated with it. Thus, as SYS1 studied the organization of the subroutine calls in the main routine of the program, SYS1 also identified all the functional components that were necessary to achieve his goal of understanding the program. Through this process, SYS1 acquired, as shown below, the static knowledge necessary to perform the **RESTORE** enhancement correctly.

- EACH RECORD CONTAINS AN ACTIVITY STATUS FIELD: Before he studied the **PDB** program in detail, SYS1 considered how a **RESTORE** enhancement might function. SYS1 generated several possibilities for the **RESTORE** enhancement and appeared to favor one that somehow kept track of records deleted during each session so that they could be restored, if necessary, during the session. To keep track of records that had been deleted during a session, SYS1 entertained the possibility of adding a status field to each personnel record that would store the information about whether the record had been deleted during the session or was still "active". When SYS1 began to study the program in detail he discovered that, in fact, each personnel record already does contain an activity status field.

    SYS1: "It [the **PDB** program] keeps track of the records, marks them "active" or "deleted"."

- **DELETE** CHANGES STATUS FIELD TO "DELETED": With the knowledge that each record contains an activity status field, SYS1 studied the **DELETE** subroutine to determine *how* the status field is changed to cause deletions. When SYS1 saw how **DELETE** performs deletions of personnel records, he observed:

    SYS1: "It [**DELETE**] marks the activity status as "deleted"."

- RECORDS ARE NEVER PHYSICALLY DELETED: Since the **RESTORE** enhancement would have to restore "deleted" records, SYS1 wanted to know whether the **RESTORE** enhancement would have access to all the records deleted in a session with the **PDB** program. Considering the purpose of the activity status field, SYS1 generated the hypothesis that records are not physically deleted from the personnel database. Rather, deletions are "virtual deletions" which leave the records physically in the database but somehow make them "invisible" to the transaction subroutines. This is how he stated that hypothesis, which he subsequently confirmed:

SYS1: "I'm thinking that the record isn't actually deleted."

- RECORD SEARCH BYPASSES RECORDS MARKED "DELETED": After SYS1 discovered that deletion of a record from the personnel database is not accomplished by physically deleting the record, but rather by changing its status from "active" to "deleted", he discovered that the search subroutines find only "active" records:

SYS1: "But it [the record] won't "exist" ... they [the record search subroutines] check if status is "active" when they search for it."

Thus, by examining the code in execution order, SYS1 acquired all four of the critical pieces of static knowledge about how the **PDB** program deletes and selects personnel records according to activity status. A-N1 also collected all these pieces of static knowledge, though using a different strategy.

5.2.2. As-Needed Strategy: A-N1

Like SYS1, A-N1 began his study of the **PDB** program by identifying some of the program's functional components. Unlike SYS1, however, A-N1 wanted to learn only as much about the program as he believed would be necessary to accomplish the **RESTORE** enhancement. As a result, after reading the enhancement assignment, and reasoning that **RESTORE** should simply reverse the action of some hypothetical record deletion functional component, A-N1 wanted to understand the record deletion function. At this point, A-N1 remarked to the interviewer that he hoped that the program was modularly organized, specifically that the record deletion functional component corresponded to a **DELETE** *subroutine*. A-N1 looked at the documentation for the program's main routine; in the documentation of the main routine, A-N1 found a list of the subroutines called by the main routine, the subroutine **DELETE** among them. In his remarks, below, A-N1 made it clear that he had now succeeded in identifying the only functional component with which he was immediately concerned, namely **DELETE**. As A-N1 put it:

A-N1: "It looks like they may have broken this [program] up functionally. Ah, [here are the] subprograms called [by the main routine]: **CREATE, DELETE, GETCMD**...Ok, good. So, there is a subprogram called **DELETE**. *So, I think I'm going to go straight to that.*"

A-N1's sentiment, expressed in this quotation, matches his behavior perfectly: He went directly to the **DELETE** module, studied it, and immediately began his **RESTORE** enhancement; he did *not* look at any other part of the **PDB** program before beginning his **RESTORE** enhancement. A-N1 learned more about the **PDB** program only as he needed to answer questions that arose as he implemented his **RESTORE** enhancement.

In the following excerpts from the interview with A-N1, we show that A-N1, like SYS1, had the critical static knowledge about the **PDB** program required for a **RESTORE** enhancement.

- EACH RECORD CONTAINS AN ACTIVITY STATUS FIELD: Though A-N1 had not studied the declaration of the array which contained the database, he inferred that references to the variable DBASE were references to the database array. Thus, when A-N1 read the **DELETE** subroutine and discovered that it changes the last field in each record of DBASE from "active" to "deleted", he reasoned that each record contains an activity status field.

A-N1: "...the status of the record, as to whether it was "deleted" or not "deleted" --it's contained in the record itself."

- **DELETE** CHANGES STATUS FIELD TO "DELETED": When A-N1 studied the **DELETE** subroutine, he was attempting to discover whether his **RESTORE** enhancement could simply reverse the action of **DELETE**. In order for **RESTORE** simply to reverse the action of **DELETE**, records must not be physically deleted from the personnel database. The following quotation shows A-N1 discovering that the record deletion mechanism alters the value of the record activity status field:

  A-N1: "...deletion consisted of a one line statement [in the **DELETE** subroutine] that just said that the contents of [the record status field]...would be the ASCII string 'deleted'..."

- RECORDS ARE NEVER PHYSICALLY DELETED: Once A-N1 discovered that deletion of a record from the personnel database is accomplished by changing the value in the record's activity status field, he needed to know whether the "deleted" record would be available for subsequent use or whether it would be physically deleted because it contained "deleted" in the activity status field. The following quotation shows that he did indeed discover that records are never physically deleted from the personnel database.

  A-N1: "Deleted records are never really deleted, so that in the process [of writing the database back to the disk], they too are rewritten..."

The fact that personnel records are never physically deleted from the database was crucial for the design of A-N1's **RESTORE** enhancement. A-N1 concluded, from the facts that records are simply marked as "deleted" and that records are never physically deleted, that **RESTORE** could, indeed, be a "mirror image" of **DELETE**.

- RECORD SEARCH BYPASSES RECORDS MARKED "DELETED": After completing his **RESTORE** enhancement, A-N1 began to investigate the rest of the program. He explored the program, not because he felt his **RESTORE** enhancement was incorrect, but because he wanted to verify his assumption that **RESTORE** was the mirror image of **DELETE**. A-N1 recognized that the **RESTORE** routine would have to obtain records from another component of the program, so he wanted to learn about the record retrieval process. He found the record search process and read the code. Later, at the end of the interview, the interviewer asked A-N1 to describe how the **PDB** program functioned. Among his remarks was this evidence that he understood that search overlooked "deleted" records:

  A-N1: "...if it [the search process] doesn't find the word "active" *then it returns "record not found"* or some other message."

In summary, A-N1 and SYS1 used similar reasoning to identify the **PDB** program's functional components. Both expected that the program was modularly organized and that the names of the subroutines would be mnemonic and reflect their function. A-N1 and SYS1, however, had different goals in studying the program. SYS1's desire to understand the whole program led him to identify almost *all* of the program's functional components and to examine the order in which they are called in the running **PDB** program *before* beginning his **RESTORE** enhancement. By examining the order in which functional components are called in the running program, SYS1 both identified the functional components, by using the mnemonic values of their names, *and* learned which functional components depend upon the results of other components to satisfy their preconditions. This knowledge of the data flow and control flow among the program's functional components gave SYS1 a framework for organizing knowledge about how the program components interact as the it runs. In contrast, A-N1's desire to understand as little as necessary about the **PDB** program led him to identify only *one* functional component before he began his **RESTORE** enhancement. A-N1 studied only **DELETE** before attempting to construct his **RESTORE** enhancement because, according to A-N1, the action of **RESTORE** most closely parallels the action of **DELETE**. A-N1 thus neither 1) identified all the functional components in the program nor 2) acquired knowledge about the causal interactions of the program's functional components before he began implementing his **RESTORE** enhancement. In the next section, we describe SYS1's use of global symbolic execution to acquire causal information about interactions in the running program; we also show the contrast to A-N1's strategy of gathering information about the program only when that information was necessary.

5.3. Acquiring Causal Knowledge
Does the programmer study the interactions of the program's components?

Though both SYS1 and A-N1 identified the functional components containing the four pieces of static knowledge essential to performing the **RESTORE** enhancement correctly, they did *not* both determine how those functional components interact with one another when the program runs: SYS1 used *global symbolic execution* to understand global data flow and control flow; as a result of his extensive global symbolic execution, SYS1 detected the interaction between the record search process and the **RESTORE** subroutine's need for "deleted" records. A-N1, prior to implementing his **RESTORE** enhancement, examined the code *only* of the **DELETE** subroutine. He did not perform global symbol execution; instead he immediately focused on the code local to the **DELETE** subroutine in order to limit his study of the program.

5.3.1. Systematic Strategy: SYS1

Like all programmers who used the systematic strategy to study the **PDB** program, SYS1 attempted to determine how the **PDB** program behaves when it runs. SYS1's desire to understand how the program behaves when it runs led directly to the goal of determining *how the functional components interact* when the **PDB** program runs. In order to determine how functional components of the program interact when it runs, programmers using the systematic strategy used extensive global symbolic execution. Global symbolic execution entails symbolically executing the program, beginning at the main routine and following the data flow and control flow of the subroutines. Because global symbolic execution requires that the programmer actually imagine the behavior of the program as if it were running in time, global symbolic execution provides the programmer with data flow and control flow knowledge and, therefore, causal knowledge about the order of actions in the program. Knowledge of the data flow, control flow, and the order of actions in the program permits the programmer to reason about precondition relationships which lead to interactions.

SYS1 began global symbolic execution of the program at the main routine, symbolically executing each line of code in the main program in the order in which it is executed at runtime. In his initial symbolic execution, SYS1 used a breadth-first strategy: he postponed symbolically executing the called subroutines until after he understood the behavior of the main routine. SYS1 gave his reason for performing global symbolic execution of the program in the following quotation:

> SYS1: "I'm tracing through the main program *to see the* flow *of the main program through its subroutines ...*"

This quote from SYS1 explains why he used global symbolic execution. SYS1 uses the term *flow* to refer to the causal sequencing of events in the **PDB** program, i.e., data flow and control flow. The quote therefore shows that SYS1 used global symbolic execution to discover *how causally dependent actions of the running program are ordered and interact*. Detection of such interactions permits the programmer to mesh the modification with the existing program.

- **RESTORE** INTERACTS WITH RECORD SEARCH: Based on his static knowledge of the **PDB** program, SYS1 understood that the record search subroutines find "active" records only. From his symbolic execution of the program's main routine, SYS1 also had the causal knowledge about data flow and control flow that each transaction subroutine is called at the same point in the **PDB** program. SYS1 realized that, if the record search process were carried out *before* the transaction subroutine were called, then the same record search process would be used for all transactions. As a result, SYS1 realized that he would have to alter the **PDB** program to enable the record search process to find "deleted" records when the user requested the **RESTORE** transaction. The following quotation shows that SYS1 was fully aware of the potential for this interaction between **RESTORE** and the record search process.

> SYS1: "If it's a **RESTORE**, I actually don't want "active" status. So if that [whether record is active] was checked in a certain place, *like before I got the command*, then I'll have to rearrange some stuff."

This piece of causal knowledge provided the key for SYS1's **RESTORE** enhancement. Since the **PDB** program carries out the record search process before, and therefore independently of, the transaction routines *and* returns only "active" records, SYS1 recognized that **RESTORE** could not obtain "deleted" records. SYS1 expressed the problem this way:

> SYS1: "Somehow, we have to tell **SEARCH** [the search process] not to look for an "active" record."

In order to "tell" the search process not to look for an "active" record, SYS1 capitalized on the fact that the **PDB** program asks for the transaction command *before* carrying out the record search: his solution used the command itself to inform the search subroutines of whether they should look for "deleted" records or "active" records. If **RESTORE** were the transaction the user requested then the search process would return "deleted" records; if any other transaction were requested, then the search process would return "active" records. SYS1 characterized his solution in this way:

> SYS1: "We know the command at that point. So, what I would do is put a check at this point [in the search subroutines] *to check if the command is* **RESTORE**."

Thus, SYS1 recognized the causal interaction of the record search process with **RESTORE**'s need for "deleted" records and invented a method for accommodating it.

In summary, SYS1's systematic strategy for studying the **PDB** program led him to acquire critical static *and* causal knowledge and thus to build a strong mental model of the program. The critical static knowledge allowed SYS1 to reason about how the program is constructed. The critical causal knowledge allowed SYS1 to reason about how the components of the program interact causally through data flow and control flow, when the program runs. Thus, the combination of the critical static and causal knowledge made it possible for SYS1 to construct a **RESTORE** enhancement that functioned correctly with the original **PDB** program.

5.3.2. As-Needed Strategy: A-N1

Immediately after reading the **RESTORE** assignment, A-N1 tried to find a local segment of code he could change to implement the **RESTORE** enhancement. Rather than examine the whole **PDB** program, A-N1 briefly read the overview of the program and, upon learning that a **DELETE** module exists, he reasoned that **RESTORE** would simply have to reverse the action of **DELETE**. When A-N1 reasoned in this way, *he had not yet examined any code and he did not know how records were deleted in the original program.* A-N1 then skimmed over the documentation of the program's main routine, confirming his expectation that each of the database transactions mentioned in the program overview corresponds to a subroutine in the program. A-N1 then turned immediately to the code and documentation for the **DELETE** module, read them, and began his modification. A-N1 verbally expressed his general strategy of trying to start a modification task immediately, without understanding how the program functions, in the following quotation:

> A-N1: *"It's best to go straight to the thing where you think you'll find a solution. And if that doesn't work, backtrack and find out where you went wrong."*

A-N1 followed this prescription exactly. A-N1 used the definition of the **RESTORE** enhancement to identify sections of the **PDB** program which might provide him with information that would allow him to make local changes to the program to implement **RESTORE**. A-N1 believed that this section of code would be a record deletion subroutine. A-N1 searched for the part of the program he expected to carry out the record deletion function, found that section in the **DELETE** subroutine, and then immediately attempted to construct a modification of the **DELETE** subroutine to implement the **RESTORE** enhancement. When A-N1 needed to know something to proceed with the enhancement, he backtracked to fill in missing knowledge, just as his quotation suggests. A-N1's study of the program was thus guided by his need to collect information directly relevant to the enhancement. Rather than being sure that **RESTORE** would fit in with the rest of the program, A-N1 adopted the strategy of modifying **DELETE** in the following way:

> A-N1: "All I need to do is take this code [DELETE] verbatim, call it **RESTORE** *and put the word "active" in it instead of "deleted"."*

This quotation shows that A-N1 believed that **RESTORE** was nothing more than a "mirror image" of **DELETE**, requiring only *local* modifications of the **PDB** program. It is especially important to realize that A-N1 never verified his assumption that local modifications would not disrupt the data flow and control flow in the program and that the existing data flow and control flow would be sufficient to implement a correct **RESTORE** enhancement. At the interviewers prompting, A-N1 examined more of the **PDB** program after implementing his **RESTORE** enhancement. As A-N1 examined the program at that time, he discovered several facts that *might have led to understanding* why his **RESTORE** enhancement was incorrect. As we will show in Section 5.3.3, however, since A-N1 had a weak mental model of the **PDB** program, he was unable to see how these facts interacted with his **RESTORE** enhancement.

A-N1's static knowledge was sufficient for him to attempt to construct a **RESTORE** subroutine, though the solution was incorrect. His solution, described in the quotation below, implements the **RESTORE** subroutine by making only local changes to the **PDB** program.

> A-N1: "All I need to do is take this code [DELETE] verbatim, call it **RESTORE** *and put the word "active" in it instead of "deleted"."*

A-N1 believed that **RESTORE** could be the exact "mirror image" of **DELETE**. A-N1's **RESTORE** enhancement was based on the assumption that the interaction of **RESTORE** with the rest of the **PDB** program would be *exactly like the interaction of* **DELETE** *with the rest of the* **PDB** *program.* This assumption, that **RESTORE** and **DELETE** have identical requirements of the **PDB** program, is fallacious. The assumption led to the failure of his **RESTORE** enhancement: though A-N1 was able to construct a **RESTORE** subroutine, he was *not* able to integrate his subroutine into the original program. As we demonstrate below, A-N1 failed to acquire the causal knowledge necessary to understand how **RESTORE** and the record search process interact in the executing program. This demonstration suggests that knowledge of the interaction between **RESTORE** and the record search process was critical to integrating the subroutine into the **PDB** program.

- **RESTORE** INTERACTS WITH RECORD SEARCH: In the debriefing phase of the interview, the interviewer asked A-N1 a series of questions about how the **PDB** program, enhanced with A-N1's **RESTORE** subroutine, behaved when it was looking for "deleted" records. A-N1's answer to the interviewer's key question shows graphically that A-N1 was completely unaware of the interaction of **RESTORE** and the order of actions in the **PDB** program.

> INTERVIEWER: "... when you write a **RESTORE** routine to restore records after **DELETE** deleted them, how does **SEARCH** [the search subroutine] find them [the "deleted" records]?"
>
> A-N1: "Well, the **RESTORE** routine puts the "active" string in the status [field]. So when **SEARCH** finds it and compares it to the ASCII string "active", ... [**SEARCH**] says 'oh, it's here' and returns the pointer back."

We know from A-N1's earlier remarks that he had the critical static knowledge about the **PDB** program required to construct a successful **RESTORE** enhancement. In this quotation, however, A-N1 showed that he did not know how his enhancement to the **PDB** program would interact with the record search process. He suggested that **RESTORE** itself solves the problem of only being able to find "active" records: according to A-N1, **RESTORE** itself changes the status of "deleted" records to "active" so that the record search subroutines can find them! Apparently, A-N1 did not know that **RESTORE** depends on the record search process to find a record *before* **RESTORE** can restore the record to active status. Hence, A-N1 did not have the key piece of causal knowledge required to construct a successful **RESTORE** enhancement.

Unlike SYS1, A-N1 never attempted symbolic execution of the main routine of the **PDB** program to discover causal interactions among subroutines. A-N1's use of the as-needed strategy led him to focus on *local* aspects of the program rather than on its global behavior. In essence, A-N1's attention to the program was guided by his need to gather information required to answer specific questions, about local program behavior, that arose during the process of performing the **RESTORE** modification. Since A-N1 focused on local behavior of the **PDB** program, he did not put together the hints of global interactions that were present in both the descriptions of the subroutines and the actual code. SYS1's use of the systematic strategy and his concern with understanding the global behavior of the program before attempting to modify it led him to acquire both static and causal knowledge about the program; A-N1's focus on local aspects of the program led him to acquire only static knowledge and to overlook the causal knowledge. Since A-N1 did not understand how the **PDB** program behaved when it executes, he failed to acquire the causal knowledge necessary to understand the way in which the **RESTORE** enhancement interacts with the existing **PDB** program.

The next section of this paper examines the statistical relationship between systematic study of the program, extensive symbolic execution of the code, and success with the **RESTORE** enhancement task. We show that our anecdotal description of SYS1 and A-N1, which portray how strong and weak mental models are built and used, is strongly supported by statistical evidence linking systematic study and success in making the **RESTORE** enhancement to the **PDB** program. The crucial feature of this link between the systematic approach and success appears to be the use of extensive global symbolic execution.

6. Statistical Evaluation of Successful Subjects

Just as SYS1's behavior led to a successful **RESTORE** enhancement, programmers who produced successful **RESTORE** enhancements behaved differently from unsuccessful programmers like A-N1. Successful programmers acquired different knowledge about the **PDB** program as well. Programmers who designed successful **RESTORE** enhancements uniformly took a systematic approach to studying the **PDB** program. They attempted to learn how the program was constructed, and how it functioned when it ran. This knowledge about how the program functioned was evidently acquired through extensive symbolic execution. The successful, systematic, programmers also had a critical piece of knowledge the unsuccessful programmers lacked: They knew how the process of searching for a record interacted with the **RESTORE** enhancement and they realized that searching for a record occurred before it was processed. Thus, successful programmers:

- used a predominantly systematic approach to studying the program
- used extensive symbolic execution when studying the **PDB** program
- understood the interaction between the record search subroutines and **RESTORE**

	Column A		Column B		Column C	
	Predominant Strategy		Extensive Symbolic Execution		Understood Interaction of Record Search & **RESTORE**	
	Systematic	As-needed	Yes	No	Yes	No
RESTORE						
Success	5	0	5	0	5	0
Failure	0	5	0	5	0	5

n=10

Table 6-1: What Successful Maintainers Did and Knew

Table 6-1 shows how success was associated with systematicity, symbolic execution, and awareness of the interaction of **RESTORE** and the record search process. Ten programmers, five of whom were successful and five of whom were not, are represented. Every successful subject used a systematic approach, performed extensive symbolic execution, and understood the interaction of **RESTORE** and the process of searching for a record. Column A, for example, shows that the use of a systematic strategy permitted all five subjects who used it to design successful **RESTORE** enhancements; all five programmers who used the as-needed strategy failed. Columns B and C, respectively, show that extensive symbolic execution of the **PDB** code, and understanding the interaction of **SEARCH2** and **RESTORE**, were also perfectly associated with success.

Each of these relationships was statistically significant, using Chi-Square analyses and significance levels corrected for performing multiple tests on the same subjects. Each of the Chi-Squares relating success and one of the three variables (i.e., using the systematic strategy, performing extensive symbolic execution, and understanding the interaction of the record search process and **RESTORE**) was significant beyond the 5% level. We conclude from these analyses that the likelihood of successfully designing a **RESTORE** enhancement was greatly increased if programmers are systematic in their approach to studying the program and perform extensive symbolic execution. Finally, we note that there was virtually no relationship between years of professional programming experience and either successfully performing the enhancement task or the programmer's choice of study strategy. The point-biserial correlation between success in the enhancement task and years of professional programming experience was -0.06, which does not approach significance. This value of the correlation coefficient is effectively zero. Since success in the enhancement task corresponded exactly to the study strategy the programmer used, this correlation coefficient also shows that there is no relationship between experience and the programmer's choice of study strategy.

7. Discussion and Conclusions

Our empirical results demonstrate that programmers who used the systematic strategy were able to construct successful **RESTORE** enhancements for the **PDB** program while programmers who used the as-needed strategy were unable to do so. We observed that programmers who used the systematic strategy performed extensive global symbolic execution of the **PDB** program; programmers who used the as-needed strategy did not perform extensive symbolic execution. We also observed that, while all programmers acquired the necessary static knowledge about the program, only programmers who used the systematic strategy acquired the causal knowledge necessary to make the **RESTORE** enhancement successfully. Thus, it appears that the use of global symbolic execution provides programmers who used the systematic strategy with necessary causal knowledge that is required to construct successful **RESTORE** enhancements.

The connection between global symbolic execution and the acquisition of causal knowledge can be understood by considering the role of knowledge about data flow and control flow in understanding programs. Successfully modifying a program requires being able to determine how proposed modifications to the code affect the data flow and control flow between program components. The programmer must be able to reason about the program's data flow and control flow in order to assess whether proposed modifications to the code would disrupt the fulfillment of preconditions, or if a proposed modification requires modifying other parts of the program to preserve the fulfillment of preconditions. By performing extensive symbolic execution of the **PDB** program, the programmer who uses the systematic strategy simulates the code in detail, imagines its behavior at runtime, and determines *how to map the program's behavior onto the program's code*. Detailed simulation of the code thus forces the programmer to imagine the data flow and control flow *across* components of the program; communication across components of a program is, by definition, the manner in which causal interactions among components are achieved. Understanding the data flow and control flow in the unmodified program permits the programmer to reason about what the data flow and control flow *should be* in the modified program. Programmers who used extensive global symbolic execution to study the program understood the data flow and control flow among the components of the **PDB** program; that knowledge permitted them to design **RESTORE** enhancements that avoided destructive interactions.

In contrast to programmers who used the systematic strategy, programmers who used the as-needed strategy to understand the **PDB** program wanted to minimize their understanding of the parts of the **PDB** program that they believed were tangential to their enhancements. Programmers who used the as-needed strategy gathered information about the program only when they needed it to resolve questions that arose as they tried to implement their enhancements. As a result, programmers who used the as-needed strategy did not perform extensive symbolic execution of the **PDB** program and therefore did not understand the data flow and control flow in the program. Since programmers who used the as-needed strategy did not understand the data flow and control flow in the program, they were unable to reason about how the components of the program interact when the program runs; thus they could not construct enhancements that avoided the destructive impact of the interactions.

The current research methodology confronted professional program maintainers with a situation and task that differed in two significant ways from their normal experience. Further research must address the effects of these two important differences.

- What role does the test and debug cycle play in program maintenance?
- What study strategies are appropriate for large programs?

Subjects in our study were not allowed to test and debug their enhancements. Testing and debugging a program bring to the programmer's attention information that was overlooked in the initial study of the program. Programmers using the as-needed strategy may depend more heavily upon testing and debugging to learn about the program's structure than programmers using the systematic strategy. If we had permitted a test and debug cycle, the programmers who used the as-needed strategy might have constructed successful **RESTORE** enhancements. If programmers using the as-needed strategy with the test and debug cycle could correctly implement the **RESTORE** enhancement, they would *at least* have to acquire the necessary causal knowledge identified in Section 3. If the programmers in our study had been allowed to test and debug their enhancements, it is possible that the mental models resulting from both strategies would have been equally strong. What, then, would recommend one study strategy over another?

Decisions about which study strategy is "best" should take into account the effects on programming efficiency of the strength of the mental model. If the mental models resulting from the use of the two study strategies were equally strong, then the programmer should use the most efficient study strategy. The most efficient study strategy may not, however, be the fastest or the one that produces immediate results. In a study of the efficiency of the software development process, Fagan [1] presents data suggesting that fixing errors as early as possible in the software development process is more efficient than fixing errors late in the development process. This suggests that finding and correcting errors in the design of an enhancement *before* implementing the enhancement is most efficient. By understanding the program prior to implementing their enhancement, programmers using the systematic strategy may be able to avoid or detect errors in the design of an enhancement more efficiently than programmers using the as-needed strategy. Programmers using the as-needed strategy may have to depend upon testing and debugging to correct errors in the design of the enhancement *after* the enhancement has been implemented. Though their initial study of the program and construction of an enhancement may be faster, they would incur the added expense of tracking down and eliminating the effects of their early, undetected mistakes. On the other hand, if the mental models resulting from the use of the two study strategies were *not* equally strong, then the programmer must consider both the amount of time spent to complete the initial enhancement, the amount of time spent to test and debug that enhancement, *and* the value to future maintenance of having a clear understanding of the program. The impact of a clear understanding of the program would be felt in two ways. Subsequent maintenance tasks depend upon 1) the programmer's ability to debug the program and 2) the continuing integrity of the modified program. If the programmer's ability to debug proposed solutions and integrate them cleanly into the existing program depend upon the strength of the mental model, then the programmer should use the study strategy that results in the strongest mental model. Since the current research does not address the impact of the test and debug cycle on the strength of the resulting mental model, this is an important area for future investigation.

The **PDB** program contains 250 lines. Clearly, it is not possible to use the systematic strategy to study a program of 100,000 lines in preparation for modifying it. On the other hand, the current research strongly suggests that causal knowledge provides a powerful basis for performing program maintenance tasks. How, then, can we assist program maintainers working with large programs to construct what we have labeled *strong mental models* of large programs? Since the systematic strategy is unworkable for studying large programs, programmers working with large programs will be forced to use study methods akin to the as-needed strategy. In order to assist maintainers faced with large programs, it will be necessary to augment their as-needed program study methods. However, the as-needed strategy appears to be comprised of a much larger, more loosely organized collection of methods which we only partially understand. Thus, further investigation of the as-needed strategy would be a productive approach to defining the ways in which the selective study of large programs can be combined with automated study tools that assist programmers in developing powerful causal models of programs. We may begin such a study by identifying the methods called on by programmers using the as-needed strategy and by identifying the knowledge that results from various components of the as-needed strategy and how to supplement it.

Our concerns about the relative efficacy of the systematic and as-needed study strategies, the role of testing and debugging in program understanding and development, and the problems of understanding large programs are largely concerns about the specifics of study strategies. Our research shows that programmers who use the systematic strategy to study the **PDB** program acquire causal knowledge about programs. It is the importance of causal knowledge in program understanding that constitutes the main contribution of our work, not the description of the study strategies themselves. We hope that the systematic strategy is not the only way to acquire causal knowledge of a program: the systematic strategy is clearly unworkable for understanding large programs. Now that we understand the importance of causal knowledge for program understanding, further research must investigate other study strategies and develop programming tools to help programmers acquire the causal knowledge necessary to build strong mental models of programs.

8. Acknowledgements

The research reported in this paper was supported by the Jet Propulsion Laboratory, California Institute of Technology under contract with the National Aeronautics and Space Administration.

We would like to express our thanks to James Spohrer and the other members of the Cognition and Programming Project for their comments and support.

9. References

1. Fagan, M.E. Design and code inspections to reduce errors in program development. *IBM Systems Journal*, 1976, *15(3)*, 182-211.

2. Fjeldstad, R.K., and Hamlen, W.T. Application program maintenance study-- Report to our respondents. In G. Parikh and N. Zvegintzov (Eds.), *Tutorial on software maintenance*. Silver Spring, Maryland: IEEE Computer Society Press, 1983.

3. Meyers, G. J. A controlled experiment in program testing and code walkthroughs/inspections. Communications of the ACM, September 1978, Volume 21, Number 9, 760-768.

4. Soloway, E., Letovsky, S., Loerinc, B. and Zygielbaum, A. The cognitive connection: software maintenance and documentation. In *Proceedings of the 9th annual workshop on Software Engineering*. NASA/Goddard, Atlanta, Georgia, 1984.

5. Weiser M. Programmers use slices when debugging. Communications of the ACM, July 1982, Volume 25, Number 7, 446-452.

CHAPTER 7

Design Activity in Developing
Modules for Complex Software

A.F. Norcio
L.J. Chmura
Computer Science and Systems Branch
Information Technology Division
Naval Research Laboratory
Washington, DC 20375-5000

ABSTRACT

Since 1978, the goal of the Software Cost Reduction (SCR) project has been to demonstrate the effectiveness of certain software engineering techniques for developing complex software. The application is the redevelopment of the operational flight program for the A-7E aircraft Also since then, the Software Technology Evaluation (STE) project has been monitoring SCR project activity in order to provide an objective evaluation of the SCR methodology. SCR project activity data are collected from SCR personnel on a weekly basis. Over 55000 hours of SCR design, code, test, and other activity data have been captured and recorded in a computer data base. Analyses of SCR module design data show that there are parameters that can be used to characterize and predict design progress. One example is the ratio between cumulative design discussing and cumulative design creating activities. This ratio is referred to as the Progress Indicator Ratio (PIR) and seems to be an accurate metric for design completeness. This and other results suggest that discussion activity among software engineers may play a major role in the software design process and may be a leading indicator of design activity progress.

INTRODUCTION

This paper presents the results of an investigation of design activities of the software engineers working on the Software Cost Reduction (SCR) project. One purpose of this study is to offer insights into understanding the design process of complex software. A second purpose is to identify parameters that characterize and predict design progress. The data analyses suggest that at least one parameter does characterize and predict design progress under the SCR approach.

The Software Cost Reduction Project

Since 1978, the Naval Research Laboratory in cooperation with the Naval Weapons Center has been redeveloping version 2 of the operational flight program for

99

the A-7E aircraft [1]. Software engineering techniques such as formal requirements specification, information hiding [2], abstract interfaces [3], and cooperating sequential processes [4] are being used. This effort is referred to as the Software Cost Reduction project.

The goals of the SCR project are to (1) demonstrate the feasibility of using selected software engineering techniques in developing complex, real-time software, and (2) provide a model for software design. The claimed advantage of the selected software engineering techniques is that they can facilitate the development of easy-to-change software. A complete discussion of the project's software requirements is provided by Heninger, et al. [5]. For a detailed description of the module design structure, the reader is referred to Britton and Parnas [6].

The Software Technology Evaluation Project

The goal of the Software Technology Evaluation (STE) project is to evaluate alternative software development technologies[1]. The approach is to monitor, evaluate, and compare software development technologies used in different software projects. The monitoring and evaluating processes consist of goal-directed data collection and analyses techniques [7]. One of the tasks of the STE project is to provide the basis for an objective evaluation of the methodology used in the SCR project. The two projects are, however, separate research investigations each with its own goals, staff, and funding.

DATA COLLECTION

Since 1978, all project engineers have been required to submit weekly reports on their project activity hours. The activity data are collected on a form called the Weekly Activity Report, the current version of which is presented in Chart 1. The boxes on the form represent different project activities.

A submitted report is usually rather sparse; typically, it has only a few boxes marked with hours spent on project activities during the week. A copy of a completed report form can be found in [8]. Once a weekly activity report is given to STE project personnel, it is validated and entered into a computer data base. An instruction sheet explaining how to report weekly activity is provided to each project engineer.

Module Development Activities

The front page of the report form is primarily used to record hours spent on module development activity, where module means information hiding module [2]. As can be seen in Chart 1, SCR development activity hours are captured for each engineer by specific module within the hierarchy (e.g., Device Interface), and by design, code, and test categories. Space is provided for project personnel to supply the names of the modules below the first two levels.

The primary product of design activity is the development of a module interface specification. A typical interface specification for the Device Interface module [9] is presented in Chart 2. Design activity is reported as hours devoted to design creating, design discussing, design peer reviewing, and design formal reviewing activities. *Design creating* activity is time devoted to thinking about a design including redesigning or

---

[1]This work is currently funded by the DoD STARS Program as Measurement Area Task G-06.

SCR Project: Weekly Activity Report

Your name: _____

Date: Friday _____

ACTIVITY AREA — Software Testing

General _____
Subset _____

(ACTIVITY HOURS — Design: Creating, Discussing, Peer Reviewing, Formal Reviewing | Pseudo Code: Creating, Discussing, Peer Reviewing | EC/C/TC Code: Creating, Discussing, Peer Reviewing, Programmer Testing | Test: Preparation, Conducting, Reviewing Results)

MISCELLANEOUS ACTIVITY | HOURS

Project Control _____
Software Requirements Document _____
Travel _____
Technology Transfer _____
Other: _____

Non SCR (Optional) _____

REVERSE SIDE

ACTIVITY AREA

Software Structures
  Module Guide
  Uses Hierarchy
Software Modules
  Hardware Hiding
  Extended Computer
  Device Interface
  Behavior Hiding
  Function Driver
  Shared Services
  Software Decision
  Application Data Types
  Physical Model
  Filter Behavior
  Data Banker
  System Generation
  Software Utility

(ACTIVITY HOURS — Design: Creating, Discussing, Peer Reviewing, Formal Reviewing | Pseudo Code: Creating, Discussing, Peer Reviewing | EC/C/TC Code: Creating, Discussing, Peer Reviewing, Programmer Testing | Test: Preparation, Conducting, Reviewing Results)

(See reverse side)

FRONT SIDE

(8 May 1985)

Chart 1. Weekly Activity Report Form

Chart 2.   Module Design Specification

DI.WOG: WEIGHT ON GEAR SENSOR

1. Introduction

The weight on gear device is a sensor that detects whether or not the aircraft is resting on its landing gear. This data can be used to infer whether or not the aircraft is airborne.

2. INTERFACE OVERVIEW

2.1. ACCESS PROGRAM TABLE

Program	Parameters	Description	Undesired events
+G_WEIGHT_ON_GEAR+	p1: boolean; O	!+WOG+!	
			None

3. LOCAL TYPE DEFINITIONS None.

4. DICTIONARY

!+WOG+!   TRUE iff weight on landing gear detected.

5. UNDESIRED EVENT DICTIONARY None.

6. SYSTEM GENERATION PARAMETERS None.

documenting. *Design discussing* activity is time devoted to discussing design issues via a computer message or directly with a colleague to assist with the design. *Design peer reviewing* activity is time devoted to reading or commenting on (informally) design documentation produced by another project member in order to assist with the design. *Design formal reviewing* activity is time spent in a formal design review, typically at the Naval Weapons Center which maintains the current operational flight program.

Coding activity is reported as hours devoted to pseudo code, Extended Computer code[2], C code, and TC code[3] activities. Pseudo code activity is further reported as hours devoted to code creating, code discussing, and code peer reviewing activities. EC code, C code, and TC code activities are reported as hours devoted to code creating, code discussing, code peer reviewing, and code programmer testing activities. *Code creating, code discussing,* and *code peer reviewing* activities have definitions similar to their design counterparts. *Code programmer testing* activity is time devoted by programmers to computer-based evaluation of their own code to convince themselves of its correctness.

Test activity is reported as hours devoted to test preparation, test conducting, and test reviewing results activities. *Test preparation* activity is time devoted to creating, discussing, and reviewing plans and procedures for computer-based testing of a module prior to formal subset testing. *Test conducting* activity is time devoted to set up and execution of module test procedures on a computer. *Test reviewing results* activity is time devoted to analyzing, discussing, and documenting results of a module test.

Other Activities

The back page of the form is used to record hours spent on software testing and miscellaneous activities. *Software testing* activity is reported as hours spent on general issues of computer-based testing and on testing of system subsets. *Miscellaneous* activity is reported as hours spent on activities not included in any of the above definitions.

OVERVIEW OF SCR PROJECT ACTIVITIES

From January 1978 to February 1985, over fifty-five thousand activity hours have been reported. Experiments have been performed to provide reasonable assurance that the reported hours accurately reflect project activity and are appropriately categorized [10]. The monthly accumulation of hours expended in the top level categories is presented in Figure 1. Software Structures (SS) effort is time spent defining and documenting hierarchical module structure in the A-7E module guide [6]. Software Modules (SM) effort is time devoted primarily to specifying and implementing modules. Software Testing (ST) effort is time spent on validation testing of subsets, and Miscellaneous (MISC) is time spent on all other activities such as travel and project control. Most SCR work so far has concentrated on software module development.

---

[2]The Extended Computer is one of the modules of the program. EC code is consists of invocations of programs on this module's interface.

[3]TC code is the assembly language code for the IBM System 4 PI model TC-2 computer. The operational flight program runs on this machine.

FIGURE 1. SCR AREA ACTIVITIES

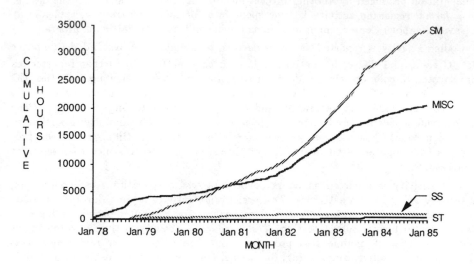

FIGURE 2. SOFTWARE MODULE ACTIVITIES

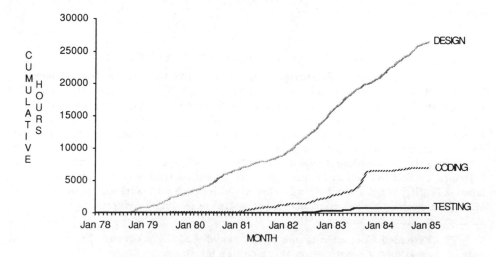

The monthly accumulation of hours expended in the Software Modules category on design, code (including pseudo-code), and test activities is presented in Figure 2. Over 75% of all reported software module activity is module design including redesign. This is consistent with the emphasis in the SCR methodology on extensive design with the expectation of significant reductions in coding, testing, and maintenance efforts [11].

There are three categories of first-level SCR modules: Hardware Hiding modules, Behavior Hiding modules, and Software Decision modules [6]. These, in turn, include ten categories of second-level modules, listed in Table 1. Each of the second-level modules is organized into several submodules (third-level modules) and some of these are further modularized. The EC module, with seven levels of submodules, has the deepest module structure.

Six of the second-level modules have accumulated more than 1000 hours of activity; these are EC, DI, FD, SS, AT, and PM. The six also have complete module interface specifications that are baselined or nearly baselined. In Figures 3 and 4, the monthly accumulation of hours expended on total activity and on design, code, and test activities are presented for Extended Computer and Device Interface modules[4]. Only the EC and DI modules have appreciable amounts of coding and testing activities. A more detailed discussion of these data is presented in [8].

Table 1. Abbreviations and Names of Second Level Software Modules

Abbreviation	Name
AT	Applications Data Type
DB	Data Banker
DI	Device Interface
EC	Extended Computer
FD	Function Driver
FLT	Filter
PM	Physical Model
SG	System Generation
SS	Shared Services
SU	System Utilities

---

[4]Vertical lines in Figures 3 through 12 represent the dates on which baselined interface specifications for the respective modules were released. The absence of these lines on a specific plot indicates that no baseline documents have been released for that module.

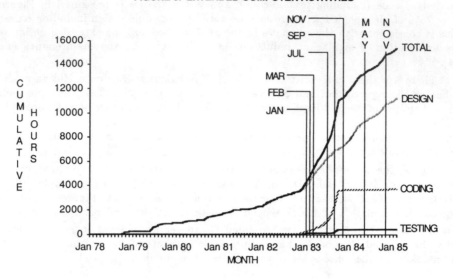

FIGURE 3. EXTENDED COMPUTER ACTIVITIES

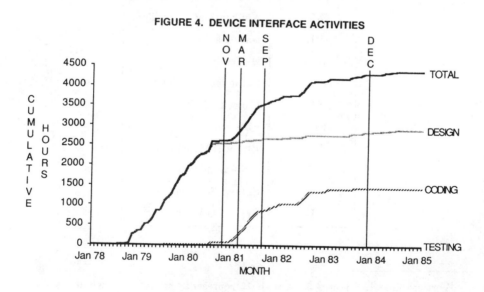

FIGURE 4. DEVICE INTERFACE ACTIVITIES

106

ANALYSES OF MODULE DESIGN DATA

As mentioned above, the SCR project emphasizes careful design which is reflected by the fact that design activity accounts for over 75% of all reported software module activity. One of the purposes of the data analyses was to identify parameters that characterize the design processes and offer predictive capabilities concerning them. Plots were constructed in order to characterize monthly hours expended on the subactivities of module design: design creating (DC), design discussing (DD), design peer reviewing (DR), design formal reviewing (DF), as well as total design (D). Unfortunately, characteristic patterns were not readily apparent.

Subsequently, it was decided to examine the accumulation of hours expended on total design and design subactivities. This approach is considered appropriate because each data point reflects the history of design activities up to that point in time. Thus, the cumulative total design hours for a module is defined by:

$$CumD_n = \sum_{i=1}^{n} D_i$$

where D_i is the monthly total of all design activities on a module for month i. (Note that D_i includes design activity on all submodules of the module.) Because data are available for all the months between January 1978 and February 1985, n has values from 1 to 86. Cumulative design creating hours for a module is defined by:

$$CumDC_n = \sum_{i=1}^{n} DC_i$$

where DC_i is the monthly design creating subactivity for a module (including all submodules) for month i. Again, n has values from 1 to 86. Similar definitions apply for $CumDD_n$ and $CumDR_n$. The significant cumulative design activities for the EC and DI modules are shown in Figures 5 and 6. Similar plots for all the modules are presented in [8].

An earlier study [10] highlighted the fact that ratios between activity categories provide valid and potentially useful metrics of SCR project activity. STE Project personnel intuitively suspected that ratios between activity categories could provide descriptive features of the SCR methodology that might be generally applicable to software design. Consequently, six ratio series between $CumDC_n$, $CumDD_n$, and $CumDR_n$ were computed. For example, the ratio between cumulative design discussing and cumulative design creating is defined as:

$$(CumDD/CumDC)_n = \frac{CumDD_n}{CumDC_n}$$

where n has values from 1 to 86. The other five, similarly defined, ratios are $(CumDC/CumDD)_n$, $(CumDC/CumDR)_n$, $(CumDD/CumDR)_n$, $(CumDR/CumDC)_n$, $(CumDR/CumDD)_n$. These ratios were correlated with $CumD_n$ over the 86 reporting

FIGURE 5. EXTENDED COMPUTER DESIGN ACTIVITIES

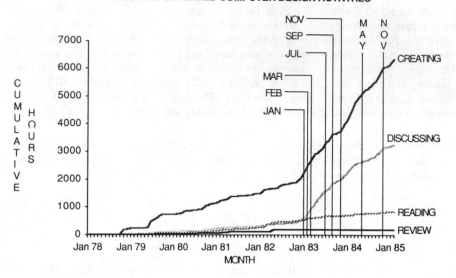

FIGURE 6. DEVICE INTERFACE DESIGN ACTIVITIES

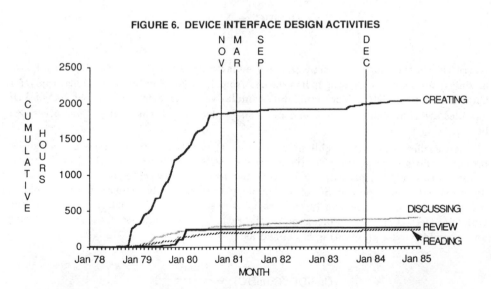

Table 2. Pearson Correlation Coefficients between CumD and Cum. Ratios

Module	$\dfrac{\text{CumDC}}{\text{CumDD}}$	$\dfrac{\text{CumDC}}{\text{CumDR}}$	$\dfrac{\text{CumDD}}{\text{CumDC}}$	$\dfrac{\text{CumDD}}{\text{CumDR}}$	$\dfrac{\text{CumDR}}{\text{CumDC}}$	$\dfrac{\text{CumDR}}{\text{CumDD}}$
AT	−0.4034	0.1245[*]	0.9774	0.9609	0.7483	−0.2006[*]
DI	0.0560[*]	−0.1998[*]	0.6574	0.1002[*]	0.8324	0.8124
EC	−0.3785	−0.3091	0.9492	0.6530	0.5436	−0.0568[*]
FD	0.7565	−0.0897[*]	0.9482	−0.0252[*]	0.1001[*]	0.9575
PM	−0.4090	−0.4144	0.9052	0.1429[*]	0.9235	0.3801
SS	0.9181	0.8665	0.5156	0.8408	−0.3675	0.5437

[*]Not significant at the $p \geq .005$ level.

months. Pearson correlation coefficients [12] are presented in Table 2. Next, for each module the ratio between monthly DC, DD, and DR were computed (e.g. DC_n/DD_n, DC_n/DR_n, and so on) and correlated with the total monthly D's and with the monthly CumD's. These coefficients are presented in Tables 3 and 4.

RESULTS

An examination of the correlation coefficients reveals that the ratio $(\text{CumDD}/\text{CumDC})_n$ correlates consistently well with CumD_n, as shown in Table 2[5]. This relationship is evident from the plots of the ratios. In Figure 7, the monthly ratio for $(\text{CumDD}/\text{CumDC})_n$ is plotted for the EC module. Comparing this with Figure 3, it can be seen that design activity surges are characterized by prior or concomitant dramatic increases in this ratio. When this ratio remains constant, it is an indication that design activity has stabilized. Increases in this ratio seem to indicate design progress. Consequently, we refer to this as the progress indicator ratio (PIR).

Even though the EC module is extremely large and complex, the relationship seems strong. A large jump in design activity follows the large rise of the PIR. However, design activity for this module is not quite stabilized and the late downward trend in the ratio indicates increasing creating time relative to discussing time.

The same patterns are also present for the DI module. As can be seen in Figures 4 and 8, the dramatic increase in design activity follows a dramatic increase in the progress indicator ratio. This same relationship holds for the FD, SS, AT and PM modules [8].

___

[5]The probability of finding this significant result is not increased because the same analyses were conducted over different data sets.

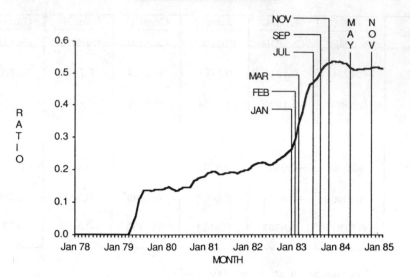

FIGURE 7. PROGRESS INDICATOR RATIO for EXTENDED COMPUTER MODULE

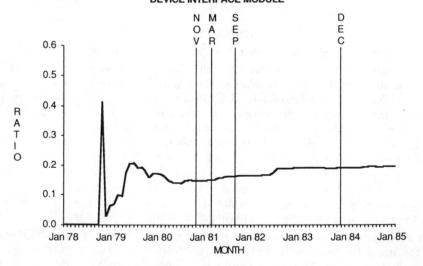

FIGURE 8. PROGRESS INDICATOR RATIO for DEVICE INTERFACE MODULE

Table 3. Pearson Correlation Coefficients between D and Monthly Ratios

Module	DC/DD	DC/DR	DD/DC	DD/DR	DR/DC	DR/DD
AT	0.3099	0.4031	0.3548	0.3048	0.3664	0.1572[*]
DI	0.3759	0.4829	0.1040[*]	0.2044[*]	0.0227[*]	0.2075[*]
EC	−0.0008[*]	0.3972	0.3401	0.5396	0.0040[*]	−0.0998[*]
FD	0.6470	0.5190	0.1305[*]	0.4813	0.1042[*]	0.3796
PM	0.3083	0.5845	0.3175	0.6581	0.0461[*]	0.3491
SS	0.6509	0.6040	0.0461[*]	0.4309	0.1248[*]	0.2578

[*]Not significant at the $p \geq .005$ level.

Table 4. Pearson Correlation Coefficients between CumD and Monthly Ratios

Module	DC/DD	DC/DR	DD/DC	DD/DR	DR/DC	DR/DD
AT	0.0532[*]	0.1667[*]	0.1169[*]	0.0843[*]	−0.0177[*]	−0.1287[*]
DI	−0.1693[*]	−0.1414[*]	0.0344[*]	−0.0879[*]	0.0683[*]	0.0352[*]
EC	−0.0932[*]	0.3933	0.3467	0.5236	−0.0248[*]	−0.0886[*]
FD	−0.0034[*]	0.0603[*]	0.1409[*]	0.0293[*]	0.1032[*]	0.1282[*]
PM	0.4034	0.3568	0.1182[*]	0.2205	0.170[*]	0.2582
SS	0.0547[*]	−0.0447[*]	0.1556[*]	−0.0531[*]	−0.0177[*]	0.0815[*]

[*]Not significant at the $p \geq .005$ level.

Coefficients of determination (r^2), as defined in [12], between $CumD_n$ and $(CumDD/CumDC)_n$ are presented in Table 5 for each module. This ratio seems to explain a high percentage of the variation of $CumD_n$.

The analyses provide supporting evidence that the ratio $(CumDD/CumDC)_n$ is an important measure of design activity progress in developing modules for complex software. When the PIR becomes constant, design activity appears to be at a very low level or even non-existent. When this ratio increases, design activity increases dramatically. The relationship between this ratio and $CumD_n$ is the strongest of all the possible relationships examined in this study. In at least one module, this ratio can explain over 95% of the variation in $CumD_n$. In the remaining modules, variations in $(CumDD/CumDC)_n$ can explain a surprisingly high degree of the variations in $CumD_n$.

CONCLUSIONS

A natural conclusion is that discussion between software designers is a critically important factor in the design of information hiding modules for complex software. When the release dates for specification baselines (e.g., [9]) are examined with the PIR, the PIR seems to be indicating the completeness of the baseline specifications. (See Figures 7 through 12.) When a baseline appears before this ratio rises sharply or during a sharp rise, the baseline is probably far from complete. Abstract interface specifications would seem to become reasonably stable only after a sharp rise and settling of this ratio. Plotting this ratio over time may provide the software manager a meaningful tool with which to track design progress. If the PIR has not surged and stabilized, the design is probably not finished irrespective of personnel claims and published baseline documents.

Table 5. Coefficients of Determination (r^2) between CumD and CumDD/CumDC

Module	r^2
AT	0.9552
DI	0.4322
EC	0.9010
FD	0.8992
PM	0.8194
SS	0.2658

All are significant at the $p \geq .005$ level.

**FIGURE 9.   PROGRESS INDICATOR RATIO for
FUNCTION DRIVER MODULE**

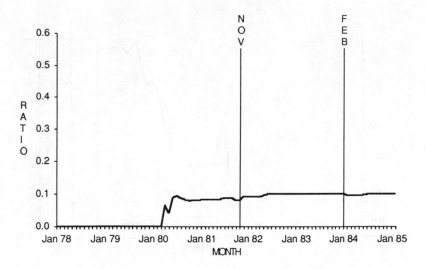

**FIGURE 10.   PROGRESS INDICATOR RATIO for
SHARED SERVICES MODULE**

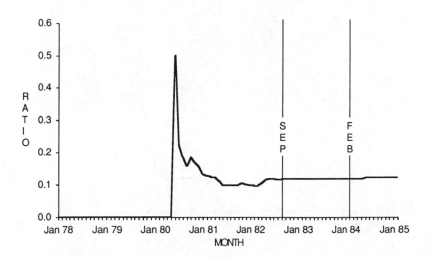

**FIGURE 11.   PROGRESS INDICATOR RATIO for
APPLICATIONS DATA TYPE MODULE**

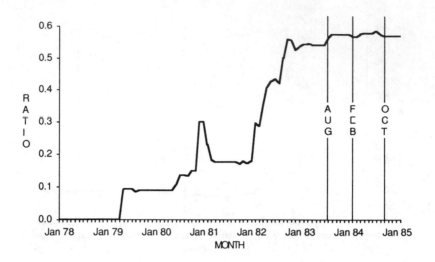

**FIGURE 12.   PROGRESS INDICATOR RATIO for
PHYSICAL MODEL MODULE**

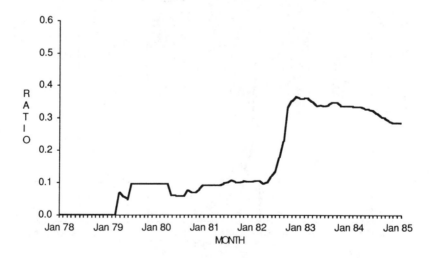

114

In addition, the PIR has an attractive property not found in a monthly plot of $CumD_n$. The range of the y-axis is constant over time and over other modules and projects. Therefore, it is possible to compare design progress on one module or project to another using this ratio. The PIR does, however, have one possible negative property. Because it involves cumulative sums, the accumulation of earlier design hours can dampen the impact of later variations in design activity. The PIR for the EC module indicates, however, that this possible flaw may be more theoretical than practical.

There is no claim that the PIR is a measure of design completeness. There are clearly other reasons why design activity on a specific software module may have stabilized. Personnel may have shifted work to another module; they may have been on vacation, and so on. However, the PIR ratio does seem to provide an indication when work on a piece of software is definitely not finished. If design completion is claimed prior to a rise and settling in this ratio, there is probably more work that needs to be done on that module.

It is necessary that this analysis be replicated on other large scale software development projects to determine whether the PIR behaves similarly in other software development environments using different design methodologies. It is intuitively appealing that discussion between project members necessarily enhances the design of software modules. It would also be useful to quantify the relative surges in the PIR. That is, there is practical importance in knowing that a given percentage increase in the PIR is customarily followed by a predicatable percentage increase in design activity. This, too, requires replicating these analyses in several different software design environments. Unfortunately, these data are difficult to collect and it is, perhaps, even more difficult to validate their accuracy.

Finally, it is logical to examine coding and testing data for these relationships. It seems reasonable to accept the importance of discussion in the design process. Its importance in the coding and testing processes is not as clear. These data exist in the SCR data base and plans are underway to examine them.

ACKNOWLEDGEMENTS

The authors owe a special debt of gratitude to Dr. Davis Weiss who first suggested that activity ratios could provide useful measures of design activities. In addition, through several readings of this paper, he offered many helpful suggestions and comments. The authors would also like to thank Mr. Jeff Sabat who prepared many data plots, Ms. Kathryn Kragh who guided many database queries, and Dr. John O'Hare and Mr. Paul Clements who offered technical advice and suggestions.

REFERENCES

1. Clements, P. C., "Software cost reduction through disciplined design," *Naval Research Laboratory 1984 Review*, pp. 79-87 (1985).

2. Parnas, D. L., "On the criteria to be used in decomposing systems into modules," *Communications of the ACM* **12**, pp. 1053-1058 (1972).

3. Parnas, D. L., *Use of Abstract Interfaces in the Development of Software for Embedded Systems*, Naval Research Laboratory Report 8047, Washington, D. C. (1977).

4. Dijkstra, E. W., "Cooperating sequential processes," pp. 43-112 in *Programming Languages*, ed. F. Genuys, Academic Press, New York (1968).

5. Heninger, K. L., Kallander, J. W., Shore, J. E., Parnas, D. L., and Staff,, *Software Requirements for the A-7E Aircraft*, Naval Research Laboratory Memorandum Report 3876, Washington, D. C. (1978).

6. Britton, K. H. and Parnas, D. L., *A-7E Module Guide*, Naval Research Laboratory Memorandum Report 4702, Washington, D. C. (1981).

7. Basili, V. R. and Weiss, D. M., "A methodology for collecting valid software engineering data," *IEEE Transactions on Software Engineering* **SE-10**(6), pp. 728-738 (1984).

8. Norcio, A. F. and Chmura, L. J., *Design Activity in the Software Cost Reduction Project*, Naval Research Laboratory Technical Report in press, Washington, D. C. (1986).

9. Parker, A., Britton, K. H., Parnas, D., and Shore, J., *Abstract Interface Specification for the Device Interface Module*, Naval Research Laboratory Memorandum Report 4385, Washington, D. C. (1980).

10. Chmura, L. J. and Norcio, A. F., *Accuracy of Software Activity Data: The Software Cost Reduction Project*, Naval Research Laboratory Report 8780, Washington, D. C. (1983).

11. Parnas, D. L. and Clements, P. C., "A rational design process: How and why to fake it," *IEEE Transactions on Software Engineering* (to appear).

12. Dixon, W. J. and Massey, F. J. Jr., *Introduction to Statistical Analysis*, McGraw-Hill Book Co., Inc., New York (1969).

CHAPTER 8

Different Logo Teaching Styles:
Do They Really Matter

Rachelle S. Heller
Department of Electrical Engineering and Computer Science
George Washington University
Washington, DC

ABSTRACT

This study has investigated whether a structured Logo experience as outlined by the Minnesota Educational Computing Consortium (MECC) and an experiential Logo setting as proposed by Seymour Papert of Massachusetts Institute of Technology (MIT) affected the level of Logo learning and the conceptual tempo of fourth grade students. Fifty-five fourth grade students from a private parochial school in suburban Washington, D.C. were divided into the two Logo learning groups. Each group met for one hour of Logo experiences each week for twelve weeks. All subjects took a Logo syntax test after three weeks and after twelve weeks of study. All subjects also took a Logo content test, a Logo concept test, a pre and post-test of conceptual tempo (MFFT:Child), and answered an opinion questionnaire after twelve weeks of study. The data from these tests were analyzed using a t-test. The attitude questionnaire data were analyzed using Chi-square (X^2) and Kendall's tau. A journal was used to record the weekly meetings.

The results revealed that the students in the structured environment scored higher on the test of Logo content. In areas of Logo syntax and allied concepts to Logo, there was no statistical difference between the groups. Furthermore, both groups improved over time in their understanding of Logo syntax as measured by the syntax test. There was a statistically significant improvement for the subjects in the Papert group as measured by their error rate on the MFFT:Child. The results from the attitude questionnaire, while not statistically significant, suggested that the subjects in a Papert environment like to work alone at the computer.

This study suggests that if the goal of exposure to Logo is a thorough knowledge of Logo, then it is expedient to use a structured approach. The study suggests that the educational community examine the goal of Logo in the classroom.

INTRODUCTION

There are currently more than 150,000 computers in schools. Experts predict that there will be more than double this amount before the end of the next year. How are these computers used in schools today? Taylor (1) says that they are used in three ways; as tutors, tools and tutees. In the tutee role the child teaches and the computer learns. When one programs a computer one teaches the computer (the tutee)how to solve the problem at hand. For example, if the problem were to add two numbers, the child would prepare the instructions necessary to solve this type of problem, put them into a language the computer can interpret, (a program) enter them into the computer, correct any errors and then direct the computer to follow the program.

Regardless of the reason for the rise of interest in teaching computer programming, the fact is that programming is part of the curriculum. Johnson (2) notes that "they (computers) will strongly impact the cognitive processes, especially in children" (p. 52). The question remains as to the actual impact of including computers in the curriculum.

The literature shows a difference of thinking concerning the direct positive relationship between learning to program and improved problem solving skills. Soloway, Lockhead & Clements (3) say there is a "common intuition among those in computer science education that programming encourages the development of good problem solving skills" (p. 171). Others (4,5,6,7) support this position. Those who did not find support for this thesis are represented by such researchers as Milojkovic (8).

Kurland et al. (9) state that the educational benefits of teaching children to program have not been "addressed adequately through systematic research" (p.4). Too little is known about its impact on a wide range of high level thinking skills. However, both intuition and preliminary research suggest that the skills acquired in learning to program will also form methodical problem solving skills.

The research results on the effect of Logo in problem solving skills, especially as they relate to planning, are divided . D. Watt (10) describes how 12 children made progress in Logo in ther own way. M. Watt (11) reports on the success with Logo by Ted, a dogged problem solver, and Stella, a creative thinker. Kull (12) sees the use of Logo as impacting a child's sense of control over the computer, an investigation of the concept of number and an understanding of the need for precision in communication. It is this last area that relates programming to problem solving.

Rieber (13) notes a statistically significant increase in systematic and procedural thinking for an experimental group exposed to Logo. Clements and Guilo, in a quantitative study (14), suggest that the act of debugging (removing the mistakes from a program) will effect the problem solving style of learners. They think that the child will become more reflective or thoughtful in his or her problem solving style. They think the child will think about the outcome of a plan before putting the plan into action.

Based on a quantitative study, Pea and Kurland (15) found no support for the view that children exposed to programming become planning oriented in their problem solving. In two different studies at the Bank Street School they reported no effects in planning due to Logo programming experience. Furthermore, they attributed improved planning ability to maturity and practice.

Since the activity programming can be considered a reflective model and exposure to reflective models have been shown to affect conceptual tempo, this research will investigate the effect of Logo programming on conceptual tempo. It has been suggested that the involvement in programming tasks in Logo leads to good problem solving skills. One measure of such skills is conceptual tempo. Adams (16) defines it as the relationship between the length of time a subject takes to make a selection from among several alternatives in a problem solving task and the accuracy of that solution

METHODOLOGY

Although intuition suggests a positive impact of learning to program a computer on problem solving styles, the research on the subject is not clear. One question that needs to be answered is what happens when children program in Logo. Does the way in which they solve problems change? Moreover, i Logo is presented

118

in different ways, will one group of children change its problem solving style differently from the other.

This study exposed two groups of children to two different Logo learning environments. One group was presented with a very open ended approach to Logo where the child could direct the course of his own experience as suggested by Papert, the designer of Logo. The second group was presented with a very tightly regulated experience as presented by the Minnesota Educational Computing Consortium (MECC). Using pencil and paper Logo syntax test at three weeks and a test of Logo syntax, content and concept at twelve weeks, the amount of specific Logo content learned by both groups was measured. This research also used the reflective or impulsive conceptual tempo as a measure of the problem solving style of these groups of children. Finally, the research investigated the attitudes of the children in each group to see if the type of Logo learning experience affected their attitudes about computers.

POPULATION

The population for this study was a group of 80 fourth grade children who were exposed to Logo for the first time. The children attend a private bilingual-school in suburban Washington, D.C. The school draws children from Northern Virginia, the District of Columbia and from the Maryland counties near the District. The children are mainly from middle and upper middle class families.

The school teaches a dual curriculum. Children spend 60% of their day in secular studies and 40% of their day studying Hebrew and religious subjects. The curriculum is ordered so that on Monday, Wednesday and Friday mornings the children are engaged in secular studies and in religious studies in the afternoon. On Tuesdays and Thursdays they study religious subjects in the morning and secular studies in the afternoon.

PROCEDURE

1. Permissions: Contact was made with the school and permission was granted to run a study of children using Logo with the fourth grade students. The parents were asked to give their permission to allow their child to participate in the study. In order for a child to remain in the study, they must agree not to engage in any computer courses outside of the study during the twelve weeks of instruction. Furthermore, any child who was absent for more than 25% of the lessons (3 sessions) would not be counted in the study although they were allowed to continue with the class.

A record was kept on each child. The record included the child's name and identification, sex, reading scores on the California Achievement Test, past Logo experience, group assignment and results on all dependent measures.

2. Pretest: All participants were pretested using the Matching Familiar Figures Test: Child (MFFT) (17) designed to determine their reflective or impulsive problem solving style. In this test children select a match for a given stimulus from among six alternatives. This test has been used successfully with children from "pre-school through elementary" (18, p. 107), and had been used with children of both sexes in grade 4. Messer (19) measured and affirmed the construct validity for the MFFT:Child.

Students with no prior Logo experience were assigned to the two groups at random. In an attempt to assess whether this random process had created two groups of essentially similar children as measured by a standardized test, a t-test was computed for the two groups using the subjects score on the CAT reading and math scores. The result based on the reading score (t (53) = 1.16, p > .05) and the result based on the math score (t (53) = .75, p > .05) indicate that there is no statistical difference between the two groups as measured by the CAT. (Table 1)

3. Scoring the MFFT:Child: Once the groups were formed the MFFT:Child was scored. A mean score for the response time was calculated for each group. A mean error score (the average number of errors) was calculated for each group. Using this scheme, a group mean for response time and for error rate was established for the Papert style group and for the MECC style group. The information obtained from this scoring was used as the basis for the hypotheses concerning the effect of Logo learning environments on conceptual tempo.

119

4. The Logo learning environments: The children had the opportunity to go to the computer lab as part of their weekly schedule. The classes met forty-five minutes a week for twelve weeks. Because of the limitation of the number of computers in the laboratory, the children are accustomed to working in pairs and continued to do so. These pairs were the same each week for the entire twelve weeks.

One group was presented with Logo following the Papert style and the other group was instructed in a style as proposed by MECC. Both groups were taught by the researcher and the classroom teacher acted as a non-participant observer. There were 25 children in the Papert group and 30 children in the MECC group.

Group One: This group was introduced to Logo in their initial contact as described by Papert et al. (20). They were shown the five commands, CLEARSCREEN, LEFT, RIGHT, FORWARD and BACK. They were instructed in how to read and interpret any error messages. The children were then free to experiment with Logo. They were encouraged to define their own tasks and to keep a notebook record of what they have done. As the children asked how to accomplish a specific task, they were guided in how to do it. This Papert style experiential learning is typified by the attempt on the part of the instructor not to suggest to the child that they approach a problem in a specific way. Requests for specific syntactic information (i.e. "Can you use abbreviations") were answered directly. Clements (21) has cautioned that the instructor not subtly guide the child to "think through what you are doing, or to slow down in their programming." A record was kept of the types of questions each child asked and notes were made of the Logo material (i.e. Logo commands or programming design) explain to each child.

Group Two: The schedule for this group included four of the 10 modules from the MECC curriculum.

Module	Topic
1	Meet the Turtle
2	Shapes
3	Patterns
5	Procedures

Each MECC module contains an overview orientation to the teacher, a detailed set of teacher notes on the featured student activities and the actual student activities. For example, in module one, the overview states that the purpose of the section is to help the student learn the initial LOGO commands of SHOWTURTLE, FORWARD, BACK, RIGHT, LEFT, HOME and CLEARSCREEN by relating them to the human body movements off the computer and to specific exercise on the computer. The teacher's notes lists the materials needed, the classroom setup, the time necessary for the activity, specific directions for the activity presentation and follow-up activities. The student activities are ditto sheets with sections to be filled in by the student. In activity two, for example, the student is directed to type.

CLEARSCREEN
FORWARD 40
RIGHT 60

and to draw, in the box provided, the results of these turtle steps.

5. Dependent measures: There were four dependent measures taken: a syntax test (22) at three weeks and a twelve weeks, a Logo content test and a concept test (8,20) at the end of the twelve weeks, and a change score on the reflective and impulsive conceptual tempo based on the pretest MFFT:Child scores and a posttest of MFFT:Child after twelve weeks.

a. After three weeks both groups were given a pencil and paper test. The purpose of this test was to see how much information about Logo syntax and content had been learned.

b. After twelve weeks both groups were retested on Logo syntax and tested for Logo content and concept knowledge. The children had one class period to finish the tests. Sample questions from these tests appear in the appendix. Copies of the full test material are available from the researcher.

The content test is designed to measure the level of Logo learned. The Papert concept test has three questions intended to measure a transference of information obtained while studying Logo to non-Logo situations.

The fact that there was no statistically significant difference between the groups as measured by the CAT reading, and math scores and the MFFT:Child conceptual tempo scores at the start of the study (Table 1) underscores the fact that the groups were essentially similar even though there were slightly more girls than boys in one group and more boys than girls in the other. This finding is in line with the finding of Kagan (23) that conceptual tempo is not dependent on sex or intelligence.

Table 1

Analyses of Group Makeup

According to CAT Reading and Math Scores and MFFT:Child Pretest

Group	No.	Mean	S.D.	S.E.	t-value	df	2-tail prob.
CAT Reading							
MECC	23	84.44	32.01	6.40	1.16	53	.250
Pap't	30	73.73	35.50	6.48			
CAT Math							
MECC	25	85.16	32.65	6.53	.75	53	.455
Pap't	30	77.97	37.29	6.81			
Latency (pretest)							
MECC	25	17.72	11.56	2.31	.76	53	.452
Pap't	30	15.62	8.95	1.64			
Error (pretest)							
MECC	25	.56	.35	.07	-.66	53	.5.3
Pap't	30	.62	.38	.07			

The two groups, MECC and Papert, were very different in style. The MECC group was a structured environment in which there was a lesson, each week, followed by hands-on computer work outlined by worksheets. The Papert group was instructed only in the four basic Logo commands (FORWARD, BACK, RIGHT, LEFT) and the interpretation of Logo error messages. From that point on the children were free to use Logo in their own way. As a result it was expected that these children would investigate different aspects of Logo.

When we examine the results (Table 2) of the Logo syntax test given to each group at the end of three weeks ($\underline{t}$ (50) = .91, p>.05), we see that there is no statistically significant difference between the groups. How can we explain this in light of the fact that the MECC group followed a very structured outline which covered many of the points on the test while the Papert group was free to follow their own interests? The first lesson to the Papert group was in fact very similar to the first lessons to the MECC group. Though neither group did very well on the test, (out of a possible total score of 34, the MECC mean score = 17.04 and the Papert mean score = 15.45), it can be argued that both environments prepare a child for the simplest understanding of Logo, the ability to write well formed Logo commands. At this level of syntax checking, both groups understand that FORWARD, BACK, RIGHT and LEFT require an input and that a space is needed between a command and its input value. Both groups can anticipate which error messages will occur if a space is omitted. Both groups can also identify the figure created by a simple sequence of these four Logo commands.

TABLE 2

Test Score on Logo Syntax at Three Weeks and Twelve Weeks

	No.	Mean	S.D.	S.E.	T-value	df	2-tail prob.
Three Weeks							
MECC	23	17.04	6.41	1.34	.91	50	.368
Pap't	30	15.45	6.19	1.15			
Twelve Weeks							
MECC	25	22.76	5.77	1.15	.90	52	.333
Pap't	30	21.28	5.38	1.00			

When we examine the results (Table 2) by both groups on the same test given after twelve weeks ($t(52) = .98$, $p > .05$) we again see no statistically significant difference. From an inspection of the mean scores (MECC = 22.76 and Papert = 21.28) we can see that each group has improved in its undersanding of Logo syntax and that that group is similar in the two groups. This suggests that time is an important factor. Nine weeks had passed from the first testing to the second testing. The children exhibited confidence in the use of the simple LOGO commands. Many of the Logo researchers suggest that a few weeks exposure to Logo is not enough. Pea (24) suggests that students need at least two years exposure before we can see any benefits. Clearly Pea is referring to benefits and understanding as related to programming. This test concerns only syntax, that is, the correct formation of a sentence or sentences in a language, but it can be argued that time is required for children to become confident about the syntax level of Logo as well as the programming level.

But the understanding of Logo syntax does not require the understanding of the effect of the Logo command (often called semantics). The study sought to investigate the effect of the learning environments on the level of Logo content learned. The results (Table 3) of the Stanford test ($t(50) = 3.82$, $p < .05$) (8) of Logo content showed statistically significant difference in the amount of Logo content learned by each group. The MECC group scored significantly higher than the Papert group on questions of Logo semantics.

Clearly the structured environment meticulously covered more aspects of Logo and offered the children drill and practice in how one uses Logo to accomplish various shapes and other outcomes. The MECC group did work-papers requiring them to investigate how to form a closed shape of many sides, how to form a star and how to manipulate the size of these figures. The Papert environment is by design more individualistic, some children will explore many aspects. Some children in the research never investigated Logo beyond moving the turtle around and around the screen. Others tried to plan and then form complicated figures and shapes. Proponents of the Logo from MIT would suggest that it is impossible to prepare a general test for Logo semantics because of the individualistic nature of the experience. Who can say that knowing the meaning of one Logo command is the measure and purpose of learning Logo. The question remains as to the goal of exposure to Logo.

When we examine the results (Table 3) on the test of Logo related concepts ($t(52) = -.12$, $p > .05$) specifically that of angle and distance, it is indicated that there is no statistically significant difference between the groups. The research does not examine whether any aligned learning takes place but does show that whatever is going on, happens equally to both groups. Many Logo researchers (15) argue that the notion that Papert offers in Mindstorms (7) that exposure to Logo does offer microworlds with which to study phenomena does not really take hold. This research does no attempt to answer that question but suggests that in order to study the question either Logo environment would be valid.

TABLE 3

Test Score on LOGO Content and Concept Twelve Weeks

	No.	Mean	S.D.	S.E.	T-value	df	2-tail prob.
Content Test							
MECC	24	6.40	2.95	.60	3.82	50	.000
Pap't	30	3.11	3.21	.61			
Concept Test							
MECC	24	13.68	2.80	.60	-.12	52	.902
Pap't	30	13.79	3.75	.70			

This research looked at the changes in conceptual tempo that might be caused by exposure to Logo. Kagan (23) suggests that the change in conceptual tempo does not happen quickly. Therefore, any change in conceptual tempo exhibited by the research groups could be said to be due to the Logo training. The statistics show (Table 4) that there is a change in the error rate for the children exposed to Logo in the Papert environment ($t(29) = 3.43$, $p<.05$). Young (25) tried to study a similar phenomena and noted that a three-week placement in Logo was not sufficient to change the classification from impulsive to reflective. The current study does not suggest a movement from impulsive to reflective but it does note an improved (reduced) error rate. This is consistent with the work of Debus (26) who suggests a trend toward more reflective behavior for children exposed to reflective models. While the MECC teams, as stated before, often hurried through the worksheets with an intent to finish the Papert teams were free to plan, try and examine the results of their efforts. This would suggest that the students in the Papert group had become more careful in their planning and execution of Logo, saw a relationship between their plan and its implementation, and therefore when measured on the MFFT:Child, exhibited fewer errors. These results could suggest to classroom teachers that some ownership or vested interest in the outcome of a project helps a child to relate the process to the product. Whichever environment is presented to the child, it should be created so that it encourages a child to participate in the process.

TABLE 4

Pre and Post Scores on MFFT:Child

	No.	Mean	S.D.	S.E.	t-value	df	2-tail prob.
MECC-Latency							
pre	25	17.72	11.56	2.31	.89	24	.383
post		16.01	10.12	2.03			
MECC-Errors							
pre	25	.56	.35	.07	1.36	24	.187
post		21.28	5.48	1.03			
Pap't-Latency							
pre	30	15.62	8.95	1.64	-.28	29	.778
post		15.93	6.98	1.27			
Pap't-Errors							
pre	30	.62	.38	.07	3.43	29	.002
post		.47	.34	.06			

At this point it is useful to relate some of the remarks and activities of the two groups. The children in the MECC group asked almost each week if they were going to receive grades on their Logo work while that question was never voiced by the children in the Papert group. The children in the MECC group were eager to finish their work papers and often shielded their answers from members of the other teams. One week the work paper involved generating a 5-point star. This was admittedly a hard task. The teams became very competitive and eager to be the first finished. Some teams wanted to settle for "close enough" just to finish first. The teams very often wanted the researcher to tell them the "right" answer, they did not want to experiment with their own ideas. Each child was given a folder in which to keep their worksheets. The worksheets build on each other and yet the children rarely went to their folders to review the work on previous sheets and to research possible solutions for the new work papers. Although the focus of this study was not to reflect on the hidden curriculum of schooling, I think it is fair to say that these children had become acculturated to an environment of right and wrong answers, product no process.

The teams in the Papert group at first did not share or venture out of their seats to see what another team was doing. They also had learned a way of acting in school that valued independent work and did not encourage sharing. After a few weeks, however, one team discovered that they had a color terminal and began to produce interesting patterns in various colors. The other teams often spent most of the period watching this team and discussing a schedule that would allow them to have a turn. As time went on, there was a lot of sharing of ideas in the Papert group.

Not all the ideas were very high minded. Most of the teams spent the twelve weeks basically wrapping the turtle around the screen. One could argue that they were investigating the limits of the turtle space or one could argue that they were overloaded by the possible LOGO effects and were becoming passive in what is otherwise an active situation. This suggests that children need some guidance in their work with Logo. The fact that Logo allows one to investigate powerful ideas does not also suggest that those powerful ideas are obvious to every student. This researcher noted that children often chose not to engage actively in Logo activities at all but to wander around the room sometimes stopping to watch other groups. These children certainly needed guidance in order to investigate the possibilities of Logo. Joyce (27) reminds us that effective teaching occurs when the teaching style is linked to the child's learning style. Therefore it would be prudent not to expect that every child will benefit from a particular environment.

In her book, The Second Self, Turkle (28) discusses a child who needs a structured environment and when exposed to Logo creates a structure by limiting herself to a small subset of commands. A similar phenomena was noted in the research journal to have occurred in the Papert group. When confronted with an open environment, some teams created very strict rules about controlling the turtle. Most of these teams were the ones that only engaged in wrapping the turtle around the screen. The rules involved what size turns and movements were allowed and who would be determined the winner when the screen was entirely covered with the turtle tracks. These teams kept track of the scores from week to week. These children also were product oriented and when the teacher did not supply a product goal, they invented one. This behavior can be said to support the claim that different children have different needs and suggests that no one environment or opportunity is appropriate for all children.

Half of the teams in the Papert group explored beyond the wrapping of the turtle. Of the teams that did such investigations most had a chief protagonist and the other team members followed. Most commonly, one team member was mildly interested in doing something and the other members wandered around the room or waited somewhat patiently for their turn. Only one team actually built a rule structure that allowed a high degree of cooperation in building any design, even to the naming of the the design from initials of each team member. Some of this difficulty could have been eliminated if there were more computers and fewer children had to be part of a team. In actual fact in most school situations it is not financially possible to reduce the student computer ratio. This would suggest that in such an environment, some structure or guidance would be appropriate. The teams in this research were formed at random. In actual classroom setting, attention to the team make-up would allow like-minded children to be grouped together. This might also contribute to effective use of the level of equipment.

A major question to consider is the goal of the Logo experience for the student. If the goal of the Logo experience is to make Logo programmers out of the children, then the research-outcome that shows that there is a statistically significant difference between the Logo learning groups as measured by a Logo content test would suggest that the MECC approach clearly outlines an attention to product. If the goal is to focus on the process of actions rather than the product, this research suggests the Papert approach should be followed. In actual fact, a blending of the two approaches, a Logo environment which teaches the Logo syntax and semantics and encourages individual experimentation, would offer the best of both worlds.

The goal of an educational setting is often to engender socialization. Both the MECC group and the Papert group exhibited measures of socialization. The types of socialization were markedly different. In the MECC group a team worked together against the rest of the teams while in the Papert group teams did share their findings with others. This research only begins to suggest that there is a different atmosphere created in each of these environments. The findings suggest that if the goal of socialization is an important outcome of an educational experience, the type of socialization must be considered. If one wants to encourage small group cohesion, the MECC group seems to engender this attitude. If the goal is to encourage wider socialization, the Papert environment should be considered.

The results (Table 5) from the attitude survey were less promising than was hoped. There is an independence between group membership and attitude as expressed on this instrument. It was expected that since the nature of the environments were very different, the survey would guide one into an under-standing of a child's reactions to the environment. A look at question 11, "I like to do Logo" alone, while not indicating a clear relationship between group membership and attitude (correlation = .20), does indicate a 'pointing' in that direction. The subjects in the MECC group were more likely to say that they disagreed, that is they liked to work with a partner. This makes sense in light of the experience of the two groups. The MECC group, as said before, very often were intent on finishing their work paper. What better way to finish than with a partner. On the other hand, the Papert group, trying to direct their own investigation into the world of Logo, would rather work along. This suggests that the standard pairing of children at a computer which is a common situation in a classroom environment may work against the child in a Papert syle Logo environment. As the relationship is not statistically strong, this research does not suggest that the Papert environment is counterproductive in a situation where a child cannot have the sole use of a computer but is does suggest that the questions be studied further.

SUMMARY

Different learning environments yield different educational outcomes. Before choosing a Logo learning environments is is crucial to determine a set of educational goals. If the goal is a thorough knowledge of Logo in a limited time frame the more prudent approach seems to be a structured environment. If, on the other hand, the goal is more broadly framed as a growth experience for the child in areas of conceptual tempo and socialization, this research suggests an experiential Logo environment. It remains to be studied whether an amalgam of these learning environments can capture the best of both situations.

APPENDIX

LOGO Syntax
(Heller, 1985)

Question 1 (8 points)
    You are to find any errors in the following LOGO statements. If you find
an error mark "yes" in the column marked "ERROR". If you do not find an error,
mark "no" in the column marked "ERROR". If you find an error, try to rewrite
it correctly in the last colmn.

    STATEMENT   ERROR   REWRITE

    FORWARD6
    BACK LOTS
    RT 12
    HOME2

LOGO Content Test
(Milojkovic, 1984)

1(a) Write a procedure to make the turtle draw a square with sides of length
      50.
1(b) Here is a picture of two squares with sides of length 50.
      Write a procedure to make the turtle draw this picture.

LOGO Concept Test
(Papert, et al, 1979)

Name _____ Class_____ Date _____

1. If the length of this line is 100   _____

    how long are these lines? (Put your answers on the dotted lines.)

    (a) _ _ _ _ _   (b) _ _ _ _ _

                                              _____

                                          (c) _ _ _ _ _ |
                                                          |
                                                          |
                                                          |

    (d) _ _ _ _ _   (e) _ _ _ _ _ |
                                          |
      _____ |

Draw lines which you think will be

(f) 150
(g) 400
(h)   99

126

REFERENCES

1. Taylor, R. The Computer in the school: Tutor, tool, tutee. Teachers College Press, 1980.
2. Johnson, C. Microcomputers in educational research. (ERIC Reproduction Service) December, 1982.
3. Soloway, E., Lockhead, J., & Clement, J. Does computer programming enhance problem solving ability? Some positive evidence on algebra word problems. In Seidel, R., Anderson, R., & Hunter, B. (Eds.) Computer Literacy. Academic Press, 1982.
4. Dolbey, J., Linn, M., & Tourniaire, R. Making pre-college instruction in programming cognitively demanding: issues and interventions. AERA Symposium, April, 1984.
5. Ehrlich, K., Abbott, V., Salter, W., & Soloway, E. Issues and problems in studying transfer effects from programming. AREA Symposium, April, 1984.
6. Howe, J. Learning mathematics through Logo programming. (University of Edinburgh A.I. Tech Report #153) Edinburgh, Scotland, 1981.
7. Papert, S. Mindstorms. Basic Books, 1980.
8. Milojkovic, J. Children learning computer programming; Cognitive and motivational consequences. Doctoral Thesis, Stanford University, 1985.
9. Kurland, D., Mawby, R., & Cahir, N. The Development of programming expertise. AERA Symposium, April, 1984.
10. Watt, D. Final report of the Brookling Logo Project: Part III. (MIT Logo Memo 354) Boston, Mass., September, 1979.
11. Watt, M. What is Logo? Creative Computing, October, 1982.
12. Kull, J. Learning and Logo. In Fein, G., & Campbell, P. (Eds.) Microcomputers in early childhood education; Conceptualizing the issues. Reston, 1984.
13. Rieber, L. The effect of Logo on increasing systematic and procedural thinking according to Piaget's theory of intellectual development and on its ability to teach geometric concepts to young children. Master's Thesis, University of New Mexico, 1983.
14. Clements, D.H., & Guilo, D. Effects of computer programming on young children. Presented at MIT Logo 84 Conference, June 1984.
15. Pea, R., & Kurland, M. On the cognitive effects of learning computer programming: A critial look. New Ideas in Psychology, Pergamon Press, 1983.
16. Adams, W. Strategy differences between reflective and impulsive children. Child Development, 1972, 43, 1076-1080.
17. Kagan, J. Reflection-impulsivity and reading ability in primary grade children. Child Development, 1965, 36, 609-628.
18. Johnson, O., & Bommarito, J. Tests and measurement in child development. Jossey-Bass Incl, 1971.
19. Messer, M. Refection-Impulsivity: Stability and school failure. Journal of Educational Psychology, 1970, 61(6) 487-490.
20. Papert, S., Watt, D., diSessa, A., & Weir, A. Final report of the Brookline Logo Project: Part II. MIT Logo Memo #53, September, 1979.
21. Clements, D.H. Supporting young children's Logo programming. The Computing Teacher, 1983, 11(5), 24-30.
22. Heller, R. The effect of MECC and Papert teaching styles on the level of Logo learning and the conceptual tempo of fourth grade students. Doctoral Thesis, University of Maryland, 1985.
23. Kagan, J. Reflection-impulsivity: The generality and dynamics of conceptual tempo. Journal of Abnormal Psychology, 1966, 71.
24. Pea, R. Programming and problem solving. (Bank Street School Tech Report #12), New York, 1983.
25. Young, L.M. An analysis of the effect of the Logo programming environment upon the reflective and impulsive cognitive styles of second grade students. University of Pittsburg, 1982.
26. Debus, R. Effects of brief observation of model behavior on conceptual tempo of impulsive children, Developmental Psychology, 1970, 2, 22-32.
27. Joyce, B. Selecting learning experiences: Linking theory and practice. Association for Supervision and Curriculum Development, 1978.
28. Turkle, S. The second self. Simon and Schuster, 1984.

CHAPTER 9

Programmer/Nonprogrammer Differences
in Specifying Procedures to People and Computers

Lisa A. Onorato
Roger W. Schvaneveldt
Psychology Department
and Computing Research Laboratory
New Mexico State University
Las Cruces, NM 88003

ABSTRACT

This paper investigates the effects of computer programming skills on the writing of ordinary instructions. Three computer experience groups (Naive, Beginner, Expert) wrote telephone directory instructions to one of three targets (another person, George Washington, or an English-understanding computer). Each subject performed this task twice, such that data could be collected from Beginners before and after one semester of computer experience. No effects of this Session variable were found, however, leading to a discussion of the learning verses selection hypotheses.

Other results indicate that overall type of instruction strategy used was only significant for the computer target. When writing for a computer, Experts were more likely to use a whole name search, Naive users to use a separate name search, and Beginners to use a letter search. These results are interpreted in terms of problem representation and in terms of expectations of a natural language computer system.

In addition, it was found that Experts used more looping and programming action statements than Naive or Beginner users, even when writing to another person. The programmer's advantages are then discussed. Also, the computer target was always the least likely to receive information in terms of alphabetization instructions, directory descriptors and fillers suggesting further burdens and expectations that users may place on natural language systems.

INTRODUCTION

In analyzing computer programming, people are beginning to conclude that the programming experience shapes and sharpens one's thought processes, one's ability to reason and one's ability to work through a problem. Golden (1) claims that "the precise orderly steps of logic required to ...program...promise to shape and sharpen the thought processes.... " (p. 56). Schank (2) states that "programming can develop your intellect and show you the benefits...of step-by-step reasoning;..the process certainly will develop your reasoning skills" (p. 6). Wirth (3) believes that abstraction-- "our most important mental tool for coping with complexity"-- is enhanced through structured programming. In essence, the common belief is that "thinking like a programmer" may be an entirely different experience than thinking like a nonprogrammer.

The present experiment attempts to examine such claims by looking at differences between expert, novice and naive computer programmers in writing instructions for either another person or a natural language understanding computer to follow. The resulting instruction data sets could prove interesting for several reasons.

Essentially, programming is the writing of instructions for another agent (the computer) to follow. Miller (4) suggests that through programming, one acquires skill at procedure specification-- the ability to specify a sequence of actions necessary to accomplish a goal. If programmers have so much practice with specifying procedures, then one might see programmer-nonprogrammer differences in ability to express oneself, ability to develop an overall general attack strategy, and in the accuracy, precision or completeness of instruction.

Miller (5), in his concentration of *au naturel* programming, began this investigation by researching the way only inexperienced programmers specify procedures. He asked nonprogrammers to write instructions for another person on how to solve problems associated with personnel files. One example would be to "write out instructions on how another person should organize a list of all people over age 50." His results indicate that nonprogrammers omit many actions from their solutions, thus requiring the "other person" to draw from some base of experience in order to follow these incomplete procedures. Miller believes that sources of difficulty may be either expressional or conceptual; either the subject knows how to solve the task but cannot put his ideas into words, or else he cannot formulate the abstract idea itself. The present experiment adds to Miller's work by examining if the experts' instruction sets illustrate similar difficulties.

Also, the subjects' instruction sets can serve as written protocols that partially reflect the sequence of mental operations stepped through in completing the task. This information can give us insight into the types of problem representations the different groups might have for ordinary tasks. Several researchers have suggested that expert and novice programmers have different representations of various programming tasks: program comprehension (Adelson (6)); program construction (Jeffries, Turner, Polson & Atwood (7)); categorization of programming problems (Weiser and Shertz (8)); and general program representation (Shneiderman (9)). Generally, it has been shown that experts use deeper, top-level, general, global, hierarchical information, whereas novices focus on the more literal low-level, specific, concrete details. This finding has been found not only for programming experts, but also for experts in chess (Chase & Simon (10)), physics (Chi, Feltovich & Glaser (11)) and algebra (Lewis (12)). This experiment investigates whether programming experts transfer their general problem solving approach from the programming environment to an everyday task.

Furthermore, through their programming experience, programmers acquire additional tools or skills such as conditionals, loops, if -then structures and other types of control-transfers. The present task also investigates whether or not these experts still think in terms of these programming constructs even when writing ordinary instructions. The task similarly investigates how nonprogrammers wish to naturally specify such constructs, if they are capable of specifying them at all. This last information would be beneficial for designers of user-friendly computer systems.

Finally, this task can be used for natural language endeavors. That is, one can observe how writing instructions to an English-understanding computer compares to writing instructions to another person. Dumais and Landauer (13) began this investigation by examining how people defined words for computer and person targets. In general, they found that experienced programmers were more terse with computers than persons, and vice-versa for novice programmers. Overall, they found that the experts were more terse than novices regardless of target. It would be interesting to see if these findings hold not only for word definition, but also for entire procedure specification.

DESIGN

The task chosen for this experiment involved a telephone directory search--writing instructions on how to look up the name Jay Smith in the telephone directory. As in Dumais & Landauer (13), subjects were asked to write out instructions to either another person or to an English-understanding computer. In addition, a third target, George Washington, was included to try to get subjects to be as specific as possible in their instruction writing to this target who was assumed to be completely naive of telephone directory usage. Often during communication, people can assume that other people have similar backgrounds and experiences and a certain knowledge base with which to understand the intended communication. They therefore tend to omit many details and obvious points from their speeches. Given the naive George Washington target, however, subjects can no longer make these assumptions about his background. Thus, through this target, one receives the opportunity to observe nearly complete and accurate instruction data sets. In contrast, no restrictions were placed on the Computer target. Through this manipulation, different targets may elicit different instructions and one can thus acquire information on the assumptions subjects make about the knowledge of the target.

The task was presented to three different groups of varying programming experience: Naive, Expert, and Beginner. The Beginner group consisted of those students enrolled in their first computer programming course. All subjects were asked to complete the task at both the beginning and end of the semester. Therefore, data was collected from Beginners before computer programming training and also after one semester experience. This manipulation is required if one wishes to show that the computer programming experience actually changes one's thought processes in writing instructions, and that differences between expert and novice groups are not necessarily due to the fact that expert programmers have different skills or cognitive abilities to begin with.

All Beginners were enrolled in an introductory Pascal course, CS 110. In this class, students usually receive their first instruction on computer usage and also receive basic training in the usage of loops, control statements, and other programming concepts.

METHOD

Subjects

Subjects in this experiment were 335 New Mexico State University undergraduate introductory psychology students who participated for partial fulfillment of experimental credit. Of these students, 138 were excluded because they were not present for the second half of the experiment. Of the remaining 197 subjects, a computer programming questionnaire determined that 108 were Naive computer users (no computer experience), 46 were Expert computer users (currently programmed at least 3 hours per week and met at least 2 of the following criteria: knew at least 2 programming languages very well; had written over 50 programs; had at least 1 year programming experience; had received at least a grade of 'B' in at least 3 programming classes), and 43 were Beginner students enrolled in their first computer programming course (CS 110 - Computer Appreciation & Introduction to Pascal).

Materials

The materials consisted of the following:
  I) Three versions of instruction forms:

(P) Please write out instructions for another person to follow on "How to look up the name Jay Smith in the telephone directory."

(G) Assume that you have just passed though a time zone and now find yourself back in the 18th century. You have just encountered George Washington and wish to tell him about modern America and all the advances of technology since his time. After having already explained to him what a telephone is and how it works, you now wish to tell him how to use a telephone directory. Please write out the instructions you would give George Washington on "How to look up the name Jay Smith in the telephone directory." Remember: George Washington can read, write, and understand English, but he has never seen or used a telephone directory before.

(C) Please write out instructions for a computer to follow on "How to look up the name Jay Smith in the telephone directory." Assume the computer is capable of understanding English. Please write out your instructions to the computer in English.

  II) A computer experience questionnaire.

Procedure

During the first week of the semester, the experimenter went to each Psychology 201 lab session with one of three instruction versions, using one randomly chosen version per lab session. Students were informed that as a chance to gain experimental credit, they could all participate in an in-class experiment. All willingly participated. The experimenter explained that the experiment dealt with how people write instructions and handed each student one of three form versions to complete. When all completed forms were collected, the experimenter informed the subjects that she would be returning with a questionnaire for them to fill out and requested that they did not discuss their answers until after these questionnaires had been completed.

During the last week of the semester, the experimenter returned to each lab session informing the students that it was necessary to re-collect the data. Students were then given the same version they had previously completed. When finished, students filled out a computer programming experience questionnaire.

The three forms (first and second instruction set and questionnaire) were then matched according to the social security number students were required to write on each. Table 1 shows the resulting number of subjects grouped according to target and to computer experience.

Table 1
Number of Subjects per Experimental Condition

Experience	Target Person	Target GeorgeW.	Target Computer	Total
Naive	34	44	30	108
Beginner	9	15	19	43
Expert	11	16	19	46
Total	54	75	68	197

RESULTS AND DISCUSSION

<u>Analysis of Strategy</u>

A scorer who was blind to the experimental conditions scored each subject's written instruction data set for statement types. This review yielded three possible categories of search strategies. The most general of these strategies, NAME, involved a whole name search (e.g., "look for his name", "look for Jay Smith"). The second strategy, 2NAME, involved a separate name search (e.g., "look for Smith, then look for Jay"). Finally, the most detailed strategy, LETTER, involved a letter search (e.g., "find the letter S, then find M, then I, T, H").

Each of the above strategies received a point for every written idea that belonged to that style search. The NAME strategy consisted of only one statement type. Subjects could thus receive either a score of 1 or 0 for this strategy.

The 2NAME search consisted of two statement types: 1) a last name search, and 2) a first name search. Subjects received a 1/2 point whenever they used either of these statement types so that, as with the whole NAME search, the highest obtainable score in this category would be 1.

Finally, the LETTER search category consisted of 8 possible statement types--reference to each of the 8 letters in the name JAY SMITH. Subjects received 1/8 point for each letter referenced, so that the resulting scores again ranged from 0 to 1.

Using the above strategy types as a repeated measures variable, an analysis of variance was performed on a 2x3x3x3 two within, two between-subjects design. The within-subjects variables consisted of the 3 strategy scores (**STR**) (NAME, 2NAME, and LETTER) and the 2 different sessions (**SESSION**) over which these scores were obtained. The between-subjects variables consisted of target (**TAR**) (Person, George Washington or Computer) and level of computer experience (**EXP**) (Naive, Beginner or Expert).

Although it was hypothesized that one semester of computer programming would affect instruction writing for the Beginner subjects, no significant effect of **SESSION** was found for any of the three experience groups. Apparently all subjects basically used the same strategy types in both sessions, and one semester of computer programming was not enough to affect the strategy style chosen. Alternatively, one semester may not have been enough time between testing, as subjects may have remembered their original answer and simply repeated it when asked to perform the exact same task in the exact same setting. Or perhaps, as one anonymous reviewer suggested, the original task may have been too simple and didn't "...push the students to use their new found ability to cope with complexity."

Hence, the following conclusions reflect results summed over **SESSION**. The mean scores for each Strategy at each Target-Experience combination are shown in Table 2.

Table 2
Means for Strategy Types

Experience	Target	NAME	Strategy 2NAME	LETTER
Naive	Person	.0	.74	.38
	GeorgeW.	.08	.76	.24
	Computer	.07	.80	.25
Beginner	Person	.11	.72	.29
	GeorgeW.	.17	.68	.22
	Computer	.0	.38	.70
Expert	Person	.05	.57	.43
	GeorgeW.	.0	.75	.31
	Computer	.21	.41	.41

Although an analysis of variance revealed significant main effects and two-way interactions, of most interest is the significant **STRxEXPxTAR** three-way interaction (F (8,376) = 3.65, $p<.0004$). This interaction is illustrated in Figure 1. As the figure shows, all subjects preferred the 2NAME strategy when writing for another person or for George W. Of interest, then, is the Computer target. Further simple effects analysis and Newman-Keuls comparisons (significant at $p<.01$) indicate that when writing for an English-understanding computer, Experts preferred a whole-name search more than did Naive or Beginner users, Naive users preferred a 2NAME search (the same they used when writing for another person or George W.), and Beginners preferred a LETTER search more than did Experts or Naive users.

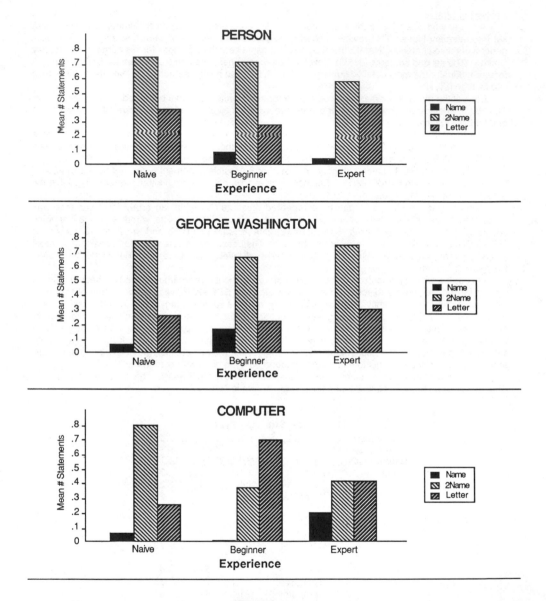

Figure 1.

Experience x Strategy across Target Levels

Problem Solving Strategies

These results are consistent with the current literature on expert-novice programmer differences. In general, previous research has shown that Expert programmers represent a given program in abstract, general, global terms, whereas the Novice programmer tends to focus on the lower level concrete details of the program. The present study similarly demonstrates that when writing instructions for a computer to follow, Experts make use of global information, and choose to work with an entire name concept, whereas Beginners focus on the specific details and concentrate on manipulating the specific letters of a name.

It should be pointed out that the strategy used by Experts in instructing a computer was apparently target-specific. Experts did not apply this strategy when instructing another person or George Washington--only the Computer. Apparently, the general problem representations typically used by experts in various fields only apply to one's specific area of expertise. Based on the analysis of strategy style, then, it would seem that the writing of ordinary instructions and the writing of instructions to a computer are two entirely different tasks for the expert programmer.

In comparison to Experts and Beginners, Naive computer users were more inclined to instruct the computer to first find a last name, and then find a first name in this telephone directory search. This separate name search was overall the most widely used strategy. Subjects at each experience level preferred this strategy when writing to George Washington or to another person. Naive users, regardless of target, preferred this strategy. While it could be inferred that people choose to begin at an intermediate level of problem-solving, for ordinary instruction writing tasks, it is also possible that this finding is task-specific and that instructing another agent to look for two names separately is simply the manner of telephone-directory instruction. Additional research employing the specification of other types of instructions (e.g., map usage, knitting instructions) is required.

It was surprising to find that these Beginners differed from the researched Naive users to begin with--even at a time prior to computer programming instruction. Perhaps a selection process is operating here, such that students who are attracted to computer science classes are a somewhat different group than those who have not signed up for such instruction. Or perhaps these subjects had some prior knowledge or outside information on the nature of computer interactions. Typically, students do not blindly enroll in a class, but probably have some idea of what is to be expected of them and what type of work will be required. Merely skimming through the course text book may have been all that was necessary for these Beginner students to gain the impression that conversing with a computer differs from conversing with another person. Thus, the Beginner's additional knowledge of computer interactions may have initially caused them to differ from Naive users in this experiment.

Natural Language Findings

The strategy findings can also be looked at in terms of requirements for a natural language system. It seems that users of differing experience have different expectations of such a system.

Experts, at least initially, expect a natural language system to understand high level abstract commands. Unless the system were truly advanced, much clarification dialogue would have to be employed in order to understand the Expert's first instructions. It might be the case that the Expert would prefer a more structured language rather than have to deal with all this backtalk. Alternatively, the Expert who is accustomed to adjusting to various different systems might readily adapt to a natural language interface after some initial period. Additional research is required in order to assess the flexibility of different user groups in adapting to the limitations of a natural language system.

Beginners expect that an English-understanding computer requires the same level of detail as a formal language system. They might believe that all computer systems are alike. Upon hearing that they were to write instructions for a computer, they then simply begin writing a program in their customary fashion, paying strict attention to details of syntax. To them, a program may always be a program regardless of the language at hand.

Naive users, people who indicated absolutely no knowledge of computer programming and have never before sat in front of a terminal, may have the misconceptions Shneiderman stresses in his book Software Psychology (1980). Shneiderman believes that the public is often deceived about what computers are and what they can be used for. He holds several groups partially responsible for these deceptions: researchers who anthropomorphize systems with names such as STUDENT, ROBOT, General Problem Solver, etc.; Science fiction writers who show robotic computers like HAL and the robots of "Star Wars"; advertisers who introduce the "office's new best friend"...etc. The point is that if these Naive users do in fact conceive of a computer in such humanistic terms, then when asked to write instructions to the computer, they would do so as if writing to another person. While the subjects in this study were not asked for their conception of a computer system, the results do suggest this belief.

Thus, it may not be enough to design a computer system that understands natural English without taking into account what users actually expect of such a system. In addition, it would be interesting to see how flexible and adaptable users could be based on their initial expectations. Further research is required in this area.

After the data was scored for strategy types, the scorer then made note of every other idea used. After all separate ideas were listed, they could be grouped into one of nine categories:

REPEAT - alternative methods of expressing the more tedious letter-by-letter or name-by-name search; the idea of a programmer's loop comes to mind. Examples: repeat the above process until finished; repeat this process as in the above process.

WITHIN - holding a certain letter or word constant while searching for the remaining letters or words. An idea such as "look for A, then look for B" is considered to be different from the idea "look for A, then WITHIN the A section look for B" such that in the first example one would end up in the B section, whereas in the second example one would end up at the AB section. Examples: hold the above letter constant or within this letter, and within this name.

ALPH - alphabetization category. Examples: first names are alphabetized, last names are alphabetized, search alphabetically, alphabetized like a dictionary, last names appear alphabetically before first names.

DIR - directory description category; includes all ideas that explain the telephone directory set-up. Examples: correct section, correct city, white pages, not yellow pages, middle initial, address, last names appear before first names, guidewords are at the top, used like a dictionary.

PROG - programming actions; includes verbs and conditionals one might encounter in programming. Examples: if more than one, if not found, stop, continue, if before, go forward, if after, go backward.

BEG and END - begin and end categories; contain all ideas that either introduced or closed the instruction set. Examples: "open the telephone directory"; "locate the number to the right of the name just found."

SUM - ideas that conclude or introduce a process. Examples: "you should have now found the letters S-M-I-T-H in order"; "you will now begin to look for the second letter."

FILL - filler (garbage) category; collection of all ideas that either did not fit into one of the above categories or were not necessary to the instruction set. Examples: "even though George Washington would never need to perform this task"; "make sure the computer understands English."

The scorer made note of each idea a subject used by placing tic marks by an idea category. If an idea applied to two categories, then each category received a point for that idea. In addition, a tenth dependent variable, TOTAL, was included, representing the sum of the above ideas.

One hypothesis of this experiment was that one semester of computer programming would have an effect on the usage of looping and transfer-of-control statements. Thus, it was predicted that Beginners would show an increase in REPEAT and PROG statements across sessions. Contrary to this prediction, there was no significant effect of **SESSION** for any of the three experience groups. Hence, scores again represent the average of the two instruction sets. Table 3 presents the mean scores obtained for each of the ten dependent measures at each of the Target-Experience conditions.

Table 3
Mean Number Statements per Category

	Category	Naive			Beginner			Expert		
		Pers	GeoW	Comp	Pers	GeoW	Comp	Pers	GeoW	Comp
T*	DIR	.79	.89	.73	.94	1.07	.47	1.59	1.16	.32
T	ALPH	1.10	1.66	.83	1.39	1.50	.71	1.09	1.94	.18
T	FILLER	.24	.77	.47	.44	1.17	.24	.18	.81	.50
E	REPEAT	.50	.25	.25	.33	.33	.58	.73	.59	.82
	WITHIN	2.41	1.52	1.88	1.83	1.37	2.63	2.54	2.25	2.13
E	PROG	.76	.91	.77	.78	1.17	1.21	2.09	1.12	1.87
	BEG	.40	.40	.50	.61	.37	.59	.68	.59	.42
	END	.46	.63	.48	.33	.60	.42	.68	.56	.50
	SUM	.13	.04	.10	.06	.00	.08	.14	.03	.10
E	TOTAL	6.79	1.07	6.02	6.72	7.57	6.92	9.73	9.06	6.84

(T = Target significant, E = Experience significant, * = T x E significant)

The Computer's Disadvantage

Of interest, as the table shows, the computer was always the least likely target to receive information about DIRectory descriptors ($F(2,188)$ = 6.62, $p<.001$) or ALPHabetization instructions ($F(2,188)$ = 23.04, $p<.0001$). In addition, both the computer and another person received less FILLER information ($F(2,188)$ = 12.82, $p<.0001$) than did George Washington. Fillers were statements that were not necessary for telephone-directory instructions. Clearly, statements such as what a telephone looks like, or how it is wired up to telephone poles, fit into this category. These telephone descriptions were the most popular filler types, and not surprisingly went mostly to George Washington.

Taking the results of DIR, ALPHA and FILLER together, one can see that subjects believed the computer to need the least amount of detailed instruction. This finding places further burdens on natural language systems, as users seem to expect a computer to already have such information built in -- at least much more knowledge than even another person.

The Programmer's Advantage

The table also shows effects of Experience on REPEAT and PROG ideas. It seems that programmers do use their programming constructs to aid them in the writing of ordinary instructions. As the table shows, overall, Experts used significantly more REPEAT statements than did Naive users ($F(2,188)$ = 3.28, $p<.0396$). Apparently, Naive users were more willing than Experts to specify step-by-step instructions than to instruct the target to simply repeat a process. One can draw several conclusions based on this finding. The first implication of this result suggests that Naive users completely lack knowledge of such repeating-processes. A second implication is that they understand the processes involved in iteration but do not know how to express them. A third implication is that perhaps Naive users do understand the mechanisms involved in repeating a process, but that they do not recognize when a later process involves the same sequence of steps as an original process. That is, perhaps Experts with their superior chunking ability recognize that searching for a second name involves the same steps as searching for a first name with the exception of a different starting location. Although the two searches involve the same sequences of steps, however, they are not entirely identical, and for this reason Naive users may not have wished to specify a repeating of processes. Perhaps if Naive users were to instruct another on how to find two separate last names, rather than a first name within a last name, they might have recognized the basically identical chunks and indeed made use of repeat statements. A fourth implication of the results could be that Naive users do in fact have knowledge of repeating-processes but perhaps are under the impression that such a style of instruction would be less thorough and more confusing to another agent than a precise, step-by-step instruction set. This reasoning seems possible because Naive users do not have the Experts' feedback that such repeat instructions are in fact capable of being followed correctly, at least by a computer.

In addition to using more REPEAT ideas, Experts also used significantly more PROGramming actions than did either Naive or Beginner users ($F(2,188)$ = 7.4, $p<.0008$). These ideas were of particular interest, so an additional analysis was performed on each instance separately. Table 4 presents the mean scores for each of the separate statements within PROGramming actions.

Table 4
Means for Programming Actions as Separate Statements

	Statement	Naive			Beginner			Expert		
		Pers	GeoW	Comp	Pers	GeoW	Comp	Pers	GeoW	Comp
E	PROG (Total)	.76	.91	.77	.78	1.17	1.21	2.09	1.12	1.87
	If Before	.07	.03	0	0	.10	.08	.18	0	.13
	Go Forward	.22	.37	.33	.44	.43	.41	.41	.50	.47
	If After	.07	.01	0	.06	.10	.08	.23	0	.10
E*	Go Backward	0	.01	0	0	.03	0	.18	0	.08
E T	If Found	.06	.02	.05	0	.03	.13	.14	.12	.29
E	If Not Found	.03	.03	.02	0	.03	0	14	.06	.24
	If More than One	.18	.19	.18	.17	.27	.24	.32	.25	.03
	Stop	.01	.07	.05	0	.03	.10	.04	.09	.21
E	Continue	.12	.16	.13	.11	.13	.10	.45	.09	.32

(E = Experience significant; T = Target significant; * = E x T significant)

Of interest, it was found that although Naive and Beginner users were just as likely to include information on what to do If More Than One Jay Smith were found, Experts were more likely to also include information on what to do if the name was Not Found at all ($F(2,188)$ = 7.07, $p<.001$). Similarly, although Naive and Beginner users were just as likely to include information on what to do if one opened the phone book to a section before the Smith's (Go Forward), Experts were more likely to also include information on what to do if one landed in a section after the Smith's (Go Backward) ($F(2,188)$ = 6.44, $p<.002$).

Thus it seems the Expert does not see such a straight line path to his goal, but rather, he is more likely to look at every possible decision and alternative that could occur along the way. It appears that programmers take less for granted when specifying instructions for other people to follow. Although nonprogrammers did not demonstrate difficulties in expressing themselves, they also did not seem to think much beyond the task at hand.

Learning verses Selection

It would be nice if one could say that the expert's programming experience with whole conditionals (not only if-then's but also if-then-else's) is responsible for his superior exception handling, as demonstrated above. It would be nice to claim that providing a computer with information on alternatives is a concept absolutely necessary to correct program construction, and perhaps has become such an ingrained way of thinking as to transfer over to everyday life. These claims can not be directly made based on the results of this experiment, however. Specifically, as was discussed previously, there was no effect of SESSION for subjects classified as Beginners. Therefore, this experiment does not directly support the claim that learning to program changes one's thought processes. Rather, based on the present results, it seems that people who succeed in becoming expert programmers may have had such superior cognitive skills to begin with.

CONCLUSION

In conclusion, regardless of whether or not the experienced programmer developed additional skills through his programming experience or initially had these skills to begin with, that programmers differ from nonprogrammers in procedural specification (or instruction writing) seems apparent from this research. It appears that experts are more likely to make use of loops and to consider more alternatives en route to their solution goal. Hence, they have an edge in both conciseness and preciseness.

This experiment not only examined programmer-nonprogrammer differences, but also looked at how people expect to communicate with a natural language computer. Although these conclusions are only tied to one set of data, at least initially it can be concluded that one natural language system may not satisfy all users. Nonprogrammers, for example, wish to talk to a computer in the same manner they communicate with each other, although they assume that the computer has more knowledge than another person. These Naive users rarely included exception-handling procedures and also assumed the computer had intact knowledge on the directory setup and alphabetization procedures. These assumptions were also made by Beginner users. But rather than communicating to a computer in the manner they communicate with other people, Beginners use the same style natural language "programs" as formal language programs. They still concentrate on low-level details. Experts, however, were more likely than other users to use top-level commands in their communication patterns. Although it may appear that Experts will place the greatest burden on designers of natural language systems, it may also be the case that Experts may be the most flexible and most willing to meet the demands of the system rather than expecting the system to adjust to them. Further research is needed in this area. Regardless, the present study does suggest that not only should a natural language computer understand English, but in order to be truly effective, it should also incorporate a user's expectations, conceptions (models) and problem solving strategies as well.

ACKNOWLEDGEMENTS

We thank Matt Anderson, Tim Breen, Nancy Cooke, Don Dearholt, Jim McDonald, and John McLean for profitable discussions. We also thank Ken Paap for his detailed review of an earlier draft. Finally, we thank several anonymous reviewers for helpful comments.

REFERENCES

1. Golden, F. (1982). Here come the microkids. Time, May 3, 50-56.
2. Schank, R. (1984). The Cognitive Computer. Reading, Mass: Addison-Wesley Publishing Co.,Inc.
3. Wirth, N. (1974). On the composition of well-structured programs. Computing Surveys, 6 (4), 247-259.
4. Miller, L. (1974) . Programming by nonprogrammers. International Journal of Man-Machine Studies, 6 (2), 237-260.
5. Miller, L. (December 1980). Natural language programming: styles, strategies and contrasts. IBM Research Report #37476.
6. Adelson, Beth (1984). When novices surpass experts: The difficulty of a task may increase with expertise. Journal of Experimental Psychology: Learning, Memory, and Cognition, 10 (3), 483-495.
7. Jeffries, R., Turner, A., Polson, P., & Atwood, M. (1981). The processes involved in designing software. In J.R. Anderson (Ed.), Cognitive Skills and their Acquisition. Hillsdale, NJ: Lawrence Erlbaum, Pub.
8. Weiser, M. & Shertz, J. (1983). Programming problem representation in novice and expert

programmers. <u>International Journal Man-Machine Studies</u>, <u>19</u>, 391-398.

9.   Shneiderman, Ben (1980). <u>Software Psychology</u>. Cambridge, Mass: Winthrop Publishers, Inc.

10.   Chase, W. & Simon, H. (1973). Perception in chess. <u>Cognitive Psychology</u>, <u>4</u>, 55-81.

11.   Chi, M. , Feltovich, P. & Glaser, R. (1981). Categorization and representation of physics problems by experts and novices. <u>Cognitive Science</u>, <u>5</u> (2), 121-152.

12.   Lewis, C. (1981). Skill in algebra. In J.R. Anderson (Ed.), <u>Cognitive Skills and their Acquisition</u>. Hillsdale, NJ: Lawrence Erlbaum, Pub.

13.   Dumais, S. & Landauer, T. (1982). Psychological investigations of natural terminology for command and query languages. In A. Badre & B. Shneiderman (Eds.), <u>Directions in Human/Computer Interaction</u>. Norwood, NJ: Ablex Publishing Corporation.

CHAPTER 10

The Effects of Program-Dependent and Program-Independent Deletions on Software Cloze Tests

Mark Thomas
Stuart Zweben
Department of Computer and Information Science
Ohio State University
Columbus, OH 43210

ABSTRACT

The cloze procedure has proven to be a reliable measure of prose comprehension and preliminary evidence suggests it could be a powerful tool for measuring software comprehensibility as well. Early work with the cloze procedure in the software domain failed to take into account some of the factors which can influence the procedure's results. Research by Hall shed light on several of these issues, and suggested that, by varying the proportion of cloze items for which program dependent knowledge is required, the outcome of a cloze test can be altered. This research further examines Hall's findings. His hypothesis that controlling these factors can determine the outcome of the test is confirmed through replication of earlier work by Cook which did not take them into account. Methods for resolving the potentially varying conclusions of these cloze tests are discussed.

INTRODUCTION

Computer scientists seeking development principles which lead to more easily understood software require techniques to accurately measure the comprehensibility of programs. Multiple-choice and short-answer comprehension quizzes are often used to assess comprehension. Unfortunately, preparing these types of tests requires considerable effort. Recently, research to determine the applicability of the cloze procedure in the area of software comprehension testing has begun. In the past, the cloze procedure has been used successfully to measure prose comprehension. The procedure involves periodically deleting words from a body of text and replacing them with an underline. The subject is then charged with the task of filling in the blanks with the word which was deleted. The subject's degree of success or failure in this endeavor provides an indication of how well the text is understood.

If the cloze procedure could be applied to software comprehension testing, several advantages over the traditional "comprehension-quiz" could be realized. Cloze tests are easier to construct, and they can be standardized so that researchers are using the same measure on different materials. They should also be more reliable since there is no possibility that a subject's score could be affected by misinterpretation of a question and more items can be included than are possible for a subject to complete on a multiple choice test in a similar amount of time (1). In addition, cloze tests appear to be a more direct measure of comprehension since they measure "comprehension in progress, not after the fact" (2).

PREVIOUS RESEARCH

Research into the use of the cloze procedure in measuring prose comprehension was begun by Taylor in 1958 (3). By the late 1960's the prose community generally regarded the cloze procedure as a proven measure of readability (4).

Examination of the applicability of the cloze procedure to testing software comprehension has only recently begun. While the cloze procedure has been used in several instances to measure the effects of certain factors on software understanding, very little research into the validity of using the cloze procedure in this way has been undertaken. Cook (5) found a positive correlation between the scores on cloze tests constructed from two functionally equivalent versions of a short sorting procedure with scores found using short-answer/multiple-choice tests for the same procedures. However, further research by Hall (6), using larger programs than those used by Cook, has shown that a closer look at the cloze procedure must be taken before it can be accepted as a valid means for measuring software comprehensibility.

Hall found that consideration must be given to the nature of the deleted items in a particular cloze test. Specifically, he stated that items deleted from a program fell into one of two categories. The first were those items which could be correctly completed without understanding the function of the program in question. These include things like structures inherent to the particular programming language being used, blanks that can be filled in using processes of elimination, and those items which can be correctly completed using simple flow analysis (variables must be defined before they are assigned to another variable, for example). Hall called these and all other items which could be correctly completed using reasoning independent of the problem in question program-independent items. In the same way, those items which required that the subject understand how the program was accomplishing its task were termed program-dependent items. Hall went on to say that the ratio of these two types of deletions to one another had a direct and predictable effect on the outcome of the test. Specifically, he found in his research that program-dependent items were more often incorrectly completed by his subjects than were those he had determined to be program-independent. Furthermore, given two candidate sets of materials whose relative comprehensibility is to be assessed using cloze testing, if the cloze tests differ substantially in their proportion of program-dependent items, then cloze scores (and hence comprehensibility) would be found significantly different. On the other hand, if the proportion of program-dependent items was similar for each of the tests, no significant difference in their respective cloze scores (and hence their respective comprehensibility) would be observed.

Hall's findings were significant for several reasons. First was the fact that early researchers of cloze testing in the software domain had concluded that the cloze procedure possessed criterion-related validity. That is, they found that the cloze procedure yielded results similar to those obtained using already established forms of comprehension testing. Hall, on the other hand, demonstrated that the cloze procedure did not always give results that corresponded to those achieved using other comprehension measures and this discrepancy could be attributed to the effects of the ratio of program-dependent to program-independent items in the different cloze tests. However, this was by no means a condemnation of the cloze procedure as a measure of software comprehensibility. In fact, researchers in the prose domain have also found that certain types of deletion items are completed more easily than others (eg. prepositions tend to be easier to complete than adverbs). Rather, Hall's results should serve as a caution to researchers wishing to use cloze testing to measure software comprehension that they must be aware of the effects of the different types of items in the tests. Moreover, Hall's findings should serve as a catalyst to encourage further research into the nature of the software cloze test in order that its inherent benefits can

139

be realized by computer scientists in need of an accurate comprehension measure. Toward this end, we hope to verify some of Hall's conclusions and to test his hypothesis regarding the effects of controlling the ratio of program-dependent and program-independent items in the procedures used in Cook's experiments.

EXAMINATION OF THE EFFECT OF DIFFERENT PERCENTAGES OF PROGRAM DEPENDENT ITEMS ON COMPREHENSION SCORES

In Cook's experiments, traditional comprehension testing showed one sorting procedure, BERZTISS, to be more difficult to understand than the other, GROGANO. In his experiment, scores on cloze tests constructed by deleting every fifth token from the program showed this same relationship. From these results Cook concluded that the cloze procedure appeared to yield similar results to those obtained using traditional software comprehension testing methods. Hall's findings, however, indicate that these results must be examined more carefully.

In reviewing Cook's results, Hall observed that the cloze tests used by Cook for his two sorting procedures contained substantial differences in the ratios of program-dependent to program-independent items. For each sorting procedure, there are five possible cloze tests which involve deleting every fifth token, depending upon whether the first token deleted is the first, second, third, fourth, or fifth token in the procedure. Since different sets of tokens will be deleted in each of these cases, it should be clear that the different cloze tests may result in different percentages of "program-dependent deletions." Specifically, Hall noted that the cloze test for the BERZTISS procedure in which deletions were started with the first token resulted in 50% program-dependent deletions while the test formed by starting deletions with the first token of the GROGANO procedure resulted in only 33% program-dependent deletions. In addition, Hall noted that if deletions in the BERZTISS procedure began at the second token, a 32% program-dependent deletion rate would result. It was Hall's contention, therefore, that scores on the cloze tests constructed from the two procedures with deletions beginning at the first token should be significantly different while no such difference should be found between scores on the GROGANO test with deletions beginning at the first token and the BERZTISS procedure with deletions beginning at the second one. The purpose of our experiment was to test this hypothesis.

Design and Overview

The experiment was constructed from the same two procedures as those used by Cook. Tokens were determined to be candidates for deletion according to the same rules as those used in the Cook experiment as well. Three different cloze tests were constructed by systematically deleting every fifth token from either the BERZTISS or GROGANO procedure. One cloze test (GROGANO 1) was formed by beginning the "every-fifth token" deletion pattern at the first token of the GROGANO procedure. A second test (BERZTISS 1) was formed by beginning the deletion pattern at the first token of the BERZTISS procedure. The third test (BERZTISS 2) was formed by beginning the deletion pattern at the second token of the BERZTISS procedure. Using the rules reported by Hall (see Appendix I for a complete statement of Hall's rules), each of the deleted tokens was classified as program-dependent or program-independent, and the ratio of the two types of deletions to one another for each of the cloze tests was verified.

The actual experiment was conducted in two parts. The first was a pilot study to test the materials and procedures of the experiment. In addition, participants in the pilot study completed a protocol analysis in which they described the thought processes that they used to complete the test. These responses were intended to give insight into common areas of difficulty for future subjects and to verify that our classification of program-dependent and program-independent items was correct. The second part of the experiment was administered following the successful completion of the pilot study. Each subject in this phase of the experiment was given one of the three different cloze tests and their scores were examined to detect any significant differences in the results of the three tests. It was hypothesized that there would be a significant difference between the scores for GROGANO 1 and BERZTISS 1 but no such difference between the scores for GROGANO 1 and BERZTISS 2. Further, it was expected that the error rate for program-dependent items would be greater than that for program-independent items, just as it was in Hall's experiments.

Subjects

The pilot study was carried out using twelve students in an advanced software engineering seminar. All but three of these subjects were graduate students. Participation in this study was a required part of their course work, as was completion of the follow-up questionnaire detailing how they arrived at their responses.

The second phase of the experiment was carried out using thirty-one subjects from upper level computer science courses. Each of these subjects completed a consent form and a background survey, which was used to balance the testing cells according to PASCAL experience, prior to participation in the experiment. All subjects in this part of the experiment participated as paid volunteers.

Materials

As discussed previously, the materials consisted of three cloze tests created from the procedures used by Cook in his experiments. The deletion rate was 1-in-5 for all three tests. Each subject was given a test booklet which consisted of the same instructions and sample problem as those given by Cook, a list of data types which were valid for the problem, and one of the three cloze tests. The cloze tests used in the experiment are given in Appendix II.

Procedure

The pilot test was administered during one of the class's regular meetings. The follow-up protocol analysis was given immediately after the test as a take home assignment. Participants in this phase of the experiment indicated no difficulties in understanding or completing either of these tasks.

In the second phase of the experiment, the majority of the tests were administered in one of three group sessions, the remainder being given on an individual basis to accommodate the students' schedules. All tests were administered within a three-day period. The subjects appeared to have no difficulty understanding their task from the materials alone so very little oral direction was given. Subjects were not given any specific time limit within which to complete the test.

Scoring for the tests was carried out in two different ways - verbatim and synonymic. For a response to be considered correct under verbatim scoring it had to be exactly the same as the deleted token. In some cases, a subject gave a response that was not exactly what had been deleted, but that still carried the proper meaning or for some other reason could still be considered valid. These responses were counted as correct under synonymic scoring. For example, several subjects used "=" instead of ":=" in assignment statements. This response showed only a lack of attention to PASCAL syntax and did not indicate that the subject did not understand the program as the "=" operator is used in several languages with which many of the subjects were familiar (PL/I for example). Another example occurred in the BERZTISS 2 procedure where the procedure name was deleted. Not surprisingly, none of the subjects filled in this blank with the name "BERZTISS". In this case, any syntactically correct procedure name was accepted under synonymic scoring. Slightly less obvious cases where a response was incorrect using verbatim scoring and valid using synonymic existed as well. In BERZTISS 2 the direction of the sort is determined by how the subject fills in the subscripts of the array inside the swapping routine. Since the procedure sorted in

141

ascending order originally, only the original subscripts were counted as correct under verbatim scoring. Subjects had not been given any program specifications prior to taking the test, however, so they could not be expected to know in which direction the procedure was intended to sort. For this reason, responses which resulted in a sort in descending order were counted as correct under synonymic scoring. While these examples are not exhaustive, they do demonstrate the differences between the two scoring techniques.

Results

Subjects who participated in the pilot study indicated no difficulty in understanding the test materials or procedures. In addition, although no firm time limit was octablichod, none of the subjects failed to complete the test in less than the allotted class period (all but one took less than 45 min). Finally, examination of their descriptions of the thought processes they used to arrive at their responses showed no problems with the classification of the deletions as program-dependent or program-independent. The subjects used program-dependent reasoning to complete program-dependent deletions and program-independent reasoning to complete program-independent deletions.

As in the pilot study, none of the subjects in the second phase of the experiment ran out of time before completing the test. The mean scores on each of the cloze tests is given in Table 1.

Table 1. Cloze Test Scores

test version	% prog. dep. cloze items	number of subjects	mean verbatim score	mean synonymic score
GROGANO 1	33%	10	76.8%	90.5%
BERZTISS 1	50%	10	69.8%	73.7%
BERZTISS 2	32%	11	75.3%	88.7%

For each test, the entries in the table indicate the average percentage of correctly completed cloze items for a given scoring method. For example, the ten subjects who took the GROGANO 1 test averaged 76.8% correctly completed cloze items when the verbatim scoring method was used to grade their tests.

Analysis of variance on these data indicated that, for each scoring method, there was a significant difference at the .05 level between the scores on the three cloze test versions ($F_{(2,28)} = 4.08$ for the verbatim method; $F_{(2,28)} = 7.71$ for the synonymic method; critical value of $F_{(2,28)} = 3.34$). Of interest, of course, are the pairwise comparisons of GROGANO 1 versus BERZTISS 1 and GROGANO 1 versus BERZTISS 2. A Newman-Keuls range test was used to determine if either pair was significantly different at the .05 level. Table 2 shows the results of the Newman-Keuls test on the verbatim scores.

Table 2. Newman-Keuls Comparison Using Verbatim Scoring

test	observed N-K statistic	critical
G vs B1	0.152	0.132
G vs B2	0.100	0.109

Using the same test and synonymic scoring the following results were obtained.

Table 3. Newman-Keuls Comparison Using Synonymic Scoring

test	observed N-K statistic	critical
G vs B1	0.166	0.114
G vs B2	0.017	0.094

The tests showed that while there was a significant difference between the means of the scores on the GROGANO 1 procedure and the BERZTISS 1 procedure, there was no significant difference between the GROGANO 1 scores and those for the BERZTISS 2 test. Furthermore, these conclusions hold regardless of the type of scoring method used. These are exactly the results that Hall predicted in his discussion of the effect of program-dependent and program-independent cloze items. Further support for his findings was found when the error rates for the two types of cloze items were compared. These results are shown in Table 4.

Table 4. Comparison of Error Rates for Program-Dependent and
Program-Independent Cloze Items

type of item	error rate (verbatim)	error rate (synonymic)
program-dependent	41.14%	32.11%
program-independent	12.41%	5.75%

In our experiment, just as in Hall's, the error rate for the program-dependent items was considerably greater than that for the program-independent items.

Discussion

Our results in this experiment confirmed Hall's hypothesis that scores on the cloze tests for the two Cook procedures would be the same if the ratios of program-dependent to program-independent deletions were equal. This gives further support to the importance of the notion of "program-dependence" and "program-independence" in assessing comprehensibility of software. Clearly the differentiation between the two types of items can have a significant effect on the results of a cloze test used for measuring software comprehensibility. Two candidate programs may appear to differ in comprehensibility when, in fact, no such difference exists (or vice versa) if the researcher using the cloze test does not take into account the effects of differences in the ratios of the two types of items to one another.

It is important to note that prose researchers also noticed differences in subjects' ability to complete cloze items depending upon the type of item in question. The fact that these differences exist should therefore not dissuade computer science researchers from using the procedure. In fact, the ultimate success of prose researchers in adapting the cloze procedure to the prose domain should encourage computer scientists who are seeking to adapt it to the software domain. Instead of concluding that cloze testing is inappropriate, it therefore seems more reasonable to examine the possibility that only cloze tests having certain characteristics are appropriate, and that these characteristics are related to the notion of program-dependent and program-independent items.

The issue of program-dependent verses program-independent items may be resolved in several ways. Certainly the possibility of merely deleting only program-dependent items exists. Results of this experiment indicated very low error rates for program-independent items. Since this experiment and those of Hall indicated that these types of items were of little use in assessing comprehension and that varying proportions of program-independent items to program-dependent ones seemed to be a principal cause of the questionable criterion-related validity of software cloze tests, excluding program-independent items from deletion might serve to raise their validity in this respect (i.e. all tests would have 100% program-dependent items). Of course, further research is needed to determine if this is true.

Another possibility when comparing different pieces of software is to use all cloze tests which are possible given a specific deletion pattern. Specifically, in our experiments a 1-in-5 deletion pattern was used which meant 5 different tests were possible. Averaging the scores over all 5 different tests (or at least some reasonable subset thereof) might minimize the effects caused by different versions having different proportions of program-dependent and program-independent cloze items. It should be noted that the percentage of program dependent cloze items for the five possible GROGANO tests ranges from 20% to 33% with an average of 28%, while the corresponding range for the BERZTISS version is between 32% and 52% with an average of 41% (see Table 5). It would therefore appear that the 1-in-5 cloze tests, on average, should conclude the BERZTISS program less comprehensible than the GROGANO, consistent with the conclusions obtained by Cook through traditional software comprehension testing methods. This argues that "every nth item" cloze testing, if done properly, would indeed possess criterion-related validity.

Table 5. Percentage of Program-Dependent Items
for Different Forms of the1-in-5 Cloze Test

Program	Token at which deletions begin	Percentage of prog. dep. cloze items
GROGANO	1	33%
	2	24%
	3	33%
	4	29%
	5	20%
BERZTISS	1	50%
	2	32%
	3	40%
	4	52%
	5	32%

On the other hand, research in the prose domain by Meredith and Vaughan (7) showed that the every-nth deletion pattern might not be stable. Specifically, they constructed ten cloze tests from the same text, five using a 1-in-5 deletion pattern and five using random deletions of 20 percent of the text. Analysis of the results showed significant differences between the the mean scores of subjects using the 1-in-5 cloze tests while no such difference was present between the mean scores of those taking the cloze tests constructed using random deletions. Investigation of the effects of such random deletion patterns is indeed warranted; they may provide a way to construct better software cloze tests.

Future research should also further examine the validity of classifying items as program-dependent or program-independent. Our protocol analysis gave preliminary indications that subjects will indeed use program-independent reasoning when completing program-independent items. However, this observation was made based on the results of cloze tests constructed from extremely short procedures. It is not obvious that subjects will use program-independent reasoning when completing certain program-independent items in larger cloze tests. Specifically, flow analysis might be quite difficult in a larger program - difficult enough to preclude using it to complete a cloze item. If this were the case, a class of "hard program-independent items" might be shown to exist. The effect of such items on larger cloze tests certainly warrants investigation.

Another problem we encountered was with respect to providing subjects with information regarding the purpose of the software they were examining. In our experiment, and consistent with Cook, we elected not to give any indication of the purpose of the procedures used to construct the tests. This resulted in the possibility that a technically correct solution was not only not the original token, it satisfied a different set of specifications! In particular, the direction of the sort was not stated and subjects could give responses which merely resulted in a sort in the direction opposite of that intended in the original procedure. In a practical situation, it seems unlikely that one would be faced with a block of code and no indication of what it was supposed to do. It is apparent that some indication of the purpose of the software being examined should be given, at least to the extent that no ambiguities like the one mentioned above exist. This is not only a problem when it comes to scoring the test but may result in confusion which may affect a subject's ability to perform on other parts of the test.

With traditional comprehension quizzes, the subject is given a complete and assumed correct piece of software to examine. Hence, the code itself is at least some form of a complete specification for the software. A cloze procedure is incomplete, however, and affords the opportunity for giving a technically correct response that does not perform the function that was intended unless some type of specification is given in advance.

Is it also possible to give too much information? In the case of our experiment, consider the difference between giving the subjects any of the following statements of objectives.

1) The procedure is a sorting procedure.
2) The procedure sorts in ascending order.
3) The procedure is a Shell sort which sorts in ascending order.

Clearly, statement 1 does not give enough information for completing the BERZTISS 2 cloze test without (as previously discussed) allowing the possibility that the subjects will give responses which result in a sort in the opposite direction of that intended. On the other hand, statement 3's degree of specification might be too great for a subject who was unfamiliar with the term "Shell sort". The additional information would at best be of no value to such a subject. Worse yet, it could confuse or frustrate the subject resulting in a lower score than would have been the case without the additional information. Clearly, experience would play a key role in determining the effect of additional information regarding program specification in this case. If comprehensibility of the the program was the issue of concern, the over-specification would have resulted in an outside factor influencing the result of the experiment. It is important, therefore, that experiments control for the "understandability of the specifications" given to the subjects. In our experiment, this factor was moot.

Finally, it is of interest to determine just what makes program-dependent items harder than program-independent items. Both our experiment and those of Hall observed substantial differences in the error rates between program-dependent and program-independent items. It could be argued that, if programmers have the knowledge, they should be able to use it to complete the cloze items whether or not the knowledge required is program-dependent. It is our contention that our programmer subjects did not in general have, nor were they able to acquire during the experiment, the necessary knowledge to complete all of the program-dependent deletions, and that they therefore did not fully understand the program. On the other hand, the small size of the program versions and the familiarity of the subjects with the Pascal language made it likely that the subjects did, in fact, have the program-independent knowledge required for the experimental task.

The fact that no specifications were given to our subjects exacerbated these differences in knowledge. While it is possible (even likely) that the programmers brought relevant program-dependent knowledge to the experimental task, they would have first had to reason about the purpose of (parts of) the program before being able to either effectively utilize that knowledge, or to acquire additional relevant program-dependent knowledge. Even once relevant program-dependent knowledge was present, it might not have been present at the right level of detail so that it could be applied by filling in a code construct. Therefore, a subject may have (eventually) known that a sort was taking place, but not that it was a method involving sub-sorting by diminishing increments. Another subject may have (eventually) known that a Shell sort was taking place, but not what constituted the upper and lower bounds for a particular increment. This would explain why Hall's experiments, in which specifications were given to the subjects, also resulted in substantial differences in the error rates between program-dependent and program-independent cloze items.

SUMMARY

Hall's research on software cloze testing strongly suggested that, in order to properly apply the cloze procedure in the software domain, it is important to distinguish between program-dependent and program-independent cloze items. Hall further conjectured that Cook's results using the cloze procedure could be altered by using a different form of cloze test. Our experiment confirmed Hall's conjecture. Our results show that attention must be focused on the nature of deleted tokens and on the form of specifications given to subjects when preparing cloze tests from computer software.

Cloze tests, however, are still an extremely attractive procedure for measuring software comprehension. They are considerably easier to construct and grade than are traditional comprehension measurement techniques. This results in a less expensive, potentially automatable testing process and consequently permits more extensive testing with a given amount of resources. In addition, cloze tests are not subject to the biases often present in multiple-choice and short-answer tests whose construction cannot be automated. While these biases may be useful in some cases, they make standardized comprehension testing extremely difficult. Furthermore, research on cloze testing in the prose domain has indicated that the cloze test is a much more direct measure of comprehension. For all of these reasons, cloze testing has the potential to be an extremely powerful tool for measuring software comprehension in the future.

The assessment of software comprehension is an important ingredient in our overall ability to assess software quality. Boehm, et al, for example, define understandability as one of the seven high-level components of the general utility of software (8). Research to determine more precisely the adaptations which are necessary before cloze testing can be used with confidence in the software domain is therefore clearly warranted.

APPENDIX I
HALL'S CATEGORIZATION RULES (ORIGINATED FOR PL/I)

If the following rules can be applied to correctly complete a deletion, then the deletion is considered program-independent.

Name on a PROCEDURE statement

1. Candidate answers are the procedures CALLed in the program in the scope of the current procedure. Since the name must be unique, all CALLed procedures with known corresponding PROCEDURE statements may be eliminated from the set of candidate answers.

2. May be specified by the name on the corresponding END of procedure statement.

3. May be determined from a corresponding CALL statement by matching the parameter list of the PROCEDURE statement to the parameter lists of all the CALL statements. The parameters should match in number, order, type, and (often) name.

Name on an END of procedure statement

1. May be specified by the name on the corresponding PROCEDURE statement.

Element in a DECLARE statement (e.g., variable name, level number, storage type, data type, precision, etc.)

1. May be specified in another DECLARE for the same variable (matched by variable name or common substructure).

2. May be specified by way variable is used (e.g., the INPUT attribute is indicated for a file if it is used only in input statements).

3. May be specified by the I/O format specifications for the variable (e.g., a format specification of F(1) suggests the variable is FIXED and has precision (1,0)).

4. The candidates for a missing variable name are all the variables referenced in the corresponding procedure, but not already DECLAREd.

Format element (e.g., data type and precision)

1. May be specified by the DECLARE statement for the corresponding variable (e.g., the DECLARE specification FIXED indicates the F format data type specification).

2. May be indicated in another format specification for the same variable.

Procedure name in a CALL statement

1. Candidate answers are all subroutine procedures within the scope of the CALL statement.

2. May be determined from a corresponding PROCEDURE statement by matching the parameter list of the CALL statement to the parameter lists of all the PROCEDURE statements. The parameters should match in number, order, type, and (often) name.

3. All subroutine procedures should be CALLed at least once.

Actual and dummy parameters

1. Candidate answers are limited to the variables DECLAREd in the corresponding procedure. All referenced parameters must be in the corresponding PROCEDURE statement parameter list.

2. May be specified in the parameter list of the corresponding CALL or PROCEDURE statement.

3. If an actual and corresponding dummy parameter cannot have the same name (because the name is not declared for both cases), then the parameter may be determined by matching the types of the parameters.

4. All variables DECLAREd with an unspecified length (indicated by a '*') must be a dummy parameter.

Name of an unreferenced substructure of a structured variable in a DECLARE statement

1. May be any syntactically correct variable name that is not the same as any other identifier not itself a part of the substructure.

Identifier in an assignment statement or conditional expression

1. Candidate answers consist of all variables DECLAREd in the corresponding procedure. All DECLAREd variables should be referenced at least once (except for substructure variables). All dummy parameters should be referenced at least once.

2. A variable itself should not be assigned to itself or subtracted from itself (i.e., there should be no statements such as A = A; or A = B - B;).

3. Both sides of an assignment statement and conditional expression should be of compatible type, structure, and precision. The common description of both sides of the assignment statement or conditional expression should also be compatible (e.g., if the candidate answers for the cloze item in the statement

        _____ = '102 N. HIGH ST.' ;

are ADDRESS and NAME, then ADDRESS should be the answer since '102 N. HIGH ST.' would commonly be described as an address and not as a name).

File name on an ON ENDFILE statement

1. Candidate answers are limited to variables DECLAREd as files in the corresponding procedure.

2. There should be only one ON ENDFILE statement for any given file used within a procedure.

3. Should be same as file name on associated input statement.

ON condition for a file

1. Should be ENDFILE condition if file used for input in corresponding procedure.

Variable in an I/O list
1. DECLAREd attributes of variable should be compatible with corresponding format specifications.

File name in an I/O statement
1. Candidate answers are limited to variables DECLAREd as files in the corresponding procedure.

2. Attributes of file from DECLARE statement (e.g., INPUT, OUTPUT, STREAM, RECORD, etc.) must match way file is used.

APPENDIX II
CLOZE TESTS USED IN THE EXPERIMENTS

GROGANO 1

```
_____ GROGANO (VAR A: _____ ; N: INTEGER);
VAR
    _____ : BOOLEAN;
   JUMP, I, J: _____ ;
   PROCEDURE MILLER (VAR _____ , Q: REAL);
   VAR
       _____ : REAL;
   BEGIN
     HOLD := _____ ;
     P := Q;
     Q _____ HOLD;
   END;
BEGIN
   JUMP _____ N;
   WHILE JUMP > _____ DO
    BEGIN
      JUMP := _____ DIV 2;
      REPEAT
        DONE _____ TRUE;
        FOR J := _____ TO N - JUMP ____
        BEGIN
          I := J _____ JUMP;
          IF A[ _____ ] > A[ _____ ] THEN
           BEGIN
             MILLER _____ A[J], _____ [I]);
             _____ := FALSE;
           END;
        END;
        _____ DONE;
    END;
END;
```

```
_____ BERZTISS (VAR A: _____ ; N: INTEGER);
VAR
_____ , I, J, L, TEMP: _____ ;
BEGIN
 D := 1;
  _____ D <= N DO
   _____ := D * 2;
  _____ := (D - _____ ) DIV 2;
 WHILE _____ <> 0 DO
  BEGIN
    _____ I := 1 TO _____ - D DO
    BEGIN
      _____ := I;
      L := _____ + D;
      WHILE A _____ L] < A _____ J] DO
      BEGIN
        _____ := A[J _____ ;
        A[J] _____ A[L];
        _____ [L] := _____ ;
        IF J - D _____ 0 THEN
        BEGIN
          L _____ J;
          J := J _____ D;
        END;
      END;
    END;
    _____ := (D - _____ ) DIV 2;
  END;
 _____ ;
```

```
PROCEDURE _____ (VAR A: ARY; _____ : INTEGER);
VAR
  D, _____ , J, L, TEMP: INTEGER;
____
  D := 1;
  WHILE _____ <= N DO
    D _____ D * 2;
  D _____ (D - 1 _____ DIV 2;
  WHILE D _____ 0 DO
  BEGIN
    FOR _____ := 1 TO N _____ D DO
    BEGIN
      J _____ I;
      L := J _____ D;
      WHILE A[ _____ ] < A[ _____ ] DO
      BEGIN
        TEMP _____ A[J];
        _____ [J] := _____ [L];
        A _____ L] := TEMP;
        _____ J - D > _____ THEN
        BEGIN
          L := _____ ;
          J := J - _____ ;
        END;
      END;
    END;
    D _____ (D - 1 _____ DIV 2;
  END;
END;
```

REFERENCES

1. Hall, W.E., and Zweben, S.H. (1985). The Cloze Procedure and Software Comprehensibility Measurement. IEEE Trans. on Software Engineering, to appear; also available as Tech. Rep. OSU-CISRC-TR-85-1, Department of Computer Science, The Ohio State University.

2. Rankin, E.F., Jr. (1978). Characteristics of the Cloze Procedure Tool in the Study of Language. In P.D. Pearsons and J. Hansen (Eds.), Twenty-seventh Yearbook of the National Reading Conference (pp. 148-153).

3. Taylor, W.L. (1953). Cloze Procedure: A New Tool for Measuring Readability. Journalism Quarterly, 30, no. 4, 415-433.

4. Robinson, C.G. (1981). Cloze Procedure: A Review. Educational Research, 23, no. 2, 128-133.

5. Cook, C.R., Bregar, W.S., and Foote, D. (1982). A Preliminary Investigation of the Use of the Cloze Procedure as a Measure of Program Understanding. Tech. Rep. 82-1-1, Department of Computer Science, Oregon State University.

6. Hall, W.E. (1984). The Cloze Procedure and Software Comprehension. Ph.D. dissertation, The Ohio State University, Columbus, Ohio.

7. Meredith, K., and Vaughn, J. (1978). Stability of Cloze Scores across Varying Deletion Patterns. In P.D. Pearson and J. Hansen (Eds.), Twenty-seventh Yearbook of the National Reading Conference (pp. 181-184).

8. Boehm, B., et al. (1978). Characteristics of Software Quality. North Holland.

CHAPTER 11

Experimental Evaluation of Program Quality Using External Metrics

Fred G. Harold

Department of Computer and Information Systems
Florida Atlantic University
Boca Raton, FL 33431

ABSTRACT

An experiment is described in which software metrics applied primarily to the source listings of COBOL programs were used to evaluate program quality. The programs analyzed were written by students exposed to structured programming concepts (experimental group) and students oriented to good programming style independent of structured programming (control group). Program quality was measured in terms of readability, maintainability, and modifiability. The metrics were applied by evaluators unaware of the experimental design. Statistical measures (frequency distributions, t-tests, discriminant analysis, and correlation coefficients) were generated from the metric data and used to distinguish the quality incorporated in the programs developed by the two groups.

BACKGROUND

The concept of program quality has traditionally been limited to internal measures of correctness and efficiency. Extension of this idea to include aesthetics and characteristics that can be measured primarily from an analysis of the source listing is a fairly recent enlargement of quality evaluation.

Coupled with the generic notion of quality is the contemporary acceptance of structured code as superior to traditional "spaghetti-bowl" programming. In the mid-1980s it may appear redundant to offer additional arguments in support of structured programming—a notion which has gained wide acceptance in the past fifteen years. The pervasiveness of the word structured in the titles of programming textbooks published in the past decade (particularly for COBOL—a language which is quite amenable to structuring, but only with conscious effort on the part of the programmer) should be sufficient to indicate the overwhelming acceptance of structured concepts as contributory to program quality. The paucity of empirical research into the benefits of structured code, however, is alarming. As recently as 1982, Gerald Weinberg stated:

> My own personal stock taking on the subject of structured programming is based on visits to some hundred installations on four continents over the past four years, plus more than a thousand formal and informal interviews with programmers, analysts, managers, and users during that same period...The first conclusion I can draw from my data is that much less has been done than the press would have you believe...All you need do is ask for examples of structured program-

ming--not anecdotes, but actual examples of structured code. If you get any examples at all, you can peruse them for evidence that they follow the "rules" of structured programming. Generally, you will find out that:

1. Five percent can be considered thoroughly structured.
2. Twenty percent can be considered structured sufficiently to represent an improvement over the average code of 1969.
3. Fifty percent will show some evidence of some attempt to follow some "structuring rules," but without understanding and little, if any, success.
4. Twenty-five percent will show no evidence of influence by <u>any</u> ideas about programming from the last twenty years.[1]

Weinberg's observations are implicitly borne out by the alarming lack of experimental support for the claims of structured programming (SP). Yet most practitioners would agree, at least in theory, with the statement that structured programming reduces software complexity, and that "Some of the benefits accompanying the reduction of program complexity are fewer testing problems, increased programmer productivity, and improved program clarity, maintainability, and modifiability."[2]

In parallel with the claims of software quality enhancements when structured techniques were used, the discipline of <u>software engineering</u> began to take shape in the 1970s. Encompassing structured programming and design methodologies under its umbrella, as well as a great variety of other concerns related to the effective development, modification, and documentation of programs (particularly large programs), software engineering also boasted a set of tools for the measurement of program characteristics. These became known as <u>software metrics</u>, frequently implemented as quantitative measures embedded in programs to evaluate efficiency or to characterize complexity.[3,4,5]

With the parallel development of software engineering in general and the dual emphases of structured programming and software metrics in particular, an increasing focus on software quality (and its updated definition) began to emerge. Traditional views of quality centered on only correctness and efficiency; evolving notions emphasized instead the features of <u>readability, modifiability</u>, and <u>verifiability</u>. In simple terms, "good" programs in the 1970s and 1980s had to be easy to understand, change, or enhance, and test. Correctness, of course, has always been the paramount concern; efficiency, however, while still important, began to be subordinated to reability, modifiablity, and verifiability (subsequently designated <u>R</u>, <u>M</u>, and <u>V</u>) in a world characterized by software maintenance costs which typically exceeded development expenditures during the life cycle.

Instrumentation of programs is frequently too costly or difficult to be practical--particularly when other means of evaluating software characteristics are available. An attempt to determine program quality externally--i.e., primarily through an examination of the source listing--became the motivating interest behind this research effort.

1. Weinberg, Gerald M. <u>Rethinking Systems Analysis and Design</u>. Boston MA: Little, Brown and Company, 1982, pp. 19-20.
2. Jensen, Randall W. "Structured Programming." <u>Computer</u>. (March 1981), p. 32.
3. Boehm, Barry W.; Brown, J.R.; Kasper, H.; Lipow, M.; MacLean, G.J.; and Merritt, M.J. <u>Characteristics of Software Quality</u> (TRW-SS-73-09). Redondo Beach CA: TRW, Inc. 1973.
4   Gilb, Tom. "Software Metrics - The Emerging Technology." <u>Data Management</u> (July 1975), pp. 34-37.
5. McCall, Jim A.; Richards, Paul K.; and Walters, Gene F. <u>Factors in Software Quality</u> (RADC-TR-77-369). Griffiss AFB NY; Rome Air Development Center, November 1977.

DESIGN OF THE EXPERIMENT

The research objective was, as implied above, primarily to assess the quality of programs by employing metrics largely outside the actual execution of the software being evaluated. An additional objective--which served also as a grounding point for the research--was to determine if the claims of structured programming advocates regarding improved program quality (readability, maintainability, and verifiablity) could be supported empirically through the application of such external metrics.

Following the establishment of these basic goals, the design process addressed the overall structure of the research. An experimental design was early chosen to provide greater validity than the simpler survey method could afford, with an acceptance of the shortcomings that the investigator's university setting imposed. Methodological questions in the following areas had to be resolved:

1) identification of metrics
2) instructional separation of experimental and control groups
3) choice of programming language
4) types and numbers of programs to be written
5) process of applying metrics
6) statistical analyses to be performed
7) formulation of a pilot study

Each of these issues will be treated in turn.

Identification of Metrics. Because the structured programming claims of enhanced readability, modifiability, and verifiability were to be evaluated, a set of metrics which could represent these three quality factors was sought. The work of Boehm[6,7,8], Clapp and Sullivan[9], Gilb[10], McCall[11], Mohanty[12], Reiter[13], Rubey and Hartwick[14], and Shneiderman[15]--all seminal contributors to software metrics -- was consulted. As a result of reviewing their early work in this discipline, the following preliminary set of metric designations was developed: Readability (quality of comments, quality of data and procedure names, sequential flow, size of modules, use of indentation, number of modules, number of conditional statements); Modifiability (program size, functionality of modules, logical module linkages, strength/clarity of module boundaries); and Verifiability (satisfaction of specifications, debugging difficulty).

6. Boehm, Barry W.; Brown, J.R.; Kasper, H.; Lipow, M.; MacLean, G.J.; and Merritt, M.J. Characteristics of Software Quality (TRW-SS-73-09). Redondo Beach CA: TRW, Inc. 1973.
7. Boehm, Barry W. "Software and Its Impact: A Quantitative Assessment." Datamation 19 5 (May 1973), pp. 48-59.
8. Boehm, Barry W.; Brown, J.R.; and Lipow, M. "Quantitative Evaluation of Software Quality." Proceedings of the 2nd International Conference on Software Engineering. San Francisco: IEEE Computer Society, 1976, pp. 592-605.
9. Clapp, J. A. and Sullivan, J.E. "Automated Monitoring of Software Quality." AFIPS Conference Proceedings 43 (1974 National Computer Conference). Montvale NJ: AFIPS Press, 1974, pp. 337-341.
10. Gilb, Tom. Software Metrics Cambridge MA: Winthrop Publishers, Inc., 1977.
11. McCall, Jim A.; Richards, Paul K.; and Walters, Gene F. Factors in Software Quality (RADC-TR-77-369). Griffiss AFB NY; Rome Air Development Center, November 1977.
12. Mohanty, Sibs M. "Models and Measurements for Quality Assessment of Software." ACM Computing Surveys 11 3 (September 1979), pp. 251-275.
13. Reiter, Robert W., Jr. An Experimental Investigation of Computer Program Development Approaches and Computer Programming Metrics. Ph.D. Dissertation. College Park MD: University of Maryland, 1979.
14. Rubey, Raymond J. and Hartwick, R. Dean. "Quantitative Measurement of Program Quality." Proceedings of the 1968 ACM Conference. New York: ACM, 1968, pp. 671-677.
15. Shneiderman, Ben. Software Psychology. Cambridge MA: Winthrop Publishers, Inc. 1980.

Tentative point values -- some binary, others ranging from 0 to 5 -- were assigned to these metrics, with the expectation that an overall quality index could be generated by summing the values allocated to any program. These initial metrics were sent for comment and suggestion to the following acknowledged experts in the area of software quality measurement: F. Terry Baker, Victor Basili, Barry Boehm, Tom Gilb, and Gerald Weinberg.

The revised metrics ultimately applied in the study resulted from the comments and suggestions offered by these practitioners and researchers. This revised complement of metrics was:

* representative of the quality characteristics R, M, and V;
* few in number, yet sufficiently comprehensive to constitute a composite quality measure;
* except for execution statistics, accessible from program source listings;
* not associated with <u>efficiency</u>, but including the essential characteristic of correctness;
* capable of being applied by a person knowledgeable in the programming language after a short orientation.

The most critical feature of each metric was its unbiased nature; it was essential that the characteristic being measured be <u>independent of the structured programming discipline</u>. In other words, each metric had to be representative of program quality whether quality was being evaluated within or outside the structured programming framework. In an attempt to assure the unbiased nature of each metric, the investigator located citations for each metric in both structured programming literature and non-structured programming references. The latter category was satisfied if a citation: appeared prior to 1970 (before the general acceptance of structured programming concepts); or regardless of date, contained no mention (or only casual mention) of structured programming.

The final set of metrics, approved by the experts named above and judged free of structured programming bias, were:

I. <u>Readability/Understandability</u>
   A. Comments: Adresses the extent and value of comment statements in the source code
      0   no comments
      1   poor comments
      2   comments slightly facilitate understanding of the program
      3   comments materially facilitate understanding of parts of the program
      4   comments materially facilitate understanding of the entire program.

   B. Data and Procedure Names: Measure of the extent to which data and procedure names clearly describe their functions
      0   not descriptive
      1   rarely descriptive
      2   occasionally descriptive
      3   frequently descriptive
      4   consistently and uniformly descriptive

   C. Sequential Flow of Logic: Specifies the extent to which program execution flows naturally from beginning to end with minimal diversion from the main line path
      0   Highly fragmented and difficult to follow
      1   frequently fragmented
      2   occasionally fragmented
      3   seldom fragmented
      4   flows cleanly from beginning to end with little or no diversion from the main path

D. Module Size: Relates the size of modules to those readily grasped by readers of the program
    0   most modules are of a length which actively inhibits readability
    1   some modules inhibit readability
    2   module size appears to work neither for nor against readability
    3   many modules appear properly sized
    4   module size actively contributes to readability

E. Indentation: Specifies the extent to which horizontal spacing within procedural code enhances readability
    0   no indentation protocol observed (or indentation detrimental to readability)
    1   indentation spotty or inconsistent
    2   indentation occasionally enhances readability
    3   indentation frequently enhances readability
    4   indentation consistently enhances readability

F. Logical Simplicity: Related to the number of conditional statements in a program, based on a predetermined optimum. This metric counts conditional statements beyond that predetermined ideal number.
    0   4 or more above optimum
    1   3 more than optimum
    2   2 more than optimum
    3   1 more than optimum
    4   optimum number of conditional statements

II. Modifiability
    A. Program Modularity: Relating to the clear functional role of each module. The function or purpose of a module should be capable of being stated as a single idea, usually expressed by an action verb.
        0   modules have no coherence or functional unity, but contain multiple functions
        1   most modules contain multiple functions
        2   some modules contain multiple functions
        3   very few modules contain multiple functions
        4   all modules appear to be functionally designed

    B. Logical Linkages: Relating to the manner in which transfer of control is made from one module to another
        0   no linkage pattern visible
        1   linkage for functional reasons but without return
        2   linkage for functional reasons with occasional return
        3   transfer of control is functional, generally with return
        4   control is transferred (with return) consistently for functional reasons

    C. Program Size: Relating to the number of non-commentary source statements in the program as compared to the number in the "school solution" (SS).
        0   over 15% more than in the SS
        1   10-15% more than in the SS
        2   5-10% more than in the SS
        3   1-5% more than in the SS
        4   less than or equal to the number in the SS

Note: The following value was determined from operating system accounting records, as was Debugging Difficulty; Satisfaction of Specifications was based on the grade assigned to the program.

    D. Empirical Modifiability: Number of runs required to incorporate a minor specification change in an already working program.
        0   more than 5 runs
        1   5 runs

```
           2    4 runs
           3    3 runs
           4    2 or fewer runs
III. Verifiability
     A.    Satisfaction of Specifications:  Relating to whether (or how well)
           the program works using standard test data.
           0    doesn't work at all
           1    works except for 2 or more flaws
           2    works except for 1 flaw
           3    works but violates formatting specifications
           4    works to specifications

     B.    Debugging Difficulty:  Relating to the number of runs necessary to
           meet the initial specifications (or to approach them as the preceding
           item indicates).
           0    15 or more
           1    12-14
           2    9-11
           3    6-8
           4    5 or fewer
```

Instructional Separation of Experimental and Control Groups. As stated earlier, the research environment was a university setting, using an introductory undergraduate programming course as the vehicle for administration of the experimental and control treatments. It was decided, because of the investigator's admitted bias towards structured programming, that some external means of instruction (for both fundamental programming concepts and specific stylistic coaching) was advisable. A self-study programming package, with ancillary readings in structured programming techniques (for the experimental group) and general concepts of good programming practice (for the control group) was selected.

Choice of Programming Language. COBOL was selected as the programming language vehicle because of its ability to be written in structured form (but only with conscious effort). Pascal, the primary language of computer majors at Florida Atlantic University, the research site, is almost incapable of being written in an unstructured form. According to Edward Yourdon, "While not as elegant and formal a language as ALGOL and PL/I, the COBOL language still includes enough features to make implementation of structured programming fairly practical."[16] An added bonus of this language decision was the availability of high-quality multi-media self-study materials for COBOL. Additionally, COBOL code, when well-written, is more readable because of its English-like nature than source code in virtually any other language.

Types and Numbers of Programs to be Written. It was desirable to have research subjects develop as many non-trivial programs of different types as was feasible within a single course. The following four programs were selected as being representative of the range of COBOL assignments appropriate for beginning students: an extract, requiring selection of records for formatted printing based on satisfaction of compound conditions; a summary and detail report of sorted data, with two levels of control breaks and page control; an edit of input data for completeness, validity, and acceptable ranges or specific values (array/table handling involved also); and a classical sequential file maintenance application in an inventory control setting, involving insertions, changes, and deletions, plus posting of issues and receipts.

   Modifications to the summary and edit programs would be required after the satisfaction of initial specifications, to provide a basis for the measurement of empirical modifiability.

---

16. Yourdon, Edward. Techniques of Program Structure and Design. Englewood Cliffs NJ: Prentice-Hall, Inc. 1975, p. 169.

Process of Applying Metrics. A group of twenty-one individuals agreed to evaluate the student programs using the selected metrics. These individuals met the following criteria: good knowledge of COBOL; operational (as opposed to classroom) COBOL experience; some formal education in computer science or information systems.

None of the scorers/evaluators was aware of the experimental design.

Statistical Analyses to be Applied. Only rudimentary statistical analysis was planned because of the exploratory nature of the experiment. Mean scores for each metric, for the R, M, and V subtotals, and for total raw score were to be computed for each of the four programming assignments—separately for experimental and control groups—and for each of the groups in the aggregate. The t-test for differences between means and the Mann-Whitney u-test for differences between independent samples were also to be calculated.

Formulation and Conduct of a Pilot Study. The complexity of the experiment made a pilot study advisable. Consequently, a preliminary study was conducted during the school term immediately preceding the one planned for the main experiment.

A regularly-scheduled four quarter-hour course was selected for the pilot study. The SRA Computer Programmer Aptitude Battery (CPAB) was administered to the students, who also completed a questionnaire designed for the research project. Based on responses and test scores, students were assigned to experimental and control groups so that there was homogeneity in aptitude and programming background. The original expectation that random assignment could be made proved infeasible because significant numbers of students indicated prior exposure to structured programming techniques. All such students were assigned to the experimental group. Each student was given a course syllabus specifying assignments and their timing, plus schedules for examinations and program submissions. All students received basic COBOL instruction through video and audio tape materials available in the university's Audio-Visual Independent Study Center (AVISC). Experimental group students were exposed to additional required multi-media materials emphasizing structured programming concepts; control group subjects were given required readings in programming style. Each student had a user identification number for the university's computer system, by means of which the metrics available through the operating system were gathered. Students used their Social Security Numbers as author identification in program source files. The instructor held an initial scheduled course meeting and subsequent class sessions only for examinations; this approach was modified for the live study to include one scheduled class meeting per week, where questions were answered and problems resolved. No planned lecture sessions were included in these class meetings, other than orientation to the four programming assignments.

A group of seven evaluators agreed to apply the metrics to source listings; each evaluator was given a one-hour briefing in the use of the metrics, and between fifteen and twenty programs to score. As in the live study, neither students nor evaluators were aware of the experimental design. Pilot study problems derived primarily from the elapsed time of about six weeks between evaluator briefings and their submission of the completed metric score sheets. Their memory of how to apply the metrics appeared to erode in that time period; consequently an improved approach was used in the live study.

CONDUCT OF THE LIVE EXPERIMENT

Based on the results of the pilot study, the live experiment was carried out during the following school term. Thirty-six students registered for the course, but early attrition reduced the group which successfully completed the course to twenty. The following profile describes the composition of the class.

Characteristic	Control	Experimental
Mean Age of Participants	24.1	23.1
Mean Years of Education Beyond High School	3.25	3.27
Mean Years of Computer-Related Work	.79	.44
Mean Years of Non-Computer Work	5.11	3.81
Mean Number of Programming Languages Known	1.77	2.22
Sex	M:12; F:6	M:12; F:6
Mean Score on Computer Aptitude Battery	82.61	83.47
Number Completing Course With C or Above	9	11
Mean Course Grade Point Average (4.0 scale)	2.88	3.18
Count of F's and D's	5	1
Count of Drops/Incompletes	4	6

As with the pilot study, the most compelling reason for inclusion of a subject in the experimental group was prior exposure to structured programming. Fifteen of the eighteen students originally placed in the experimental group had received some instruction in structured programming; nine had actually used structured programming concepts in either school or work assignments. The remaining group assignments were made to assure homogeneity of computer aptitude and experience to the extent possible with the rather small number of participating subjects.

Because of the learning process from the pilot experiment, the study proceeded smoothly. At the one scheduled class meeting per week, both groups met with the instructor, who responded to substantive COBOL questions, distributed and discussed assignments, administered examinations, and resolved any problems (which rarely occurred). Meetings of the instructor with individual students were not permitted to address stylistic considerations.

The output of the completed course was the source listing of programs completed by the students. 122 programs -- 59 from the control group and 63 from the experimental group -- were evaluated. These programs were given coded designations as follows:

Extract (X)	Update (U)
Basic Summary (S)	Modified Summary (T)
Basic Edit (E)	Modified Edit (F)

THE SCORING SESSION

Over a year elapsed between the completion of the course and the application of metrics to the programs. During this time the investigator solicited volunteer scorers, improved the scoring forms to be used, gathered the operating system statistics and quantitative metric information to be recorded on the scoring sheets, and planned the mechanics of the scoring process. Problems in the scoring of pilot study programs derived mainly from the elapsed time between the orientation given to scorers and the actual application of the metrics. After some deliberation it was decided that a concentrated evening scoring session, preceded by a dinner and a briefing on the application of the metrics, would provide the best control of the experiment. Potential scorers from the university and from business and government organizations were invited to participate; twenty-one individuals agreed to attend the scoring session, twenty of whom actually participated. The format of the scoring session, held in the meeting room of a local restaurant, was designed as follows:

    5:30-6:00 pm Social Hour
    6:00-6:45   Dinner

	Minutes Allocated
6:45–7:30	Briefing on Application of Metrics
7:30–10:30	Scoring Session
10:30–?	Commentary and Social Hour

The briefing session, on which the success of the scoring process depended, was planned as follows:

	Minutes Allocated
Introduction to the research (without disclosure of the experimental design)	5
Orientation to the metrics	10
Description of programming assignments and their scoresheet identification	5
Orientation to the scoresheet	5
Dry run (researcher scores a program)	5
Participants score and discuss a program	15

(In the last two exercises above, the researcher evaluated a high-quality unstructured program and the participants then scored a moderate-quality partly structured program, both from the pilot study).

As might be expected, the briefing session lasted longer than its allocated time (by about fifteen minutes); otherwise the scoring session proceeded on schedule. The program listings were distributed in a manner assuring that each scorer would evaluate a mix of program types from each of the two groups. The session ended only when each program had been evaluated by three scorers.

Immediately after the scoring session, the investigator added to the scoresheets the metric values for the five items not entered by the scorers (Roman numeral and alphabetic designations refer to the detailed descriptions of metrics earlier in this paper):

I.F.	Logical Simplicity
II.C.	Program Size
II.D.	Empirical Modifiability
III.A	Satisfaction of Specifications
III.B.	Debugging Difficulty

STATISTICAL ANALYSIS

The 366 metric scoresheets generated during the scoring session (three for each of the 122 programs evaluated), after being completed by the recording of ratings for the five items above, were entered as data cases for processing by SPSS (Statistical Package for the Social Sciences). Statistical analysis centered around the following null hypothesis:

As evaluated by the application of selected software metrics, the quality of computer programs written by students exposed to both COBOL and structured programming concepts cannot be shown to be significantly superior to the quality of programs written by students exposed to both COBOL and general programming style guidelines.

Scoresheet data for each of the twelve uniquely identifiable program categories (the six specific programming assignments for each of the two groups) was designed an SPSS subfile; where appropriate, each statistical measure was applied both in the aggregate for each group and to each subfile. The SPSS subprograms invoked were: (1) Frequencies; (2) T-Tests; (3) Discriminant Analysis; (4) Pearson Product-Moment Correlation. Sixteen variables were evaluated by these subprograms:

Readability
1. COM (Comments)
2. NAM (Data and Procedure Names)
3. SEQ (Sequential Flow of Logic)
4. MSZ (Module Size)
5. IND (Indentation)
6. LOG (Logical Simplicity)
7. RST (Readability Subtotal: sum of scores for metrics 1-6)

Modifiability
     8. MDL (Program Modularity)
     9. LNK (Logical Linkages)
    10. PSZ (Program Size)
    11. EMM (Empirical Modifiability)
    12. MST (Modifiability Subtotal: sum of 8-11)
Verifiablity
    13. SAT (Satisfaction of Specifications)
    14. DEB (Debugging Difficulty)
    15. VST (Verifiability Subtotal: sum of 13 and 14)
    16. TOT (Total Raw Score: sum of 7, 12, and 15)

Note: The EMM metric was recorded only on scoresheets for the two modified programs -- the Modified Summary and the Modified Edit. Similarly, the DEB metric applied only to the Extract, the Update, and the basic versions of the Summary and Edit. In other words, empirical modifiability was the sole measure of debugging difficulty for the two modified programs.

Frequencies: A summary of the output from the Frequencies subprogram, aggregated for all programs of the control group and all programs of the experimental group, appears in Table 1. Modifiability and Verifiability Subtotals do not sum directly from their component metrics because of the selective recording of the EMM and DEB metrics just discussed.

Table 1
Grouped Means for Individual Metrics
(Individual scores range from 0 [low] to 4 [high])

Metric	Control Group Mean	Experimental Group Mean	Number of Assignments in in Which Means of Experimental Group Were Larger
COM	.678	.529	1
NAM	2.503	2.439	2
SEQ	2.559	2.587	3
MSZ	2.316	2.550	5
IND	1.514	1.772	4
LOG	2.627	2.683	4
RST	12.198	12.561	4
MDL	2.486	2.603	4
LNK	2.384	2.656	6
PSZ	1.559	2.048	4
EMM	2.222	2.316	1 (of 2)
MST	7.107	8.005	5
SAT	3.322	3.587	4
DEB	2.537	2.409	1 (of 4)
VST	5.085	5.270	4
TOT	24.390	25.836	6

It can be readily seen that thirteen of the sixteen means (including all three subtotals and the overall total) are higher for the experimental group than for the control group, indicating the likelihood that higher quality is reflected in the programs written using structured programming techniques. Subsequent SPSS runs were designed to test this possibility further.

T-Test: Because relatively few cases were available within each subfile, the t-test was selected to show possible significance in the differences between program scores recorded for the two groups. Like the Frequencies analysis, T-Test was applied both to each subfile and to the aggregated scores for each group. A .90 confidence level for one-tailed tests of significance was selected as a realistic point of discrimination.

Results of t-test processing were mixed. Single program scores were somewhat inconclusive (see Table 3), while aggregate scores (see Table 2) showed more distinct characteristics in the data. The SPSS files were sequenced so that control group cases preceded experimental group data; consequently, t-values are negative where experimental group data has a higher mean and positive where control data reflects higher quality.

Table 2
Aggregate T-Test Results

Variables	T-Value	Confidence Level (if significant)	Degrees of Freedom
COM	1.32	.90	364
NAM	.60		364
SEQ	-.23		364
MSZ	-2.10	.975	364
IND	-1.83	.95	364
LOG	-.46		364
RST	-.90		364
MDL	-1.04		364
LNK	-2.31	.975	364
PSZ	-4.05	.99	364
EMM	-.33		109
MST	-3.73	.99	364
SAT	-3.38	.99	364
DEB	.72		253
VST	-.94		364
TOT	-2.42	.99	364

Table 3
Program-By-Program T-Test Results

Metric	Extract	Basic Summary	Program Modified Summary	Basic Edit	Modified Edit	Update
COM	.29	.82	.94	.60	.81	-.83
NAM	1.19	.64	.13	1.05	-.94	-1.00
SEQ	-1.01	.12	.73	-.07	-2.04***	.48
MSZ	-2.18***	-.55	-.38	.40	-1.22	-1.75**
IND	-2.44****	.28	-.68	.03	-1.71**	-.09
LOG	2.91****	.78	-1.28	-.84	-.82	.16
RST	-.78	.23	-.19	.30	-1.73**	-.64
MDL	-1.03	-.70	.00	-.10	-.11	-.59
LNK	-1.81**	-1.01	-.63	-.76	-1.42*	-.31
PSZ	-4.31****	1.10	.84	-2.62****	-5.37****	-2.67****
EMM	.00	.00	1.55*	.00	-2.36***	.00
MST	-3.26****	-.57	1.02	-2.19***	-3.59****	-1.46*
SAT	.00	-2.31***	-3.75****	-2.04***	.65	-1.52*
DEB	-1.99**	.53	.00	.68	.00	1.41*
VST	-1.99**	-.52	-3.75****	-.66	.66	-.61
TOT	-2.43****	-.17	-.20	-.66	-2.89****	-.81

These results suggest several characteristics of the data: - Total Raw Score figures provided a t-value significant not at the .90 level chosen, but at the more discriminating .99 level. Experimental group aggregate figures proved superior to control group totals with 99% certainty.

Five of the twelve component t-scores for the aggregate data--all above the .90 confidence level--indicated higher quality for experimental group data. Control group aggregate scores were significantly higher (at the .90 level) for only Comments, which are frequently used to compensate for the absence of other quality attributes.

For the 90 program-by-program t-values (15 for each of the six programs), 27 were statistically significant; 25 of these favored the experimental group.

Discriminant Analysis: Stepwise introduction of variable into a linear discriminant function was employed both to isolate variables which most consistently distinguished between control and experimental groups and to attempt a predictive classification into groups based on the values of key metric scores. The following variables, listed in their order of inclusion, contributed significantly to the discriminant function; all were significant at or above the .90 level:

PSZ, SAT, EMM, IND, COM, NAM, SEQ, AND LNK

An attempt to predict group membership for individual programs met with an overall success rate of 77.05%. The data used in this discriminant analysis run excluded all subtotal and total figures because of their strong correlation with the component metric variables in their category. Individual program figures are shown in Table 4:

Table 4
Discriminant Analysis Prediction of Group Membership
(Program by Program Data)

Program	Actual Group	Number Of Cases	Predicted Group Control	Experimental
Extract	Control	36	31 (81.1%)	5 (13.9%)
(81.9% total)	Experimental	36	8 (22.2%)	28 (77.8%)
Basic Summary	Control	33	22 (66.7%)	11 (33.3%)
(74.2% total	Experimental	33	6 (18.2%)	27 (81.8%)
Mod. Summary	Control	30	21 (70.0%)	9 (30.0%)
(71.7% total)	Experimental	30	8 (26.7%)	22 (73.3%)
Basic Edit	Control	27	18 (66.7%)	9 (33.3%)
(70.2% total)	Experimental	30	8 (26.7%)	22 (73.3%)
Mod. Edit	Control	24	23 (95.8%)	1 (4.2%)
(90.2% total)	Experimental	27	4 (14.8%)	23 (85.2%)
Update	Control	27	21 (77.8%)	6 (22.2%)
(75.0% total)	Experimental	33	9 (27.3%)	24 (72.7%)

This data indicates that proper prediction of group membership occurred consistently in at least 70% of the instances.

Pearson Product-Moment Correlation: Because the mean figures for Empirical Modifiability (EMM) yielded by the Modified Summary and the Modified Edit were in opposition--1.90 and 2.50 respectively for Experimental and Control Groups for the Summary, and 2.78 and 1.88 respectively for the Edit--the supposedly related Debugging Difficulty (DEB) ratings were correlated with EMM figures. Results are shown in Table 5:

Table 5
Correlation Coefficients: DEB and EMM

Program	Experimental Group	Control Group
Summary	.86	-.028
Edit	.51	.28

These figures indicated a much stronger linkage between the two metrics for the Experimental Group, with even a modest negative value for the Summary program within the Control Group. When Satisfaction of Specifications (SAT) was incorporated, findings indicated a significant (at the .95 level) <u>negative</u> correlation between EMM and SAT for both groups. This indicates that perseverance in the debugging of modifications led to a <u>successful</u> change implementation--if a costly one. This shifts our view of modifiability from emphasis on ease to emphasis on success.

    <u>Inversely Correlated Metrics</u>: The detailed output from the Pearson Product-Moment Correlation run included several statistically significant (.90 level or above) negative correlations between metric pairs. Table 6 provides counts for both groups on a program-by-program basis and specifies those pairs common to the same programs for the two groups:

Table 6
Significant Negatively Correlated Metric Pairs (Counts)

Program	Control	Experimental	Common Pairs
Extract	5	7	COM-LOG
Basic Summary	8	7	IND-PSZ
Modified Summary	11	6	COM-PSZ EMM-IND
Basic Edit	19	9	DEB-IND DEB-LOG IND-VST MDL-PSZ
Modified Edit	10	14	EMM-LOG EMM-SAT EMM-VST LOG-MST LOG-SEQ MST-SAT MST-VST
Update	0	14	None

Certain observations regarding these negative correlations are in order:

    a. There is little duplication between significant negative correlations for control and experimental groups within the same program. The specified pairs are from a non-redundant total of 120 correlations per program (all pairings of the 16 metrics).

    b. Program Size (PSZ) was the most common metric appearing in negatively correlated pairs. A resulting conjecture is that a compact program may inhibit quality in other areas.

    c. Where no significant inverse correlations occurred for the Update within the control group, 14 were present in the experimental group. This suggests (conjecture only) a tighter coupling between quality characteristics in this most complex of the programs. Perhaps, by the end of the programming

    Because the most convincing figures are derived from aggregating the subscores, selective use of structured programming concepts would seem to be

assignments, the experimental group had so optimized each of the characteristics measured by these 14 pairs that any shift in one caused a reactive opposite shift of the other in the pair.

d. The patterns of such correlation counts for the two groups (viewed chronologically--i.e., in the assignment order of the six programs) show real differences. Control group counts assumed a generally bell-shaped distribution; for the experimental group, a rising curve was generated (conceivably a type of learning curve indicating an increased facility for exploiting each quality attribute fully as experience with structured programming increased).

CONCLUSIONS AND FUTURE RESEARCH RECOMMENDATIONS

Results of the statistical analysis show a strong basis for rejection of the null hypothesis; in other words:

As evaluated by the application of selected software metrics, the quality of computer programs written by students exposed to both COBOL and structured programming concepts can be shown to be significantly superior to the quality of programs written by similar students exposed to both COBOL and general programming style guidelines.

If subordinate null hypotheses had been postulated for the specific quality characteristics of Readability, Modifiability, and Verifiability, the only one which could be rejected would be the Modifiability hypothesis (and only after a careful examination of the apparently disappointing metrics in that area).

less productive than a global application of structured techniques. There may, in fact, be an interaction among such programming guidelines that results in a synergistic contribution to program quality.

Future research might include experiments to:

1) identify a smaller number of metrics which might yield equally good results;

2) develop metric categories beyond the Readability, Modifiability, and Verifiability classifications;

3) replicate the project in a different language environment;

4) focus on the potentially rich area of program maintenance/modification;

5) study the interaction of structured programming with other software engineering techniques; and

6) apply the same controlled research format to the concepts of structured design.

7) conduct a similar experiment in an environment of "programming in the large." Basili and his colleagues have initiated such an endeavor at the Software Engineering Laboratory sponsored by NASA's Goddard Space Flight Center and the University of Maryland. Their research there also has the distinction of being carried out with production programmers rather than students. Their initial plans are described by Basili.[17]

In summary, this project supported the claims of structured programming advocates regarding the enhancement of programs quality through application of structured programming techniques. In addition, it developed a set of software quality metrics that operate generally independent of program execution.

17. Basili, Victor R.; Zelkowitz, Marvin V.; McGarry, Frank E.; Reiter, Robert W.; Truszkowski, Walter F.; and Weiss, David L. The Software Engineering Laboratory (Technical Report TR-535) College Park MD: University of Maryland 1977.

REFERENCES

1. Weinberg, Gerald M. Rethinking Systems Analysis and Design. Boston MA: Little, Brown and Company, 1982, pp. 19-20.

2. Jensen, Randall W. "Structured Programming." Computer. (March 1981), p. 32.

3,6. Boehm, Barry W.; Brown, J.R.; Kasper, H.; Lipow, M.; MacLean, G.J.; and Merritt, M.J. Characteristics of Software Quality (TRW-SS-73-09). Redondo Beach CA: TRW, Inc. 1973.

4.   Gilb, Tom. "Software Metrics - The Emerging Technology." Data Management (July 1975), pp. 34-37.

5,11.   McCall, Jim A.; Richards, Paul K.; and Walters, Gene F. Factors in Software Quality (RADC-TR-77-369). Griffiss AFB NY; Rome Air Development Center, November 1977.

7.   Boehm, Barry W. "Software and Its Impact: A Quantitative Assessment." Datamation 19 5 (May 1973), pp. 48-59.

8.   Boehm, Barry W.; Brown, J.R.; and Lipow, M. "Quantitative Evaluation of Software Quality." Proceedings of the 2nd International Conference on Software Engineering. San Francisco: IEEE Computer Society, 1976, pp. 592-605.

9.   Clapp, J. A. and Sullivan, J.E. "Automated Monitoring of Software Quality." AFIPS Conference Proceedings 43 (1974 National Computer Conference). Montvale NJ: AFIPS Press, 1974, pp. 337-341.

10.   Gilb, Tom. Software Metrics Cambridge MA: Winthrop Publishers, Inc., 1977.

12.   Mohanty, Siba M. "Models and Measurements for Quality Assessment of Software." ACM Computing Surveys 11 3 (September 1979), pp. 251-275.

13.   Reiter, Robert W., Jr. An Experimental Investigation of Computer Program Development Approaches and Computer Programming Metrics. Ph.D. Dissertation. College Park MD: University of Maryland, 1979.

14.   Rubey, Raymond J. and Hartwick, R. Dean. "Quantitative Measurement of Program Quality." Proceedings of the 1968 ACM Conference. New York: ACM, 1968, pp. 671-677.

15.   Shneiderman, Ben. Software Psychology. Cambridge MA: Winthrop Publishers, Inc. 1980.

16.   Yourdon, Edward. Techniques of Program Structure and Design. Englewood Cliffs NJ: Prentice-Hall, Inc. 1975.

17.   Basili, Victor R.; Zelkowitz, Marvin V.; McGarry, Frank E.; Reiter, Robert W.; Truszkowski, Walter F.; and Weiss, David L. The Software Engineering Laboratory (Technical Report TR-535) College Park MD: University of Maryland 1977.

CHAPTER 12

An Empirical Study of the Effects of Modularity on Program Modifiability[1]

Timothy D. Korson
Department of Computer Science
Southern College of Seventh-Day Adventists
Collegedale, TN 37315

Vijay K. Vaishnavi
Department of Computer Information Systems
Georgia State University
Atlanta, GA 30303

Abstract

An empirical study of the effects of modularity on adaptive program maintenance is reported. A discussion of methodological issues in empirical studies using programmers is also included.

The study provides strong evidence that a modular program is faster to modify than a non-modular, but otherwise equivalent version of the same program, when one of the following conditions hold:

   (a)   Modularity has been used to implement "information hiding" which localizes changes required by a modification.
   (b)   Existing modules in a program perform useful generic operations, some of which can be used in implementing a modification.
   (c)   A significant understanding of, and changes to, the existing code are required for performing a modification.

In contrast, the study provides evidence that modifications not fitting into the above categories are unaided by the presence of modularity in the source code.

1. INTRODUCTION

Over the past decade many changes have taken place in how programming is taught. Emphasis has shifted from machine efficiency to human efficiency. Unstructured, non-modular approaches are being replaced by highly structured, modular ones.

Claims made for these new techniques include:

   (a)   Enhanced reliability
   (b)   Easier and more thorough testing possibilities
   (c)   Reduced number of "bugs" in new programs
   (d)   Shortened program development time
   (e)   Ease of modification of programs created using such techniques

Some of these claims are in dispute, while others have substantial anecdotal evidence, case histories, and intuitive appeal in their favor (12, 14).

Some empirical work has been done (3), but, in general, modern programming practices are in a poor state empirically (22). In other words, there has not been very much empirical research in this area, and much of what has been done has failed to support commonly held hypotheses. Excellent critical reviews of the current state of empirical research in programming practices are provided by

---

[1] This research is partially supported by a grant from Borland International.

Vessey and Weber (22), Sheil (14), and Brooks (2).

Most empirical studies dealing with the new methodologies have focused on language characteristics (3), but as Sheil (14) notes, these studies have found few clear effects of changes in programming notation. Since many of the studies conducted have dealt with language characteristics, and more importantly, since most of these studies have been so inconclusive, the study reported in this paper does not attempt to further consider language characteristics. Instead, it deals with the issue of modularity.

Case histories suggest that there are ways to increase programmer productivity. The psychological arguments presented in (6) indicate that limiting the amount of information the programmer must consider simultaneously while developing, debugging, or modifying a program should yield considerable benefits. Since modularity is a tool programmers use to try and achieve the above, proper modularity should yield these benefits.

Further theoretical support for the hypothesis that modularity should yield measurable benefits comes from classical complexity theory. Complexity theory states that a system's chance of survival is increased if it is composed of a hierarchy of subsystems which are loosely coupled but each of which is internally cohesive.

Stevens, Myers, and Constantine's "Theory of Modularity" (referred to as structured design) (20) can be thought of as arising from an application of complexity theory to software design. This paper uses their terminology and framework in discussing modularity. It may be noted the this "Theory of Modularity" (20) has not been empirically tested in a controlled experimental setting. In other words, there is no empirical evidence to help answer the question, "What, if any, benefits are gained by a modularity such as suggested by Stevens, Myers, and Constantine?" This question addresses a whole area of research which must be necessarily limited to a much more fundamental sub-question. To narrow the above question, one must focus upon:
    (a) Which benefits are to be studied
    (b) What levels of modularity
The present study focuses on ease of modification (also called maintenance) as this is the area in which structured design is claimed to have the most benefits (20). Furthermore, given the long life cycle of software today, ease of modification is an important economic question.

Vessey and Weber (21) classify all maintenance activity as:
    (a) Repair maintenance
    (b) Productivity maintenance
    (c) Adaptive maintenance
Repair maintenance is really an extension of the debugging stage and is not further considered.

Productivity (sometimes called perfective) maintenance is concerned with reducing the amount of computer resource required to run a program. Ideally, concern for a program's efficiency should be incorporated into that program's original development. Profiles should be run on the source code and changes needed to enhance efficiency should be made before the program is put into production. Besides the fact that efficiency considerations should be taken care of before the maintenance stage, statistics (7) indicate that productivity maintenance is not nearly as significant a problem as adaptive maintenance.

A survey of 486 managers of large commercial data processing centers (7) revealed that their number one concern in maintenance is demand for enhancement and extensions. Because of its relative importance, this study focuses on adaptive maintenance. Therefore, unless otherwise noted, this paper uses the term maintenance (or modifications) to mean one of the following activities:
    (a) Enhancing existing features of a program
    (b) Adding new features to a program
    (c) Changing existing features of a program to meet new specifications
Due to the difficulty in doing research in human factors, and because of the lack of other research in the area, the levels of modularity compared in the present study are the fundamental ones of:
    (a) Presence of "good" modularity, with
    (b) Absence of modularity.
A program exhibiting "good" modularity means that it is composed of a

hierarchy of loosely coupled modules each of which is internally cohesive.

Thus the sub-question investigated in the present study is: Does a modularity such as suggested by Stevens, Myers, and Constantine (20) allow a program to be modified more quickly than a non-modular, but otherwise equivalent version?

The rest of this paper is organized as follows: In section 2, we elaborate on the objectives, importance, and scope of the present study. In section 3, we relate the study to previous research. We go into the methodological problems faced in conducting research in the area and put the study in its proper perspective. In section 4, we describe the experimental setting, experimental design, nature of the specific experiments, and the research hypotheses. In section 5, we discuss results from the experiments and their validity. In section 6, we elaborate on certain lessons learned from the study. Some of these lessons are general in nature in the area of conducting empirical human factors research, while others are more specific. In the concluding section, we summarize the results of the study and provide suggestions for future research.

2. PRESENT STUDY

Research Objectives

The goal of this study is to empirically examine some of the relationships between the level of modularity and the time taken to perform adaptive maintenance on reasonably complex programs.

Clearly there is an infinite number of modifications one can make to any given program. This study proposes that, given the modular version of the source code of a specific program, one can classify a particular modification to that program and then use that classification to predict whether the modular version will be faster to modify than an equivalent non-modular version.

Specifically, this study is designed to give some empirical evidence that a modular program is faster to modify than a non-modular, but otherwise equivalent version of the same program, when one or more of the following conditions hold:
(a) Modularity has been used to implement "information hiding" which localizes changes in the source code required by a modification.
(b) Existing modules in a program perform useful generic operations, some of which can be used in implementing a modification.
(c) A significant understanding of, and changes to, the existing code are required for performing a modification.

In contrast, this study also gathers evidence that modifications not fitting into the above categories are unaided by the presence of modularity in the source code.

It may be noted that the above paragraphs outline a model that is useful not only for prediction, but also for understanding why and when modularity is important. This has implications for how the original coding of programs should be performed. This issue is further discussed in the concluding section.

The theoretical background for the hypotheses examined in this study is treated in depth in (6) which also reviews the relevant literature in "human factors in software development."

In a larger sense, it is the objective of this study to contribute to the understanding of methodological issues of conducting empirical research with programmers. Thus it is our hope to help provide a basis for doing further work in this area of software engineering--an area that is so critical to programmer productivity.

Importance of the Study

Maintenance costs account for 40 - 75 percent (21) of the total life cycle costs of a system. Proponents of modular programming claim that these costs can be substantially reduced by proper program design. These claims have such intuitive appeal that modular programming has become a de facto standard in many educational and "enlightened" industrial circles.

In spite of the wide acceptance of modular programming, there are still reasons why empirical research in this area is important:

- Theory may lead one believe that modular programming is beneficial, but one needs empirical results to determine the magnitude of these effects.
- Some still doubt the benefits of modular programming and acceptance of modular programming is far from universal (14).

Moreover, any discipline has an obligation to validate claims made by its theoreticians. This is especially true when these claims affect:

- The way courses are taught in colleges and universities across the nation.
- Forty to seventy-five percent of the expenditures of a multi-billion dollar industry
- The development of new languages such as Ada
- Much of the research and direction of a relatively new discipline.

Thus, the literature is full of exhortation to do empirical research in this basic area of software engineering (1, 12, 14, 21).

In reviewing the empirical literature in the field, We have been unnerved to find how often others have failed to demonstrate commonly held beliefs. Therefore, if this study can document a replicable experimental framework in which certain benefits of modularity can be observed and measured, then it will have provided an important basis for further research.

Scope and Limitations

Type of Programs. Consideration is limited to non-recursive implementations of straightforward applications in accounting, inventory control, purchasing, scheduling, etc.

Size of Programs. All programs have at least 450 lines of source code.

Language. Even though COBOL is the most popular business language, Pascal is used throughout the experiments, as it facilitates a more direct implementation of the theory we are examining.

Factors held constant. There are many other factors besides modularity that can have an effect on modifiability. These factors include:

- Type of control structures employed
- Variable naming conventions
- Use made of comments
- Indentation conventions
- Length of the program

In this study, all of the above variables are held constant. As the experimental procedures outlined in Section 4 explain, one group of programmers is given a "modular" version of a program to modify. A second group is given an "equivalent monolithic" version of the same program. The "monolithic" version is identical to the equivalent "modular" version except for the in-line expansion of all function and procedure calls. Thus, no matter what types of control structures, etc. are employed, any difference in the time taken to modify the two versions of a program can only be attributed to the level of modularity (or to factors external to the source code, such as difference in programmer ability).

Given this fact, it might seem that the choice of control structures, etc. might be irrelevant. In a sense, this is true. But these other factors may have an interaction effect with modularity. For example, it may be that the modular code is not any faster to modify if restricted control structures are employed, but if unrestricted use of GOTOs is allowed then the modular code might be consistently faster to modify. The present study does not intend to draw any conclusions about such interaction effects. Their possibility is pointed out only to underline the fact that any conclusions about the benefits of modularity are stated within the context of these other fixed variables. For this reason, the types of control structures employed, variable naming conventions, etc., all follow current recommended programming practices.

Modifications. The modifications to be performed are substantial examples of adaptive maintenance.

Design. Besides providing a theoretical background on modularity, Stevens, Myers, and Constantine (20) have developed structured design tools. As important as design is, this research is limited to considering existing source code.

Authors	Independent Variable(s) Control Structures	"Readability" (i.e., indentation variable names, comments)	Modularity	Activity Studied Comprehension	Coding	Debugging	Maintenance	Method Laboratory Experiment	Archival Study
1 Sime et al [17]	X							X	
2 Lucus & Kaplan [9]	X				X			X	
3 Sime et al [18]	X				X			X	
4 Soloway et al [19]	X				X			X	
5 Green [1977]	X			X				X	
6 Sheppard et al [15]	X			X				X	
7 Shneiderman et al [16]		X		X				X	
8 Weissman [23]	X	X		X				X	
9 Love [8]	X	X		X				X	
10 Sheppard et al [15]	X	X				X		X	
11 Lucas & Kaplan [9]	X						X	X	
12 Sheppard et al [15]	X						X	X	
13 Vessey & Webber [21]	X		X				X		X
14 Present Experiment		X	X				X	X	

Relationship to Previous Research

FIGURE 1

3. RELATIONSHIP TO PREVIOUS RESEARCH

Figure 1 forms the basis for this section's comments. It is a summary of the empirical research most closely related to the current study. The table provides a framework that makes it easy to compare and contrast the different studies, as well as to show how the empirical work described in this paper relates to previous empirical research.

Figure 1 is organized according to the claims each researcher is trying to validate. The first four studies examine the effects of different levels of control structures on coding performance. The next two references are about experiments on the effects of control structures on program comprehension, while Shneiderman et al. (16) study the effects of readability (level of indentation) on comprehension. It is evident from **Figure** 1 that most of the studies have focused on the effects that varying the type of control structures has on program coding and comprehension.

Typically, the comprehension experiment consists of randomly dividing a class of computer science students into two groups, and giving each group a different version of a small (10-40 line) program to study. Students are then expected to recall (or explain) the program. Students given the "readable" structured version of the program are expected to outperform the control group. In the coding experiments, two groups of programmers are given the same specifications for a small program, but each group is supposed to use/avoid certain methods/control structures. Again, those students using "readable", structured methods are supposed to produce code more quickly, with less errors and have more fun doing it.

A Methodological Problem

Surprisingly, <u>less</u> than one-third of the hypotheses in these studies have been supported by the statistics derived from the empirical data. This does not imply that these hypotheses are necessarily wrong. Programming methodology is but one factor in determining the ease of understanding, coding, or modifying a program. The differences in programmers' native and acquired abilities are often so large as to obscure any difference due to a particular methodology or construct one may be studying. In experiment number 10 of **Figure** 1, one programmer took 67 minutes to discover a bug found by another programmer in only 6 minutes (4). That is a ratio of 22 to 1. Other studies have documented similar (20 to 1) ratios (13). In comparison, the effects of structured programming are often so small as to be statistically undetectable without using an experimental design that allows for one to control for (i.e., statistically factor out) these extraneous variations. In a carefully controlled experiment (No. 5 in **Figure** 1), Green was able to demonstrate an eleven percent time increase in programmer performance due to the use of structured selection constructs as opposed to using GOTO's. To detect an eleven percent variation among groups, when dealing with a within-group variation of 20 to 1, calls for a very well designed and carefully controlled experiment. In this situation, the simple two group comparison, as used in most of the existing research, is not appropriate. Some statistical method such as paired comparison, blocking, or covariant analysis, must be used so that the large differences in human programming ability do not statistically obscure the differences in the variable of interest. Lack of attention to this area is one of the major criticisms to be leveled at the existing research. However this variation among programmers is also one of the most difficult problems to solve in experimental design. The reason for this is that there is no reliable covariant with programmer ability. Management ratings, test scores, years of experience, GPA, and various other measures have all failed to successfully predict programmer performance. Given the fact that there is no reliable covariate with programmer ability, The empiricist may have to use a simple two group comparison. If he does, however, he must take care to insure:

- As much homogeneity of programming ability as possible among the programmers used in the experiments.
- That there exists theoretical reasons to believe that the treatment effect is large enough to be detected using this simple statistical design.

Structured, "readable", code **is** most likely beneficial in understanding,
developing, debugging, and maintaining programs, but in view of the relatively
unsophisticated state of existing research, methodological problems have
prevented the empiricist from obtaining convincing evidence of these benefits.
Because the relative size of the effects is so much smaller than was assumed, the
empiricist will have to work much harder to demonstrate them.

Why Another Empirical Study

Of more practical and economical importance is the study of factors that are
believed to have a larger relative effect on productivity. It has already been
noted that programmer ability is one of these factors. The level of modularity
of the code is another such factor. We believe that the design of a program as a
loosely coupled hierarchy of internally cohesive modules has a greater effect on
a large programs modifiability than does adherence to a structured methodology in
the internal coding of these modules.

There is little formal data to support the above position. It is based
primarily upon the arguments developed in Chapter III of (6). The human
information processing capacity is limited to simultaneous consideration of
7 ($\pm$2) chunks of information. In a well designed modular program, each module is
of such limited size and complexity that it is within human capacity to process
it without the need to resort to some swapping algorithm. If the human brain is
at all like a computer, then its internal processing speed is orders of magnitude
faster than the time it takes to shift its attention, swap information in and
out, find where it left off, and resume processing. Therefore, any technique
(such as modularity) that will reduce the programmer's need to use a swapping
algorithm will result in gains in productivity which should be orders of
magnitude greater than techniques (such as structured programming) which simply
increase the rate at which a given 7 ($\pm$2) chunks of information can be processed.

Sheppard et al. (Nos. 6, 10, and 12 in **Figure** 1) studied the effects of
three different types of control structures – "strictly structured", "naturally
structured", and "deliberately convoluted". "Strictly structured" programs used
only the three basic control constructs (WHILE; IF–THEN–ELSE; and SEQUENCE),
while the "naturally structured" version allowed for the use of GOTO's, mid-loop
exits from a DO, and multiple returns. They hypothesized that subjects would
perform best with the "strictly structured" version; but the data showed no
statistically significant differences between the "strictly structured" and the
"naturally structured" versions. The "convoluted" version did result in poorer
performance than either of the other two versions. The programs they studied
were about 50 lines long, just the size of a typical well designed module.

The relatively small increase in performance (only eleven percent) reported
by Green (5), with the fact that Sheppard et al. (15) could not detect any
difference in performance unless the code was deliberately convoluted, correlates
well with the theoretical position taken above. Thus, it is not the purpose of
this study to conduct another study similar to references 1-9 of **Figure** 1. And
yet, the literature is full of case histories and other anecdotal evidence which
indicates that significant gains in programmer productivity are possible. Theory
suggests that these large gains can be made by the proper use of program
modularity. The next section describes the experiments used to test this theory.

4. EXPERIMENTAL DESIGN AND HYPOTHESES

Experimental Setting

Programmers participate in a controlled laboratory setting with each
participant assigned to a complete microcomputer workstation.

Participants

Sixteen "experienced" programmers have consented to participate. Seven are
professional programmers. The other nine are advanced computer science students
at Southern College of Seventh-day Adventist. The participants have been chosen
according to the following criteria:
- Fluency in Pascal
- Knowledge of the IBM-PC
- Amount of programming experience

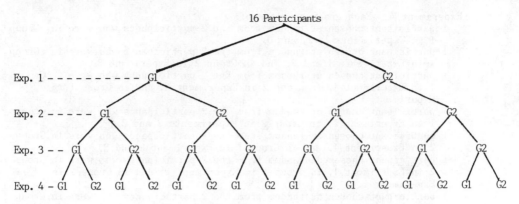

16 Participants

Exp. 1 - - - - - - - - - G1   G2

Exp. 2 - - - - - G1   G2   G1   G2

Exp. 3 - - G1   G2   G1   G2   G1   G2   G1   G2

Exp. 4 - G1 G2 G1 G2 G1 G2 G1 G2 G1 G2 G1 G2 G1 G2 G1 G2

(G1 is the group receiving modular code; G2 is the group receiving the monolithic code)

Assignment of Participants to Experimental Treatments

FIGURE 2

A participant is classified as a professional programmer if he has the equivalent of at least one year's experience as a full time programmer. Among the professional programmers are two systems programmers, four applications programmers, and the head of a data processing department.

Experimental Design

Each programmer participates in five experiments.

The first experiment is a pretest simply for the purpose of familiarizing the participants with the experimental environment. This includes exposure to the hardware and software used, as well as the experimental setting.

During the pretest, all participants modify a small, one-page, program. The pretest program cannot bias the participants for, or against, modularity because modularity is not a factor when a program is short enough to be a one-page mainline program.

Since, during the pretest, all participants are given an identical task, neither is there a need to control for "learning" during the pretest.

Assignment of Participants to Experimental Treatments. There are four experiments, corresponding to the four research hypotheses. For each of these experiments there are two groups: Group 1 receiving modular code and Group 2 receiving equivalent monolithic code. The sixteen participants are assigned to groups as follows (See **Figure 2**):

Experiment 1. Each group consists of:
    8 participants chosen at random from the 16 participants.

Experiment 2. Each group consists of:
    4 participants chosen at random from the 8 participants who were in Group 1 (receiving modular code) in Experiment 1.
    4 participants chosen at random from the 8 participants who were in Group 2 (receiving monolithic code) Experiment 1.

Experiment 3. Each group consists of:
    2 participants chosen at random from the four participants who were in Group 1 in Experiments 1 and 2.
    2 participants chosen at random from the four participants who were in Group 1 in Experiment 1 and in Group 2 in Experiment 2.
    2 participants chosen at random from the four participants who were in Group 2 in Experiment 1 and in Group 1 in Experiment 2.
    2 participants chosen at random from the four participants who were in Group 2 in Experiments 1 and 2.

Experiment 4. Each group consists of:
  1 participant chosen at random from the 2 participants who were in Group 1 in Experiments 1, 2, and 3.
  1 participant chosen at random from the 2 participants who were in Group 1 in Experiments 1 and 2, and in Group 2 in Experiment 3.
  1 participant chosen at random from the 2 participants who were in Group 1 in Experiment 1, in Group 2 in Experiment 2, and in Group 1 in Experiment 3.
  1 participant chosen at random from the 2 participants who were in Group 1 in Experiment 1, in Group 2 in Experiments 2 and 3.
  1 participant chosen at random from the 2 participants who were in Group 2 in Experiment 1, and in Group 1 in Experiment 2 and 3.
  1 participant chosen at random from the 2 participants who were in Group 2 in Experiment 1, in Group 1 in Experiment 2, and in Group 2 in Experiment 3.
  1 participant chosen at random from the 2 participants who were in Group 2 in Experiments 1 and 2, and in Group 1 in Experiment 3.
  1 participant chosen at random from the 2 participants who were in Group 2 in Experiments 1, 2, and 3.
This assignment of subjects to treatments is used to control for both "background" and "learning effect".

Experimental procedures. In each of the four modification experiments, participants receive one of two standard source code listings. Participants in Group 1 receive a modular version of the program to modify. Participants in Group 2 receive an equivalent monolithic version of the program. This version is created by replacing each procedure, or function call with the code for that procedure or function.

All participants are given the same specifications of a modification to be made to the program.

The modification process consists of four phases. The number of minutes for each phase is recorded for each participant. The time is determined by direct observation.

Phase 1:
  On paper, the modifications are coded noting deletions, additions, and changes to the original source code.

Phase 2:
  At the computer, the original program is edited to reflect the modifications made on paper; this is just an exercise in typing.

Phase 3:
  The syntax errors are interactivly removed from the modifications.

Phase 4:
  Logic errors are interactivly debugged until the program passes a standard test.

A copy of the experimental material is available from the authors. It consists of the instructions, documentation, and specifications of the required modifications given to the participants, as well as the modular and monolithic versions of the source codes that are to be modified.

To simplify the discussion of the experiments and hypotheses, the following definitions are given. By "modularity" or "modular program" it is meant that the program is composed of a loosely coupled hierarchy of modules each of which exhibits high inner module cohesion. Using the theory of Stevens, Constantine, and Myers (20), "loosely coupled" means that no pair of modules are more than stamp coupled unless they are both part of an information cluster, in which case they may be common coupled. "High inner module cohesion" means that at least ninety percent of the modules have a level of cohesion that is among the top three (functional, sequential, or communicational) according to the ranking given by Stevens, Myers, and Constantine. The other ten percent may descend to the procedural or temporal level, but none of the modules may descend to the logical or coincidental level.

Description of the Experiments

Experiment 1 – Information hiding. Due to the work of David Parnas (10,11), the concept of information hiding has become well known. The thrust of his argument is that a program ought to be coded so that design decisions likely to be subject to later modification are "hidden" in a single, or small number of modules.

Experiment 1 seeks to demonstrate the value of information hiding. For this experiment, participants are asked to modify an inventory tracking, point of sale, program. The modification calls for all inventory accesses to be made directly to the inventory file rather than to an intermediary array. The inventory accessing mechanisms are localized to three modules in the modular program, but spread over the entire program in the monolithic version.

Experiment 2 – Reusable Modules. Software libraries are maintained so that programmers don't have to continually reinvent the wheel. Compilers provide a standard set of functions and procedures so that each programmer won't have to waste his time coding them.

Every program uses some data structures, and has some particular application domain. If the original program is designed so that modules exist that perform the primitive operations on the program's data structures, and application domain, then in some cases the maintenance programmer should be able to use those existing modules to save time in making a modification.

Experiment 2 uses a workstation scheduling program to demonstrate the advantage of reusable modules. The modification calls for adding a feature to enable a user to remove himself from a waiting list. The modular version has procedures that implement some of the primitive operations necessary for accomplishing this task.

Experiment 3 Chunking effect. There are psychological arguments (6) to support the hypothesis that a modular version of a large program is easier for a programmer to understand and work with, than an equivalent monolithic version. Therefore, if a given modification requires the maintenance programmer to understand and interact with a large program, then the modular version should be faster to modify simply because the programmer's cognitive structures are better adapted to the modular version.

Experiment 3 uses a calendar program to test this theory. The modifications specify widening the calendar, and allowing for more messages per day. Implementing these modifications calls for about the same number of lines of code to be added and changed in the modular version as in the monolithic. In both cases the changes and additions are spread throughout the code.

Experiment 4 – Adding a feature. There are theoretical reasons for believing in modular programming. The applicability of these reasons to program maintenance has been discussed in the settings of Experiments 1 through 3. If however, none of the above reasons that favor modular programming are applicable to a particular modification, then our preliminary research has indicated there is no reason to predict that the modular program will be faster to modify. This is true even when the implimentation of a new feature necessitates additions that are spread throughout the source code of the original program.

Experiment 4 uses a purchasing program to exemplify such a situation. The modification specifies adding a feature to allow the input file to be edited interactivly. This feature interacts very little with the rest of the program. It is an addition, not a localized change, and there are no existing modules in the original program to facilitate its implementation.

Research Hypotheses

The research hypotheses are the following:

Experiments 1 through 3. The mean time taken to complete the modifications by Group 1 (having the modular code) is less than the time taken by Group 2 (having the monolithic code).

Experiment 4. The mean time to complete the modifications is the same for Groups 1 and 2.

The mean time taken to complete the modifications is calculated using the sum of the times taken to complete Phases 1, 3, and 4. Phase 2 is only an exercise in typing and is not included.

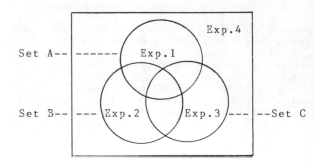

Set A is the set of modifications localized to a small number of modules which are called throughout the program.

Set B is the set of modifications that can make use of existing modules.

Set C is the set of modifications requiring a significant understanding of the original code.

Experimental Framework

FIGURE 3

Figure 3 illustrates the interaction between modularity and modification, and shows the placement of the modifications used in each of the above experiments according to this framework.

5. RESULTS
The data collected during the experiments are summarized in **Figures 4** through **7**.

Experiment 1 – Information Hiding
The mean time for the modular group is 19.3 minutes. The mean time for the monolithic group is 85.9 minutes. Assuming as a null hypothesis that information hiding has no effect on maintainability, the probability of obtaining means as different as these due to chance is less than 0.001. Therefore one must reject the null hypothesis and conclude that under these conditions a modular program is faster to modify than an equivalent monolithic version.

Experiment 2 – Reusable Modules
The mean time for the modular group is 44.1 minutes. The mean time for the monolithic group is 259.8 minutes. Assuming as a null hypothesis that the presence of reusable modules has no effect on maintainability, the probability of obtaining means as different as these due to chance is less than 0.001. Therefore one must reject the null hypothesis and conclude that when reusable modules are present, a modular program is faster to modify than an equivalent monolithic version.

Experiment 3 – Chunking Effect
The mean time for the modular group is 127.8 minutes. The mean time for the monolithic group is 215.8 minutes. Assuming as a null hypothesis that the chunking effect has no effect on maintainability, the probability of obtaining means as different as these due to chance is less than 0.025. Therefore one must reject the null hypothesis and conclude that if a given modification requires of the maintenance programmer a significant level of understanding and interaction with a large program, then a modular program is faster to modify than an equivalent monolithic version.

Experiment 4 – Adding a Feature
The mean time for the modular group is 82.5 minutes. The mean time for the monolithic group is 82.3 minutes. The data from this experiment do not give any rationale for rejecting the null hypothesis of equality of the means of the modular and monolithic groups. Therefore, until there is evidence to the contrary, we must conclude that a modular program is no faster to modify than an equivalent monolithic version if the modification is not a member of the union of sets A, B, and C of **Figure 3**.

Register Program — Information Hiding

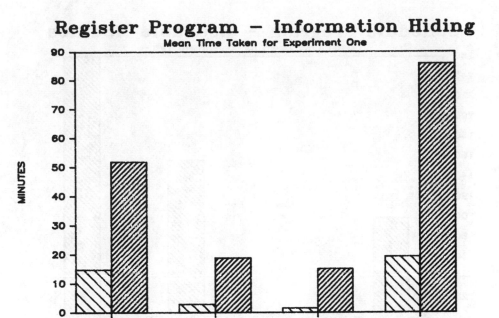

Mean Time Taken for Experiment One

Group 1 (Modular)

		code	syntax	logic	Total
Participant	2	8	1	1	10
Participant	3	10	2	1	13
Participant	4	9	3	1	13
Participant	5	10	1	5	16
Participant	6	19	6	1	26
Participant	7	16	1	1	18
Participant	9	32	1	1	34
Participant	11	15	8	1	24
Mean (minutes)		14.9	2.9	1.5	19.3

Group 2 (Monolithic)

		code	syntax	logic	Total
Participant	1	35	6	8	49
Participant	8	54	13	16	83
Participant	10	73	32	2	107
Participant	12	42	1	1	44
Participant	13	48	75	69	192
Participant	14	54	10	3	67
Participant	15	53	3	2	58
Participant	16	56	11	20	87
Mean (minutes)		51.9	18.9	15.1	85.9

$P < .001$

FIGURE 4

179

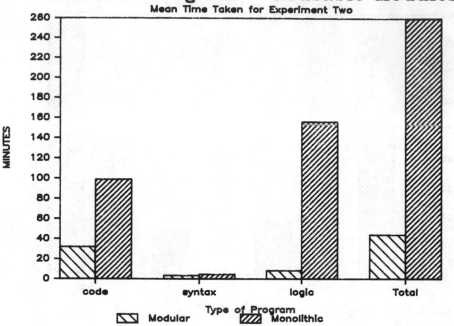

Schedule Program — Reusable Modules
Mean Time Taken for Experiment Two

Group 1 (Modular)

		code	syntax	logic	Total
Participant	2	18	1	2	21
Participant	6	12	8	5	25
Participant	8	49	2	40	91
Participant	9	31	1	3	35
Participant	10	44	1	1	46
Participant	11	29	10	6	45
Participant	12	34	2	5	41
Participant	14	40	3	6	49
Mean (minutes)		32.1	3.5	8.5	44.1

Group 2 (Monolithic)

		code	syntax	logic	Total
Participant	1	33	4	100	137
Participant	3	107	1	172	280
Participant	4	99	2	23	124
Participant	5	104	2	158	264
Participant	7	59	1	170	230
Participant	13	184	17	220	421
Participant	15	152	9	44	205
Participant	16	55	1	361	417
Mean (minutes)		99.1	4.6	156.0	259.8

$P < .001$

FIGURE 5

Calendar Program – Chunking Effect

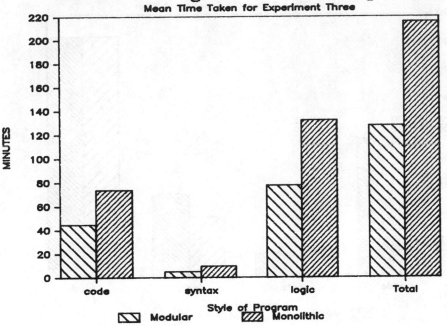

Mean Time Taken for Experiment Three

Group 1 (Modular)

		code	syntax	logic	Total
Participant	1	21	3	87	111
Participant	2	21	2	15	38
Participant	3	33	5	105	143
Participant	6	11	5	181	197
Participant	7	85	2	67	154
Participant	8	55	12	59	126
Participant	10	86	11	60	157
Participant	13	47	1	48	96
Mean (minutes)		44.9	5.1	77.8	127.8

Group 2 (Monolithic)

		code	syntax	logic	Total
Participant	4	66	1	24	91
Participant	5	79	12	43	134
Participant	9	88	26	149	263
Participant	11	60	6	200	266
Participant	12	65	10	239	314
Participant	14	70	4	115	189
Participant	15	89	12	85	186
Participant	16	74	6	203	283
Mean (minutes)		73.9	9.6	132.3	215.8

$P < .025$

Figure 6

181

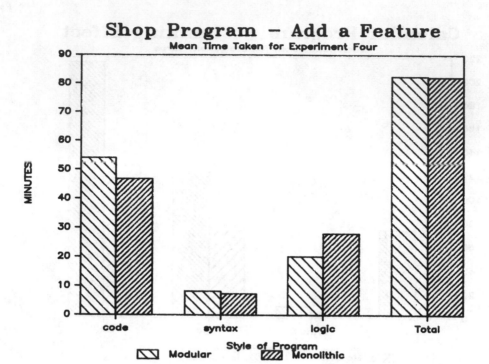

Shop Program – Add a Feature
Mean Time Taken for Experiment Four

	Group 1 (Modular)			
	code	syntax	logic	Total
Participant 4	53	9	19	81
Participant 6	14	3	33	50
Participant 7	40	5	6	51
Participant 9	69	13	48	130
Participant 10	99	12	3	114
Participant 12	51	2	5	58
Participant 13	57	15	27	99
Participant 16	49	7	21	77
mean	54.0	8.3	20.3	82.5

	Group 2 (Monolithic)			
	code	syntax	logic	Total
Participant 1	31	2	5	38
Participant 2	30	8	7	45
Participant 3	34	2	32	68
Participant 5	60	8	40	108
Participant 8	65	8	46	119
Participant 11	35	7	57	99
Participant 14	62	8	9	79
Participant 15	57	16	29	102
mean	46.8	7.4	28.1	82.3

Figure 7

Participants not finishing in the first setting

All of the experiments take place from 6:00 PM - 10:00 PM. In Experiments 2 and 3, two programmers having the monolithic version are unable to finish in the allocated time. They return and finish at the next available time.

At the beginning of the second setting the participants are given time to refamiliarize themselves with the program before being clocked in. Nevertheless, because of the possibility that the participants forget some of the program between setting one and two, we include only one half of the time taken in the second setting in calculating the times.

The four cases when programmers having the monolithic versions do not finish in the first setting are:

Experiment 2, Participant 13 (220 minutes of logic = 153 + 134/2)
Experiment 2, Participant 16 (361 minutes of logic = 310 + 102/2)
Experiment 3, Participant 9 (220 minutes of logic = 79 + 140/2)
Experiment 3, Participant 12 (220 minutes of logic = 88 + 302/2)

In every case, programmers having the modular versions finish in the allotted time.

Validities

Internal Validity. The differences between the mean times of the modular and monolithic groups are large and consistent. The only reasonable explanation for these consistent differences is that they are due to the differences in difficulty of modifying the modular vs. the monolithic versions of the programs.

If the differences between the modular and monolithic groups are due to differences in programming ability between the two groups, then one would **not** expect to see that difference persist from experiment to experiment given the successive reassignment of participants to groups as explained in the previous section.

Another possible explanation for the differences between the modular and monolithic groups is that all the programmers are biased against monolithic programming. The counter argument against this comes from Experiment 4. If the programmers' biases cause them to do better on the modular versions, then why don't those biases have the same effect in Experiment 4?

As stated above, it must be concluded that the observed differences are due to the difference in the level of modularity in the programs.

External Validity. The fact that about one half of the participants are professional programmers enhances the experiments' external validity. This, coupled with the fact that production size programs and realistic modifications are used, means that the experiments have relevance to real business settings.

Statistical Validity. The first test performed on the data for each experiment is Bartlett's test for homogeneity of variance. In Experiments 2 and 3 this test indicates that the variance of Group 1 is significantly smaller than that of Group 2. Since an assumption underlying the t-test is that the variances of the two groups be equal, all probabilities stated in this paper are calculated using the non-parametric, Wilcoxon Rank Sum test for equality of means.

Actually the t-test is a very robust test and is often used even when the underlying mathematical assumptions are not met. In these experiments the t-test yields the same results as does the Wilcoxon Rank Sum, but since the Wilcoxon Rank Sum test does not require homogeneity of variances it is, in this instance, the more appropriate test to use.

In any case, the statistical results are not marginal. There are clear grounds for accepting the research hypotheses.

Validity due to Replication. In preparation for this research, several preliminary experiments were conducted with a second semester programming class at Southern College of Seventh-Day Adventists. Studies similar to Experiments 1 and 4, but using different test materials, were conducted. The same results were obtained.

Another round of experiments was conducted using a graduate software engineering class at Georgia State University. Experiments 1, 2, and 3 of the present study were first conducted there. The class had about twenty students, but due to different language and programming abilities, only eight of the students were able to finish the pretest in the allotted time. The magnitude and direction of the results were the same as in the present study but since data was collected on only eight of the students, the statistics were not as clean (P values ranged from 0.03 to 0.07).

That the magnitude and direction of the results of these earlier replications of the experiments are the same as those reported in this paper, adds to the validity of the conclusions of this study.

6. LESSONS FROM THIS STUDY

Statistical Design

In planning this research, it was realized that the variability among the programmers might be so large as to obscure the treatment effect. Therefore it was decided to use a statistical design such as paired comparisons or analysis of covariance, that allows one to factor out the variation due to different levels of programming ability among the participants. Since there is no good covariate with programming ability that could have been used to accomplish this, it was decided to run a series of pretests. The times taken to modify these pretests would be an actual measure of programming ability. These times could then be used in an analysis of covariance, or to rank and pair the participants. However, this turned out to be impossible. In our preliminary research, the rankings varied wildly from pretest to pretest. Sometimes the programmer who finished first in one test would finish last in the next test. Therefore we did not use a series of pretests in this study. It is worth noting that the phenomenon persists during the experiments reported in this paper. Participant 2 was an exception to the above observations. He consistently finished first.

The implications of this are serious. It means that the classical "paired comparisons" design is not readily available to persons doing research with programmers. Evidently there exist strong interaction effects between a given programmer and any program on which he might be working. These interactions could have to do with the program domain, type of algorithm, type of data structures, and how easy the maintenance programmer finds it to follow the original programmer's logic (i.e. how well their cognitive processes match).

Students as participants

In spite of the practical advantage of using students as subjects, we feel that working exclusively with a class of students is often not adequate when conducting empirical research with programmers. The variability in programming ability in the typical class is too large to permit most treatment effects to be detected. Furthermore, using an intact class means that the research must be conducted within the constraints of the class schedule, objectives, and grading scheme. Perhaps the most important factor is that, even though some students have significant experience and are thus competent programmers, the average student is not representative of a professional programmer.

It is often advantageous to use a class of students for a preliminary set of experiments to test the soundness of one's hypotheses and experimental design. These experiments should be conducted with the usual rigor, and sometimes they will yield meaningful results. Often, however, the results will be ambiguous due to the constraints imposed by working with an intact class. Before reporting these ambiguous results in the literature, we encourage the researcher to conduct another set of similar experiments in an environment free from the constraints imposed by a class.

Summary of Factors Contributing to the Success of this Research

Magnitude of the treatment effect. On the average, the programmers having the monolithic versions took 4.02 times longer to finish than those having the modular versions. Had the treatment effect been smaller, these experiments might have failed to demonstrate the research hypotheses.

Homogeneity of the programmers. If the last programmer to finish a given experiment (in a given group) had taken twenty times as long as the programmer finishing first, then the statistics would not have indicated a significant difference between Groups 1 and 2. But since all the participants of these experiments were experienced, competent, pascal programmers, the average ratio of the longest to the shortest time taken was 3.72 : 1.

Use of Dedicated Microcomputer Workstations. The research hypotheses concerned the time taken by a programmer to modify a program. Using Turbo Pascal on IBM-PC's helped insure that the time taken was actually spent making the modifications and not attributable to system overhead. If a timesharing computer had been used, the differing response times, and possible down times, would have biased the results. Furthermore, the participants would have spent a considerable amount of time waiting for compilations of the relatively large programs on which they were working. Further bias would have resulted from some of the participants using this time more profitably than others. Using Turbo Pascal eliminated this problem, as it compiled our largest program in about 20 seconds.

7. CONCLUDING REMARKS

In this paper we have reported on an empirical study of the effects of modularity on adaptive program maintenance. In addition to the important specific results obtained, the study has demonstrated that a carefully designed empirical study using programmers can lead to replicable, unambiguous conclusions.

The study, comprising four experiments, has provided strong evidence that under certain conditions modular programs are faster to modify than their equivalent monolithic versions. Specifically, it has shown that if (a) the modifications are substantial enough (average time taken across Experiments 1 to 4 is 114.6 minutes), (b) the program to modify is long enough (average length of programs used in Experiments 1 to 4 is 995 lines), and (c) The modification is an element of A U B U C (see **Figure** 3), then a modular program is faster to modify than the equivalent monolithic version. On the other hand, if the modification is a member of U - (A U B U C), then this study has shown that there is no reason to expect the modular version to be faster to modify.

The study has also shed some light on how the modules should be designed in order to minimize their adaptive maintenance cost. The following guidelines have emerged: (a) All design decisions subject to future modification should be localized to a single or a small number of modules. (b) The modules should, whenever reasonable, be designed as generic operations on the data structures representing the problem domain. (c) The whole program should be designed as a loosely coupled hierarchy of short modules, each of which is internally cohesive.

These results may seem intuitively obvious. To put them in their proper perspective, consider the first preliminary experiment conducted in preparation for this research. The same experimental procedures were followed as outlined in this study. The authors hypothesized that the modular version would be faster to modify. The mean time for the monolithic group, however, turned out to be slightly <u>less</u> than for the modular group. This unexpected result led to a careful reexamination of the theoretical basis underlying modularity which resulted in the development of the framework illustrated in **Figure** 3 and the realization that the modification was an element of U - (A U B C). Thus contrary to our original expectations, even well designed modular programs are not always faster to modify than their monolithic counterparts. This is true even when the modification calls for additions that are spread throughout the source code of the original program.

Suggestions for Future Research

This research has only examined the presence of modularity verses the absence of modularity. Further research needs to be done concerning the levels of modularity. A next step could be to test the rankings of different kinds of modules as theorized by Stevens, Myers and Constantine (20).

One could also look at the effect of modularity on program development time. Is development time really shortened due to earlier and more thorough testing possibilities? Are modular programs less error prone?

There is a pressing need for basic psychological research on programmers and experimental design for testing software engineering theory. Until some of these basic problems are solved, successful empirical research in software engineering will remain limited to areas where the magnitude of the treatment effects is very large.

Acknowledgments

The authors are indebted to Bill Cotterman, Bikram Garcha, Robert Elrod,

Martha Hansard, Roger Lamprey, Arthur Nevins, Mark Rice, William Richardson, and James Senn for invaluable help at various stages of the work reported in the paper.

REFERENCES

1. G. D. Bergland, "A Guided Tour of Program Design Methodologies," _Computer_, Vol 12 (1981), 13-37.
2. R. E. Brooks, "Studying Programmer Behavior Experimentally: The Problems of Proper Methodology," _Communications of the ACM_, Vol 23 (1980), 207-213.
3. Bill Curtis, _IEEE Tutorial: Human Factors in Software Development_, IEEE, New York, 1981.
4. Bill Curtis, "Substantiating Programmer Variability," _Proceedings of the IEEE_, Vol 69 (1981), 846.
5. T. R. G. Green, "Conditional program statements and their comprehensibility to professional programmers," _Journal of Occupational Psychology_, Vol. 50 (1977), 93-109.
6. T. D. Korson, "An Empirical Study of the Effects of Modularity on Program Modifiability," Ph.D. dissertation proposal, Georgia State Univ., unpublished, 1985.
7. B. Lientz, "Issues in Software Maintenance," _ACM Computing Surveys_, Vol 15 (1983), 271-278.
8. L. T. Love, "Relating individual differences in computer programming performance to human information processing abilities," Ph.D. Dissertation, University of Washington, Unpublished, 1977.
9. H. C. Lucas and R.B. Kaplan, "A Structured programming experiment," _The Computer Journal_, Vol. 19 (1974), 136-138.
10. D. L. Parnas, "On the Criteria to Be Used in Decomposing Systems into Modules," _Communications of the ACM_, Vol 15 (1972), 1053-1058.
11. D. L. Parnas, "Designing Software for Ease of Extension and Contraction," _IEEE Transactions on Software Engineering_, Vol 5 (1979).
12. Svend Ryge, "Evaluating Structured COBOL as a Software Engineering Discipline," _Data Base_, (1981), 3-6.
13. H. Sachman, W.T. Ericson, and E.E. Grant, "Exploratory experimental studies comparing online and offline programming performance," _Communications of the ACM_, Vol 11 (1968), 3-11.
14. B. A. Sheil, "The Psychological Study of Programming," _Computing Surveys_, Vol 13 (1981), 101-120.
15. S. Shepard, B. Curtis, P. Milliman, and T. Lowe, "Modern Coding Practices and Programmer Performance," _Computer_, Vol. 12 (1979), 41-49.
16. Ben Shneiderman, R. Miara, J. Musselman, and J. Navarro, "Program Indentation and Comprehensibility," _Communications of the ACM_, Vol. 26 (1983), 861-867.
17. M. E. Sime, T.R.G. Green, and D.J. Guest, "Psycological evaluation of two conditional constructions used in computer languages," _International Journal Man-Machine Studies_, Vol. 5 (1973), 123-143.
18. E. Sime, T.R.G. Green, and D.J. Guest, "Scope marking in Computer Conditionals - A Psychological evaluation," _International Journal Man-Machine Studies_, Vol. 9 (1977), 107-118.
19. E. Soloway, J. Bonar, and Kate Ehrlich, "Cognitive Strategies and Looping Constructs: An Empirical Study," _Communications of the ACM_, Vol. 26 (1983), 853-860.
20. Stevens, Myers, and Constantine, "Structured Design," _IBM Systems Journal_, Vol 13 (1974), 115-139.
21. Iris Vessey and Ron Weber, "Some Factors Affecting Program Repair Maintenance: An Empirical Study," _Communications of the ACM_, Vol 26, (1983), 128-134.
22. Iris Vessey and Ron Weber, "Research on Structured Programming: An Empiricist's Evaluation," _IEEE Transactions on Software Engineering_, Vol SE-10 (1984), 397-407.
23. L. Weissman, "Psychological Complexity of Computer Programs: An Experimental Methodology," _SIGPLAN Notices_, Vol. 9 (1974), 25-36.

CHAPTER 13

Experiments on Slicing-Based Debugging Aids*

Mark Weiser
Jim Lyle
Computer Science Department
University of Maryland
College Park, MD 20742

ABSTRACT

Programming slicing is a method for reducing the amount of code looked at when debugging or understanding programs. Previous work concentrated on showing that programmers mentally slice during debugging. We present new work which concentrates on evaluating automatic tools for presenting slices to the debugging programmer. For one such tool, an online window-based editor/compiler/slicing system, we were unable to show that slicing helped. A second experiment, pencil and paper this time, presented programmers with *dices* of programs. A dice is a slice on incorrect variables from which slices on correct variables have been removed. Programmers using the dicing tool debugged their programs significantly faster than unaided programmers.

1. Introduction

Debugging and maintaining computer programs, especially programs written by someone else, is a difficult and time consuming task. Among other things, the programmer needs to understand how a program produced a particular result so that the program behavior can be modified.

One aid to understanding is to reduce the amount of detail a programmer sees by extracting only relevant information. An application of data-flow analysis, program slicing, can be used to transform a large program into a smaller one containing only those

---

*Research supported in part by AFOSR contract #82-0303 and by the NASA Goddard Human Factors Committee.

statements relevant to the computation of a given output [12].

A previous experiment showed that programmers mentally construct slices when debugging[11]. However, in spite of some preliminary experiments[9, 5] the efficacy of slicing-based tools remains to be proven. We present here studies of debugging with the aid of two different automatic slicing tools.

2. Debugging Tools

Psychological theories of debugging and tools for debugging are not often linked. Before describing the tools we built based on slicing theory it is useful to review the range of other debugging tools, including that most common one: no tool at all.

2.1. Debugging Without Tools

A study of software engineering practices of 30 companies found only 27 percent using some type of testing tool[14]. They attributed the low usage to several factors, among them a perceived high cost of tool usage, managers lacking software experience, and previous experience with incomplete and poorly documented tools. One is therefore not surprised to find that often the reaction to the question, "are there any debugging tools available on our computer" is not "yes, and it works great," but instead "well, yes, but you don't want to use it." This somewhat negative reaction to debugging tools and experimental results [3] that suggest code reading may be the most effective debugging approach, has lead some authors, Myers, for example, to advocate avoiding automatic tools except as a last resort [8]. What Myers does advocate is a cycle of think, generate hypotheses from the program behavior and other known facts, and test the generated hypotheses until the error is found.

2.2. Debugging With Tools

Debugging tools have evolved through three generations from the first memory dump programs to sophisticated systems that sometimes can locate faulty statements.

The first generation of tools provides information in terms of the underlying machine architecture. These tools, often called *low level debuggers,* are the memory dumps and absolute instruction traces found on most systems. An example of an interactive first generation tool is the Unix **adb**[7].

The second generation of tools provides information in terms of the programming language used to write the program. The information provided by these tools, often called *high level debuggers* or *symbolic debuggers,* is available immediately for the programmer's use. He does not need to determine answers to questions like "what is the memory address of variable X", so that he can examine the value of X from the memory dump. Examples of this kind of tool are the Unix sdb and dbx, VAX DEBUG[1], and the PLUM system[13].

The third generation of tools does more than provide raw information. These tools try to make some deduction about the presence and location of faults in the program. Two examples of third generation tools are DAVE [2] a tool that finds likely errors by examining the data-flow relationships of variables, and FALOSY [10] a debugging expert-system.

A fourth kind of system, not so much a debugging tool as a tool for understanding bugs, is represented by the Proust system[4]. Systems like Proust could eventually evolve into intelligent debugging aids.

3. Debugging With Program Slices

A program slice is computed on a set of variables at a given statement. The resulting subset of program statements are all statements relevant to the computation of the set of variables at the given statement.

Since a program slice contains all statements that could have influenced the value of a variable at some statement, if the printed value of some variable is incorrect then the *bug* should be evident somewhere in the slice on that variable at that print statement (but see exception, below). As an example, consider the following program intended to compute some simple statistics.

The right hand side of line 8 of the program in Figure 1 should have "sum + x(i)" instead of "x(i)." If we have a *reliable* testing method, i.e., one that shows the existence of faults, then we would discover through testing that the value computed for *avg* was incorrect. At this point the usual approach is to examine the entire program to try to locate the fault. Using program slicing we would first compute the slice on *avg* at line 16 and examine the resulting program slice for the fault. Figure 2 presents the slice on *avg* at line 16. All reference to the *std* computation that is irrelevant to the computation of *avg* has been removed so that the programmer can examine a smaller program in search of the fault.

A slice computed at the output statement on an incorrectly valued output variable does not always contain the fault. For example, if the statement at line 8 in the program of Figure 1 were changed to:

$$8 \quad 20 \quad ssq = sum + x(i)$$

then a slice (see Figure 3) on *avg* at line 16 would not contain line 8, the incorrect statement. However, comparison of the slice on *avg* with the program specifications in Figure 3 would show that the computation of *avg* does not meet the specifications. Further slicing would cast suspicion on lines 7 and 8 since these lines do not appear in the slice of any output variable. Also, data-flow analysis would show that the value of *ssq* computed by lines 7 and 8 is never used (line 9 assigns *ssq* before the value could be used) and hence an error should be suspected on those lines.

4. A slicing environment – no significant advantage

Our first experiment evaluating slicing-based aids had no statistically significant results. It is nonetheless a useful lesson in the problems of evaluating tools, and so worth discussing briefly. More details are in Lyle's thesis[6].

In evaluating a new tool the Hawthorne effect is a constant menace. In the short time of the experiment subjects may react more to the newness of the tool than to any specific quality. To control for this we created a completely new multi-window programming environment called Focus. Subjects performing both slicing and non-slicing tasks were required to work in Focus, which had its own editor, compiler, and user interface (including help system). The only user interface difference between treatments is that during some tasks users had an extra command, *slice*, in their pop-up menu.

In spite of this careful control, a randomized order within-subjects design, and learning trials, we were unable to show that having a slicing tool helped reduce debugging time. If anything the trend was the other way: slicer users took a little longer to debug, possibly because they were playing with their new command.

This experimental result was disappointing because it had seemed to follow from the mental use of slices that a slicing aid would be useful. Perhaps more learning time, or larger programs (ours were around 100 lines) would have given a different result. In post-experiment interviews subjects did say they liked having the slicing command. Or, perhaps, slicing is like watching a beautiful sunset – a computer *can* do it, but it just isn't the same.

Figure 1
Stat: Program to Compute Average and Standard Deviation

```
1                subroutine stat(n,avg,std)
2                real x(20)
3                read (8,100)n
4                do 10 i = 1,n
5        10      read (8,200)x (i)
6                sum = 0
7                do 20 i = 1,n
8        20      sum = x (i)
9                ssq = 0
10               do 30 i = 1,n
11       30      ssq = ssq + x(i)**2
12               avg = sum/n
13               std = sqrt(ssq - n*avg**2)/(n-l))
14               print 300,n
15               print 600,(x(i),i = 1,n)
16               print 400,avg
17               print 500,std
18               return
19       100     format (15)
20       200     format (f10.0)
21       300     format ('n =',15)
22       400     format ('avg =',f10.4)
23       500     format ('std =',f10.4)
24       600     format ('x = ',15f4.0)
25               end
```

Figure 2
Slice from Stat on avg at Line 16

```
1                subroutine stat(n,avg,std)
2                real x(20)
3                read (8,100)n
4                do 10 i = 1,n
5        10      read (8,200)x(i)
6                su, = 0
7                do 20 i = 1,n
8        20      sum = x(i)
12               avg = sum/n
16               print 400,avg
18               return
19       100     format (i5)
20       200     format (f10.0)
22       400     format ('avg = ',f10.4)
25               end
```

Figure 3

Slice from Incorrect Program Does Not Contain Fault

(Slice on avg at 16)

```
1        subroutine stat(n,avg,std)
2        real x(20)
3        read (8,100)n
6        sum = 0
12       avg = sum/n
16       print 400,avg
19 100        format (i5)
22 400 format ('avg =',f10.4)
25       end
```

Figure 4

Specifications for Program of Figure 3

INPUT:

n Number of elements in array X

X Array of n real numbers

OUTPUT:

n Number of elements in array X

avg Sum of elements in X divided by n

std Standard deviation of elements in X

5. Evaluation of Dicing – it seems to help

Our second experiment was more successful. Previous work on using slicing for debugging uses only the information that some variables are computed incorrectly. It does not use the other information gained from testing that some variables might be correct.

5.1. Introduction to Dicing

We propose a method, called *dicing, which combines multiple slices to further refine the location of* program faults. Dicing is a heuristic only, but in practice [6] seems to be a good one. Dicing starts like slicing, with a slice on variables with incorrect values. The fault is likely in this slice. Dicing then separately slices on variables with correct values, and makes the assumption that the fault is unlikely to be in this slice. Combining these two slices gives the basic dice: the slice on incorrect variables *less* the slice on correct variables.

In discussing dicing it is convenient to distinguish two sets of variables. The first set, called *KBI* (known to be incorrect) contains all the variables which testing has identified as containing incorrect values. The second set, call *CSF* (correct so far) contains variables which testing has identified as correct. *Dicing* is the following procedure: (1) slice on KBI. (2) slice on CSF. (3) Remove from slice (1) the statements in slice (2). The result is a dice. (More details are in Lyle [6]).

Dicing depends on three assumptions:

(1) Testing has been reliable and all incorrectly computed variables have been identified.

(2) If the computation of a variable, v, depends on the computation of another variable, w, then whenever w has an incorrect value then v does also.

(3) There is exactly one fault in the program.

191

The three assumptions are necessary for the correct operation of dicing. If testing has not identified all incorrectly computed variables then we could have the following situation: A single fault could cause two variables to be incorrectly valued while unreliable testing identifies only one variable as a member of KBI and incorrectly places the other variable in CSF. If these two variables are used for dicing the faulty statement would not be included in the dice.

If the second dicing assumption does not hold then variables that depend on the faulty statement could be placed in CSF and hence dicing would fail to include the faulty statement. This could also happen if a second fault canceled the incorrect value for some of the output variables.

As an example of dicing, consider the program fragment in Figure 5.

If the intended output for Y is $2A^2$ and the intended value for Z is A^2-2 instead of A^2+2, we would go through the following steps to isolate the fault to line four.

(1) Execute the program with reliable test data. The result of such a test would be that the value for Z was not correct and that the value for Y was correct.

Figure 5
Dicing Example

```
1        Get (A);
2        L := A**2;
3        Y := L*2;
4        Z := L + 2;
5        Put (Y,Z);
```

---

(2) Slice on the incorrectly valued variable Z, at line 5. This restricts our attention to lines, 1,2,4, and 5.

(3) Slice on the correctly valued variable, Y at line 5. This identifies lines 1,2,3, and 5 as being correct.

(4) Considering the specification and the two slices together, the dice is statement 4, which contains minus instead of plus in the expression.

We are left with three issues:

(1) In general, how should we select the variables for slicing and dicing?

(2) How useful is dicing when the above assumptions are relaxed?

(3) How useful is dicing when people try to use it?

(1) and (2) are addressed in [6]. An experiment to evaluate (3) is discussed below.

5.2. An Experiment With Dicing

We evaluated how well programmers can use the information gained from dicing by introducing three faults into a program and timing how long ten programmers took to find the error, given the listing of a slice on a KBI variable with the dice highlighted. These times were compared to the times of ten programmers given the entire program listing without slicing as a debugging aid.

5.2.1. Hypotheses

Our central hypotheses is that programmers using the dicing information find faults faster than programmers using traditional methods. We also would like to check the hypothesis that there is no significant difference in the debugging ability of the control and experimental groups. Debugging ability is difficult to accurately measure so we tested the hypothesis that the background and experience between the two groups was not significantly different.

5.2.2. Subject Selection

We recruited subjects from the computer science graduate student population at the University of Maryland. We also recruited some subjects from the University of Maryland Computer Science Center's System Support staff and one physics graduate student with many years of FORTRAN experience.

Each subject was asked the following background questions:

(1) How long have you been programming?

(2) How many CMSC classes in your BS/BA?

(3) How many other CMSC classes?

(4) What programming languages are you familiar with?

(5) On a scale from 0 to 10, how good are you with FORTRAN?

We found that the subjects had a wide range and variety of experience. Table 1 summarizes the subject's responses.

Table 1 Background Summary						
Experimental Group Background						
name	N	mean	sd	min	max	median
years	10	9.7	6.4	2.0	19.0	7.5
bs-classes	10	7.2	4.4	0.0	13.0	7.5
other-classes	10	7.6	6.4	0.0	20.0	9.5
tot-classes	10	14.9	7.5	3.0	25.0	15.5
languages	10	5.9	2.5	3.0	12.0	5.5
skill	10	6.7	2.4	2.0	10.0	7.5
Control Group Background						
years	10	8.3	3.4	3.0	13.0	9.0
bs-classes	10	7.4	5.7	2.0	20.0	6.0
other-classes	10	4.3	5.8	0.0	15.0	1.0
tot-classes	10	11.7	8.7	2.0	27.0	8.5
languages	10	8.5	4.1	1.0	15.0	9.0
skill	10	7.2	2.6	2.0	10.0	7.0
Total Group Background						
years	20	9.0	5.0	2.0	19.0	9.0
bs-classes	20	7.3	5.0	0.0	20.0	6.5
other-classes	20	5.9	6.2	0.0	20.0	4.5
tot-classes	20	13.3	8.1	2.0	27.0	13.0
languages	20	7.2	3.6	1.0	15.0	6.5
skill	20	6.9	2.5	2.0	10.0	7.0

All subjects had at least two years experience programming and most subjects had at least nine. All subjects claimed to "know some FORTRAN", and most subjects claimed to feel "comfortable with FORTRAN," the language of the programs in the experiment. Table 2 shows how many subjects claimed

to be familiar with the given language. Some languages such as ALGOL and Forth had only one or two claimants and were omitted. In Table 2, assembler means any assembly language. Fifteen subjects were familiar with at least one assembler and six subjects with two or more. One likely difference between these subjects and real world programmers is that if the distribution of language familiarity for the subjects were compared with real world programmers, the frequency of PL/I and COBOL would be higher and the distribution of Lisp and C would be less.

A Mann-Whitney statistic, $U < 23$, is significant at the 0.05 level for a two tailed test with ten subjects in each group. As Table 3 shows, we found no significant difference between the background of the experimental and the control group subjects. We feel that we can conclude that any difference in performance between the two groups would be from the treatments applied to the groups.

Table 2	
Language Frequency	
Language	Number of Subjects
FORTRAN	20
Pascal	16
Assembler	15
C	13
Lisp	10
Basic	8
COBOL	6
SNOBOL	6
APL	6
PL/I	5

Table 3		
Mann-Whitney U for Background		
Variable	U	Low Group
years	48.0	cont
bs-classes	45.5	cont
other-classes	37.5	cont
tot-classes	39.5	cont
languages	28.0	exp
skill	43.0	exp

5.2.3. Procedures

The subject first answers a background questionaire and takes a practice treatment. They then are given an explanation of the program to be debugged and finally locate each of three bugs in a FORTRAN program. The goal of the practice treatment is to get the subject in the frame of mind for debugging, and remove any confusion about what he should be doing.

The practice treatment for the experimental group is an explanation of slicing and dicing and why they should help locate a program fault. The subject then locates a fault in a FORTRAN program that computes mean and standard deviation.

The control group is told that the experimenter is collecting data on how programmers debug programs and would he debug a small program, explaining what he is doing and thinking as he goes.

After the practice treatment, the experimenter gives an informal specification of the program to be debugged to both groups of subjects. The subject and experimenter discuss a sample correct output, variable naming conventions and the general algorithm used in the program until the subject understands the materials.

The procedure for measuring fault location time is to identify to the subject a variable as having been shown incorrect by testing. The subject is given (face down) a listing of the relevant slice with the diced set highlighted (the control group received a listing of the entire program). Timing begins when the subject turns over the listing and ends when he states that he has found the fault. If the subject has not correctly identified the fault, he is so informed and timing continues until the fault is correctly identified.

5.2.4. Materials

The experimental materials used are a survey form, the listing of a practice program, a description of how to use slicing and dicing for debugging, documentation to a FORTRAN program to compute statistics on letters, words, lines and sentences in a file, a listing of this program with three planted faults, and the listing of a program slice for each fault.

The practice program is a mean and standard deviation program written in FORTRAN with a fault installed in the initialization of the variable *sum*. This program was chosen because it is a practical program, easy for the subjects to understand, and yields clear slices. This program also refreshes the subject on statistics used in the experimental program so that, some learning (or maybe relearning) effects are removed.

Only the experimental group receives a description of how to use slicing and dicing along with sample slices from the practice program.

The documentation includes a description of what the program is supposed to do, a sample input, a sample correct output for the given input, and a table of major variables and their meaning. Since all three faults introduced into the experimental program involve minimums or maximums, included in the description is a generic explanation of how to compute a minimum or maximum. We want the subject to know what he is looking for; we do not want to measure how long it takes for him to remember how to compute a minimum.

The experimental program reads a file of text and computes descriptive statistics on the letters, words, lines, and sentences in the file. Since many algorithms follow a pattern of initialization, intermediate computation, result, we installed in the experimental program a fault in each one of these locations. A fault was placed in the result phase of the computation of the variable XWTS (maximum words per sentence), the intermediate computation phase of MLETTL (minimum letters per line), and the initialization of MWTL (minimum words per line).

5.3. Experimental Results

Warm-up is the time spent from beginning to fill out the questionaire until the subject is ready to start looking for the faults in the experimental program. Total-time is the total time spent looking for faults (XWTS + MLETTL + MWTL). The Table 4 summarizes the raw data on debugging times.

The Table 5 presents Mann-Whitney U statistics for testing the null hypothesis that there is no difference in performance between the two groups. A U value < 23 is significant at the 0.025 level for a one-tailed test. As shown in Table 5, we found a significant difference between the experimental and control group performance on two of the three faults and for the time to locate all the faults.

Table 4 Debug Times Summary						
Name						
Experimental Group						
XWTS	10	97.4	131.3	22.0	461.0	53.5
MLETTL	10	162.8	106.2	69.0	413.0	123.0
MWTL	10	19.0	16.2	6.0	54.0	12.0
Warm Up	10	761.1	237.2	453.0	1160.0	744.0
Total Time	10	279.2	239.4	111.0	928.0	207.0
Control Group						
XWTS	10	192.9	112.3	54.0	364.0	174.0
MLETTL	10	309.9	181.1	87.0	651.0	267.0
MWTL	10	67.2	97.7	7.0	312.0	23.5
Warm Up	10	642.7	124.9	416.0	879.0	630.5
Total Time	10	570.0	257.3	273.0	1026.0	508.5
Total Group						
XWTS	20	145.1	128.6	22.0	461.0	85.0
MLETTL	20	236.4	163.0	69.0	651.0	192.5
MWTL	20	43.1	72.5	6.0	312.0	17.0
Warm-Up	20	701.9	194.2	416.0	1160.0	641.5
Total-Time	20	424.6	284.2	111.0	1026.0	325.0

It should be pointed out that the non-statistically significant fault (MWTL) is on the boundary of the critical region (U < 27) for the 0.05 level of significance, and that the median time to locate this fault was less than 20 seconds. We observed that the subjects who took the longest to find this fault were members of the control group using a backward search method. Since the fault was with the initialization of MWTL, the subjects took much time working back to the beginning of the program.

Table 5 Mann-Whitney U for Debugging Times		
Variable	U	Low Group
XWTS	19.0	exp
MLETTL	20.0	exp
MWTL	27.5	exp
Total-Time	13.0	exp
Warm-Up	37.0	control

6. Summary and Conclusions

A pencil and paper based simulation of a slicing-based tool was shown to be useful. Despite great effort at designing a homogeneous interactive environment and data collection tool, a slicing tool in that environment could not be shown useful. Possibly the novelty of that environment added enough noise to make any differences among individual tools. Others attempting to measure tools in new environments should be wary of the environmental noise. Dicing was quite successful and may one day be found in every programmer's toolkit.

REFERENCES

[1]   Bert Beander. "VAX DEBUG: An interactive, symbolic multilingual debugger." *SIGPLAN Notices* **18**, 8, pp. 173-179, August 1983. (Proceedings of the ACM SIGSOFT/SIGPLAN Software Engineering Symposium on High-Level Debugging)

[2]   L. D. Fosdick and L. J. Osterweil. "Data flow analysis in software reliability." *ACM Computing Surveys* **8**, 3, pp. 305-330, September 1976.

[3]   J. D. Gould and P. Drongowski. "An exploratory study of computer program debugging." *Human Factors* **1**, 6, pp. 258-277, 1974.

[4]   W. L. Johnson and E. Soloway. "PROUST: Knowledge-Based Program Understanding." *IEEE Transactions on Software Engineering* **SE-11**, 3, pp. 267-275, March 1985.

[5]   Herbert D. Longworth. Sliced-based Program Metrics. M.S. Thesis, Michigan Technological University 1985.

[6]   J. Lyle. "Evaluating Variations on Program Slicing for Debugging." Ph.D Dissertation, Computer Science Dept University of Maryland, Dec 1984.

[7]   J. F. Maranzano and S. R. Bourne. "A tutorial introduction to Adb." pp. 323-350 in *Unix Programmer's Manual Volume 2,* Holt, Rinehart, and Winston, 1983.

[8]   Glenford J. Myers. *The Art of Software Testing.* John Wiley and Sons, 1979.

[9]   K.J. Ottenstein and L.M. Ottenstein. "The Program Dependence Graph in a Software Development Environment." pp. 177-184 in *Proceeding of the ACM SIGSOFT/SIGPLAN Software Engineering Symposium of Practical Software Development Environments,* ed. P. Henderson, ACM SIGPLAN, SIGSOFT Engineering Notes, Pittsburgh, Penn., April 23-25, 1984.

[10]   Robert L. Sedlmeyer and William B. Thompson. "Knowledge-based fault localization in debugging." *SIGPLAN Notices* **18**, 8, pp. 30-41, August 1983. (Proceedings of the ACM SIGSOFT/SIGPLAN Software Engineering Symposium on High-Level Debugging)

[11]   Mark Weiser. "Programmers Use Slices When Debugging." *Communications of the ACM* **25**, 7, pp. 446-452, July, 1982.

[12]   Mark Weiser. "Program slicing." *IEEE Transactions on Software Engineering* **SE-10**, 4, pp. 352-357, July 1984.

[13]   Marvin V. Zelkowitz. *PL/I Programming with PLUM.* Paladin House, Geneva, Illinois, 1976.

[14]   Marvin V. Zelkowitz, Raymond T. Yeh, Richard G. Hamlet, John D. Gannon, and Victor R. Basili. "Software engineering practices in the US and Japan." *Computer* **17**, 6, pp. 57-65, June 1984.

CHAPTER 14

A Model of Novice Debugging in LISP[1]

Claudius M. Kessler
John R. Anderson
Department of Psychology
Carnegie-Mellon University
Pittsburgh, PA 15213

ABSTRACT

This paper reports an investigation of novice programmers trying to debug one-line LISP functions. We present a model of debugging based on protocol data and introduce a production system simulation of the ideal novice debugger. We conclude with a discussion of the applicability of such a model to the teaching of programming in LISP.

INTRODUCTION

A large part of the professional activity of a computer programmer consists of debugging programs. In programming courses, however, debugging is hardly ever treated as a skill that needs to be taught. Although it is generally acknowledged that bugs occur frequently and slow down the programming of novices as well as experts, the novice must acquire the skill to correct bugs on his own. There is some help available in the form of debugging tools that exist in most programming languages. Frequently, however, these tools are based on an advanced understanding of the language, and novices do not even know about their existence. In many programming courses, structured programming is explicitly taught with the implication that it will make debugging of programs easier, but there is no actual instruction in debugging itself.

Debugging has been the target of previous research in cognitive science. However, the outcome of this research usually is geared towards developing programming tools for debugging. Rich & Waters (1), for example, propose a programmer's apprentice that, among other things, helps to debug programs. They represent the knowledge about programs as programming plans. Debugging consists of modifying plans so they fit a given programming situation. These plans can then be translated into code by the apprentice. The PROUST model by Johnson & Soloway (2) examines Pascal programs and discovers bugs if they violate certain programming structures such as looping constructs. In this way it develops a model of the programmer's intentions that allows it to pinpoint errors in the code. The basic knowledge of PROUST rests in programming plans similar to those discussed by Rich & Waters (1).

---

[1]

This research has been supported by Contract MDA903-85-K-0343 from the Army Research Institute.

There have been a number of psychological studies looking at novice-expert differences in debugging (3, 4, 5, 6) and subjects' ability to deal with different kinds of bugs (7, 8, 9, 10, 11). However, to date, the only detailed process model of debugging is that proposed by Carver & Klahr (12). They developed an ideal production system model for debugging LOGO programs. The model is ideal in the sense that it is not based on data, but on a task analysis. It is supposed to capture the processes that go into debugging as done by an experienced, but not yet expert programmer. Carver & Klahr distinguish four phases in the debugging process: program evaluation, bug identification, bug location, and bug correction. The program evaluation phase compares the program output and the expected correct output. The bug identification phase creates one or more discrepancy descriptions which help to narrow the search for the program statement containing the bug. The bug location process actually searches the code for the buggy statement. Its effectiveness depends largely on the specificity of the descriptions created in the previous phase. In the bug correction phase, the buggy code gets replaced by new code, and a new evaluation is initiated. The productions in the model draw on four sources of information: the correct solution, the program output, the code, and knowledge of the programming language.

Studies on novice programmers tend to use a rather lenient definition of novice. Most so-called novices have received about a semester's course worth of instruction in the language they are tested in. True novices, people who have received little or no instruction in the language might show the difficulties inherent in debugging more clearly than these more experienced subjects. Furthermore, the effectiveness of instructional manipulations such as the timing of instruction, and teaching subskills can be more readily investigated if novices are tested in the process of acquiring a language.

In our study, we use true LISP novices, people with no previous instruction in LISP, to study the process of debugging. We want to present a theoretical outline of debugging based on data from protocol studies on the behavior of these novices. To make this theory more tractable, we formulated a production system model of debugging based on these results. The data consist of eight protocols of novice programmers who were taught the first two lessons of a LISP course sequence, which covered the basic LISP functions and the writing of simple function definitions in LISP. Instead of letting our subjects write functions, they were given buggy functions and they had to find and correct the errors.

METHOD

Materials

The buggy and the correct versions of the LISP functions we used in this experiment are listed in the Appendix. The functions were selected from lesson 2 of the LISP tutor (13 (chapter 2), 14). They were designed to be simple, but increasingly more challenging exercises in writing LISP function definitions. In each of the functions, one and only one bug was introduced. The bugs were taken from protocols of students that went through the LISP tutor. All of the bugs seemed to present difficulties to students having their first encounter with the material covered in lesson 2. Six bugs were used, each appearing in two different LISP functions, resulting in a total of 12 buggy functions. Six more functions were taken from lesson 2 in their correct form. They served as distractor items.

Two of the six bugs were syntactic bugs. One parenthesized a variable, the other quoted a variable. Four of the bugs were of a semantic nature. In one case, functions that should have been embedded were not. The three remaining bugs dealt with list combination problems. In one case, the 'list'-command was omitted, in the second, 'append' was used instead of 'list', and finally, a 'reverse'-command was omitted in a list manipulation that included several command steps.

While the first five bugs were completely isomorphic for both functions they appeared in, the 'reverse'-bug was an exception. In the SNOC-problem (see the Appendix), the 'reverse' that was deleted was the outermost 'reverse', while in the ROTATER-problem (see the Appendix), the innermost reverse was deleted. Table 1 demonstrates the output obtained from the six bug types.

Table 1
The Output of the Bugged Functions

```
=>(first '(a b c))
Error: eval: Undefined function  x

=>(replace 'rings '(ties hats pants))
(x hats pants)

=>(ftoc 32)
17.77777777777778

=>(sqr 2)
4

=>(back '(a b c))
((c b a) (c b a))

=>(snoc 'd '(a b c))
(d c b a)

=>(rotater '(a b c d))
(d d c b)
```

Design and Procedure

The subjects in our study were eight Carnegie-Mellon University undergraduates who participated for course credit or pay. They did not know any LISP and their previous college level programming experience was limited to at most one introductory Pascal class.

Two sequences of functions were made up for each subject. Each sequence consisted of six different bugs in a fixed order. The order in which the bugs were presented was the same as shown in the Appendix. The functions were assigned randomly to the first or second sequence, with the exception of SNOC and ROTATER. SNOC always was the last function in the first sequence, and ROTATER was the last function in the second sequence. This was done because our experience from tutoring lesson 2 indicated that the ROTATER problem was more difficult than any of the other problems in lesson 2. Furthermore, it seemed to us that the bug in ROTATER was harder to discover than the corresponding bug in SNOC.

The experiment was done over two days. On the first day, subjects went through an instruction booklet covering the material of lesson 1 of the LISP tutor. Basically, this included an introduction to LISP functions and the use of variables. They had to do exercises on a terminal using a LISP environment with some added user-friendly features. Each subject was run individually.

On the second day, subjects went through an instruction booklet that explained how to write function definitions in LISP. The experimenter then gave an introduction to the verbal protocol technique, including an example of going through the process of writing a function call. Subjects were then asked to solve the problems in the instruction booklet on the terminal, using the same LISP environment as on day 1. Each subject received two sequences of nine functions, containing six buggy and three correct functions. While all of the bugs were presented in the same order in each sequence, the correct functions that were used as distractors were distributed semi-randomly, with the restrictions that no two correct problems could follow one another, and that they were neither in the first nor in the last position of a sequence.

The buggy functions were loaded into the LISP environment. Thus, the subjects were able to call the function they were working on. Before calling the function, however, they had to predict if the code was correct or not. The subjects were requested to talk aloud about their problem solving during the debugging process. The experimenter made sure that the subject did not stay silent for a prolonged period of time by prompting them to talk. The subjects were told that they should feel free to ask the experimenter for assistance if they found a problem unsolvable. Assistance was given in the form of different kinds of hints: if subjects followed a wrong path, they were told to back up, otherwise they were given an explanation of a part of the code. This explanation was the same for all subjects, and was constructed as to not give away the solution directly. This process was repeated until the subjects arrived at the correct solution. One of the verbal protocols was lost due to equipment failure.

In addition to the protocols, we obtained data from the terminal interactions which were recorded and time stamped. Each terminal interaction was either a completed command to run a function with some arguments or a function definition typed in by the subject.

RESULTS AND DISCUSSION

The average solution times and the number of terminal interactions for our eight subjects are shown in Table 2. These measures seemed more informative than the number of hints given per problem, since, due to the simplicity of the functions, there were hardly more than two hints given for each function. The time and terminal interaction data were submitted to analyses of variance with sequence and tasks as within-subject factors. There was a main effect of sequence for both times and terminal interactions (times: $F(1, 7) = 39.73$, $p < .001$; terminal interactions: $F(1, 7) = 8.28$, $p < .05$). Subjects took longer to work through the initial sequence of six tasks and typed in more statements overall. While there were no further significant results for the terminal interaction data, the solution times showed a main effect of tasks ($F(5, 35) = 13.16$, $p < .001$) and a significant interaction between sequence and tasks ($F(5, 35) = 9.34$, $p < .001$). However, if the first and last problems of the sequence are excluded from the Anova, the interaction between sequence and task goes away. Subjects speed up much more on the first problem, presumably reflecting the fact that they are adjusting to the task on the first problem. The last problem was the only problem that was not counterbalanced for the two sequences, with the more difficult problem always occuring in the second sequence. Individual t-tests for speedup between sequence 1 and 2 revealed a significant speed-up only for tasks 1, 2,and 4 (1: $t(7) = 5.49$, $p < .001$; 2: $t(7) = 3.31$, $p < .05$; 4: $t(7) = 3.02$, $p < .05$). Speed-up on tasks 3 and 5 falls just short of significance (3: $t(7) = 1.97$, $p < .09$; 5: $t(7) = 1.89$, $p < .1$). The speed-up for task 6 is quite weak statistically ($t(7) = .61$).

The main effect of tasks seems to be tied to task 1 in the first sequence and to the last task in the second sequence. An analysis of variance for

Table 2
Mean Completion Times and Terminal Interactions (in Parentheses)

Bug	First Pass	Second Pass
1 Parentheses	28:19 (7.62)	5:49 (3.75)
2 Quote	6:23 (3.50)	3:03 (2.87)
3 No Embedding	6:48 (4.87)	2:56 (2.75)
4 No Combiner	13:33 (5.00)	4:53 (5.00)
5 Wrong Combiner	8:59 (6.87)	4:42 (3.37)
6 Missing Reverse	10:39 (6.37)	9:26 (3.75)

Note: N = 8 for each cell. Times in minutes and seconds.

sequence 1, with the first task excluded, shows only a marginal effect of tasks ($F(4, 28) = 2.28$, $p < .09$). Similarly, an analysis of variance for sequence 2 with the last task (ROTATER) excluded, does not show a main effect of tasks at all ($F(4, 28) = 1.79$, $p < .16$).

The reason subjects took so long to complete the first problem was that they did not really understand how to write function definitions in LISP. They had extracted virtually nothing from reading the problem instructions. This finding ties in with other research on learning to program in LISP, e.g. (15). Anderson (16) found that subjects show over a 50% speed-up from the first function they code in lesson 1 of the LISP tutor to the second function. In our experiment, most of the time in the first problem was taken up by the experimenter giving a hands-on demonstration of a LISP function definition. Once subjects seemed to have grasped the LISP function definition form, their behavior in problem 1 followed pretty much the same course as in the other problems.

The ROTATER problem proved to be the most difficult in the experiment. As mentioned before, there are two factors contributing to this. First, the function is more complex than any other of the 12 problems, and second, the bug in ROTATER was harder to find than the bug in the related problem, SNOC. The process of debugging ROTATER will receive more consideration below.

The quantitative data give a fairly obvious picture of the subjects' performance. Subjects take an extraordinarily long time to do the very first problem, then spend about the same time on all the other problems in the first sequence. When the bugs are repeated, subjects speed up considerably, with the exception of the last problem, ROTATER which has a slightly different bug and which we had predicted would be more difficult. Since the terminal interaction data do not add any further information, they will not be considered here.

A THEORY OF DEBUGGING

In order to find an explanation for the pattern of results we obtained, and to get a better idea of the processes that go on in debugging, we considered protocol data from our subjects. The six bugs we used seemed to be sufficiently distinct to produce no transfer of debugging from one bug to the other. Yet, the protocols lead us to believe that most subjects used the same debugging strategy for all problems. We now want to characterize this general debugging strategy we could extract from the protocols.

The debugging process could essentially be broken down into four episodes.

These were code comprehension, bug detection, bug localization, and bug repair. The first two of these episodes were usually short, and there is not much evidence about the mental processes taking place in the protocols. The bug localization and bug repair episodes provide the bulk of our protocol data. We now turn to a discussion of the processes going on in the different episodes.

The Debugging Episodes

Code Comprehension. Most subjects started out by trying to understand what the code was doing. The reading of the code at this time was rather superficial. Subjects often gave wrong judgments when asked to predict if the code was correct before they were allowed to run it. In the best case, they came out of this comprehension process with correct hypotheses of the code's behavior; in the worst case, they skipped the code comprehension and just took a guess about the correctness of the function. In general, they formed wrong hypotheses about the code, either because they did not try hard enough to understand it, or because they did not have the necessary LISP knowledge available at this point.

Bug Detection. The next step subjects took was to run the code. This was an obvious step, which usually led the subjects to detect the error. Subjects made very few comments during this stage. Since bug detection includes the process of describing the difference between the desired and the obtained results, it is possible that our tasks were sufficiently simple that subjects did not need to go through an elaborate process in order to compare the correct and the buggy answer.

Bug Localization. This episode consisted in actually finding the piece of code that was responsible for the error. For most subjects, this was a difficult problem solving process. The difficulty of this episode was enhanced, of course, if subjects had done the previous episodes improperly or not all. However, subjects usually could locate the bug in the code after going through some iterations of creating and rejecting hypotheses.

Bug Repair. This phase proved to be difficult independent of what had been going on in the previous phases. Even if subjects had found the bug and knew the faulty part of the code, it proved to be a hard task to come up with the correct code. This was the phase where most hints were given. If subjects made a correction that turned out to be wrong, there was a danger that they would get lost when they tried to correct their own initial correction. In these cases, the experimenter intervened and put them back on the track of the original function. Thus, while we estimate that this phase took longest for all our subjects, the time spent in correcting an identified error might be underestimated by our experimental procedure.

Evaluation

The sketch of the debugging process outlined above is supported by six of the seven protocols we obtained. There were no debugging episodes in these protocols that could not be accommodated by this scheme. There were of course additional processes going on, that in our view were less central to the debugging process. For example, subjects often looked for LISP function definitions they could not retrieve in memory, or they did checks on the syntax of the code they were writing. Subjects also made meta-comments about how hard or easy certain problems were.

The debugging process as described so far is by no means the only way to debug, even at a beginner's level of proficiency. In fact, one of our subjects displayed an entirely different strategy. The first thing he did when reading the problem was to actually generate the code in his mind. He then compared his code with the code actually presented. To the extent that he generated the correct code, his strategy proved more efficient than the one outlined so far. This strategy would work only for simple problems such as ours, of course.

Before we look into some issues concerning specific bugs, we have to address the question where the savings in time are coming from when going from the first to the second sequence. First we must note that sequence and bugs are confounded in our experiment, so that this result may be of limited validity. We believe, however, that we would have obtained some speed-up even with randomized repeated bug sequences, for an obvious reason: our subjects could remember at least some of the bugs. The protocols show some anecdotal evidence of bug recognition on the second pass. Since we did not explicitly give a recognition test, we do not know how frequently bugs actually were recognized. As the error data will show, bug repetition did not generally facilitate comprehension of the code. As it stands, we do not know if bug recognition is the only cause for the speed-up. However, the fact that we could not observe any speed-up within the two sequences favors the bug recognition explanation.

Bug Data

We conclude this section with a closer look at the bugs and the errors they triggered in our subjects. While we try to interpret the data in terms of our theory, it should be remembered that bug type was confounded with presentation sequence in our experiment. We therefore cannot exclude the possibility that the error distribution we obtained is at least in part due to the specific presentation sequence we used. Our main interest here is in the qualitative nature of the errors, and not so much in their distribution over tasks. Table 3 gives an overview of how the errors subjects made were distributed over the six bug types. The first column gives the comprehension errors, where subjects assumed that the function was working correctly, before they actually ran the code. The second column gives the errors in the bug location phase, and the third column gives the wrong repairs. Repair errors were only counted when a bug had been located correctly, and when a subject actually typed in the code as a correction for the bug. If an error had been made in the location phase, the

Table 3
Number of Errors for each Bug

Bug	First Pass			Second Pass			Overall		
	C	L	R	C	L	R	C	L	R
Parentheses	2	1	3	4	0	0	6	1	3
Quote	2	1	0	1	0	0	3	1	0
No Embedding	0	0	2	0	0	0	0	0	2
No Combiner	1	1	4	1	0	2	2	1	6
Wrong Combiner	1	2	3	1	0	2	2	2	5
Missing Reverse	0	2	3	1	1	1	1	3	4
Sum	6	7	15	8	1	5	14	8	20

Note: N = 7 for each cell. C = Comprehension, L = Location, R = Repair. See text for further explanations.

wrong repair that followed it was not counted as a repair error. The table gives the number of subjects that went wrong on a given problem in a given phase. Repeated errors within a phase were not counted. It should be noted that our subjects found the debugging process much harder than this error measure indicates. Subjects often made repeated errors on a problem, and considered many erroneous alternatives before they settled for one.

As can be seen, there is a 50% reduction of errors between the first and the second sequence. Interestingly, this reduction occurs only for the errors in the location and the repair phase, while errors in comprehension stay at the same level. In addition, the errors were not distributed evenly across tasks. The comprehension errors concentrated on the syntactic bugs, while the repair errors occured mainly with bugs that had to do with list manipulation. Locating a bug once an error had been detected was the easiest problem in all of our tasks. Below we discuss the bugs in the order they were given to the subjects, noting is in which particular debugging episode subjects had difficulty with the bug.

Parenthesized Variable. This bug was very difficult to detect, even when it occured for the second time. Of all six bug types given to them, subjects most often accepted this bug as a correct solution (see Table 3). Once the bug was found (frequently with hints from the experimenter), correction was a problem only the first time around, when subjects were still unsure about how to write and evaluate function definitions.

Quoted Variable. This bug also turned out to be hard to detect. However, most subjects noted the quote in the function body as being rather unusual. Subjects seemed to detect the bug just because nothing else was wrong with the function. Again, correcting the bug was easy once it was detected.

No Embedding. This turned out to be the easiest bug for most of our subjects. They recognized immediately that to translate the mathematical formula, the LISP code had to be embedded. Some subjects had to think hard about how the correct embedding was to be done, but all came up with the correct solution in the end.

No Combiner. There was some problem in detecting this bug, but it turned out to be even harder to fix it. Subjects had trouble with the concept of creating a list to output two numbers, and often needed a hint to find the bug. Once the bug was found, there was the problem of finding the right combiner. Most subjects iterated at random through the three combiner functions they knew, without having an idea about their differences.

Wrong Combiner. Essentially, this problem showed the same characteristics as the previous one. However, this time some subjects had to be alerted to the fact that the combiner used produced a wrong parenthesization. Once parenthesization was detected as the problem, localization was not too difficult. To fix the problem, some subjects went through the same kind of combiner iteration they had used in the previous problem.

Missing Reverse. There are actually two bugs to consider. In SNOC, the outer 'reverse' was left out, while in ROTATER, it was the inner 'reverse' (see the Appendix). Nobody had problems in detecting the error in SNOC. The main problem in SNOC was to detect the systematic relation between the correct answer and the output. Some subjects seemed to bypass this analysis and went straight to changing the code. This resulted in an inadequate correction, leading the subjects back to consider alternatives. At this point, two of the subjects decided to rewrite the code by using an (append <list> (list <atom>)) construction. The other subjects went back to the code, and discovered, with or without hints from the experimenter, that all they had to do was to reverse the output.

ROTATER posed a different problem. By the time they got to this problem, subjects had gathered some experience in debugging. Most of the subjects quickly located the error as being in the second argument to append. Opinions on how to

fix this error differed widely, however. Most subject found the correct
solution after exploring several erroneous paths and getting hints from the
experimenter. The complexity of the code left more correction paths open for the
subjects than the previous problems. This seems to account for the additional
time needed to solve this problem.

To summarize, it seems that we are able to attribute most of the typical
errors on a particular function to one of the debugging episodes we described.
The debugging process we presented thus should be able to serve as an ideal
model for novice debugging. The errors students make could be thought of as
deviations from this ideal model. The next section will describe a
computational model of the debugging process.

A PRODUCTION SYSTEM MODEL OF DEBUGGING

Overview

We developed a simulation of the student debugger written in GRAPES (17), a
goal-restricted production system language intended to implement an aspect of
the ACT* theory (18)[2]. GRAPES is distinguished from other production system
languages by its goal structure - productions must match to particular goals
before they can fire. One of the actions of a production can be to actually
create goals and subgoals. Thus, the goal-structure itself is created by
productions. This feature of GRAPES makes it particularly useful for modeling
the goal-directedness of human problem solving behavior. Figure 1 gives the goal
structure for the model.

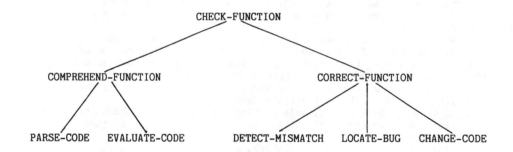

Figure 1
The Goal Tree

The model is started up by giving it a problem and initializing a top goal.
When the top goal is initialized, two subgoals are set up. The first subgoal
demands an evaluation of the function in order to comprehend it, while the
second one demands to find and correct the bug. To satisfy the comprehension
goal, the function is first parsed into the smallest units that can be

_____

2

The actual productions used and traces of their performance can be obtained
by writing to Claudius Kessler, Department of Psychology, Carnegie-Mellon
University, Pittsburgh, Pa 15213.

evaluated. The function is then evaluated according to the rules of LISP, with the result of every LISP function call being stored in working memory. The output that a given function call would produce is the final result of the comprehension phase.

Under the second subgoal, code correction, further subgoals are set up that in turn detect a bug, locate it, and finally change the code. This phase starts out with a goal to check the output for correctness. If it is found to be incorrect, the checking productions return a description of the discrepancy between the output and the correct answer. Under the localization subgoal, the evaluation results of all LISP function calls can then be compared to the discrepancy description, and the buggy part of the code can be located in this way. Once the bug is located, a final goal to change the buggy part of the code is instantiated. If a change can be made, the production system goes again through the evaluation cycle. If the output now matches the correct answer, the production system halts with a success message. If not, the system can go through another debugging cycle if its knowledge base indicates another possible change. If all possibilities are exhausted, the system halts with a failure message.

Examples

The production system was designed so it could handle all the bugs in the Appendix. These bugs could appear in any user-defined function as long as no other than the basic LISP functions were used. In order to see how the model works, examples of the functions FIRST, SQR, and ROTATER are given. In addition to the general working principles of the productions system, the FIRST function illustrates how syntactic bugs are handled, while SQR and ROTATER demonstrate how two aspects of suboptimal debugging that we observed in our protocols have been built in the model.

FIRST. The top-level production sets up the subgoals to parse the function and to match the output and the correct answer. Following LISP syntax, the parsing productions parse the code into the basic functions "car" with the argument "(x)" and, since "x" is in parentheses, it is further parsed as a function with no argument. Obviously, "x" is not a basic LISP function, and the evaluation productions cannot evaluate it. Thus, an error message is returned as the result of the first subgoal and the location of the error is marked as "x".

Since there is no answer to be matched, and the error is already located, the only thing that is left to do under the second subgoal is to change the code. This is done by the matching production that fires when there is a syntax error. It corrects the code, and on the second iteration of the debugging process, the code is recognized as correct.

SQR. In this case, the first subgoal returns with an evaluation. The result is a number, not a list. The match productions then evoke the DETECT-operator which gives the discrepancy description that there is no list. The discrepancy description is then used in the locate-productions to locate the error as a statement to make a list. Under the change-goal, a combiner function is inserted in the code. In this case the production system has incomplete knowledge about combiner functions. It randomly picks a combiner that has not been used yet. This turned out to be a typical novice strategy. Since there are only 3 possible statements, the debugging is guaranteed to succeed on the third iteration at worst.

ROTATER. Again, the first subgoal is completed with the return of an evaluation. The match-productions again evoke the DETECT operator which returns with a discrepancy description pointing to the part of the answer list that is wrong. The locate-productions then locate the part of the code which is responsible for the wrong part of the answer list. The system then goes off into a simple means-ends analysis, trying to substitute code so it gets the correct second element of the list. This is another novice strategy we observed. Since this approach does not produce the correct code, it is abandoned. Our students also tended to give up this strategy when it did not lead to immediate success. It then sets a goal to use the functions in the code in order to find the right answer, a strategy that was given as a hint when students got lost. In this way, it finally arrives at inserting the missing reverse. The function is then checked again and is found correct.

GENERAL DISCUSSION

The model completely specifies the processes necessary to debug the functions in the Appendix. It does so by breaking down the debugging processes into episodes. These episodes closely match the performance of human novices on the same tasks. While we tried to implement some of the ineffective strategies human novices show, we did not impose other limitations on the production system. Our system, for example, does not have any working memory limitations that lead to a buggy performance. Anderson & Jeffries (19) have shown that these working memory limitations account for a large part of the inferior performance of novices. It is possible and highly likely that the knowledge our subjects had about LISP was in a state where it was highly capacity demanding. Thus, working memory limitations probably account for some of the performance we observed in our subjects. This goes for forgetting the exact specification of a LISP function as well as for forgetting intermediate results or goals that have been established.

Another aspect of our system that may not be true of the human novices is the strict goal hierarchy. The behavior of our novices was not as goal-directed as our system is. Subjects often floundered and went off into some trial-and-error behavior until they were brought back on track by the experimenter. We think that our model nevertheless captures all the steps a novice is in fact going through when debugging a problem flawlessly.

In our protocols, we observed several ways in which our subjects' performance was suboptimal. Our model captures some of the ways in which a novice can perform ineffectively. It further allows us to identify the subskill in which the performance flaw is occuring. We know for example that detecting a bug does not guarantee that it also can be corrected, and vice versa, that a person who has enough knowledge of LISP to write functions correctly, does not necessarily recognize a given bug. Since the model attributes performance lapses to different episodes, it could be useful as a diagnostic tool for identifying weaknesses in a beginning programmer's knowledge.

The research reported in this paper also has implications for the teaching of debugging. It became clear that debugging is a skill that does not immediately follow from the ability to write code. Rather, it consists of several subskills that can and must be taught in addition to instructions about how to write programs. These subskills include the ability to evaluate code correctly, to be able to locate errors by parsing the code and matching it with the results obtained, and the ability to generate correct code to fix the bug.

In our model, we could simulate the debugging process as we extracted it from the protocols, including some inefficient strategies our novice subjects were using. With more data on the debugging behavior of novices on different functions, we should get a more complete picture of the possible strategies and novice inefficiencies associated with debugging subskills. An extended production system could model these skills, incorporating the ideal debugger and the strategy differences and errors of the novices. As such, it would form the core of a debugging tutoring system that could complement programming instruction.

REFERENCES

1. Rich, C., & Waters, R. C. (1981). <u>Abstraction, inspection, and debugging in programming</u> (Tech. Rep. AI Memo 634). Massachussetts Institute of Technology, Boston, MA.

2. Johnson, L., & Soloway, E. (1984). Intention-based diagnosis of programming errors. <u>Proceedings of the 1984 Conference of the AAAI</u>.

3. Youngs, E. A. (1974). Human errors in programming. <u>International Journal of Man-Machine Studies</u>, <u>6</u>, 361-376.

4. Soloway, E., Ehrlich, K., Bonar, J., & Greenspan, J. (1983). What do novices know about programming? In B. Shneiderman & A. Badre (Ed.), <u>Directions in Human-Computer Interaction</u>. Norwood, NJ: Ablex Inc.

5. Jeffries, R. (1981). Computer program debugging by experts. Paper presented at the Psychonomics Society Meeting.

6. Jeffries, R. (1982). A comparison of the debugging behavior of expert and novice programmers. Paper presented at the American Educational Research Association Annual Meeting.

7. Gould, J. D., & Drongowski, P. (1974). An exploratory study of computer program debugging. <u>Human Factors</u>, <u>16</u>, 258-277.

8. Gould, J. D. (1975). Some psychological evidence on how people debug computer programs. <u>International Journal of Man-Machine Studies</u>, <u>7</u>, 151-182.

9. Atwood, M. E., & Ramsay, H. R. (1978). <u>Cognitive structures in the comprehension and memory of computer programmers: An investigation of computer program debugging</u> (Tech. Rep. TR-78-A21). U. S. Army Research Institute.

10. Soloway, E., Bonar, J., & Ehrlich, K. (1983). Cognitive strategies and loopin constructs: An empirical study. <u>Communications of the ACM</u>, <u>26</u>, 853-860.

11. Katz, I. R., & Anderson, J. R. (1985). An exploratory study of novice programmer's bugs and debugging behavior. Unpublished Manuscript. Carnegie-Mellon University, Pittsburgh, PA.

12. Carver, S. M., & Klahr, D. (in press). Children's acquisition of debugging skills in a LOGO environment. <u>Journal of Educational Computing Research</u>.

13. Reiser B., Anderson J. R., & Farrell, R. (1985). Dynamic student modelling in an intelligent tutor for LISP programming. <u>Proceedings of the International Joint Conference on Artificial Intelligence</u>.

14. Anderson, J. R., Corbett, A. T., & Reiser B. J. (in press). <u>Essential LISP</u>. Reading, Ma.: Addison-Wesley.

15. Anderson, J. R., Farrell, R., & Sauers, R. (1984). Learning to program in LISP. Cognitive Science, 8, 87-129.

16. Anderson, J. R. (1985). Production Systems, Learning, and Tutoring. In D. Klahr, P. Langley, & R. Neches (Ed.), Self-modifying Production Systems: Models of Learning and Development. Cambridge, Ma.: Bradford Books/MIT.

17. Sauers, R., & Farrell, R. (1982). GRAPES User's Manual ONR Technical Report. Carnegie-Mellon University, Pittsburgh, PA.

18. Anderson, J. R. (1983). The Architecture of Cognition. Cambridge, MA: Harvard University Press.

19. Anderson, J. R., & Jeffries, R. (1985). Novice LISP errors: Undetected losses of information from working memory. Human-Computer Interaction, 1, 107-131.

APPENDIX

The Bugged and the Correct Function Versions

BUG: Parenthesized Variable

This function is called first. Given any list, it should return the first element of that list. For instance, (first '(a b c)) should return a.

wrong: (defun first (x) (car (x)))

correct: (defun first (x) (car x))

This function is called extract. It should return the second element of a list. For instance, extract called on (a b c) should return b.

wrong: (defun extract (x) (car (cdr (x))))

correct: (defun extract (x) (car (cdr x)))

BUG: Quoted Variable

This function is called replace. It should replace the first element of a list with a new element. This function takes two parameters - the new element and the list. For instance, (replace 'rings '(ties hats pants)) should return (rings hats pants).

wrong: (defun replace (x y) (cons 'x (cdr y)))

correct: (defun replace (x y) (cons x (cdr y)))

This function is called pair. It takes as its argument an element x and a list y. It should return a list consisting of two elements, x and the first element of the list y. For example, (pair 2 '(4 5 6)) = (2 4).

wrong: (defun pair (x y) (list 'x (car y)))

correct: (defun pair (x y) (list x (car y)))

BUG: Wrong Embedding

This function is called "ftoc". It takes as its argument a degree reading in
fahrenheit and should return the celsius equivalent. The formula for
converting fahrenheit (f) to celsius (c) is: c = ((f - 32) / 1.8)).

wrong: (defun ftoc (x) (difference x 32)(quotient x 1.8))

correct: (defun ftoc (x) (quotient (difference x 32) 1.8))

This function is called "ctof" . It should convert celsius degrees to
fahrenheit degrees. The equation to convert celsius (c) to fahrenheit (f) is:
f = (c * 1.8) + 32).

wrong: (defun ctof (x) (times x 1.8) (plus x 32))

correct: (defun ctof (x) (times (plus x 32) 1.8))

BUG: No Combiner

This function is called sqr. It should return a list of the perimeter and the
area of a square, given the length of one side. So, (sqr 2) should return
(8 4).

wrong: (defun sqr (x) (times x 4) (times x x))

correct: (defun sqr (x) (list (times x 4) (times x x)))

This function is called polar. It takes one argument that is a radius of a
circle that is situated at the origin of a cartesian co-ordinate plane and
another argument that is the angle away from the x axis. The radius and angle
are measurements in a polar co-ordinate system that are converted to cartesian
(x and y) co-ordinates and then returned in a list by this function. The x
co-ordinate is the radius times the cosine of the angle and the y co-ordinate
is the radius times the sine of the angle. For example, (polar 10 60) =
(5.0 8.66).

wrong: (defun polar (x y) (times x (cos y)) (times x (sin y)))

correct: (defun polar (x y) (list (times x (cos y)) (times x (sin y))))

BUG: Wrong Combiner

This function is called back. It should return two copies of a list, where
each copy is the original reversed. Thus, (back '(a b c)) should return
(c b a c b a).

wrong: (defun back (x) (list (reverse x) (reverse x)))

correct: (defun back (x) (append (reverse x) (reverse x)))

This function is called pal. It takes a single list as an argument and should return a palindrome that is twice as long. A palindrome is a list that reads the same forward and backward. For instance, (a b c c b a) would be the palindrome made from (a b c).

wrong: (defun pal (x) (list x (reverse x)))

correct: (defun pal (x) (append x (reverse x)))

BUG: Missing Reverse

This function is called snoc. It is the opposite of cons. Instead of inserting an item into the front of a list, it should insert the item at the end. So, (snoc 'd '(a b c)) = (a b c d).

wrong: (defun snoc (x y) (cons x (reverse y)))

correct: (defun snoc (x y) (reverse (cons x (reverse y))))

This function is called rotater. Its argument is always a list. It should return a list that is the same as the argument except that the former last element becomes the new first element. Thus, it rotates the list one to the right. For example, (rotater '(a b c d)) = (d a b c).

wrong: (defun rotater (x) (append (last x) (reverse (cdr x))))

correct: (defun rotater (x) (append (last x) (reverse (cdr (reverse x)))))

CHAPTER 15

Fragile Knowledge and Neglected Strategies
in Novice Programmers

D.N. Perkins
Fay Martin
Educational Technology Center
Harvard Graduate School of Education
Cambridge, MA 02138

ABSTRACT

Many students have great difficulty mastering the basics of programming.
Inadequate knowledge, neglect of general problem-solving strategies, or both
might explain their troubles. We report a series of clinical interviews of
students taking first year BASIC in which an experimenter interacted with
students as they worked, systematically providing help as needed in a
progression from general strategic prompts to particular advice. The results
indicate a substantial problem of "fragile knowledge" in novices -- knowledge
that is partial, hard to access, and often misused. The results also show
that general strategic prompts often resolve these difficulties.
Recommendations for teaching more robust knowledge and general strategies are
made. Implications for the impact of programming on general cognitive skills
are considered.

INTRODUCTION

Plentiful evidence speaks to the difficulties encountered by beginning
students of programming in primary and secondary. Linn (1) reported only
modest achievement in BASIC in most schools in a study ranging over a number
of school systems. Research conducted by Pea and Kurland documented the
minimal competency achieved by students learning Logo under relatively
nondirective conditions (2, 3). Perkins and his colleagues have discussed
patterns of behavior displayed by many novice programmers as part of their
partial mastery, patterns such as haphazard tinkering where a student
attempts to repair a buggy program by a series of almost arbitrary changes
(4). While reasonably successful efforts to teach youngsters programming
have been reported from time to time (1, 5-7), typical results at the primary
and secondary level seem disappointing and call for efforts to understand the
nature of the difficulties and remedy them.

We gratefully acknowledge the collaboration with teachers and school systems
that made possible the research reported here. Preparation of this report
was supported in part by the National Institute of Education (contract number
NIE 400-83-0041). Opinions expressed herein are not necessarily shared by
NIE and do not represent Institute policy.

One natural approach to defining the difficulties asks what students typically know and what they do not. Do they understand the basic operations of the computer language in question? Do they possess problem solving strategies for managing an attack on a problem, as has proved important in mathematical problem solving for example (8-11)? Do they have in their repertoires prototypical programming plans such as nested FOR-NEXT loops or recursion (12, 13)? Do they know the symptoms that signal when a particular operation or programming plan might serve? One can speak roughly of a continuum between low-level knowledge of the particular commands a language offers and rather abstract and general tactics of problem solving (1). With such a continuum in mind, is the shortfall principally in low-level knowledge or high-level strategic repertoire?

The question has some interest not only for the pedagogy of programming in itself, but for the possibility explored by many that learning to program might impact on learners' general cognitive skills (e.g. 1, 14, 15). Consider two extreme cases. Perhaps novice programmers have ample general cognitive skills for the relatively easy problems they face, but their mastery of the primitives of the language is so poor that they cannot apply those skills effectively to solve programming problems. In this case, instruction in programming cannot be expected to boost learners' cognitive skills until it moves beyond the fundamentals and into problems that pose higher order challenges. On the other hand, perhaps novice programmers have the details of the language under control but lack the general cognitive skills required to marshall their knowledge. In this case, from the first programming affords a natural training ground for the development of those higher order skills, although it may be questioned whether students will develop them without strong mediation (16-19).

The broad issues seem clear enough. However, in pursuing them one has to recognize a certain oversimplification in the questions: Knowledge comes across as a "you have it or you don't" attribute. The student may know some things about the language, but not other things and perhaps not enough. However, common experience testifies that often a person does not simply "know" or "not know" something. Rather, the person sort of knows, has some fragments, can make some moves, has a notion, without being able to marshall enough knowledge with sufficient precision to carry a problem through to a clean solution. One might say that learners in such a state have <u>fragile</u> knowledge.

Understanding in what ways students' knowledge of programming might be fragile -- neither here nor there, reliable nor random, possessed nor lost -- could help in grasping the nature of students' difficulties and designing instruction that affords better learning opportunities. In particular, under the general label of fragile knowledge a number of questions can be addressed. Do students have knowledge of operations they do not succeed in retrieving? Is the problem of retrieval radical, or can strategic prompts trigger retrieval? Is it that students do not have certain knowledge or do they get confused about what knowledge to use when?

In this paper, we report on a series of clinical case studies done with high school students taking a first year BASIC course. Working one-on-one with a number of students, the experimenter observed and interacted in defined ways as the students attempted to solve programming problems. While a few students managed the problems well, most evinced considerable difficulty at some points. In this paper, we offer some simple descriptive statistics and close examinations of a number of programming episodes in quest of a view of novice programming that highlights the interaction between strategies and fragile -- not just partial -- knowledge.

We interpret the students' difficulties as manifesting fragile knowledge of BASIC commands in four senses. <u>Missing knowledge</u> is the straightforward case of an impasse due to knowledge the student has either not retained or never learned, as revealed by clinical probes disclosing no sign of the

214

knowledge. Inert knowledge refers to situations where the student fails to retrieve command knowledge but in fact possesses it, as revealed by a clinical probe. Misplaced knowledge designates circumstances where a student imports command structures appropriate to some contexts into a line of code where they do not belong. Conglomerated knowledge signifies situations where a student produces code that jams together several disparate elements in a syntactically or semantically anomalous way in an attempt to provide the computer with the information it needs. The four will be more sharply defined and distinguished and their connections to the literature examined as they are discussed in turn.

We also made tallies of certain fragile knowledge events that show to what extent general strategic prompts helped students over their difficulties. This, along with some features of the individual case studies, allows appraising the relative contributions of fragile knowledge and lack of general problem-solving skills to students' difficulties and points to prospects for a better pedagogy of programming.

A CLINICAL METHODOLOGY

To investigate the locus of novices' programming difficulties, we devised a procedure that would reveal whether particular difficulties reflected the failure of high-level problem management skills or a poor understanding of particular commands in the programming language. The experimenter presented a student with a choice of eight increasingly difficult programming problems. The problems built on one another, each preparing the way for the next. Each student selected a problem that seemed manageable, attempted it in interaction with the experimenter until completing it, and proceeded to the next problem, continuing this process until the end of a session of about 45 minutes. Some details follow.

Subjects. Twenty high school subjects enrolled in the second semester of a year-long first BASIC course participated in the study. The students ranged from 10th to 12th graders, including 11 females and 9 males. Each student participated for one 45 minute session. In our view, the instruction at the site was quite careful and conscientious, from a teacher with a very good understanding of BASIC in particular and programming in general. Nonetheless, while some of the students had developed considerable programming skills others displayed substantial difficulties, as will emerge.

Programming tasks. The sequence of eight programming tasks, ranging from easy to difficult, centered on the FOR-NEXT loop. All the problems asked for programs that produced patterns of stars (asterisks) on the screen. For example, problem 1 called for a program to produce a column of ten stars; problem 3 called for a program that would ask for a number and then print a column with that many stars; problem 4 did the same except that the row of stars was to be horizontal. Problem 5 required a program that asked for a number and then produced a square of stars. For instance, with an input of 5 the program would produce:

```
* * * * *
* * * * *
* * * * *
* * * * *
* * * * *
```

Problem 8 called for a hollow square of stars of any size.

It should be noted that the exact character of the challenge posed by these problems depends somewhat on the programming environment and the commands students know. In particular, we designed the sequence knowing that the students in our sample did not have at their disposal cursor control commands and consequently needed to produce the patterns of stars through print statements, line by line from the top to the bottom of the pattern. This prevents, for example, solving the hollow square of stars problem by way of a program that guides the cursor around the sides of the square, printing asterisks along the way.

   Procedure. The experimenter explained the purpose of the study -- to come to understand how people learn programming, what difficulties they have, and how to help people to overcome them -- and explained that the experimenter would watch and help as the student worked some programming problems. The experimenter introduced the student to the sequence of problems and invited the student to choose one to begin with that would be "challenging, not too easy, but not too hard."

   The experimenter watched and asked occasional questions to track the student's thinking until and if the student encountered a significant difficulty. Then the experimenter intervened, asking questions and providing information to help the student to overcome the difficulty. The experimenter worked with the student until the student attained a program that performed the task in question. Then the experimenter asked the student to attempt the next problem, and so on until time ran out.

   When the student faced an impasse, the experimenter's first questions, called prompts, were high-level strategic questions one might ask oneself. By definition, prompts were questions that did not require any foreknowledge of the true nature of the difficulty: People in principle could prompt themselves. Some typical prompts were, "What's the first thing you need to tell the computer to do; how would you describe the problem to yourself; what does this (e.g., a semicolon) do?" As the examples suggest, some prompts were phrased generally and could be used in any problem-solving situation, even one outside of programming, while others were particularized to mention semicolons or other elements of the programming situation. The prompts were generated by the experimenter according to the experimenter's judgment of the level of specificity needed.

   If a couple of prompts did not help the student to overcome the difficulty, the experimenter resorted to "hints." Hints by definition reflected the experimenter's understanding of the solution, nudging the student toward a resolution with leading questions or bits of information. Some characteristic hints would be, "Can you think of a command to get the computer to ask you for a number; your problem is to repeat something several times, so do you know a command for that; could you use a comma or semicolon somehow?"

   If a couple of hints did not provoke progress, the experimenter provided an exact solution to the immediate dilemma so that the student could get on with the rest of the program. These were called "provides." Characteristic provides were: "Write INPUT 'How many stars per side' N; use a FOR-NEXT loop; put a semicolon after the print statement." The experimenter did not just provide answers, of course, but also attempted to explain them.

   The escalation from prompts to hints to provides not only helped the student but served as a probe of the student's level of mastery and understanding. The more support the student required, the less the student could accomplish solo. A successful prompt suggested that the student could succeed by learning self-prompting strategies -- good questions to ask oneself in programming situations. At the other extreme, a provide preceded by several unsuccessful prompts and hints indicated very limited knowledge and understanding relevant to the particular difficulty.

   Although the experimenter generally attempted the progression from prompts to provides, sometimes the experimenter moved directly to hints or provides. This occasionally happened by mistake, but more often because the general performance of the student and spiraling frustration suggested that more direct help was needed to maintain the student's attention and involvement.

Data collection. The data collected during a session included notes
taken by the experimenter, code written by the student and transcribed by the
experimenter, and an audiotape of the conversation. The audiotape was
transcribed later and notes and code interpolated to yield a verbatim
protocol of the session. Case studies were drawn from the protocols; a
number of examples will be discussed below. In addition, the protocols were
scored for certain events as discussed later.

SOME DESCRIPTIVE STATISTICS

As already indicated, in this paper we emphasize clinical discussion of
examples. Nonetheless, some general descriptive statistics can help to
clarify the character of the experiment and the import of our results. Of
the 20 subjects, 9 chose to begin with problem number one, while the
remainder chose to begin anywhere from problem 2 to 7 with problem 4 most
frequently selected. In the course of the interview, a subject completed on
the average 3.45 problems. Of course, the interviewer helped a student
whenever necessary, so this represents a considerably higher figure than one
would expect had the students been working alone.

A judge scored interactions between the experimenter and the subject on
a 4 point scale according to whether the subject's progress was spontaneous,
the consequence of a prompt, a hint, or a provide. A second judge scored
blindly a random subsample of the data. The correlation between the two
judges was .92, N=183, p<.001, over all doubly scored interactions.

The entire sample presented 163 episodes culminating in a provide or a
successful prompt or hint, an average of a bit more than 8 episodes per
subject. We focus on these for the remainder of the analysis. Each
resolution by way of a prompt, hint, or provide was preceded by some sort of
inadequate handling of the programming problem by the subject -- else there
would have been no difficulty to prompt, hint, or provide for. We wanted to
know more about the character of those difficulties resolved by a prompt or a
hint. A judge classified the subject's immediately prior response into one
of four categories, followed by blind cross-checking by a second judge on a
randomly chosen subsample of the data; the second judge agreed with the first
76% of the time.

The categories were as follows. "Omissions" were failures to provide a
needed element or any substitute element, as for example in leaving out a
semicolon on a PRINT or leaving out a FOR statement altogether. "Migrations"
were cases where a syntactic element from one command intruded into another,
as in for example PRINT S STEP 2. "Sequence errors" were cases where an
element was mispositioned in a program, as in placing sequentially FOR loops
that should be nested. "Mistakes" were responses not classified into any of
the prior categories. The analysis disclosed 26 omissions, 15 migrations, 12
sequence errors, and 25 mistakes immediately preceding resolution by a prompt
or hint. Of course, the subjects made many more mistakes than this; similar
difficulties often preceded resolution by a provide and prompts and hints
that did not yield a resolution, but we do not need statistics on those for
the present discussion. The figures mentioned along with some further
information will be used to estimate the frequency of the types of fragile
knowledge to be discussed.

MISSING KNOWLEDGE

Knowledge might be fragile in many ways, each telling us something about
students' shortfalls of understanding and pointing to ways to remedy them.
Perhaps the simplest sort of fragile knowledge is partly missing knowledge: A
student knows something about a command or other element of programming but
has minor gaps that impair the student's functioning. Since this sort of
fragility is so straightforward, we will not treat it extensively but simply
mention a couple of examples.

The programming tasks that asked the students to produce one or more horizontal lines of stars of varying length all called for the use of a semicolon at the end of a PRINT "*" to suppress the usual carriage return. While some students recalled this tactic spontaneously or upon prompts or hints, others found themselves at a loss. When the experimenter provided the semicolon, some even showed no familiarity with its function although all the students had been exposed to it in their class.

For a more advanced example, the problems calling for multiple rows of stars required a bare PRINT statement after the NEXT of the inner FOR loop to force a carriage return after each line of stars. The students in their class had used bare PRINT statements to create blank lines in formatting output. However, apparently many associated a bare PRINT with blank lines specifically, not recognizing its general function of outputting a carriage return, which could also be used to terminate a line.

How often did students' difficulties reflect missing knowledge pure and simple? When a prompt or hint resolved a problem, this showed that the student had at least some further knowledge he or she had not used. Also, when a provide resolved a problem at a level above that of writing a line of code (for instance, retrieving what command to use), if the student could follow through with the line of code this also demonstrated unaccessed rather than missing knowledge. Consequently, we estimated the number of episodes of missing knowledge by subtracting off those cases from the total number of episodes. This yielded a figure of 60 out of 163, 37%, or a bit more than a third. To be sure, some of this third might constitute knowledge "really" there but not retrieved despite the prompts and hints; one could consider the figure an upper estimate, or alternatively one could say that knowledge so hard to retrieve is "functionally missing" so far as the enterprise of programming goes.

The estimate, rough though it is, suggests that missing knowledge indeed plays a substantial role in students' difficulties. If that were the whole story, there would be little point of speaking of fragile knowledge: One might just as well refer to partial knowledge. However, another two-thirds remains to be accounted for: The larger portion of the troubles afflicting students generally proves more complex. To consider missing knowledge as the only explanation would be both to miss much about the structure of students' knowledge and to underestimate how much knowledge they have. With this in mind, we turn to other species of fragility.

INERT KNOWLEDGE

One particularly straightforward kind of fragility has been called "inert knowledge." This refers to knowledge that a person has, but fails to muster when needed. For example, Bereiter and Scardamalia (20) discuss the problem of inert knowledge in the context of writing. They note that youngsters asked to write on a topic typically only manage to access a fraction of their relevant knowledge. Conventional tactics of fluency such as brainstorming ideas seem to offer little help; however the strategy of listing words that might be used in an essay considerably increases students' retrieval of relevant information. The authors suggest that this occurs because the bare terms activate a network of associations more effectively than lists of points, which have a more particular nature.

Broadly speaking, the problem of inert knowledge is a problem of transfer. Knowledge acquired on one occasion fails to bridge the slight or substantial gap to another occasion of application. Belmont, Butterfield, and Ferretti (21) emphasize that knowledge often tends to remain bound to the context of initial learning unless the learner deploys self-monitoring strategies that help to carry the knowledge across to other applications. Salomon and Perkins recently have presented a general theory of the mechanisms of transfer that identifies both "high road" and "low road" ways that transfer can occur (17, 19). The former requires mindful abstraction and application in new contexts. The latter requires skills practiced to near automaticity on a variety of cases, so that new contexts spontaneously evoke the skills in question. In typical instructional situations, neither the conditions for low nor high road transfer are met. Consequently, knowledge that otherwise might serve the learner in a new context remains inert.

How does all this apply to the context of our study? Inert knowledge was implicated whenever a subject, after an omission or mistake, responded successfully to a prompt or hint, or a subject followed through on a provide that did not simply give a solution at the code level. This occurred in 76 of the 163 episodes, 47%, or almost half. However, such numbers do little to convey the character of the phenomenon -- the main focus of this paper. Consider these cases, for instance. Brenda was working on a program to print a column of ten stars. She had coded:

```
10   X = "*"
20   FOR X = 1 TO 10
30   PRINT X
40   NEXT X
```

When she ran the program, she received the error message, "Type mismatch in 10." She asked what a type mismatch was and the experimenter directed her to look at line 10.

E: What kind of symbol is the star, a number or a character?

Brenda: A number, no a character.

E: Okay, and what is X? What does it stand for?

Brenda: Oh, a number.

She then recoded: 10   X$ = "*". So the experimenter's hint lead Brenda to retrieve knowledge that in fact she possessed but had not accessed.

Dennis was working on the more advanced problem 5, which called for a solid square of stars. He had coded two nested FOR loops but his output resulted in a horizontal row of stars. Dennis pondered his output for a while.

E: How many stars did you get?

Dennis: Twenty-five. That's the right number.

E: What do you need to do?

Dennis: Put them into a block.

E: Right.

Dennis then coded a bare PRINT after the first NEXT statement to force a carriage return and make rows of stars. Here the experimenter's general queries led Dennis to see through to the nature of the problem and retrieve a command that would solve it.

These examples illustrate that knowledge needed to generate a solution can be inert, but so can knowledge needed as a critical filter to assess a candidate solution. We term the activity of reading back expressions in a computer language to discern exactly what they tell the computer to do "close tracking" (Perkins, Hancock, Hobbs, Martin, & Simmons, in press). There is a strategic side and a low-level knowledge side to close tracking. On the strategic side, students need to attempt to close track in order to apply the

219

critical filter. On the knowledge side, even when a student tries to close track, problems of fragile knowledge can stand in the way.

For an example of this sort, consider how Abby began a program to print out a column of N stars:

```
3   INPUT "How many stars do you want"; N
4   PRINT
5   N = 8
10  FOR X = 1 TO N
```

When she ran the program with an input of 5, she could not figure out why she got 8 stars. The experimenter then asked her to describe what the program did line by line.

> Abby: Okay, at line 3 it's going to input how many stars do you want and then it's going to stop so I can put it in. On the next line it's going to skip a line 'cause of the print. Then on number 5 I'm telling it how many I want, the little stars. I'm telling it how many stars I want to print out, and the next line is the loop.

Even in reading through the program, Abby did not realize that her assignment of 8 to N would overwrite her input. Yet this would appear obvious once pointed out. Odd as such slips may seem, they proved quite common, preventing students from filtering out their errors by close tracking.

With these examples in mind, what factors might explain the occurrence of inert knowledge in programming? One obvious cause is the failure to execute certain strategic actions that marshall particular knowledge. A programmer may fail to close track an expression to check it, for example. On the other hand, even when students ask themselves appropriate higher order questions, the retrieval process may fail for any number of reasons. Abby, for, instance, seemed to be interpreting what each line did by reading in her intention to get N set to a reasonable value rather than by thinking about the exact actions prescribed by the code. For another instance, a student failing to retrieve a bare PRINT to force a carriage return at the end of a row of stars may know in principle that such a print statement outputs a carriage return but associate the action strongly with making blank lines. In general, one should recognize that an experienced programmer will have a rich network of associations linking various commands and programming plans; if retrieval does not succeed by one route, it will probably succeed by another. In contrast, the network of connections in the novice inevitably is sparse; if retrieval by one route fails for whatever reason, there may be no other ready way.

MISPLACED KNOWLEDGE

Another phenomenon of fragility might be called misplaced knowledge. Here, knowledge suitable for some roles invades occasions where it does not fit. Like inert knowledge, misplaced knowledge occurs commonly in human experience. For instance, one's steering habits lead to trouble when one's car skids, since the best corrective calls for steering with rather than against the direction of the swerve. Toddlers frequently overgeneralize the application of new words and individuals learning a second language experience interference from terms and syntactic structures in their native language (22). Functional fixedness, where people have difficulty in applying an object in an unconventional way, and the classic Einstellung effect, where problem solvers carry forward a solution method for a series of problems to new problems allowing a much simpler solution, offer other examples (23, 24). As with inert knowledge, the connection with transfer should be plain. All these examples amount to instances of negative transfer, where the knowledge or know-how in question impairs rather than abets performance through application in an unsuitable context.

How does misplaced knowledge appear in the present study? For the sake of counts, we merged misplaced knowledge and conglomerated knowledge, identifying them with the categories of "migration" and "sequence error" discussed previously. The reason for the merging was that misplaced knowledge and conglomerated knowledge really lie along a continuum with mixed cases in the middle, a point discussed explicitly in the next section. In all, 27 episodes, 17%, involved misplaced or conglomerated knowledge.

Although characterizing a modest portion of the episodes, misplaced knowledge provides considerable insight into students' problems of knowledge representation. For one point, misplaced knowledge can <u>cause</u> inert knowledge: Sometimes relevant knowledge remains inert because misplaced knowledge has intruded. For example, Stan began working on the program to print a vertical column of N stars. He coded a FOR loop and then paused, pondering how to handle the print statement. When asked about his worry, he said he wanted to set up the format line in order to "print out the stars the way you want it." He was referring to formatted printing with the print using command. The experimenter quickly steered him away from this cumbersome method.

E: What if you didn't use a format. Is there any other way you can think of to print a star?

Stan: Print and then just write an asterisk.

For another example, Dan was working on the program to print out a row of N horizontal stars. He coded:

```
10   INPUT "How many stars do you want?"; S
15   LET S$ = "*"
20   PRINT S STEP 2
```

When asked how the program would work, he explained that STEP 2 would print across so that somehow the star would be printed S times horizontally. Clearly Dan misplaced the STEP command from a FOR loop. Moreover, he was unable to retrieve the FOR loop itself even after the experimenter hinted. When the experimenter prompted him to think of another way to print across, he did produce PRINT S$;, but still no FOR loop. Moreover the semicolon also migrated inappropriately: When the experimenter directly suggested using a FOR loop, Dan coded 12 FOR X = 1 TO S;, with the semicolon at the end of the FOR statement.

As with inert knowledge, we should ask what explains the occurrence of misplaced knowledge. Overgeneralization -- or underdifferentiation to put it another way -- provides one obvious cause. Recall how Dan had not sharply differentiated the proper applications of STEP or the semicolon. Recency of learning often figured in such difficulties, the students apparently feeling that whatever they had studied lately must somehow apply. This was probably the cause of Stan's misapplication of print using. Throughout the course of data collection, we noted how different intrusions seemed to crop up as a function of topics in class. Early in our observations, we saw print using and read data statements appear in students' code. A few weeks later the step command was interpreted as causing both horizontal and vertical printing, somehow always in association with print statements rather than loops. In the final sessions, we began to see students try to apply arrays in coding the square designs.

In situations where the learner has difficulty finding a reasonable solution, misplaced knowledge may amount to a desperation measure. Precedent for this appears in mathematical and other problem solving contexts, where the general point has been made that students commonly try to provide some kind of a response, even if a dubious one (25), or to repair a response they think to be inadequate as best they can (26, 27). For example, Alice was having great difficulty programming the vertical column of ten stars. She realized that she needed to print a star ten times going down, but could not retrieve an appropriate command for doing so. Her first idea for repeating involved the use of a GOSUB, but the experimenter steered her toward the idea of a FOR loop. Then to take care of the printing she suggested using READ, but realized there were no data to read. Finally, she coded a print statement inside the loop but become stuck over whether to code ten print statements instead of just one. Ultimately the experimenter had to provide Alice with the correct code. It seems fairly clear that in this instance Alice's misplaced knowledge reflected her being at a loss.

CONGLOMERATED KNOWLEDGE

Another manifestation of fragile knowledge might be called "conglomerated knowledge." This appears when the young programmer composes code that expresses loosely the intent without following the strict rules that govern how the computer actually executes code. Dan's use of STEP in the midst of a PRINT statement offers an example not only of misplaced but also conglomerated knowledge.

Another example independently produced by several students concerned the problem of printing five stars in a horizontal row. In one episode, Gail coded:

```
10   INPUT "How many stars do you want"; X
20   PRINT "*"; X
```

Her idea was that the star would print ten times across.

This example illustrates well the peculiar character of conglomerates. They certainly show signs of the programmer's mindful engagement in the activity of programming; the programmer plainly has sought to encode information the computer would need to carry out the task in question. On the other hand, conglomerates are syntactically or semantically ill-formed. Either they are far from being legal code in the language in question, as with STEP in the midst of PRINT, or although accidentally legal direct the computer to do something very different from the programmer's intent, as with "PRINT "*"; X" to print a row of X stars.

Consider another more complex example. Ellie was working on the same problem, but she coded:

```
1    FOR X = 1
10   "Print how many stars do you want"; N
20   INPUT NUMBER
30   X = (*) * NUMBER
40   NEXT X
```

Her conglomerate aimed to multiply the asterisk times whatever number she put in. There are several other difficulties with her program as well, of course.

As indicated in the previous section, there is no sharp borderline between misplaced and conglomerated knowledge, and we have not tried to make separate counts of them, locating both within the same 27 episodes, 17%. The problem is that many conglomerates involve misplaced knowledge -- elements from one programming construct or context showing up in the midst of an expression from somewhere else entirely. But a broad distinction can be drawn. Pure cases of misplaced knowledge involve knowledge intruding into contexts without any sense of a conglomerate jammed together out of ill-fitting parts, as in the earlier example of seeking to use a print using statement in a situation calling for a simple print. Pure cases of conglomerates occur when the expression in question does not show components obviously misplaced from some other context. For instance, in the "PRINT

"*"; X" example, one does not particularly feel that the X is misplaced from anywhere, from a FOR-NEXT loop for example. Rather, the programmer simply means to let the computer know that X stars are required and hopes that putting the X in the print expression will do so.

As with inert and misplaced knowledge, one wants an explanation for conglomerates. Why do they occur? Plainly they reflect the active effort of young programmers to solve the problem. Unsure exactly how to command the computer, a programmer takes a stab at it, putting together code that provides the computer with at least some of the information the computer would need to perform the task. The remaining question asks why programmers take such stabs rather than doing the "right thing?" Several answers seem relevant. First of all, the "right thing" often involves knowledge inert or not possessed at all, leaving the programmer no proper recourse. Second, the programmer often works from an underdifferentiated knowledge base, leading to misplacements that yield conglomerates. Third, the programmer fails to close track tentative conglomerates or may be unable to do so with precision. Fourth, the programmer lacks the general critical sense that one simply cannot expect to throw things together in a programming language and have them work. That is, the programmer treats the programming language as much looser, less restrictive, more expressive and more like a natural language than in fact it is. Finally, we do well to remember the lesson of "repair theory" -- students will try to patch a response they suspect to be inadequate, although the patches themselves typically are inadequate (26, 27).

PROMPTS AS A GAUGE OF STRATEGIC SHORTFALL

One of our running themes in this paper has been the contribution to programming of relatively high level strategic knowledge versus relatively low level knowledge of the details of the language. Successful prompts in particular show that a student possesses knowledge the student might have retrieved and applied autonomously. In other words, prompts are the high level strategic questions one might ask oneself. To the extent that a student needs help but proves responsive to prompts, the student displays a strategic shortfall but sufficient lower level mastery.

How often did this happen? Of the 163 episodes, 53 were resolved by prompts, 25 by hints, and 85 by provides. This amounts to 33% prompts, 15% hints, and 52% provides. This actually underestimates the efficacy of prompts a little bit, because the experimenter from time to time gave a hint without a prior prompt or a provide without a prior hint; had the experimenter actually given prompts or hints in those cases, a few of them probably would have succeeded, raising the percentage of effective prompts and hints. So one can say that at least a third of the time, prompts were effective and prompts and hints together were effective something like half the time. This shows that students had considerably more knowledge resources than they accessed without help and that much of the time they might help themselves to access that knowledge by self-prompting.

Now let us examine the character of prompts. Particularly notable is their range. Here are some samples selected for variety: "What's the first thing you need to tell the computer to do?" "Are there any other ways to make the computer (print across, repeat something, whatever)?" "How would you describe the problem to yourself?" "What is your plan?" "Do you know a command for repeating?" (after the student has indicated a need to repeat; otherwise this would be a hint). "What do you need to do next?" "What does a semicolon do?" (when the student is reading back a statement with a semicolon; otherwise this would be a hint). Note how much these prompts vary in seeming generality and yet how alike they are. While some are phrased much more specifically than others, these bind a very general question to particular circumstances. For instance, "What does a semicolon do?" is a special case of "What does _this_ do?" where the _this_ might be a symbol in an algebraic equation or a part of a carburetor. In type, the question is a probe for the exact function of a part.

Of course, whether a prompt succeeds depends not just on the prompt itself but on the accessibility and organization of the knowledge the prompt seeks to activate. The very same prompt can succeed on one occasion and fail on another. For example, in attempting the filled-in square program, a number of students coded only one FOR loop and two PRINTs, one with a semicolon "to go across" and another without "to go down." Through a series of prompts, the experimenter usually got the students to realize that the program needed to repeat N rows of N stars per row. But this was not always enough. When asked, "Do you know a command that might help you repeat something," Dennis, for example, replied, "Oh yeah. FOR-NEXT." But Randy's response was "GOTO."

We have saved one type of prompt for separate discussion because it occupies a pivotal position in programming: The prompt to close track, which may be seen as a special case of the prompt to check one's work in relation to one's objectives. As mentioned earlier, close tracking ideally functions as a critical filter applied to candidate solutions. While some students had difficulty close tracking with precision, others succeeded. When students close tracked either spontaneously or upon prompting, they did so accurately about 50% of the time, correctly forecasting a problem or explaining a bug. However, only about 20% of the episodes of close tracking were spontaneous; the rest had to be prompted. This almost certainly underestimates the frequency of spontaneous close tracking, since we only tallied episodes where students were plainly close tracking; a couple of seconds staring at the program with no tracking-like comments would not be counted, although the student might have been close tracking rather than just generally looking over the program. Nonetheless, the numbers suggest that students do not spontaneously close track as often as they might benefit from it.

Naomi presented us with an exception to this trend. Naomi was working on a programming problem from our sequence that asked for a triangle of stars. She wrote a program involving nested loops but no use of the iteration variable of the first loop as the upper limit of the second, to yield lines of increasing length. But even before running the program she paused, pondered her program for a moment, and realized, "It's going to end up like a square." Naomi's inclination and ability to read back her program and forecast what it would do, rather than presuming it would do as she intended, enabled her to reject plans and seek other alternatives. As noted, this was relatively infrequent among the students.

In addition to forecasting, the critical filter of close tracking can serve as a debugging aid. One can adopt the general strategy of close tracking the whole program or likely segments of it not just to predict what the program will do but to try to explain bugs: Why did the program misbehave in exactly this way? Often students prompted to attempt this strategy managed to follow through. For example, Dick was working on the filled-in square problem with one loop and two print statements, PRINT "*"; to print across and PRINT "*" to print down. When he ran his program he got a column of pairs of stars. The experimenter prompted him to trace why that result occurred. Dick spent a few moments contemplating the program and then replied, "It prints that and that and then goes down, prints that, then that, goes down, prints that and that." The experimenter asked what Dick needed to get the desired result. Dick: "Keep on printing that row. So after it prints a row, it goes on to print the same row, that many times." Dick thus reached a sharper formulation of what needed to happen. The figures and such examples as these argue that students would do well to prompt themselves to close track more often.

CONCLUSION: ISSUES OF KNOWLEDGE AND STRATEGY

We began this paper by noting the modest programming achievement reported by other investigators and asking whether students' lack of low-level programming knowledge or high-level strategies was to blame. Even in asking the question, we recognized its presumption: (1) Both could be implicated; (2) lack of low-level knowledge might describe too simply the nature of students' knowledge difficulties. The case studies and general findings reported here suggest a perspective on novices' programming difficulties somewhat more subtle than knowledge versus strategies. That perspective and its implications lend themselves to discussion by way of four questions. What characterizes novices' difficulties with programming? Are the difficulties just a consequence of poor instruction? What are the implications for the teaching of programming? What are the implications for programming's impact on cognitive skills?

What Characterizes Novices' Difficulties with Programming?

The data reviewed here suggests this answer: <u>fragile knowledge exacerbated by a shortfall in elementary problem-solving strategies.</u> As to fragile knowledge, both the case studies and the tallies of the effectiveness of prompts and hints in marshalling students' knowledge demonstrated that viewing novices' knowledge as partial was too simple. Besides problems of missing knowledge, students displayed inert knowledge that they could not readily muster, misplaced knowledge that migrated to inappropriate contexts, and conglomerated knowledge that mixed together commands in syntactically or semantically anomalous ways. The causes of such fragile knowledge seemed varied but comprehensible. Among the factors discussed were a sparse network of associations, underdifferentiation of commands, binding of commands and programming plans to customary contexts without recognizing their generality, treating a programming language more like a natural language where one can say what one means in many ways, and, of course, underuse of general strategic questions to prompt oneself to better marshall one's knowledge.

The range of difficulties posed by fragile knowledge might seem dismaying, but there is another way to look at it. The phenomena of fragile knowledge say that students know more than you might think. To be sure, that knowledge is often inert, underdifferentiated, undergeneralized, and so on, but at least it is there in some nascent form. Moreover, the fragile knowledge phenomena of misplaced and conglomerated knowledge catch students in the midst of seeking to cope with the task in an exploratory way. If the misplacements and conglomerates will not do the job hoped for, at least they signal the students' efforts to muster what they know and apply it somehow. Note that while misplacements and conglomerates by definition will not work, they are never nonsensical. While "PRINT "*"; X" will not print X *'s in a row, and a student with a good understanding of PRINT would know that, nonetheless one can see how such a format <u>might</u> perform such an action.

Now consider problem-solving strategies. The strategic shortfall implicated by the clinical work involves rather elementary strategies. Prompts in the spirit of "what now," "what other ways," "how can you describe the problem," "what's the plan," "do you know a command to do that," and "what will this command do," dominated. These concern several aspects of problem solving -- formulating goals, generating solutions, evaluating solutions, breaking set. However, they contrast with many efforts to enumerate problem solving heuristics that emphasize somewhat more sophisticated strategies, in effect taking such simple prompts as these almost for granted (8-10, 28).

Why elementary problem-solving strategies come to the fore here seems plain enough. The students' fragile knowledge will not sustain any very sophisticated problem solving. On the contrary, in light of their fragile knowledge, students' principal problem becomes how to muster that knowledge

most effectively. Elementary prompts rather than sophisticated strategies
that take much more for granted fit the bill. For this reason, we say that
the strategic shortfall exacerbates the fragile knowledge problem. It is not
enough just to conclude that students need both more robust knowledge and
more strategies as though the two were independent dimensions of programming.
One must appreciate how knowledge and strategies work together to support one
another, weaknesses in either finding partial compensation in the other.

Are the Difficulties Just a Consequence of Poor Instruction?

We have already noted that in our judgment the students we studied were
taught in a careful and conscientious way by a teacher with excellent mastery
of BASIC. Yet anyone familiar with programming must be taken aback by some
of the errors students committed in our case studies. "How could any
well-instructed student think that would work?" someone might ask. On this
interpretation, one need only teach programming in the solid way we at least
sometimes teach many another subjects and the difficulties will recede. In
our view, this reading of the circumstances underestimates the difficulty of
programming and learning to program. Although programming achievement of
students certainly varies according to the ability of the students and the
expertise of the teachers (1), it seems to us that too many students display
substantial difficulties too often to justify attributing such troubles
solely to teaching.

Consider for a moment what a challenge programming is. Unlike most
school subjects, programming is problem solving intensive. One cannot even
come close to getting by just by knowing answers. Moreover, as the phenomena
of misplaced and conglomerated knowledge demonstrate, a freewheeling
manipulation of one's knowledge will not suffice either, as it might to some
extent in the arts or literature for instance. The demands of a computer
that cannot discern what a program means are inevitably more stringent than
the demands of a reader who not only can see through to meanings but may
appreciate exploratory and playful extrapolations and stretchings of
concepts. Moreover, programming calls for extraordinary perfection. If you
get 90% of the words right on a spelling test, you score a 90; if you make
90% good points on an essay, you probably get an A. But if you get only 90%
of your commands right in a program, it will not do anything like what it is
supposed to. Moreover, the remaining 10% may well introduce several
interacting errors that make tracking down the bugs a demanding and
frustrating task.

For these reasons and no doubt others, we suggest that normally
responsible and knowledgable instruction does not suffice to give students a
reasonable mastery of programming, particularly the students who do not show
a flair for programming. Just as programming makes extraordinary demands on
students, so does the teaching of programming make extraordinary demands on
pedagogy.

What are the Implications for the Teaching of Programming?

With this challenge in mind, how should programming be taught? It would
be glib to propose that the present findings can offer anything like a full
formula for so complex an enterprise. Nonetheless, our observations suggest
three broad recommendations. First of all, teach programming so as to reduce
the problem of fragile knowledge. This general directive translates into a
number of particular objectives. One needs to highlight the functional roles
of commands in their generality in order to work against inert knowledge.
For instance, a FOR loop needs to be seen as a way of repeating anything any
number of times that can be calculated as the loop is entered; PRINT needs to
be seen as outputting a carriage return character that hence either
terminates a line or creates a blank line. Also, one needs to convey an
understanding of exactly what commands do. For instance, a FOR loop does not

226

just repeat something in a holistic sense but goes through a particular iteration process with a particular end-test, making possible nonstandard applications such as transferring out of a loop before it is complete. One needs to caution students about freewheeling and treating the computer language as though it were a natural language that could get across an intended meaning in many ways.

Second and somewhat paradoxically, teach programming so as to preserve the exploratory use of the language. It would be a shame to convey such a stringent image of programming that students became fearful of making conjectures, as indeed some students seem to be (see the discussion of "stoppers" versus "movers" in 4). The solution to the paradox involves what might be called "controlled exploration," exploratory thinking filtered by a precise appreciation of what the programming language affords. For instance, we think this to be a good principle: "When in doubt, take a stab at a solution; but check your stab by close tracking." This encourages students to attempt cycles of invention and critical filtering from which they can learn. For example, a couple of times a student in our clinical work proposed "PRINT "*"; X" or a slight variant, close tracked what would happen upon execution, and realized it would not behave as desired. We see such episodes not as unfortunate sidetracks but as important learning experiences wherein students enlarge their own understanding of the language by generating possibilities and testing those possibilities against the knowledge they already have. However, such exploratory learning cannot go well unless the students have enough knowledge to be able to close track well.

Third, encourage the use of elementary problem-solving strategies. As our data demonstrate, students would gain by prompting themselves more often with simple strategic questions such as "what does the program need to do next," "what command do I know that might help to do that," "what will what I have written really do," or "how did my program get that wrong answer?" The last two, prompts to close track, have special importance. As stressed before, close tracking is the critical filter that allows detecting programming errors with understanding. To be sure, running the program to see what happens also acts as a critical filter: If the program fails, there is something wrong. However, the critical filter of running the program provides far less information than the critical filter of accurate close tracking. While the former simply presents the programmer with the fact of an error, and perhaps an error message or some anomalous output, the latter leads the student through the program's action blow by blow.

What are the Implications for Programming's Impact on Cognitive Skills?

The present findings in no way document an impact of programming on general cognitive skills. On the contrary, if anything they suggest that students of programming need stronger general problem solving skills in the first place in order to best build upon their fragile knowledge. Rather than expecting programming instruction of itself to boost cognitive strategies, one should teach cognitive strategies as part of better programming instruction.

However, the findings do support the idea that beginning programming is a natural arena for the development of general cognitive skills. To see this point, consider what the present study might have found instead. High level prompts could have proved quite ineffective. Only hints might have succeeded in marshalling students' fragile knowledge. Such a finding would suggest that even elementary problem-solving strategies had no very important role to play until students achieved a substantial mastery of the basics of the computer language in question. However, this was not the finding. Instead, it appears that certain general problem-solving strategies can contribute from early on.

227

In sum, we suggest a distinction between programming as an arena for the development of cognitive skills and programming as an activity whose pursuit automatically develops cognitive skills. Our data argue for the former and against the latter. Direct teaching or indirect encouragement of strategic self-prompting and other tactics should help students to learn to program better and increase the likelihood of transfer from programming as well.

REFERENCES

1. Linn, M. C. (1985). The cognitive consequences of programming instruction in classrooms. Educational Researcher, 14, 14-29.

2. Pea, R. D., & Kurland, D. M. (1984a). On the cognitive effects of learning computer programming. New Ideas in Psychology, 2(2), 137-168.

3. Pea, R. D., & Kurland, D. M. (1984b). Logo programming and the development of planning skills (Report no. 16). New York: Bank Street College.

4. Perkins, D. N., Hancock, C., Hobbs, R., Martin, F., and Simmons, R. (in press). Conditions of learning in novice programmers. Journal of Educational Computing Research.

5. Clements, D. H. (1985, April). Effects of Logo programming on cognition, metacognitive skills, and achievement. Presentation at the American Educational Research Association conference, Chicago, Illinois.

6. Clements, D. H., & Gullo, D. F. (1984). Effects of computer programming on young children's cognition. Journal of Educational Psychology, 76(6), 1051-1058.

7. Nachmias, R., Mioduser, D., & Chen, D. (1985). Acquisition of basic computer programming concepts by children (Technical report no. 14). Tel Aviv, Israel: Center for Curriculum Research and Development, School of Education, University of Tel Aviv.

8. Polya, G. (1954). Mathematics and plausible reasoning (2 vols.). Princeton, New Jersey: Princeton University Press.

9. Polya, G. (1957). How to solve it: A new aspect of mathematical method (2nd ed.). Garden City, New York: Doubleday.

10. Schoenfeld, A. H. (1980). Teaching problem-solving skills. American Mathematical Monthly, 87, 794-805.

11. Schoenfeld, A. H. (1982). Measures of problem-solving performance and of problem-solving instruction. Journal for Research in Mathematics Education, 13(1), 31-49.

12. Anderson, J. R., & Reiser, B. J. (1985). The LISP tutor. Byte, 10(4), 159-175.

13. Soloway, E., & Ehrlich, K. (1984). Empirical studies of programming knowledge. IEEE Transactions on Software Engineering, SE-10(5), 595-609.

14. Feurzeig, W., Horwitz, P., & Nickerson, R. (1981). Microcomputers in education (Report no. 4798). Cambridge, Massachusetts: Bolt, Beranek, & Newman.

15. Papert, S. (1980). Mindstorms: Children, computers, and powerful ideas. New York: Basic Books.

16. Delclos, V. R., Littlefield, J., & Bransford, J. D. (1985). Teaching thinking through LOGO: The importance of method. Roeper Review, 7(3), 153-156.

17. Salomon, G., & Perkins, D. N. (1984, August). Rocky roads to transfer: Rethinking mechanisms of a neglected phenomenon. Paper presented at the Conference on Thinking, Harvard Graduate School of Education, Cambridge, Massachusetts.

18. Perkins, D. N. (1985). The fingertip effect: How information-processing technology changes thinking. Educational Researcher, 14(7), 11-17.

19. Perkins, D., & Salomon, G. (in press). Transfer and teaching thinking. In Bishop, J., Lochhead, J., & Perkins, D. (Eds.). Thinking: Progress in research and teaching. Hillsdale, New Jersey: Erlbaum.

20. Bereiter, C., & Scardamalia, M. (1985). Cognitive coping strategies and the problem of inert knowledge. In S. S. Chipman, J. W. Segal, & R. Glazer (Eds.), Thinking and learning skills, Vol. 2: Current research and open questions (pp. 65-80). Hillsdale, New Jersey: Erlbaum.

21. Belmont, J. M., Butterfield, E. C., & Ferretti, R. P. (1982). To secure transfer of training instruct self-management skills. In D. K. Detterman & R. J. Sternberg (Eds.), How and how much can intelligence be increased? (pp. 147-154). Norwood, New Jersey: Ablex.

22. de Villiers, J. G., & de Villiers, P. A. (1978). Language acquisition. Cambridge, Massachusetts: Harvard University Press.

23. Adamson, R. E. (1952). Functional fixedness as related to problem solving. Journal of Experimental Psychology, 44, 288-291.

24. Luchins, A. S. (1942). Mechanization in problem solving. Psychological Monographs, 54(6).

25. Davis, R. B. (1984). Learning mathematics: The cognitive science approach to mathematics education. Norwood, New Jersey: Ablex.

26. Brown, J. S., & VanLehn, K. (1980). Repair theory: A generative theory of bugs in procedural skills. Cognitive Science, 4, 379-426.

27. VanLehn, K. (1981). Bugs are not enough: Empirical studies of bugs, impasses and repairs in procedural skills. Palo Alto, California: Cognitive and Instructional Sciences Group, Palo Alto Research Center, Xerox.

28. Wickelgren, W. A. (1974). How to solve problems: Elements of a theory of problems and problem solving. San Francisco: W. H. Freeman and Co.

CHAPTER 16

Analyzing the High Frequency Bugs in Novice Programs

James G. Spohrer
Elliot Soloway
Department of Computer Science
Cognition and Programming Project
Yale University
New Haven, CT 06520

ABSTRACT

In this paper, we provide a detailed analysis of the bugs that novice programmers most frequently made while solving a set of introductory programming problems. First, we show the special status of high frequency bugs: Lots of students learning to program make the same bugs. Second, we show that most of the high frequency bugs do not arise because students have a misconception about some language construct. The implications of these two results for teaching programming are discussed.

INTRODUCTION: MOTIVATION AND GOALS

There is much folklore surrounding the teaching of programming to people. For example, one quite popular piece of folklore deals with the ostensible mental damage that students undergo when they learn to program in BASIC. In this paper, we will focus on the following two bits of folk wisdom that deal with the types of bugs that students make when they learn to program.

- Just a few types of bugs are made by lots of students learning to program.
- Most bugs arise because students have some misconception about some language construct.

We will argue, based on our empirical study, that 1) yes, a few bug types account for a large percentage of program bugs, and 2) no, misconceptions about language constructs do not seem to be as widespread or troublesome as is typically believed.

Recently, there has been a great deal of interest in understanding bugs in programs (e.g., [1],[2],[3],[4],[5],[6],[7]). Interest in program bugs usually derives from one of three perspectives:

- Engineers: Improve programmer productivity and program reliability.
- Educators: Improve novices' understanding of programming, and the novices

ability to rapidly learn to generate correct, maintainable programs.

- Cognitive scientists: Improve our understanding of the acquistion and performance of complex problem solving skills and determine how misconceptions, problem solving strategies, and cognitive constraints on processing can lead to errors.

In this paper we are primarily concerned with the educator's perspective. Our data and theory of programming bugs can provide educational leverage for instructors in three ways:

- By providing a vocabulary for discussing programs, bugs in programs, and the problems which arise for novices.

- By identifying the high frequency bugs across a range of introductory programming problems.

- By giving a sense of why some of the bugs may have occurred.

The organization of this paper is as follows: Section 2 describes how our buggy program data were collected; in Section 3 the goal and plan structure of novice programs is explained and how we identify bugs in terms of this structure is presented; Section 4 examines two commonsense notions about bugs in novice programs that many educators have, evaluates whether or not our data support the notions, and makes recommendations to educators based on our findings; in Section 5 we summarize the results of our analysis and their implications.

DATA COLLECTION

The descriptions of bugs that we report in this paper are based on actual student generated programs. We augmented the operating system of the VAX 750 that the students were using and, with their permission, obtained a copy of each syntactically correct program they submitted for compilation. We call such data *on-line protocols*. We have collected this type of data from students for a number of introductory Pascal programming courses at various universities. The data reported in this paper were collected during the Spring 1984 semester at Yale University in an introductory Pascal programming course specifically designed for non-science, humanities oriented students.

```
Programming Assignments -- Some Critical Issues

 1. Cricket Chirp Problem    -- Input Reals and Integers, Arith. Calc., Output
 2. Electric Bill Problem    -- Nested If-Then-Else, Single Boundary Data Guard
 3. Reformatting Problem     -- Loop, Interval & Set Data Guards, Read Characters
 4. Averaging Problem        -- Average, Counters, Running Total Accumulators
 5. Fibonacci Problem        -- Nested Loops, Saving Previous Value In Loop
 6. Rainfall Problem         -- Maximum, Average, Division-by-zero Guard
 7. Bank Problem             -- Command Selection Loop
 8. Tax Problem              -- Dispatch Loop, Procedures
 9. License Plate Problem    -- Functions, Random Numbers
10. Decoder Problem          -- Input from File
```

Figure 1: The Spring 1984 CS110 series of programming assignments.

During this course, students were assigned ten programming problems (see Figure 1). Three of the programming problems were selected for further study:

- *The Electric Bill Problem*: An early assignment in which the students had to use nested IF-THEN-ELSE constructs for the first time.

231

- *The Reformatting Problem*: The first problem in which students had to use a loop.

- *The Tax Problem*: One of the later problems, and one in which the students were required to use procedures for the first time.

In addition to introducing students to one main programming concept for the first time, the problems also required students to use in new ways some of the concepts that they had previously learned, as illustrated in assignment summaries in Figure 2.

The Electric Bill Problem

1. Input Customer_Number and Usage, and guard against negative Usage.
2. Calculate the customer's electric Bill based on various Usage ranges.
3. Output the Customer_Number, Usage and Bill.

The Reformatting Problem

1. Input experiment data; in case of typos, give the user a second chance.
2. Calculate the Elapsed_Time of the experiment based on start and end times.
3. Output reformatted experiment data with Elapsed_Time.
4. Process multiple experiments.

The Tax Problem

1. Input Marital_Status and Income, and guard against typos.
2. Dispatch to appropriate formula based on Marital_Status.
3. Calculate Tax and Net_income (in subroutines) based on Marital_Status.
4. Output Marital_Status, Income, Net_Income, and Tax.
5. Perform multiple tax computations.

Figure 2: Summary of the three problem specifications.

Sixty-one students' first syntactically correct programs for the three problems were selected for detailed analysis. We selected the first syntactically correct version because we are primarily interested in non-syntactic errors, and the first version contains more bugs than later versions (i.e., the novices had not yet debugged their programs). Of the 183 programs chosen in this manner, twenty-five programs were excluded from the analysis because the students had not tried to solve enough of the problem in their first attempt (e.g., merely printing an introductory message). In addition to these data, we have analyzed novice programs for other problems and from later versions; see Johnson et al. [8], Joni and Soloway [9], and Spohrer et al. [10] for a more complete analysis.

IDENTIFYING BUGS IN TERMS OF GOALS AND PLANS

If a program is syntactically well-formed, then the program can be executed, but functional errors or *bugs* may prevent the program from behaving in an appropriate manner or from producing the correct output. Run-time error messages such as "attempted division by zero", "attempted access of uninitialized variable", or "array index out of bounds" indicate that a program has functional errors. In addition, deviant program behavior such as "never returning" (an infinite loop) or producing the wrong output on test input also indicate functional errors. To understand how we identify bugs in novice

232

programs, we must first describe the *goal and plan* structure of a program.

```
01 PROGRAM Reformatting(INPUT,OUTPUT);
02 VAR Id, Start_Hour, Start_Minute, Start_Second, End_Hour, End_Minute,
03     End_Second, Elapsed_Time, Start_Time, End_Time : INTEGER;
04     Problem_Type, Accuracy, Sentinel, Whitespace1, Whitespace2 : CHAR;
05
06 BEGIN
07 +------[ P:SEPARATE-LOOP-CONTROL-CHARACTER ]-----------------+
08 |WRITELN('Type "y" to process data ("n" to stop)');          |
09 |READLN(Sentinel);                                           |
10 |IF ((Sentinel <> 'y') and (Sentinel <> 'n'))               |
11 |   THEN BEGIN                                               |
12 |        WRITELN('Type "y" or "n"');                |-- G:LOOP
13 |        READLN(Sentinel);                                   |
14 |        END;                                                |
15 |WHILE (Sentinel = 'y') DO                                   |
16 | BEGIN                                                      |
17 +-----------------------------------------------------------+
18 | +---------[ P:INPUT-ALL/GUARD-ALL/RETRY-ALL ]-------------+
19 | |WRITELN('Enter: Id Type Start(h m s) End(h m s) Accuracy');|
20 | |READLN(Id, Whitespace1, Problem_Type,                   |
21 | |       Start_Hour, Start_Minute, Start_Second,          |
22 | |       End_Hour, End_Minute, End_Second,                |
23 | |       Whitespace2, Accuracy);                          |
24 | |IF ((Id < 0)  OR  ((Problem_Type <> 'a') AND            |
25 | |   (Problem_Type <> 'b') AND (Problem_Type <> 'c')) OR  |
26 | |   ((Start_Hour   < 1) OR (Start_Hour   > 12)) OR       |
27 | |   ((Start_Minute < 0) OR (Start_Minute > 59)) OR       |
28 | |   ((Start_Second < 0) OR (Start_Second > 59)) OR    |-- G:VDE
29 | |   ((End_Hour   < 1) OR (End_Hour   > 12)) OR           |
30 | |   ((End_Minute < 0) OR (End_Minute > 59)) OR           |
31 | |   ((End_Second < 0) OR (End_Second > 59)) OR           |
32 | |   ((Accuracy <> '+') AND (Accuracy <> '-')))           |
33 | |   THEN BEGIN                                           |
34 | |        WRITELN('BAD DATA: Try again.');                |
35 | |        READLN(Id, Whitespace1, Problem_Type,           |
36 | |             Start_Hour, Start_Minute, Start_Second,    |
37 | |             End_Hour, End_Minute, End_Second,          |
38 | |             Whitespace2, Accuracy);                    |
39 | |        END;                                            |
40 | +-------------------------------------------------------+
41 | +--------[ P:STANDARDIZE-WRAPAROUND-DIFFERENCE ]---------+
42 | |Start_Time := Start_Hour*3600 + Start_Minute*60 + Start_Second;|
43 | |End_Time   := End_Hour*3600   + End_Minute*60   + End_Second; |
44 | |IF (Start_Time >= End_Time)                          |-- G:CALC
45 | |    THEN End_Time := End_Time + 12*3600;                |
46 | |Elapsed_Time := End_Time - Start_Time;                  |
47 | +-------------------------------------------------------+
48 | +--------------[ P:OUTPUT-ALL ]-------------------------+
49 | |WRITELN('Result:',Id,Problem_Type,Elapsed_Time,Accuracy);|-- G:OUTPUT
50 | +-------------------------------------------------------+
51 +----------[ P:SEPARATE-LOOP-CONTROL-CHARACTER ]--------------+
52 |  WRITELN('Type "y" to process data ("n" to stop)');        |
53 |  READLN(Sentinel);                                         |
54 |  IF ((Sentinel <> 'y') and (Sentinel <> 'n'))             |
55 |     THEN BEGIN                                             |
56 |          WRITELN('Type "y" or "n"');              |-- G:LOOP
57 |          READLN(Sentinel);                                 |
58 |          END;                                              |
59 | END;                                                       |
60 +-----------------------------------------------------------+
61 END.
```

Figure 3: A sample solution to the Reformatting Problem.

We have been developing a theory of the knowledge that programmers use in generating and interpreting programs. Two key types of knowledge for which we have found empirical support are *programming goals and programming plans* [11],[12],[2]. Programming plans are stereotypic sequences of code that accomplish some programming goal. In short, goals are *what* must be accomplished to solve a problem, and plans are *how* the goals can be achieved. For example, consider the summary specification of the Reformatting Problem in Figure 2; the four top-level goals that must be achieved are:

- *G:VDE*: This is the G:VALID-DATA-ENTRY goal of inputting experiment

233

data, and in case of errors, giving the user a second chance to enter correct data.

- *G:CALC*: This is the G:CALCULATION goal of computing the elapsed time of the experiment in seconds.
- *G:OUTPUT*: Write out the reformatted data.
- *G:LOOP*: Process multiple records of information.

Each of these goals must be achieved using a particular programming plan. For example, consider the sample solution to the Reformatting Problem shown in Figure 3:

- P:INPUT-ALL/GUARD-ALL/RETRY-ALL is used to achieve G:VDE (lines 19-39).
- P:STANDARDIZE-WRAPAROUND-DIFFERENCE is used to achieve G:CALC (lines 42-46).
- P:OUTPUT-ALL is used to achieve G:OUTPUT (line 49).
- P:SEPARATE-LOOP-CONTROL-CHARACTER is used to achieve G:LOOP (lines 8-16, 52-59).

Many alternative plans exists for achieving these four goals. For example, instead of achieving G:VDE for all the input variables at once (i.e., P:INPUT-ALL/GUARD-ALL/RETRY-ALL, as in Figure 3), G:VDE could have been achieved for each input variable separately, as shown below for the first two variables:

```
P:INPUT-GUARD-RETRY-EACH
01 WRITELN('Enter subject number.');              <-- G:INPUT
02 READLN(Id);
03 IF (Id < 0) THEN BEGIN                          <-- G:GUARD
04                WRITELN('Bad Data: Try again.'); <-- G:RETRY
05                READLN(Id)
06                END;
07 WRITELN('Enter Problem Type.');                 <-- G:INPUT
08 READLN(Problem_Type);
09 IF ((Problem_Type <> 'a') AND (Problem_Type <> 'b') AND  <-- G:GUARD
10     (Problem_Type <> 'c'))
11            THEN BEGIN
12                WRITELN('Bad Data: Try again.'); <-- G:RETRY
13                READLN(Problem_Type);
14                END;
15 ...
```

Both plans organize the same set of subgoals (i.e., G:INPUT, G:GUARD, and G:RETRY for each data item), but each interleaves the subgoals differently.

We use the goal and plan structure of a program to identify bugs. Our position is: *Given a goal and plan vocabulary for describing the structure of a program, we can identify bugs in novice programs as the differences between one of the correct plans for achieving a goal and the observed plan for achieving a goal.* For example, Figure 4 shows an incorrect implementation of the P:INPUT-ALL/GUARD-ALL/RETRY-ALL. Because we have the correct plan (left side of Figure 4), we can compare it to the observed implementation used by the novices and note the differences. The buggy plan is missing certain variables that are contained in the correct plan. The problem with the buggy plan is that the whitespace (that is used to separate the input values) will be read in instead of the intended character values. In line 3 of the buggy plan, the Problem_ Type variable will read the space just before the character a, which is the intended input for Problem_ Type. However, note that in line 3 of the correct plan an extra variable, Whitespace1, has been added to capture the whitespace character before the character a. The problem also exist in line 18, when the G:RETRY subgoal is achieved, and in line 6 and 21 for the Accuracy variable. All together there are four plan differences, as indicated by the arrows in Figure 4. Because all four of these differences result from the same underlying misconception

SAMPLE INPUT: *23 a 10 45 30 10 57 02 +*   ;Note spaces between input values

```
+-[ CORRECT P:INPUT-ALL/GUARD-ALL/RETRY-ALL ]--------------+    +------------[ OBSERVED BUGGY PLAN FOR G:VDE ]---------------+
|WRITELN('Enter: Id Type Start(h m s) End(h m s) Accuracy').|    |WRITELN('Enter: Id Type Start(h m s) End(h m s) Accuracy').|
|READLN(Id, Whitespace1, Problem_Type, -------------------->|READLN(Id, Problem_Type,                                   |
|       Start_Hour, Start_Minute, Start_Second,             | |       Start_Hour, Start_Minute, Start_Second,             |
|       End_Hour, End_Minute, End_Second,                   | |       End_Hour, End_Minute, End_Second,                   |
|       Whitespace2, Accuracy);                             | |       Accuracy);                                          |
|IF ((Id < 0) OR ((Problem_Type <> 'a') AND                 | |IF ((Id < 0) OR ((Problem_Type <> 'a') AND                 |
|    (Problem_Type <> 'b) AND (Problem_Type <> 'c)) OR       | |    (Problem_Type <> 'b') AND (Problem_Type <> 'c')) OR     |
|    ((Start_Hour   < 1) OR (Start_Hour   > 12)) OR         | |    ((Start_Hour   < 1) OR (Start_Hour   > 12)) OR         |
|    ((Start_Minute < 0) OR (Start_Minute > 59)) OR         | |    ((Start_Minute < 0) OR (Start_Minute > 59)) OR         |
|    ((Start_Second < 0) OR (Start_Second > 59)) OR         | |    ((Start_Second < 0) OR (Start_Second > 59)) OR         |
|    ((End_Hour    < 1) OR (End_Hour    > 12)) OR           | |    ((End_Hour    < 1) OR (Start_Hour    > 12)) OR         |
|    ((End_Minute  < 0) OR (End_Minute  > 59)) OR           | |    ((End_Minute  < 0) OR (Start_Minute  > 59)) OR         |
|    ((End_Second  < 0) OR (End_Second  > 59)) OR           | |    ((End_Second  < 1) OR (Start_Second  > 59)) OR         |
|    ((Accuracy <> '+') AND (Accuracy <> '-')))             | |    ((Accuracy <> '+') AND (Accuracy <> '-')))             |
|  THEN BEGIN                                               | |  THEN BEGIN                                               |
|      WRITELN('BAD DATA: Try again.');                     | |      WRITELN('BAD DATA: Try again.');                     |
|      READLN(Id, Whitespace1, Problem_Type, -------------->| --> READLN(Id, Problem_Type,                              |
|             Start_Hour, Start_Minute, Start_Second,       | |             Start_Hour, Start_Minute, Start_Second,       |
|             End_Hour, End_Minute, End_Second,             | |             End_Hour, End_Minute, End_Second,             |
|             Whitespace2, Accuracy). --------------------->| --> Accuracy);                                            |
|  END.                                                     | |  END;                                                     |
+----------------------------------------------------------+ |  +--------------------------------------------------------+
```

Figure 4:   Identifying bugs as plan differences.

about reading characters embedded in other input data, we identify the following bug:

- G:VDE[P:INPUT-ALL/GUARD-ALL/RETRY-ALL]/G:TYPE&G:ACCURACY :: MALFORMED G:INPUT&G:RETRY

The bug name serves to locate where the bug occurred: In the top-level G:VDE goal, when the P:INPUT-ALL/GUARD-ALL/RETRY-ALL plan was employed, the G:TYPE&G:ACCURACY subgoals were not successfully achieved due to malformed plans to achieve the G:INPUT&G:RETRY subgoals.

ANALYSIS OF THE DATA

Figure 5 summarizes some of the results of our analysis of the first syntatically correct programs for these three problems.

Type of Statistic	Elec. B. (KWH)	Reformat. (REF)	Tax (TAX)
Number of Subjects Analyzed	55	46	57
Total of Observed Bugs (TOKENS)	85	140	59
Number of Unique Bugs (TYPES)	28	46	27
Bugs per 1st Synt. Correct Version			
Mean	1.5	3.0	1.0
Standard Deviation	1.4	2.2	1.3
Assignment Number (in sequence)	2	3	8
Lines of Pascal per Program (mean)	27.8	73.1	68.6

Figure 5:   Statistical overview of the three problems.

The first row of Figure 5 shows that about fifty novices' programs were analyzed for each of the three programming problems. In order to provide a better appreciation of the three programming problems, we have included information in the table about when the problems occurred in the curriculum and an indication of the size of the programs. We found the most bugs in the Reformatting Problem, the Electric Bill Problem was the next buggiest problem, and the Tax Problem was the least buggy. An important distinction to be aware of when counting bugs is the type-token distinction. A *bug token* is an instance of a bug in some program. A *bug type* is a name for a group of identical bug tokens. The total number of bug tokens found in all the novice programs is 85, 140 and 59, respectively, while the number of bug types for each problem is 28, 46, and 27, respectively. So on average, for each bug type there were about three example bug tokens. In the next section, we will evaluate one commonsense notion of programming bugs.

The Relative Frequency of Bugs

Anyone who has taught programming and seen a large number of buggy programs has probably made the following observation:

- *All bugs are not created equal. Some bugs occur over and over again in a group of novices programs, while others occur only rarely.*

In order to evaluate this observation, we kept track of the frequency of each bug in our analysis. For an even distribution, 10% of the bug types would account for 10% of the bug tokens. However, as Figure 6 shows just 10% of the bug types account for between 32% and 46% of the bug tokens. A few high frequency bug types account for the bulk of the observed tokens.

```
          |  KWH  |  REF  |  TAX  |   <----- Problem
       --+-------+-------+-------+
  %   10% |  44%  |  46%  |  32%  |   <--|
       --+-------+-------+-------+       |
  T   20% |  55%  |  64%  |  46%  |   <--|
  Y    --+-------+-------+-------+       |
  P   25% |  62%  |  69%  |  56%  |   <--|-- % Tokens accounted for
  E    --+-------+-------+-------+       |
  S   50% |  80%  |  84%  |  77%  |   <--|
       --+-------+-------+-------+
```

Figure 6:   Table of percent of tokens accounted for by specified percent of types.

On average for the three problems, one fifth (20%) of the bug types account for over half (55%) of the bug tokens. These data support, and quantify, the intuition that not all bugs are created equal. The fact that a relatively few bug types account for so many bug tokens has implications for educators:

- *Educators can most effectively improve their students' performance by changing instruction to address and to eliminate the high frequency bugs.*

In this case, a commonsense notion about the nature of bugs in novice programs has been confirmed. In the next section, we will examine another commonsense notion about the bugs in novice programs.

Sources of High Frequency Bugs

In most introductory textbooks each successive section covers a new language construct. Instructors teach the course by describing successive language constructs and then showing how to use the construct in a program. Because of this emphasis on language constructs, one might suspect that:

- *Most bugs arise because the novice does not fully understand the semantics of particular programming language constructs.*

Certainly, extensive evidence does exist that novices have many misconceptions about constructs. For instance, Bayman & Mayer [13] showed that novices possess a wide range of misconceptions concerning individual statements or constructs from the programming language they had learned. These misconceptions reflected differences between novices' mental models of individual BASIC statements and an expert's framework for describing the function of the statements [14]. However, these studies were designed to test novices ability to interpret single statements after taking a three-session self-instruction course. To evaluate the notion that most bugs arise from misconceptions about a construct, more representative data is required. Our data which was collected in a more natural setting during a semester-long introductory programming course can be analyzed to provide a more complete picture of novice programmers and the types of bugs they make.

In predicting where bugs might occur in a program, this commonsense notion would suggest that high frequency bugs might be associated with the main language construct that was being introduced in each of the problems. This view derives from a general heuristic, that mistakes occur most frequently in novel situations or when something new is being used. If programming is viewed as composing language constructs, then one would expect many bugs in the most novel constructs. The main language constructs introduced in each of the three problems we analyzed are:

- *Electric Bill Problem*: IF-THEN-ELSE
- *Reformatting Problem*: WHILE-DO, AND, OR, READLN (for characters)
- *Tax Problem*: PROCEDURE

Of the 101 types of bugs found in the three problems, we have selected the 10% most frequently occurring bugs to analyze in detail to evaluate the notion that most bugs arise when novices misunderstand the semantics of language constructs. For this purpose, we selected 11 bugs in all (see Figure 7): 3 from the Electric Bill (abbreviated BILL), 5 from the Reformatting (REF), and 3 from the Tax (TAX) Problems. None of the most common bugs occurred in WHILE-DO loops or in using a PROCEDURE. In fact, as we will show, *only 1 of the 11 bugs seems clearly to result from a misunderstanding of the semantics of a construct*; 3 of the 11 bugs might result from misunderstanding the semantics and the remaining 7 bugs most probably did not involve any misunderstanding of a language construct. These data indicate that while some bugs do result from misunderstanding the semantics of particular constructs, by no means do the data indicate that this is the dominant source of bugs in novice programs. We will examine each of the bugs in Figure 7 in more detail and explain why we have classified the bugs as we have.

Problem	Rank Order	Frequency (# subjects)	Description	Semantics of Construct Dominant Problem?
BILL	1	13	Zero is excluded (Figure 8)	NO
	2	13	Output frag. (Figure 9)	NO
	3	11	Output frag. (Figure 11)	NO
REF	1	20	Off-by-one (Figure 12)	NO
	2	18	Space gets read (Figure 13)	YES
	3	13	OR-for-AND (Figure 14)	MAYBE
	4	11	Off-by-one (Figure 15)	NO
	5	7	Wrong constant (Figure 16)	NO
TAX	1	7	Wrong formula (Figure 17)	NO
	2	7	Needs parentheses (Figure 18)	MAYBE
	3	5	OR-for-AND (Figure 19)	MAYBE

Figure 7: The 10% most frequent bugs for the three programming problems.

237

Eleven High Frequency Bugs. The 11 bugs selected for detailed analysis represent just 10% of the types of bugs that we found, but account for well over a third of all the bug tokens we observed. To get a better idea of how common these bugs actually are, consider that on average for any particular one of these bugs one out of every five students generated it (some bugs were made by about one out of every two students).

In order to evaluate the commonsense notion that most novice programming bugs are due to a misunderstanding of the semantics of some particular language construct, we must try to identify the underlying source of each bug. In effect, we are trying to guess what the student was (or was not) thinking about that lead to the bug. We term explanations of the origins of bugs *plausible accounts*. For example, the bug described in section 3 (see Figure 4) might have arisen because the student thought that since whitespace between numeric input is ignored, the whitespace between character input would be ignored as well. Developing and evaluating the veracity of such plausible accounts is clearly a difficult activity. We have drawn on the work of Bonar and Soloway [2], Sleeman et al. [6], and Pea [5], who interviewed students as they were attempting to write programs, in developing and evaluting the plausible accounts presented in this section. The verbal reports they gleaned often shed light on why the students were writing the programs in the way they were. Nonetheless, extreme care must be exercised in using such verbal reports to both develop and evaluate plausible accounts. For example, simply asking a student what he/she was thinking about as they were creating the buggy program (or after the fact), may or may not provide particularly useful data; oftentimes when someone is confused, they do not know why they are confused, and their verbal report may not be accurate. We have also drawn on our not inconsiderable experience in analyzing and tutoring students in programming (e.g., [8],[15],[10]) in developing and evaluating the plausible accounts in this section. Thus, while these plausible accounts must be subjected to further scientific inquiry, they were by no means created from whole cloth; we feel that they have considerable grounding in psychological reality. In what follows, then, we will use these plausible accounts to explore the question -- are most bugs the result of misconceptions about language constructs?

```
G:VDE/G:GUARD :: MALFORMED G:COND
01 +-------------------+
02 | IF (Usage <= 0)   |
03 +-------------------+
04      THEN WRITELN('Illegal Usage!');
05      ELSE ...
```

Figure 8: BILL1: An off-by-one bug.

BILL1: Boundary Problem. Figure 8 shows an example of the most frequent bug that occurred in the Electric Bill Problem. The students who made this bug did not include zero in the range of allowed values for the amount of electricity used by a customer. This type of bug is commonly called an *off-by-one* bug, and is characteristic of problems novices have in deciding on appropriate boundary conditions.

One might try to argue that the students that made this bug simply did not understand the semantics of the relational operators (e.g., <= or <) they were using. However, in the Electric Bill Problem relational operators had to be used elsewhere in the program to select the various rate ranges in the calculation, and in these situations the relational operators were usually correct. More likely, the off-by-one bug in the Electric Bill Problem results from a conscious decision on the part of some students to exclude zero from being a legitimate value for the usage variable. Possibly, the students reasoned that if there was no usage, then there would be no need to calculate a bill (because, after all, the bill would come out zero, no charge for no usage). Note that this is fundamentally different from excluding negative values of usage, which are impossible. Apparently, the

238

distinction between impossible values and trivial or unlikely values of a variable were blurred in the students' minds as they attempted to define a set of legal or valid values.

The issue of how best to handle boundary points concerned other students who did not make this particular bug. While some students included zero usage in the lowest rate range, other students explicitly tested to see if the value of usage was zero. If it was, then they printed out a special message indicating that no electricity had been used. Novices had difficulty deciding whether a boundary point should be handled separately, or like values in one of the two ranges it divides.

We have classified this bug (see BILL1 in Figure 7) as probably not the result of any misunderstanding of language constructs. Most students who generated this bug had successfully used relational operators in other parts of the program. The bug appears to be symptomatic of a more general problem novices have when they try to categorize and handle boundary points.

```
G:VDE/G:GUARD :: MALFORMED G:SCOPE-FOR-VALID
01 BEGIN
02 +------------------------------------------------------+
03 |WRITELN('Please input customer id, and kwh used.');  |-- G:INPUT
04 |READLN(Id,Usage);                                    |
05 +------------------------------------------------------+
06 +------------------------------------------------------------------+
07 |IF (Usage < 0)                                                    |
08 |   THEN                                                           |
09 |       +------------------------------------------------+         |
10 |       | WRITELN('Negative kwh used is impossible!');    |-- G:ERROR |
11 |       +------------------------------------------------+         |
12 |   ELSE                                                           |
13 |       +------------------------------------------------+         |
14 |       | IF (Usage < 350)                              |         |-- G:VALID-DATA-GUARD
15 |       |    THEN Bill := Usage * 0.09                   |         |
16 |       | ELSE IF (Usage < 625)                          |         |
17 |       |         THEN Bill := 350 * 0.09 + (Usage - 350) * 0.05 | |
18 |       | ELSE IF (Usage < 850)                          |-- G:CALC |
19 |       |         THEN Bill := 350 * 0.09 + 275 * 0.05    |         |
20 |       |                         + (Usage - 625) * 0.04  |         |
21 |       | ELSE Bill := 350 * 0.09 + 275 * 0.05 + 225 * 0.04 |       |
22 |       |                         + (Usage - 850) * 0.03; |         |
23 |       +------------------------------------------------+         |
24 +------------------------------------------------------------------+
25 +----------------------------------------------+
26 |WRITELN('Customer number    = ', Id);         |
27 |WRITELN('KiloWatt Hours used = ', Usage:0:2); |-- G:OUTPUT
28 |WRITELN('Electric bill      = $', Bill:0:2);  |
29 +----------------------------------------------+
30 END.
```

Figure 9:   BILL2: An output fragmentation bug.

BILL2: Plan-Dependency Problem.   Figure 9 shows an *output fragmentation* bug. Under certain circumstances, a program with this type of bug generates an "attempt to output uninitialized variable" error message. Note that the normal output (lines 26-28 in Figure 9) will always be done, even if the value input for Usage is not a valid number. When the value of Usage is bad (i.e., negative), the error message will be printed (line 10), but the bill will not be computed. Unfortunately, the normal output will be executed anyway, and the program will fail in an attempt to write out the value of the uninitialized Bill variable (line 28). The output plan depends on the calculation plan to compute a value for the Bill variable, so when the calculation is skipped, the normal output should be skipped as well.

One might try to explain this type of bug as a misunderstanding of the semantics of the IF-THEN-ELSE construct: Novices appear to think that the statements that occur after the ELSE will all be a part of the ELSE clause. If ELSE clauses were really scoped this way then the code would be correct, because the normal output would only be done after the calculation. However, one piece of evidence indicates that the novices did in fact know the actual scope of the ELSE clause. The way novices organize their code on a page (using indentation, etc.) says a lot about how they expect the code to be executed. Note that the output code is not aligned with the start of the ELSE clause, but instead is aligned with the IF statement for the valid data guard. In other situations where novices left out a BEGIN-END pair, the intended scoping was easily inferred from indentation and alignment. For example, a few of the novices used two WRITELN statements in the THEN clause (see line 10 of Figure 9), but left out the BEGIN-END pair which is necessary to group the two statements. In these situations, the two WRITELN statements were aligned with each other, indicating the scoping intended by the novices. Because of the alignment of the output code, it appears that the novices who made this output fragmentation bug were not misunderstanding the scope of the ELSE clause.

```
01    Program Cricket_Chirp(input, output);
02    VAR Chirps_In_Ten_Seconds: INTEGER;
03        Temperature: REAL;
04
05    BEGIN
06    +-------------------------------------------------------+
07    |Writeln('Input Number of cricket chirps in 10 seconds.');|-- G:INPUT
08    |Readln(Chirps_In_Ten_Seconds);                         |
09    +-------------------------------------------------------+
10    +-----------------------------------------------+
11    |Temperature := (Chirps_In_Ten_Seconds*6 + 40)/4;|-- G:CALC
12    +-----------------------------------------------+
13    +---------------------------------------------------------+
14    |Writeln('Chirps In Ten Seconds', Chirps_In_Ten_Seconds);|
15    |Writeln('Temperature =', Temperature:0:2);              |-- G:OUTPUT
16    +---------------------------------------------------------+
17    END.
```

Figure 10: Sample solution to the Cricket Chirp Problem.

Instead, it is our sense that the bug occurs because novices are unable to anticipate all of the implications of combining programming plans. In particular, the novices generate programs in which the output is always done, even though the output should not be done if the input data is invalid. The programming problem that novices solved just before the Electric Bill Problem was the Cricket Chirp Problem. As the solution to the Cricket Chirp Problem in Figure 10 illustrates, the plan structure of this program is fairly straightforward: Get the input (lines 7-8), do the calculation (line 11), and print the outputs (lines 14-15). In contrast, the plan structure of the attempted solution to the Electric Bill Problem in Figure 9 is more complex. The most fundamental difference between the two problems is that in the Cricket Chirp program only one sequence of goals can occur, while in the Electric Bill program two sequences of goals can occur, one for valid data and the other for invalid data. For example, consider the following sequences of goals required to solve each of the two problems:

- *Cricket Chirp Goal Sequence:*
  - ▸ SEQUENCE 1: G:INPUT -> G:CALC -> G:OUTPUT
- *Electric Bill Goal Sequences:*
  - ▸ SEQUENCE 1: G:INPUT -> G:VALID-DATA-GUARD -> G:CALC -> G:OUTPUT
  - ▸ SEQUENCE 2: G:INPUT -> G:VALID-DATA-GUARD -> G:ERROR

Before looking at why the novices might have generated the buggy code shown in Figure 9, it is informative to look at the reasons why the novices may not have detected any problem with their code. In verifying the code in Figure 9, to make sure that both possible goal sequences were achieved, the novices may have reasoned as follows:

SEQUENCE 1: After getting the inputs (lines 3-4), I check to see if the Usage is valid (line 7), and if it is, I do the calculation (lines 14-22). After that's done I do the output

240

(lines 26-28). Yep, that works.

SEQUENCE 2: After getting the inputs (lines 3-4), I check to see if the Usage *is valid (line 7), and if it's not, I print out an error message (line 10). Yep, that works too. Both possibilities check out fine, so I am done.*

The problem with the verification in SEQUENCE 2 is that while all of the explicit goals in the sequence check out, there is a final implicit goal in the sequence, G:STOP, that is not verified. Stopping after reporting an error condition is so natural that the novices may not have bothered to check for the stop because it is implicit, or they may have had the *Bad-is-stop* misconception which attributes to the computer the ability to "do the reasonable thing" when an error message is printed. If the novices had been explicitly requested to verify that G:STOP was achieved after G:ERROR, then some of them might have foreseen the possible negative interaction with G:OUTPUT (i.e., attempted output of the uninitialized Bill variable). In essence, the novices had the "whole 'sequence'", but not "nothing but the 'sequence'."

While these verification scenerioes may explain why the novices did not detect the output fragmentation bug in Figure 9, they do not address the question of why the novices generated the buggy code in the first place. One reason is that, in keeping with their previous experience with the Cricket Chirp Problem (see Figure 10), the novices had overgeneralized the basic structure of all programs and developed the *Output-goes-last* misconception. Novices with this misconception always place the code to achieve output at the very end of the program in the same way that people put the closing (e.g., "Yours truly...") of a letter at the end -- "that's the place where it goes." Alternatively, the novice may have reasoned as follows:

- *First, I have to get the input, then I check to make sure it's valid. If it's not valid then I want to print out an error message, otherwise the next thing to do in the other case is the calculation (*puts this in ELSE clause*). Finally, after the calculation is completed, the output can be done.*

In this case G:ERROR and G:CALC were symmetric alternatives, each being the first goal that had to be achieved in the sequences when the two sequences became different. If the novices had thought of the calculation and output as a unit, then the novices might have placed the combined calculation-output in the ELSE clause. Expert programmers would consider the calculation and output as a unit, because experts are aware of the plan dependency between the two -- the calculation produces a result (i.e., the value of Bill), that the output depends on. The novices' view of the calculation and output is more fragmentary. To correct the problem in Figure 9, the output plan should be nested along with the calculation plan in the valid-data-guard plan. In general, plan dependencies arise when one plan produces a result that is used by another plan, and plan dependencies have implications for how the plans should be combined. As this example illustrates, when a novice ignores, or overlooks, the calculation-output plan dependency and guards only the calculation, but not the combined calculation-output, an *output fragmentation* bug results.

We classified this bug as probably not arising from a misunderstanding of any construct (see BILL2 in Figure 7). The alignment evidence argues against a misconception about the scope of the ELSE clause. Instead, it appears that the novices did not consider the implications of the calculation-output plan dependency, and the resulting error-output interaction.

BILL3: Plan-Dependency Problem. In Figure 11 another form of the output fragmentation bug for the Electric Bill Problem is shown. The problem is the same in this case as in the last bug described: If usage is negative, then an attempt will be made to output the uninitialized bill variable. However, note in this case that the novice has

```
MISPLACED G:OUTPUT
01 BEGIN
02  WRITELN('Please input customer id, and kwh used.');
03  READLN(Id,Usage);
04  IF (Usage < 0)
05      THEN WRITELN('Negative kwh used is impossible!');
06      ELSE BEGIN
06          IF (Usage < 350)
07              THEN Bill := Usage * 0.09
08          ELSE IF (Usage < 625)
09                  THEN Bill := 350 * 0.09 + (Usage - 350) * 0.05
10          ELSE IF (Usage < 850)
11                  THEN Bill := 350 * 0.09 + 275 * 0.05
12                              + (Usage - 625) * 0.04
13          ELSE Bill := 350 * 0.09 + 275 * 0.05 + 225 * 0.04
14                              + (Usage - 850) * 0.03;
15              <------------+
16      END;                |
17                          |
18 +----------------------------------------------------+
19 | WRITELN('Customer number    = ', Id);              |
20 | WRITELN('KiloWatt Hours used = ', Usage:0:2);      |
21 | WRITELN('Electric bill       = $', Bill:0:2);      |
22 +----------------------------------------------------+
23 END.
```

Figure 11: BILL3: An output fragementation bug.

explicitly included a BEGIN-END pair to scope the ELSE clause. To repair this bug, the output code (lines 19-21 in Figure 11) should be moved inside the BEGIN-END block (around line 15).

Once again, it seems reasonable to conclude that the novices did not have a misconception about the scope of the ELSE clause, based on both the alignment of the output code and the presence of the BEGIN-END pair. For these reasons, we have classified this bug as we did the previous output fragmentation bug -- probably not caused by a misunderstanding of any language construct's semantics, but instead the result of not detecting a plan dependency.

REF1: Boundary Problem. In Figure 12 the most frequent Reformatting Problem bug is shown. The condition that is used to guard against invalid times is not quite correct. When the value of the hour variable is 12, then the input will be considered invalid, even though it is in fact a legal value. If either the upper bound for hours was changed from 12 to 13 (see line 4 in Figure 12) or the relational operator was changed from >= to > (and the constant was left 12), then the code would be correct. This is another off-by-one bug (recall BILL1), because one of the boundary values is not handled properly.

```
G:VDE/G:START-HOUR/G:GUARD :: MALFORMED G:COND (12 for 13)
01      WRITELN('Enter start hour, minutes, and seconds');
02      READLN(Start_Hour,Start_Minute,Start_Second);
03 +--------------------------------------------------------+
04 | IF ((Start_Hour    <=  0) OR (Start_Hour   >= 12) OR   |
05 |     (Start_Minute <= -1) OR (Start_Minute >= 60) OR    |
06 |     (Start_Second <= -1) OR (Start_Second >= 60))      |
07 +--------------------------------------------------------+
08      THEN BEGIN
09          WRITELN('Error: Rtype hour minute second');
10          READLN(Start_Hour,Start_Minute,Start_Second);
11          END;
```

Figure 12: REF1: An off-by-one bug.

The students who generated this bug probably understood the semantics of the relational operators. In Figure 12 all of the other relational operators are correct; only the one for the upper hour boundary is inappropriate. This off-by-one bug may have arisen because of an inconsistency between the various times units. Hours range from 1 to 12, while minutes and seconds range from 0 to 59. Note that the lowest value in each range is different, so while 12 is both the number of allowed values and the highest value for hours,

60 is the number of allowed values and 59 is the highest value for minutes and seconds. The number of allowed values in a range (12 and 60) are important constants because they are used in conversion rules which relate quantities measured in one time unit to quantities measured in another time unit. The problem is that if the novice wants to use these two constants in the upper bound guard, then a different relational operator is needed for hours as well as for minutes and seconds. So the novices might generate this bug because they tend to use seemingly related constants (i.e., 12 and 60, rather than 13 and 60), while at the same time trying to use the same relational operator to make the terms more parallel. Alternatively, the novices might be confusing the number of values in a range with the maximum value in a range; the former is needed to convert between units and the latter is needed to construct a valid data guard.

In sum, the source of the bug seems to be a problem that novices experience while reasoning about a group of related boundary conditions. The novices may want the constants to be semantically related and at the same time they are trying to exploit certain forms of parallelism in their code, but it seems unlikely that they would misunderstand relational operators -- misusing only the relational operator for the upper hour boundary. For this reason, we have classified this bug as most likely not arising from a misunderstanding of the semantics of any language construct (see Figure 7).

```
INPUT:
23 a 10 45 30 10 57 02 +

Buggy Code to achieve G:INPUT:

G:VDE[P:I-A/G-A/R-A]/G:TYPE&G:ACCURACY :: MALFORMED INPUT
01  WRITELN('Enter Id, Type, Start (h ▪ s), End (h ▪ s),Accuracy');
02  +------------------------------------------------+
03  |READLN(Id,                                      |
04  |       Problem_Type,                            |
05  |       Start_Hour, Start_Minute, Start_Second,  |
06  |       End_Hour, End_Minute, End_Second,        |
07  |       Accuracy);                               |
08  +------------------------------------------------+

Corrected Code to achieve G:INPUT: (note additional whitespace variables)
09  WRITELN('Enter Id, Type, Start (h ▪ s), End (h ▪ s),Accuracy');
10  +------------------------------------------------+
11  |READLN(Id,                                      |
12  |       Whitespace1, Problem_Type,               |
13  |       Start_Hour, Start_Minute, Start_Second,  |
14  |       End_Hour, End_Minute, End_Second,        |
15  |       Whitespace2, Accuracy);                  |
16  +------------------------------------------------+
```

Figure 13: REF2: A space as seperator, not character bug.

REF2: Data-Type Inconsistency Problem. In the case of the bug shown in Figure 13, apparently the novices did not see that the whitespace a character that could be read, not just a separator that would be ignored. One could convincingly argue that this bug is in fact caused by a misunderstanding of how READLN works in the context of characters. Possibly, some novices think that READLN ignores all whitespace when it is parsing an input line and assigning values to a sequence of variables. When a READLN is used to input a sequence of numeric values, this is certainly the case. For this reason, we have classified this bug as probably resulting from a misunderstanding of the semantics of the READLN language construct (see Figure 7).

The novices had previously used the READLN construct successfully in other problems on different types of input data. In predicting where bugs will occur, knowing that a particular construct has been used successfully before does not imply that it will be used correctly in future problems. The key issue is not the particular construct that was being used, but the programming plan in which the construct played a role. In the case of the whitespace bug in Figure 13, the new plan involves reading character values on the same line with numeric values. Previously, either character values were read alone on a line or just numeric values were read on a line.

```
G:VDE/G:TYPE/G:GUARD :: MALFORMED G:COND (OR For AND)
01    WRITELN('Enter problem type');
02    READLN(Problem_Type);
03    +--------------------------------+
04    | IF ((Problem_Type) <> 'a') OR  |
05    |     (Problem_Type) <> 'b') OR  |
06    |     (Problem_Type) <> 'c'))    |
07    +--------------------------------+
08       THEN BEGIN
09           WRITELN('Type "a", "b", or "c"');
10           READLN(Problem_Type);
11           END;
```

Figure 14: REF3: An OR-for-AND bug.

REF3: Negation and Whole-Part Problem. Figure 14 shows an *OR-for-AND* bug that occurred in novices' Reformatting programs. The boolean connective that is used in the guard (lines 4 and 5) should be AND, rather than OR. The bug occurred during the composition of a P:SET-MEMBERSHIP-EXCLUSION plan for the Problem_Type variable. The data item in question could take on one of a small set of character values that were members of a set of valid inputs. For instance, the valid values for a problem type are 'a', 'b', or 'c'. The data guard was intended to determine if the input value was outside the valid set, and if so give the user a second chance to enter the data correctly.

While the OR-for-AND bug seems to indicate that novices did not understand the semantics of OR, two pieces of evidence contradict this conclusion. First, novices usually used the OR boolean connective correctly in the P:INTERVAL-EXCLUSION plans required to guard the hour, minute, and second data items in the Reformatting Problem as shown below:

```
01 IF ((Start_Hour < 1) OR (Start_Hour > 12) OR
02     (Start_Minute < 0) OR (Start_Minute > 59) OR
03     (Start_Second < 0) OR (Start_Minute > 59))
04 THEN ...data_ok...
05 ELSE ...retry...
```

Secondly, some of the novices used a P:SET-MEMBERSHIP-INCLUSION plan to guard the data items as shown below:

```
01  IF ((Problem_Type = 'a') OR
02      (Problem_Type = 'b') OR
03      (Problem_Type = 'c'))
04  THEN ...data_ok...
05  ELSE ...retry...
```

The novices who chose the P:SET-MEMEBERSHIP-INCLUSION plan used the OR boolean connective correctly. In order to explain why we think that many of the novices may actually understand the semantics of OR, we introduce the following two terms:

- *good-thing:* a term in a boolean expression, which either partially or totally implies that the value of the data item is valid.

- *bad-thing:* a term in a boolean expression, which either partially or totally implies that the value of the data item is invalid.

From our perspective, it appears that the novices may have the following notion concerning the use of OR: If each term corresponds to a whole *good-thing* or a whole *bad-thing*, then connect the terms with the boolean connective OR. In the case of P:INTERVAL-EXCLUSION, since (Start_Hour > 12) is a whole *bad-thing*, OR should be used. In the case of P:SET-MEMBERSHIP-INCLUSION, since (Problem_Type = 'a') is a whole

244

good-thing, OR should be used. If the novices mistakenly reasoned that since (Problem_Type = 'a') is a whole *good-thing*, by simple negation (Problem_Type <> 'a') is a whole *bad-thing*, then OR would have been the appropriate connective to use. In this case, the student's problem would not be in misunderstanding when to use the OR boolean connective, but in thinking that something was a whole *bad-thing* when in fact it was just one piece of a *bad-thing*. (Problem_Type <> 'a') is just a part of a *bad-thing* because, even if the problem type is not equal to 'a', it still may be valid because it could still be equal to 'b' or 'c' instead. Therefore, what on the surface appears to be a misunderstanding of the semantics of a construct may in fact be the result of some other error.

As shown in Figure 7 we have classified this bug as maybe arising from a misunderstanding of the semantics of the language. While we feel some students did in fact understand the semantics of OR, but had the misconception that Problem_Type <> 'a' was a whole *bad-thing* due to faulty reasoning about the effects of negating a term, some students may not have understood the semantics of OR. Those students who did not understand the semantics of OR may have simply always used the boolean connective OR to connect terms in a boolean expression, or have assumed, based on their linguistic intuitions, that if they could understand the intent of the boolean expression, then so could the computer.

```
G:VDE/G:START-MINUTE&SECOND/G:GUARD :: MALFORMED G:COND (60 for 59)
01    WRITELN('Enter start hour, minutes, and seconds');
02    READLN(Start_Hour,Start_Minute,Start_Second);
03   +-----------------------------------------------+
04   | IF ((Start_Hour    < 1) OR (Start_Hour   > 12) OR |
05   |      (Start_Minute < 0) OR (Start_Minute > 60) OR |
06   |      (Start_Second < 0) OR (Start_Second > 60))   |
07   +-----------------------------------------------+
08      THEN BEGIN
09           WRITELN('Error: Retype hour minute second');
10           READLN(Start_Hour,Start_Minute,Start_Second);
11           END;
```

Figure 15: REF4: An off-by-one bug.

REF4: Boundary Problem. In Figure 15 we have yet another off-by-one bug (see bugs BILL1 and REF1). This bug is very similar to the other Reformatting Problem off-by-one bug (see Figure 12). However, in this case the upper bound for the hour variable is correct, but the upper bound for the minute and second variable is wrong. The guard shown in Figure 15 will permits minute and second values of 60. The highest legal value for these two time units should be 59. To repair this bug, either the constants could be changed from 60 to 59, or the relational operators for the minute and second upper boundaries could be changed from > to >=.

As in the analysis of the bug REF1, we feel it is unlikely that the students who made this bug misunderstood the semantics of the relational operators. Instead, our experience favors the view that the students were trying to produce parallel code (same relational operator) for a group of boundary guards, and the constants 12 and 60 seemed a more coherent choice than the correct constants 12 and 59.

```
G:CALC/G:SINGLE,G:MARRIED/G:NET/G:HI-RANGE :: MALFORMED G:ARITH
01   Start_Time := Start_Hour*3600 + Start_Minute*60 + Start_Second;
02   End_Time   := End_Hour*3600   + End_Minute*60   + End_Second;
03   IF (Start_Time >= End_Time)
04      +------------------------------------+
05      | THEN End_Time := End_Time + 4320;  |
06      +------------------------------------+
07   Elapsed_Time := End_Time - Start_Time;
```

Figure 16: REF5: An incorrect constant bug.

REF5: Duplicate Tail-Digit Problem. In Figure 16 an incorrect constant bug is shown. The correct constant is 43200 (i.e., the number of seconds in a twelve hour clock period), not 4320. Several students dropped the duplicate tail digit when they produced the wrap-around compensation for the Reformatting Problem's elapsed time calculation. This bug is clearly not caused by a misunderstanding of the semantics of any particular language construct. Perhaps the student made an error while calculating the constant, or merely made the error while typing the constant in their program. In other problems, not described here, we have noted a similiar bug in which students use the constant 9999 instead of the correct constant 99999.

An alternative plausible account for this bug is suggested by the presence of another high frequency incorrect constant bug in novice programs for the Reformatting Problem. Many novices used the constant 360 instead of 3600 for converting from hours to seconds. If 360 is used instead of 3600 in the conversion, it is consistent that 4320 would be used instead of 43200 in the wrap-around compensation. The novices may obtain 360 as the result of multiplying 60 times 60, because they think the answer will be 36 followed by some zeroes. They tack on one zero, obtaining 360, and then see if this is a reasonable answer. Because 360 is the number of degrees in a complete circle, and they may be visualizing the hand of a clock sweeping out a complete circle for an hour, the novices may be biased to accept this result as the correct answer. Thus, a related constant may have interferred with the production of the correct constant.

Relevant portion of assignment:
```
01 Assume that a tax table specifies that married people pay 30% of their
02 combined salary for the first $10,000 and 32% for any amount over that.
```

Correct:
```
01   IF (Income < 10000)
02      +--------------------------------------------------------+
03      | THEN Tax := Income * 0.30                              |
04      | ELSE Tax := 10000  * 0.30 + (Income - 10000) * 0.32;|
05      +--------------------------------------------------------+
```

Incorrect:
```
G:CALC/G:MARRIED/G:TAX/G:HI-RANGE[P:STRAIGHT] :: INCORRECT PLAN
01   IF (Income < 10000)
02      +----------------------------+
03      | THEN Tax := 0.30 * Income  |
04      | ELSE Tax := 0.32 * Income; |
05      +----------------------------+
```

Figure 17: TAX1: A correct and incorrect interpretation of the tax formula.

TAX1: Expectations and Interpretation Problem. Figure 17 shows an example of the most frequently occuring bug in Tax Problem programs. The wrong formula has been used to calculate the tax. The correct formula does not use a "straight rate" formula, but instead uses one rate for the portion of the income below the cut-off (i.e., $10000) and another rate for the portion of the income above the cut-off. Probably, some students selected the wrong formula because most taxes (sales, income, etc.) that the students were familiar with are computed using a "straight-rate" formula, like the one they used in their programs. For this reason, we classified this bug as not the result of misunderstanding the semantics of any language construct. Instead, the students most likely misinterpreted the assignment due to their expectations about tax calculations.

```
G:CALC/G:SINGLE,G:MARRIED/G:NET/G:HI-RANGE :: MALFORMED G:ARITH
01   IF (Income < 10000)
02      +--------------------------------------------------------+
03      | THEN Tax := Income * 0.30                              |
04      | ELSE Tax := 10000  * 0.30 + Income - 10000 * 0.32;|
05      +--------------------------------------------------------+
```

Figure 18: TAX2: An operator precedence bug.

TAX2: Coincidental Ordering Problem. The bug shown in Figure 18 (missing parentheses to over-ride operator precedence evaluation order) might be explained as a misunderstanding of the operator precedence rules for the language. Maybe the students did not know about operator precedence, but instead assumed that the computer (like an intelligent human who was aware of the programming assignment) would be able to figure out the correct ordering. If this were the case, then the students would not have to learn about operator precedence hierarchies -- the operators precedence ranking would dynamically be altered in response to the assignment and the particular ordering of operators in the arithmetic expression. However, this explanation seems less likely in light of the fact that in the Electric Bill Problem a similar sort of arithmetic expression had to be constructed (i.e., a series of multiply-accumulates with a threshold cut-off as part of the last term in the series; a*x + b*(y-z)), and omitting the parentheses was not a common bug. However, the Electric Bill Problem description did warn students to be sure to parenthesize expression in a conditional statement. Perhaps this warning made the novices more aware of the need for parentheses in arithmetic expressions as well.

The intended grouping of the second term was (Income - 10000) * 0.32: First do the subtraction and then do the multiplication. Assuming that the students who made this error wrote the expression from left-to-right, then the generation order (i.e., the left-to-right order that they wrote in) also had the subtraction come first and the multiplication come second. So the intended order of evaluation was the same as the generation order. Consequently, the novice may have simply never detected any problem. If the generation order had been different than the intended evaluation order, the novice may have seen the need for parentheses to ensure the proper evaluation of the arithmetic expression. For example, after writing 0.32 * Income, the novice might have realized that he/she didn't want the to multiply 0.32 times the income, but the income minus $10000 instead. After realizing this the novice might go back and add parentheses. We classified this bug as maybe caused by a misunderstanding of language semantics (see Figure 7).

```
G:VDE/G:STATUS/G:GUARD :: MALFORMED G:COND (OR For AND)
12    WRITELN('Enter marital status');
13    READLN(Marital_Status);
14    +--------------------------------+
15    | IF ((Marital_Status <> 's') OR |
16    |     (Marital_Status <> 'm'))   |
17    +--------------------------------+
18        THEN BEGIN
19            WRITELN('Type "m" or "s"');
20            READLN(Marital_Status);
21            END;
```

Figure 19: TAX3: An OR-for-AND bug.

TAX3: Negation and Whole-Part Problem. Figure 19 shows an example of another OR-for-AND bug, this time occurring in the Tax Problem programs (recall that REF3 was an OR-for-AND bug in the Reformatting Problem programs). In the Tax Problem, the valid data guard for the Marital_Status variable can be achieved using a P:SET-MEMBERSHIP-EXCLUSION plan, since a legal value of marital status is either 'm' for married, or 's' for single. Based on an argument similar to that for the bug REF3, we classified this bug as maybe caused by a misunderstanding of language semantics.

Summary of Plausible Accounts. In summary, an examination of the plausible accounts for the 11 most frequent bugs from the three problems reveals the following: The 7 bugs in the NO category have what we term *non-construct-based* plausible accounts. The 1 bug in the YES category has a *construct-based* plausible account. The 3 bugs in the MAYBE category have both construct-based and non-construct-based plausible accounts. We can reject the hypothesis that the categories are equally likely ($\chi^2 = 5.1$, $p < .05$), and in the clear cut cases (i.e., just NO and YES) the data suggest that non-construct-based

```
    Does the bug indicate that the novices misunderstood
       the semantics of a particular language construct?
```

```
            | CATEGORY | NUMBER OF BUGS |
            +=====================================+
            |    NO    |        7       |
            +------------+-----------------+
            |  MAYBE   |        3       |
            +------------+-----------------+
            |   YES    |        1       |
            +=====================================+
```

Figure 20: Results of analysis of plausible accounts for the top 11 bugs.

plausible accounts dominate (7 to 1; $p < .10$ by sign-test). Even making the most conservative assumption possible (all MAYBE are added to YES), the construct-based plausible accounts can not be shown to dominate (7 NO to 4 MAYBE-YES). Therefore, based on our analysis of the high frequency bugs, we find no support for the notion that misconceptions about the semantics of language constructs are the dominant cause of novice bugs.

Based on our detailed analysis of these 11 bugs, we can identify three problems that may interfere with novices attempts to understand the semantics of programming language constructs:

- *Data-Type Inconsistency Problem*: Because whitespace between numeric input values is ignored by READLN constructs, some novices assumed that whitespace between character values would also be ignored. Consider the space-as-separator-not-character bug: REF2.

- *Natural Language Problem*: Because many programming language constructs are named after related natural language words, some novices become confused about the semantics of the construct in the programming domain (see Bonar and Soloway, 1985). Consider the OR-for-AND bugs: REF3 and TAX3.

- *Human Interpreter Problem*: Because novices know how they intend a construct to be interpreted, they assume the computer will be able to arrive at a similar interpretation; and they infer semantics for a construct that will make the human interpretation possible (see Sleeman, Putnam, Baxter and Kuspa, 1985). Consider the OR-for-AND bugs, and the missing parentheses bug: REF3, TAX3 and TAX2.

Most of the plausible accounts for these 11 bugs did not indicate that the understanding the semantics of the language constructs was the dominant underlying problem. Instead, several other types of problems were identified:

- *Boundary Problem*: Novices have difficulties deciding what the appropriate boundary points are. Consider the three off-by-one bugs: BILL1, REF1, and REF4.

- *Plan Dependency Problem*: Novices have difficulties detecting plan-dependencies that constrain how plan nesting should be done. Consider the two output fragmentation bugs: BILL2 and BILL3.

- *Negation and Whole-Part Problem*: Novices mistakenly infer that the negation of a whole *good-thing* is a whole *bad-thing*. Consider the OR-for-AND bugs: REF3 and TAX3.

- *Expectations and Interpretation Problem*: When novices read a programming assignment, their expectations about how certain quantities should be calculated may cause them to misinterpret the specifications. Consider the incorrect formula bug: TAX1.

248

- *Duplicate Tail-Digit Problem*: When novices use constants that have repeated tail-digits, they may drop the final digit. Consider the incorrect constant bug: REF5.

- *Related Knowledge Interference Problem*: Sometimes the correct response may be very similiar to a related, but incorrect, response. Consider the 360 instead of 3600 bug which may precede another incorrect constant bug: REF5.

- *Coincidental Ordering Problem*: When novices generate an expression and the intended evaluation order is the same as the generation order, they may not detect any need for explicit grouping plans to be used. Consider the missing parentheses bug: TAX2.

The main implication to educators of these other kinds of non-construct-based problems is:

- *Educators may help eliminate certain frequently ocurring bugs by making students explicitly aware of the problems they may come up against; not just construct-based problems, but non-construct-based problems as well.*

Awareness of the problems may help students identify where to be extra cautious when they generate programs.

All Bugs

While the previous section looked at just 11 out of the 101 bug types, in this section we will examine all 101 bug types. Figure 21 shows the number of bugs in each of the three categories:

- NO: The bug probably did not result from a misunderstanding of the semantics of a language construct.

- MAYBE: The bug might have resulted from a misunderstanding of a construct's semantics.

- YES: The bug probably resulted from a misunderstanding of the semantics of a language construct.

```
Problem            ||  NO    MAYBE    YES  ||
-------------------+------+---------+-------++
BILL    (N = 28)   ||  19      9       0    ||
                   ||                       ||
REF     (N = 46)   ||  20     21       5    ||
                   ||                       ||
TAX     (N = 27)   ||  13     10       4    ||
-------------------+------+---------+-------++
OVERALL (N = 101)  ||  52     40       9    ||
-------------------+------+---------+-------++
```

Figure 21: Distribution of bugs into the three categories: NO, MAYBE, and YES.

The 52 bugs in the NO category are best explained in terms of non-construct-based plausible accounts. The 9 bugs in the YES category are best explained in terms of construct-based plausible accounts (i.e., misconceptions or lack of knowledge about the semantics of language constructs). The 40 bugs in the MAYBE category have both construct-based and non-construct-based plausible accounts. We can reject the hypothesis that the categories are equally likely (χ^2=29.2, p<.01), and in the clear cut cases (i.e., just NO and YES) the non-construct-based plausible accounts are significantly more common than the construct-based plausible accounts (52 to 9; p<.001 by sign-test). Even making the most conservative assumption possible (all MAYBE are added to YES), the construct-based plausible accounts can not be shown to dominate (52 NO to 49 MAYBE-YES). Therefore, based on our analysis of all 101 bug types, we still find no support for the notion that misconceptions about the semantics of language constructs are the dominant cause of novice bugs.

CONCLUDING REMARKS

In short, our data support one commonsense notion about bugs in novice programs, while not supporting another:

- *SUPPORTED: All bugs are not created equal. Some occur over and over again in many novice programs, while others are more rare.*

- *NOT SUPPORTED: Most bugs result because novices misunderstand the semantics of some particular programming language construct.*

The main implications these findings have for educators is that: 1) The high frequency bugs are "hot-spots" that must be attended to, and 2) simply making the semantics of constructs clearer will not address many of the problems novices are having.

ACKNOWLEDGEMENTS

This work was sponsored in part by the National Science Foundation, under NSF Grant DPE-8470014, and by the Army Research Institute, under contract MDA903-85-K-0188.

The views, opinions, and findings contained in this report are those of the authors and should not be construed as an official Department of the Army position, policy, or decision, unless so designated by other official documentation.

A condensed version of this paper will appear in the CACM.

We wish to thank David Littman, Jeannine Pinto, Sheryl Slossberg and Andy Liles for their comments on drafts of this paper.

REFERENCES

1. Anderson, J.R. and Jeffries, R. (1985) Novice LISP errors: Undetected losses of information from working memory. *Human-Computer Interaction, 1(2))*, 107-131.

2. Bonar, J. and Soloway, E. (1985) Preprogramming knowledge: A major source of misconceptions in novice programmers. *Human-Computer Interaction, 1(2)*, 133-161.

3. Domingue, J. (1985) *Towards an automated programming advisor.* (Technical Report No. 16). Milton Keynes, MK7 6AA, England: Human Cognition Research Laboratory.

4. Johnson, L., and Soloway, E. (1983, August) *PROUST: Knowledge-based program understanding.* (Technical Report 285). New Haven, CT: Department of Computer Science, Yale University.

5. Pea, R.D., (1985) *Language-independent conceptual "bugs" in novice programming.* (Manuscript). New York, NY: Bank Street School.

6. Sleeman, D., Putnam, R.T., Baxter, J.A., Kuspa, L.K. (1985) *Pascal and high-school students: A study of misconceptions.* (Manuscript). Stanford, CA: School of Education, Stanford University.

7. Spohrer, J.C., Soloway, E., and Pope, E. (1985) A goal/plan analysis of buggy Pascal programs. *Human-Computer Interaction, 1(2)*, 163-207.

8. Johnson, L., Soloway, E., Cutler, B. and Draper, S. (1983, October) *BUG CATALOGUE: I.* (Technical Report 286). New Haven, CT: Dept. of Computer Science, Yale University.

9. Joni, S. and Soloway, E. (1985) But My Program Runs! *Journal of Educational Computing Research*, Fall. (In press).

10. Spohrer, J.C., Pope, E., Lipman, M., Sack, W., Freiman, S., Littman, D., Johnson, L., and Soloway, E. (1985, May) *BUG CATALOGUE: II,III,IV.* (Technical Report 386). New Haven, CT: Dept. of Computer Science, Yale University.

11. Soloway, E., Ehrlich, K., Bonar, J., Greenspan, J. (1982) What do novices know about programming? In B. Shneiderman and A. Badre (Eds.), *Directions in Human-Computer Interactions*, Norwood, NJ: Ablex. 27-54.

12. Soloway, E., Ehrlich, K. (1984) Empirical studies of programming knowledge. *IEEE Transactions on Software Engineering*, 5, 595-609.

13. Bayman, P. and Mayer, R.E. (1983, September) A diagnosis of beginning programmers' misconceptions of BASIC programming statements. *Communications of the ACM*, 26, 677-679.

14. Mayer, R.E. (1979, November) A psychology of learning BASIC. *Communications of the ACM*, 22, 589-593.

15. Littman, D., Pinto, J., Soloway, E. (1985) Observations on tutorial expertise. *Proceedings of Conference on Expert Systems in Government.* MacClean, VA.

PANEL: FUTURE DIRECTIONS

CHAPTER 17

A Plan for Empirical Studies of Programmers

Victor R. Basili
Department of Computer Science
University of Maryland
College Park, MD 20742

ABSTRACT

For any area which requires experimental evidence, a high-level long range plan is needed. The plan should (1) classify the problems that need to be addressed, (2) provide for the development of appropriate theories and models of explanation, (3) offer a research framework that permits experiments to be categorized and evaluated, and (4) provide a feedback mechanism so that knowledge can be incorporated into the knowledge base of the research and user communities.

PROBLEMS AND THEORIES

How we classify the problems that need to be solved depends upon the maturity of the area. In a mature field, it may be possible to lay out the problems and isolate the particular variables for study. In an emerging area, like programming, the problem is more difficult. We do not have a satisfactory understanding of the programming process and product in order to delineate its domain.

The study of programmers involves an understanding of cognitive models of human behavior as well as the environment in which programmers work and the interaction of the two. Psychologists have a great deal to say about the human thought process in general and will continue to provide us with deeper insights as their research progresses. However, we really know very little about the domain of human thought as it applies to programmers and their environment.

For example, we know very little about such things as design and the effect of design methods on various product characteristics, such as modularity and ease of change. We do not know whether certain methods provide better modularization or are easier to understand and change than others. The problem is even deeper than that; we do not even know what better modularization is or what makes a program easier to change. Before we can articulate our problems, we need to evolve theories and create realistic models of the programming process and product.

This makes it all the more important to proceed in an organized manner to state the problems and develop theories about programming. The problems should lead to goals for experimentation. For example, one problem is that programmers make errors in developing a software product. The goal might then be to minimize the number of errors a programmer makes. This goal requires a model of how programmers solve problems (a cognitive model), a model of errors as they appear in the product (e.g. a set of fault classification schemes), and a model of how errors translate into faults. We must then translate this goal into a set of experimental hypotheses based upon the models used.

The experimental hypotheses articulate the goal in a manner that lends itself to study. They define the goal in measurable terms and specify the kind of data that needs to be collected in order to perform the experiment.

It is important to establish a set of goals for the empirical study of programmers so that we can define our experiments appropriately, communicate our results, and put them in the proper perspective. It has been acceptable in the past to run small independent experiments about the effects of a particular variable on some aspect of programming. These experiments have been useful in an exploratory sense. They have shown us that we can experiment with programmers and have given us some insights into the problems confronting us. However, we now need to step back and lay out a framework of high level goals, to attack the problem top down.

The goals may start out vague and ambiguous, expressed at an imprecise level of abstraction, they need to be iterated. The process of going from goals to hypotheses to data requires a basic paradigm that traces the goals to the actual data needed for the experiment.

The paradigm can be viewed as a diagram:

```
    Goal 1                    Goal 2            ...        Goal n
      . . .                     . . .                       . . .

        . . .                      . . .                   . .   .
          .       .         .          .             .   .       .
Hypothesis1 Hypothesis3 Hypothesis4      .             .     Hypothesis8
   .        .      .          .        .    Hypothesis6           .
   .Hypothesis2 .        .  Hypothesis5     .        Hypothesis7  .
   d1  . . .  m9      d2    . . .        .              . . .  m5

      .      .   .                    .  .         .   .     .
      m1  m2  m3            m4  m2  d3      m6       m1  m6  m7
```

Here there are n goals shown and each goal generates a set of hypotheses that attempts to define and quantify the specific goal which is at the root of its goal tree. The goal is only as well defined as the hypotheses that it generates. Each hypothesis generates a set of metrics (mi) or distributions (di). Again, the hypothesis can only be analyzed relative to and as completely as the available metrics and distributions allow. As is shown in the above diagram, the same hypotheses can be used to define different goals (e.g. hypothesis6) and metrics and distributions can be used to test more than one hypothesis. Thus hypotheses and metrics are used in several contexts.

The paradigm is important not just for focusing research investigations but also for interpreting the hypotheses and the metrics. For example, m6 is collected in two contexts and possibly for two different reasons. Hypothesis6 may ask for the number of faults found in system test of the product (m6) as part of the goal to model error analysis (Goal2). But m6 may also be used as part of a hypothesis about the complexity of the product (e.g. hypothesis7) related to a goal on ease of modification (e.g. Goaln).

It is possible that some hypotheses can only be partially tested. Some data may be needed that is not available. It is important, however that the hypothesis and data be included in the goal/hypothesis/metric diagram. This is so that the other metrics that are needed for testing the hypothesis can be viewed in the proper context and the hypothesis interpreted with the appropriate limitations. The same is true for hypotheses being asked that may not be answerable with the data available.

SCOPE OF EVALUATION

We must begin to categorize experiments, based upon the the scope of evaluation. One such classification scheme is discussed in Basili, Selby & Hutchens (1). Experiments are classified with respect to the number of projects and the number of teams (or individuals as data points). A single team and single project is a case study; a single team and a set of projects represent a multi-project experiment; multiple teams and a single project represent a replicated project experiment; and a multiple team and set of projects permit a blocked subject-project experiment.

As we move from a case study to a blocked single project experiment, we get more statistical confidence in the results of our analysis. However, our experiments become more expensive and the domain of study must shrink. For example, it is possible to study a hundred thousand line project as a case study or a set of such programs in a multi-project experiment, but we could not possibly replicate those projects or control the variables sufficiently to perform a replicated project or blocked subject-project experiment on anything but a reasonably small project. Thus each experimental scope has its benefits and drawbacks.

If we think of various hypotheses being tested in different experimental forms, we can begin to add to our confidence level with respect to certain goals. For example, running a blocked-subject-project experiment on the effects of a testing technique on programmers may provide statistical confidence in the results but it will not be clear that the approach will scale up for large projects. If we combine the carefully controlled experiment with a case study and witness the same results, we raise our confidence in the results and begin to believe that the testing technique scales up.

The different approaches also lend themselves to different types of analyses. Quantitative analysis may be more appropriate for a controlled experiment while qualitative analysis may be more useful on a case study.

FEEDBACK MECHANISM

All the research needs to be performed in a framework that permits researchers to add to the existing knowledge and permits organizations to use the knowledge that has been gathered so far. It is important that the ideas to improve the environment for programmers be transferred into practice so they may be tested in a variety of situations and case studies performed in specific environments.

This leads us to the following basic mechanism for bringing new ideas into practice and continuing the experimentation using production environments as the laboratory for case study analysis:

1. Characterize the approach/environment.

This step requires an understanding of the various factors that will influence the project development. This includes the problem factors, e.g. the type of problem, the newness to the state of the art, the susceptibility to change; the people factors, e.g. the number of people working on the project, their level of expertise, experience; the product factors, e.g. the size, the deliverables, the reliability requirements, portability requirements, reusability requirements; the resource factors, e.g. target and development machine systems, availability, budget, deadlines; the process and tool factors, e.g. what techniques and tools are available, training in them, programming languages, code analyzers.

2. Set up the goals, hypotheses, data for successful project development and for study.

It is at this point the organization and the project manager must determine what the goals are for the project development. Some of these may be specified from step 1. Others may be chosen based upon the needs of the organization, e.g. minimizing the number of faults, evaluating the effect of a testing technique. In this context empirical studies may be performed to test the hypotheses in practice.

3. Choose the appropriate methods and tools for the project that satisfy the project goals and take advantage of the knowledge gained from previous research.

Once it is clear what is required and available, methods and tools should be chosen and refined that will maximize the chances of satisfying the goals laid out for the project. Tools may be chosen because they facilitate the collection of the data necessary for evaluation, e.g. configuration management tools not only help project control, but also help with the collection and validation of error and change data.

4. Perform the software development and maintenance, collecting the prescribed data and validating it.

This step involves the collection of data by forms, interviews, and automated collection mechanisms. The advantages of using forms to collect data is that a full set of data can be gathered which gives detailed insights and provides for good record keeping. The drawback to forms is that they can be expensive and unreliable because people fill them out. Interviews can be used for qualitative analysis, to validate information from forms, and gather information that is not easily obtainable in a form format. Automated data collection is reliable and unobtrusive and can be gathered from program development libraries, program analyzers, etc. However, the type of data that can be collected in this way is typically not very insightful and one level removed from the issue being studied.

5. Analyze the data to evaluate the current practices, determine problems, record the findings, make recommendations for improvement and possibly generate new hypotheses.

This is the key to the mechanism. It requires a post mortem on the project. Project data should be analyzed to determine how well the project satisfied its goals, where the methods were effective, where they were not effective, whether they should be modified and refined for better application, whether more training or different training is needed, whether tools or standards are needed to help in the application of the methods, or whether the methods or tools should be discarded and new methods or tools applied on the next project.

6. Proceed to step 1 to start the next project, armed with the knowledge gained from this and the previous projects.

This procedure for developing software has a corporate learning curve built in. The knowledge is available to researchers and can be stored in a corporate data base available to new and old managers to help with project management, method and tool evaluation, and technology transfer.

CONCLUSION

The time has come for us to organize our approach to experimentation in the programming domain. We have been able to demonstrate that we can learn from experiments, but we need to solidify our approach and work from the top down, not from the bottom up. We need to add on to each other's work and create a framework for doing so both in the laboratory with controlled experiments and in the industrial setting with case studies. We can fill in the pieces of the puzzle of programming only by starting with the template of a set of goals, theories and models, working on the larger pieces first (e.g. showing the effects of possibly a set of variables) and then refining those larger pieces until we better understand the effects of individual variables. From this process, we will gain the knowledge necessary to help mature the field and obtain truly useful results.

REFERENCES

1.   Basili, V. R., Selby, R. W., and Hutchens, D. H., Experimentation in Software Engineering, IEEE *Transactions on Software Engineering,* April, 1986.

CHAPTER 18

By the Way,
Did Anyone Study Any Real Programmers?

Bill Curtis

Software Technology Program
Microelectronics and Computer Technology Corporation (MCC)
Austin, TX 78759

ABSTRACT

The relevance of the current empirical research on programming to the
pressing problems of software development is challenged. A review of research
since 1980 shows a trend toward greater methodological rigor. However, at the
same time most studies concentrate on novice programming, and fail to offer
guidance in developing advanced software development environments. Several
crucial questions are posed for future empirical research on programming and two
exploratory studies under way in the author's laboratory are described.

GENESIS OF THE FIELD

The earliest empirical studies of programmers were conducted to evaluate
tests of cognitive skills for selecting programmers. By the end of the 1960s,
these efforts were generally regarded as successful in predicting training
performance (Mayer & Stalnaker, 1968), but less so in predicting job performance
(Reinstedt et al., 1967). The problem centered around the use of tests of
general cognitive skills rather than performing a professional job analysis to
determine the specific skills that should be tested for. Further, there was no
model of how this skill mix changed across different jobs in system development
or over time with an individual's career path.

Testing materials were improved in the early 1970s, as tests were
developed to assess the specific tasks programmers performed (Wolfe, 1972).
This improvement benefitted in part from the Equal Employment Opportunity
Commission's scrutiny of testing's role in discrimination. The increased
professionalism needed to avoid charges of discrimination caused a deeper look
at the relationship between what the tests measured and the skills required to
perform the job. Unfortunately, even with better tests much of the skepticism
fostered by earlier disappointments remained. Currently, the better tests
provide information on aptitudes for performing some of the tasks in a
programmer's job (Bloom, 1980). However, they should be used as only one input
to an overall screening and selection procedure for programmers.

In the early 1970s another form of empirical research on programmers
emerged. This research took a human factors approach and investigated how the
tools programmers used affected their performance. Some of the earliest

256

programs of this type were developed at the University of Sheffield (Sime et al., 1977) and at IBM's T.J. Watson Research Center (Thomas & Carroll, 1977). After a few more years these were joined by concentrated programs at the University of Maryland (cf. IEEE Computer, Dec. 1979), at Science Applications Inc. (Ramsey & Atwood, 1978), and in General Electric's Space Division (Sheppard et al. 1979). By the end of the 1970s, a small literature had emerged studying such factors as structured programming, the features of programming languages, software metrics, and the format of procedural specifications.

A SHIFT TO COGNITIVE SCIENCE

1980 and 1981 were turning points for the experimental study of programming. In 1980, Ben Shneiderman summarized this fledgling literature in four chapters of his book Software Psychology. And in 1981, I published an IEEE tutorial containing 51 of these early reserach contributions. Yet, there was a waterfall around the bend. Brooks (1980) and Sheil (1981) attacked the subjects, methods, and tasks employed in many of these studies and questioned whether this literature was relevant to real programming. Indeed, this form of research was extremely expensive and difficult to conduct rigorously, but useful information had emerged even though the research methods needed improvement.

The problem in these early empirical studies was that the computer scientists who were conducting much of the research had little formal background in behavioral research methodology. The psychologists who had come into the field were unsure of what the important questions were and how to attack them. The result was that, as Sheil argued, empirical studies of programmers were having little impact on computer science, because the results lagged rather than preceeded the major movements in programming. Computer science was little interested in weak empirical justifications for directions it had already taken, such as structured programming. Computer scientists cared more for deductive proofs than for the rejection of null hypotheses.

Yet, in 1981 a wave of papers began to appear that were the precursors to the empirical work we see in this workshop. These developments had been foreshadowed in a dissertation by Brooks (1977), in Atwood and Ramsey's (1978) attempt to apply Kintsch's theory of text comprehension to programming, and in Mayer's (1981) work on learning computer languages. These trends, represented in papers by McKeithan et al. (1981) and by Adelson (1981), signalled a shift away from the human factors paradigm toward a more cognitive psychological approach to programming. Soloway's group at Yale have been prolific contributors to this cognitive science orientation (Soloway & Ehrlich, 1984).

This body of research has concentrated on expert-novice differences in programming. Yet, too often the "experts" were seniors or graduate students, and in general they had little professional experience. Thus, expert-intermediate differeces would be a more appropriate nomenclature. We see at this workshop a set of papers that tell us how novices understand programing and how they make mistakes. To prove valuable, this reserach must be translated into better teaching methods and tools. We see several papers here that show promise of this happening.

Nevertheless, there are two dangers I see in the current empirical research on programming. The first and greatest problem is to believe that what is being presented here is research on programming in the large. A better title for this workshop, given the preponderence of the data presented, is "Empirical Studies of Student Programming". The processes observed in these experiments are only a subset of the factors that affect programming on large projects, where those involved are no longer novices to programming.

The second danger is that the empirical research will continue to focus on demonstrating already established cognitive phenomena and on refining research methodology. This focus will produce elegant research that misses important questions. To some extent the current empirical research represents the discovery by cognitive psychologists that programming is an interesting testbed for cognitive theories because of its procedurality. Futher, more cognitive psychologists are learning to program out of necessity, and find in their frustration the grist for research.

Many of the results obtained are not surprising, since they represent the demonstration in programming of cognitive phenomena that had already been demonstrated in other areas. For instance, much of the expert-novice differences research merely extends results to programming that Herbert Simon and his colleagues had demonstrated in other areas such as chess (Chase & Simon, 1973) and physics (Larkin et al., 1980). Much of the research on programming bugs made by novices revolves around the "repair theory" developed by Brown and Van Lehn (1980) in looking at children's subtraction errors. It will not be surprising to see a new research area emerge on learning strategies in programming that will use Anderson's (1983) ACT* theory of cognitive skill acquisition as a point of departure.

The value of this research is that it has introduced computer science to a source of explanation for programming phenomena. However, empirical research needs to take the next step to ensure its continued value to computer science. Much of the current research is descriptive, in that it simply seeks to describe what occurs in programming. The next step is to show how these findings can be used to guide new programing technology.

THE OTHER WORLD OF EMPIRICAL RESEARCH ON PROGRAMMERS

In the latter half of the 1970s, a second type of empirical study of programmers began to appear. In 1977, Walston and Felix published a study of how different factors affected the productivity of IBM Federal Systems Division's software development projects. Boehm (1981) published similar data from TRW's Defense and Space Group on the front cover of his 1981 book Software Engineering Economics. Since then, other studies have been published by McGarry (1982), Lawrence (1981), and my programming measurements team at ITT (Vosburgh et al., 1984). The Boehm and McGarry data were overwhelming in their implication of individual differences as the major factor in programming performance. These differences far outweighed the impact of programming practices, languages, and tools in affecting project outcomes.

These data were not published as experimental studies. They were performed at an organizational level rather than a cognitive level. Nevertheless, they point to factors that make programming particularly difficult on real projects. For instance, Walston and Felix (1977) found that the complexity of the interaction with the customer was crucial in determining the performance of the project. This factor involves processes that are psychological, but are rarely the focus of experimental research on programming. Current research investigates how people express solutions, but not how they learn what the real problem was to begin with. In fact, one of the greatest problems on large projects is that customers do not state their full requirements, because they are unable to determine them. Research on helping people elaborate their full desires (i.e., more fully defining the problem structure) may have dramatic payoff to real programming environments.

Many of thoseperforming experimental research on programming, especially on novice student programming, are not familiar with these project level data. This is unfortunate, because these data present evidence on which factors exercise real control over programming performance in professional environments. Experimentalists who want to ensure their research is relevant to real programming issues should become familiar with this other empirical literature.

AN EXPLORATORY PROGRAM OF EMPIRICAL RESEARCH ON PROGRAM DESIGN

Designing the software to fly the space shuttle requires teams of designers, each of whom is an expert in a different area. Yet, processes emerge in developing systems of this size that cannot be captured by studying the writing of small programs. Getting a team of experts to agree on design

258

decisions which force crucial tradeoffs in their differing areas of expertise is one of these processes. Getting them to agree on the structure of the problem they are trying to solve is an even more intriguing process.

The Software Technology Program at MCC is charged with providing its shareholders with technology that will produce dramatic increases in programming productivity and quality on large projects. A portion of this program has been devoted to experimental research. These experiments are being conducted in both the computer science and psychological traditions. That is, some of these experiments represent an attempt to build a piece of technology and learn from it. In such computer science experiments, there are no controls and the lessons derived are often subjective. Other experiments are being conducted in the tradition of behavioral science. There are two types of experiments that will be conducted over time in the Software Technology Program. The first consists of exploratory attempts to gather data that will contribute to models of the design process. The second type of experiment is a controlled evaluation of the technology being created. Obviously, these two types of studies will be conducted at different points in the program.

In order to justify investing in experimental studies, we are assuming that there is information that we can get faster, cheaper, or more thoroughly from experimental data than from other sources. This in itself is an experiment; what is the value of empirical research in a technology development effort? From the empirical data collected on large projects to date, it appears that the front end of the software life-cycle contains the greatest leverage for affecting gains in productivity and quality. Thus, we have chosen to focus on creating a computer-aided environment for software requirements and design. This environment needs to support cooperative design activity by teams of experts, each representing a different area of specialization. Some additional goals are to capture the history and rationale of the design, to promote the reuse of many forms of information, and to encourage the exploration of design alternatives. We have chosen to use distributed, real-time systems as an application area, since such systems will account for an increasing portion of future business.

Currently, we are concluding the analysis of our first two exploratory experiments. The first experiment has been conducted at the individual level by Herb Krasner to explore the behavioral characteristics of designers solving a distributed systems problem. In this experiment, Herb presented professional software engineers with a specification for an elevator system and told them to create the design for the software to control it. This study is similar to those by Kant and Newell (1984), Jeffries et al. (1981), and Adelson and Soloway (1985). Our interest, however, is in watching how professionals structure their approach to a computational problem.

Even though we only used professionals, the individual differences in approaches taken to the problem were substantial. Many of the participants did not recognize the opportunity for distributed control in this system, and instead designed a centralized system. Only among extremely experienced system designers did Herb observe an approach that could be described as a design methodology. However, it is possible that the two hour time limit caused them to deviate from their normal approach to decomposing systems problems. Most of the participants did little to consider alternatives to the design they began pursuing initially. Herb concluded that although many individuals explore design alternatives, they do so in depth rather than breadth. The designers who were most successful in specifying a design for this problem were characterized by 1) being able to rapidly switch their attention between the structure of the problem and the structure of thier solution, and 2) stating and challenging their own assumptions.

Although the literature on software design methods stresses the independence of problems and methods for designing their solutions, in practice much of programming knowledge seems to be instantiated in known solutions for classes of problems. Basili et al. (1985) observed a similar problem when experienced Fortran programmers learned to use Ada, but failed to write programs using some of the advanced concepts made available in Ada such as packages. We are currently focusing on how the participants chose to represent the problem, in the hope that we can gain insight into how different representations might encourage exploring design alternatives.

In our second experiment, Vincent Shen, Jeff Conklin, Herb Krasner, Micheal Evangelist, and I have been videotaping every group meeting of both the customer and design teams on a medium-sized project (in addition to several smaller design meetings and post-project interviews). This project was to produce an object-server for use with an object-oriented information base. We are aware that the generalizability of our observations must be tempered by the fact that 1) this was a single rather than multiple team project, 2) the members in each of the customer and design teams were working with each other for the first time, and 3) only team meetings were recorded.

Our initial observations are beginning to suggest to us that the rate at which teams make design decisions on systems with which they have little past experience is influenced by the extent to which they share common models of the task domain and of the computing knowledge necessary to design a solution. Within the design team, factions form around these shared models. The social behavior of the team is frequently played out on a foundation created by the amount of diversity in these models. Within factions (which may consist of only a single individual) exploration tends to be a matter of elaborating the effects of a design decision to sufficient depth to determine its stability. However, exploration of alternative approaches to the design does not appear to be characteristic of these factions.

The exploration of high level design alternatives seems to occur most frequently when differing task or computational models among team members leads to a challenging of assumptions or a proposing of new constraints relevant to the design. We are now in the initial stages of developing a model of the competing forces that both enhance and inhibit the exploration of design alternatives. There are many other effects in these tapes that we are currently investigating, but which I do not have space to discuss here. In some cases these observations are sufficiently raw that we are not confident yet in presenting them. These observations need to be confirmed by further study before we can talk about conclusions.

Our primary goal in this second experiment was to develop a method for studying design teams. We believe that data can be derived from these tapes for building models of at least part the design process. Many important parts of the design process are not visible in such tapes, but we have been able to develop some early notions of the benefits and limitations of team processes for designing software. There were some negative effects of using this data gathering technique, mostly due to the inconvenience of the planning and setup of meetings to be videotaped. It is possible to overcome this and other negative effects with experience.

As the experiment progressed, it became apparent to members of both the customer and design teams that the videotaping could become more than just a data collection medium. There were three ways in which having videotapes would assist the design process. First, videotape provides complete and accurate documentation of meetings. It does not suffer some of the incompleteness or biased interpretation problems that meeting notes or formal minutes often exhibit. Second, videotape allows a designer to recapture the context in which an idea may have fleetingly sprung to mind, but which was lost while continuing to listen to the speaker. The several word notes typically taken in such situations are frequently not enough to help a designer recapture the context and regenerate the idea. For both of these first two purposes, videotape would require a dynamic indexing technique, so that the entire tape would not have to be searched to get at that portion that was desired.

Finally, videotape can serve as a way of communicating across teams that would otherwise not interact. Thus, the tape of a customer meeting where scenarios of use were described prior to formal requirements being abstracted from them, would provide the design team with information they would later need. The current state-of-the-art in videotape technology may not be adequate to satisfy many of these purposes, but the potential exists for this technology to be a valuable part of a project database.

As of this writing we are only part way through this research project and our results must be considered tentative. We are experimenting with a new way to gather data on programming, especially on the design process. We are identifying both the strengths and weaknesses of this method. Nevertheless, we are derivng some interesting observations about design decision-making from that portion of the design process that we are able to capture.

SUMMARY

The empirical study of programming will need new data gathering techniques, such as the one we are experimenting with, if it is to pave the way for advancements in computer science rather than lagging them (Curtis, et al., in press). Further, those running experimental studies must learn more about the factors controlling programming performance, if the field is to become more than an academic diversion. This conference is encouraging in that we see many scientists actively conducting research. Nevertheless, it is also clear from these papers that this research must move beyond the carefully developed methods learned from cognitive psychology if it is to contribute timely knowledge about the crucial issues in software development.

REFERENCES

Adelson, B. 1981. Problem solving and the development of abstract categories in programming languages. Memory and Cognition, 9(4), 422-433.

Adelson, B. & Soloway, E. 1985. The role of domain experience in software design. IEEE Transactions on Software Engineering, 11(11), 1351-1360.

Anderson, J.R. 1983. The Architecture of Cognition. Cambridge, MA: Harvard.

Atwood, M.E. & Ramsey, H.R. 1978. Cognitive Structures in the Memory and Comprehension of Computer Programs: An Investigation of Computer Program Debugging (TR-78-A21). Alexandria, VA: Army Research Institute.

Basili, V.R., Katz, E.E., Panlilio-Yap, N.M., Ramsey, C.L., and Chang, S. 1985. Characteristics of an Ada software development. IEEE Computer, 18(9), 53-65.

Boehm, B.W. 1981. Software Engineering Economics. Englewood Cliffs, NJ: Prentice-Hall.

Bloom, A.M. 1981. Advances in the use of programmer aptitude tests. In T.A. Rullo (Ed.) Advances in Computer Programming Management (Vol. 1). Philadelphia: Hayden, 31-60.

Brooks, R. 1977. Toward a theory of cognitive processes in computer programming. International Journal of Man-Machine Studies, 9, 737-751.

Brooks, R. 1980. Studying programmer behavior experimentally: The problems of proper methodology. Communications of the ACM, 23(4), 207-213.

Brown, J.S. & VanLehn, K. 1980. Repair theory: A generative theory of bugs in procedural skills. Cognitive Science, 4(4), 379-426.

Chase, W.C. & Simon, H.A. 1973. Perception in chess. Cognitive Psychology, 5(1), 55-81.

Curtis, B. 1981. (Ed.) Human Factors in Software Development. Washington, DC: IEEE Computer Society. (2nd ed., 1986)

Curtis, B., Soloway, E., Brooks, R., Black, J.B., Ehrlich, K., & Ramsey, H.R. in press. Software psychology: The need for an interdisciplinary program. Proceedings of the IEEE.

Jeffries, R., Turner, A.A., Polson, P.G., & Atwood, M.E. 1981. The processes involved in designing software. In J.R. Anderson (Ed.) Cognitive Skills and Their Acquisition. Hillsdale, NJ: Erlbaum, 255-283.

Kant, E. & Newell, A. 1984. Problem solving techniques for the design of algorithms. Information Processing and Management, 28(1), 97-118.

Larkin, J., McDermott, J., Simon, D.P., & Simon, H.A. 1980. Expert and novice performance in solving physics problems. Science, 208, 1335-1342.

Lawrence, M.J. 1981. Programming methodology, organizational environment, and programming productivity. Journal of Systems and Software, 2(3), 257-269.

Mayer, R. 1981. The psychology of how novices learn computer programming. ACM Computing Surveys, 13(1), 121-141.

Mayer, D.B. & Stalnaker, A.W. 1968. The use of psychological tests in selecting computer programmers. Proceedings of SHARE XXXI/GUIDE 27, 1.146-1.167.

McGarry, F.E. 1982. What have we learned in the last six years? In Proceedings of the Seventh Annual Software Engineering Workshop (SEL-82-007). Greenbelt, MD: NASA Goddard Space Flight Center.

Reinstedt, R.N. et al. 1967. Computer personnel research group programmer performance prediction study. Proceedings of the Fifth Annual Computer Personnel Reaearch Conference. New York: ACM.

Sheil, B. 1981. The psychological study of programming. ACM Computing Surveys, 13(1), 101-120.

Sheppard, S.B., Curtis, B., Milliman, P., & Love, T. Modern coding practices and programmer performance. IEEE Computer, 12(12), 41-49.

Shneiderman, B. 1980. Software Psychology: Human Factors in Computer and Information Systems. Cambridge, MA: Winthrop.

Sime, M.E., Arblaster, A.T., & Green, T.R.G. 1977. Structuring the programmer's task. Journal of Occupational Psychology, 50, 205-216.

Soloway, E. & Ehrlich, K. 1984. Empirical studies of programming knowledge. IEEE Transactions on Software Engineering, 10(5), 595-609.

Thomas, J.C. & Carroll, J.M. 1979. The psychological study of design. Design Studies.

Vosburgh, J., Curtis, B., Wolverton, R., Albert, B., Malec, H., Hoben, S., & Liu, Y. 1984. Productivity factors and programming environments. In Proceedings of the 7th International Conference on Software Engineering. Washington, DC: IEEE Computer Society, 143-152.

Walston, C.E. & Felix, C.P. 1977. A method of programming measurement and estimation. IBM Systems Journal, 16(1), 54-73.

Wolfe, J.M. 1971. Perspectives on testing for programmer aptitude. Proceedings of the 1971 Annual Conference of the Association for Computing Machinery. New York: ACM, 268-277.

CHAPTER 19

What to Do Next:
Meeting the Challenge of Programming-in-the-Large

Elliot Soloway
Department of Computer Science
Cognition and Programming Project
New Haven, CT 06520

INTRODUCTION: MOTIVATION AND GOALS

In [1], David Parnas recently presented researchers with the following clear challenge: how can we improve the process of *programming in the large*? While there has been work on describing *what* happens on projects of reasonable size (e.g., [2],[3],[4]), there has been precious little research directed towards understanding *how* and *why* individuals and teams actually go about designing, building, and maintaining large software systems. In this brief position paper, I first argue why research into *programming in the small* has been a reasonable --- and important --- enterprise, and how the insights gained in that research can directly lead to effective, productive research into *programming in the large*. In particular, I will argue that research in the former domain has led to the formulation of specific questions that need to be examined in the latter domain. Next, I argue that, since our current state of understanding about issues in programming-in-the-large is nonetheless still in its infancy, we need to adopt a research methodology for exploring programming-in-the-large that supports theory building, as opposed to methodologies that support theory testing.

THE IMPORTANCE OF STUDYING PROGRAMMING-IN-THE-SMALL

There are two major reasons why the study of programming-in-the-small is a reasonable first approach to the study of programming-in-the-large:

- *Identify baseline issues:* We need to first identify the salient behaviors that "programmers"[1] exhibit, and understand their functionality. For example, our research ([5],[6],[7]), as well as that of others (e.g., [8],[9]), has shown that effective designers and maintainers[2] *repeatedly* carry out some sort of simulation on their partial design, code enhancement, etc. Why? With respect to both the designers and the maintainers, we suggest that simulation helps these individuals identify, among other things, the subtle and often undesired interactions among the modules that might result from their design/enhancement. Observations of interactions (among other events) then seem to drive the designers/maintainers in their subsequent steps in the design/enhancement process.

Thus, in identifying and understanding the functionality of such recurrent and/or important behaviors of expert programmers (and, by comparison, of less expert programmers), we have identified key skills that differentiate experts from non-experts. In turn, at a minimum, this knowledge can enable us to make prescriptions for how to (1) educate non-experts, and (2) build tools to help both non-experts and experts do their jobs more effectively.

- *Develop confidence in methodologies:* Given the acknowledged pitfalls in carrying out empirical research about programmers (e.g., [10],[11]), the field needs to establish some confidence in its research methods. For example, developing the stimulus materials for a controlled experiment (e.g., see [12]) is no mean feat: if subjects are to see 2 or 3 different programs all containing the same manipulation, how can we guarantee that other factors in the programs are held constant --- especially when we are uncertain of what those other factors might be! Thus, shortish programs are, not unreasonably, typically the programs of choice in carefully controlled studies. Therefore, by focusing on programming-in-the-small, the field is sharpening its methodological skills, and it is my sense that we are starting to see when it is appropriate (and inappropriate) to use a particular experimental method.

While the above observations may not have been explicit in the minds of researchers, I think that these two points are nonetheless guiding research about programmers. In sum, then, it appears eminently reasonable that considerable effort should have been expended --- and will continue to be expended! --- in studying aspects of programming-in-the-small.

THE BRIDGE TO PROGRAMMING-IN-THE-LARGE RESEARCH: AN EXAMPLE

Besides having payoffs for programming-in-the-small, research in this domain provides the critically needed context in which to initiate research in programming-in-the-large. That is, imagine if we didn't have research on programming-in-the-small; where would one start exploring programming-in-the-large? The alternatives are

---

[1]When I use the term "programmer" I mean it generically to refer to all participants in the various aspects of the software life-cycle: designer, coders, testers, maintainers.

[2]Similar research clearly needs to be done with coders, testers, etc.

enormous. However, our current research provides the important bridge to the new domain. For example, do the behaviors we observed in programming-in-the-small recur in programming-in-the-large? While we are under no illusion that programming-in-the-large will be just like programming-in-the-small (e.g., there surely will be new behaviors in the new domain), nonetheless, current research provides a rich base from which to explore out.

Let me play out this research approach by continuing with the example about designers/maintainers carrying out simulation. The studies in which simulation was observed were clearly programming-in-the-small (e.g., enhancing a 500 line program; designing an electronic mail system). Recall we suggested that maintainers acquired critically important "temporal knowledge" (interactions during execution) about the program via simulation. In fact, those maintainers who did not employ a global simulation of the components did not make the enhancement correctly! (Similarly, designers who did not carry out a global simulation of their design-in-progress overlooked critically important interactions.) Question: what happens to simulation when maintainers are confronted with large programs (10,000 lines and up)? This is a particularly interesting question because of a claim Parnas [1] makes:

> It should be clear that writing and understanding very large real-time programs by "thinking like a computer" will be beyond our intellectual capabilities.

Is simulation used during programming-in-the-large? Parnas, in fact, has some interesting observations on this question:

> In recent years many programmers have tried to improve their working methods using a variety of approaches. However, when they get down to writing executable programs, they revert to the conventional way of thinking.

Why do programmers revert to their old, and presumably bad, habits? One reasonable suggestion is that the new methods they are attempting to use simply do not play the same functional role that simulation does. The programmers *need* to get information about interactions --- and the new methods don't facilitate the acquisition of this information.[3] Thus, while it might well be that simulation is a poor technique for programming-in-the-large, we had better understand its role before its use is forbidden. Based on the observations made about simulation in programming-in--the-small then, we are in a fine position to start our study of programming-in-the-large: what techniques would serve programmers better than simulation? In sum, then, rather than venturing

---

[3]One might reasonably argue: well, if the programmer had only used the new design methods appropriately, he would not have had to worry about unwanted interactions. The interesting question then is: *why* and *how* do these new methods prevent unwanted interactions?

forth into the vast unknown of programming-in-the-large, studies of programmers can, at least initially, build directly on work done in programming-in-the-small.

METHODOLOGICAL ISSUES IN STUDYING PROGRAMMING-IN-THE-LARGE

The key issue to keep in mind when studying programming-in-the-large is that we are essentially in a *theory formation* mode, as opposed to a *theory testing* mode. That is, we have only recently begun to develop even modestly detailed conjectures at the level of cognitive processing models of aspects of programming-in-the-small (e.g., [13]). I am not aware of any models of similar depth for aspects of programming-in-the-large. Thus, in studying programmers carrying out programming-in-the-large, we need to choose research methodologies that are appropriate for the state of our understanding.

For example, while controlled studies have proved very useful in studying programming in the small, controlled studies may not be all that useful for initially studying programming-in-the-large. This type of methodology requires that carefully worked out hypotheses be developed first, before the experiment. Since hypotheses deal with individual factors, controlled studies are most effective in a theory testing mode: one needs the theory first in order to develop the hypotheses. Moreover, since controlled studies require a substantial number of subjects, one had better be sure that one is testing something important, and that the results obtained can have at least some pretense of generality. Without some sort of theory underlying the hypotheses, the importance and generality issues are in doubt. Finally, controlled studies require a confined setting in which as few factors as possible are allowed to vary. If generating several 100-line matched programs is hard, then one wonders about developing several 10,000-line matched programs! Almost by definition, programming-in-the-large violates the basic premises for a controlled study.

In contrast, protocol studies, of subjects "talking-aloud" as they carry out some task, can provide a rich source of data for the theory building enterprise.[4] Here the experimenter is trying to identify basic behavior patterns, and confront the robustness and diversity of behaviors. Moreover, protocol data quickly dissuades one from developing simplistic cognitive or social interaction theories: in observing experts in action, one is readily reminded of the amazing skills that people can and do possess! The

---

[4]Note that statistical arguments can be made using protocol data, e.g., [6]; however, this is not the norm.

downside of this methodology is that one quite quickly can become overwhelmed and mired in data: it is often hard to see the forest fore the trees. As practioners of this methodology have pointed out (e.g., [14],[15]) there are other dangers in gathering and analyzing protocol data, e.g., the particular choice of subjects may not be "representative" of the population in general. Thus, care must be exercised in gathering and analyzing protocol data. In sum, then, given that we are more in the theory building mode than in the theory testing mode, I think the protocol methodology will, quite naturally and reasonably, become the major source of data in initially studying aspects of programming-in-the-large.[5]

CONCLUDING REMARKS

We clearly need to take up the challenge of studying programming-in-the-large. However, we must recognize the magnitude of the task: studying the processes that are involved in writing a 1,000,000 line program goes way beyond present day studies of problem solving. Nonetheless, as I tried to illustrate with the "simulation" example above, programming-in-the-small research can provide provide powerful anchors for research into programming-in-the-large. Moreover, researchers and consumers of research may have to come to understand alternative research methodologies: controlled studies may not necessarily be the only effective way to explore programming-in-the-large with some degree of effectiveness and confidence. While it is trite to say, "we are living in exciting times," it is nonetheless true. The scope of the problem is enormous; there is room for lots and lots of players. Jump in!

ACKNOWLEDGMENTS

This work was sponsored by the National Science Foundation under NSF Grant IST-8505019.

REFERENCES

1. Parnas, D. (1985) Software Aspects of Strategic Defense Systems. *American Scientist, 73*, 432-440.

2. Basili, V., Selby, R., Philips, T. (1983) Metric Analysis and Data Validation Across Fortran Projects. *IEEE Transactions of Software Engineering, SE 9, 6*, 652-663.

---

[5]For example, in what seems to me to be a perfect match between problem and research method, B. Curtis and colleagues at MCC are using protocol techniques in studying a multiple person design team as the team is engaged in the process of design.

3. Basili, V., Reiter, R. (1979) An Investigation of Human Factors in Software Development. *Computer*, December, 21-38.

4. Boehm, B., Brown, J., Kaspar, H., Lipow, M., Macleod, G., Merrit, M. (1978) *Characteristics of Software Quality.* North-Holland Publishing Co., Amsterdam.

5. Adelson, B., Soloway, E. (1984) A Cognitive Model of Software Design. In *The Nature of Expertise*, Chi, M., Glaser, R., Farr, M., (Eds.), to appear. Also Technical Report #242, Dept. of Computer Science, Yale University.

6. Littman, D., Pinto, J., Letovsky, S., Soloway, E. (1986) Software Maintenance and Mental Models. In *Empirical Studies of Programmers*, Soloway, E., Iyengar, S. (Eds.). Ablex, Inc.

7. Adelson, B., Soloway, E. (1985) The Role of Domain Experience in Software Design. *IEEE Transactions on Software Engineering*, November.

8. Jeffries, R., Turner, A., Polson, P., Atwood, M. (1981) The Processes Involved in Designing Software In *Cognitive Skills and Their Acquisition*, J.R. Anderson (Ed.). Lawrence Erlbaum Associates. Hillsdale, New Jersey.

9. Kant, E., Newell, A. (1982) *Problem Solving Techniques for the Design of Algorithms.* CMU-C S-82-145. Carnegie-Mellon Unversity.

10. Brooks, R. (1980) Studying Programmer Behavior Experimentally: The Problems of Proper Methodology. *Communications of the ACM, 23*, 207-213.

11. Sheil, B. (1981) The Psychological Study of Programming. *Computing Surveys, 13*, 101-120.

12. Shneiderman, B. (1980) *Software Psychology: Human Factors in Computer and Information Systems.* Winthrop Publishers, Inc.

13. Letovsky, S. (1986) Processes in Program Comprehension. In *Empirical Studies of Programmers*, Soloway, E., Iyengar, S. (Eds.). Ablex, Inc.

14. Ericsson, K., Simon, H. (1980) Verbal Reports as Data. *Psychological Review, 3*, 215-251.

15. Lewis, Clayton (1982) *Using the "Thinking aloud" Method in Cognitive Interface Design.* RC 9265. IBM Watson Research Center, Yorktown Heights, NY.